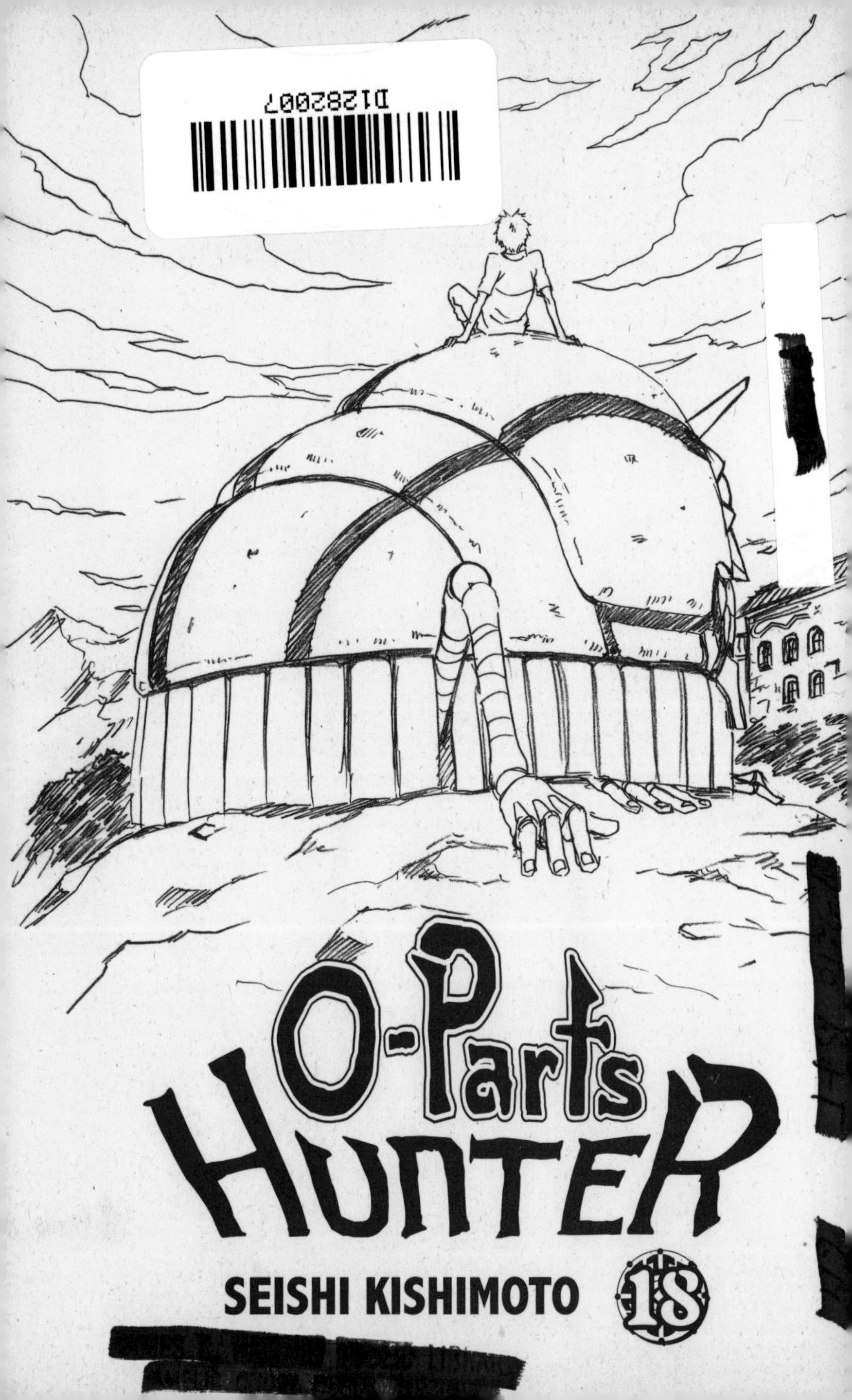

O-Parts HUNTER

SEISHI KISHIMOTO

18

CHARACTERS of O-Parts HUNTER

...to help you guys.

Having gotten close to her true Angel form, she is now able to wield Sandalphon's powers, but her true powers are yet to be seen...

Ruby Crescent: A treasure hunter in search of the Legendary O-Part and her missing father. Rescued from Stea HQ, she turns out to be a Recipe for the Kabbalah. Jio brings her back into this world.

Satan: An alternate personality that exists inside Jio's body. The ultimate weapon of the Kabbalah who holds earth-shattering powers.

Jio Freed: A wild O.P.T. boy whose dream is world domination. He has been emotionally hurt from his experiences in the past but has become strong after meeting Ruby. Ever since the Rock Bird incident, he has had Ruby's soul inside him.

Jio's Friends

Kirin: An O-Part appraiser and a master of dodging attacks. He trained Jio and Ball into strong O.P.T.s.

Ball: He is the mood-maker of the group and the kind of person who cares about his friends.

Cross: He used to be the Commander in Chief of the Stea Government's battleship. His sister was killed by Satan.

Master Zenom & the Big Four
The Zenom Syndicate claims that their aim is to bring chaos and destruction upon the world, but...

Pursuing the Powers of the Kabbalah
Amaterasu Miko
The leader of the Stea Government and the person who turned it into a huge military machine. Miko is collecting the recipes of the Formal Kabbalah.

the keyword of 666

A legacy left by the Ancient Race who are said to have co[me] from the Blue Planet. The Kabbalah is the Ultima[te] Memorization Weapon, which absorbs every kind [of] "information" that makes up this world, and evolves alon[g] with the passing of time! It consists of two counterparts: the Formal Kabbalah and the Reverse Kabbalah.

10i Nahema (Materialism)
9i Lilith (Instability)
8i Adramelech (Avarice)
7i Baal (Lust)
6i Belphegor (Odious-ness)
5i Asmodeus (Cruelty)
4i Astaroth (Apathy)
3i Lucifuge (Rejection)
2i Beelzebub (Stupidity)
1i Satan (Atheism)

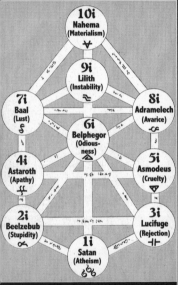

Reverse Kabbalah

The symbol of destruction with the names of the powerful archdemons listed on the sephirot from one to ten.

1 Metatron (Crown)
2 Raziel (Wisdom)
3 Zaphkiel (Understand-ing)
4 Zadkiel (Benevo-lence)
5 Samael (Might)
6 Michael (Beauty)
7 Haniel (Victory)
8 Raphael (Splendor)
9 Gabriel (Foundation)
10 Sandalphon (Kingdom)

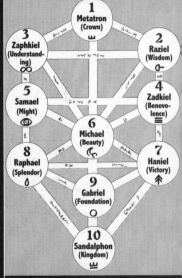

Formal Kabbalah

The symbol of creation with the names of the great archangels listed on the sephirot from one to ten.

STORY

Ascald: a world where people fight amongst themselves to get their hands on mystical objects left behind by an ancient civilization…the O-Parts.

In that world, a monster that strikes fear into the hearts of the strongest of men is rumored to exist. Those who have seen the monster all tell of the same thing–that the number of the beast, 666, is engraved on its forehead.

***

Jio rescues Ruby following a fierce battle at Stea Government headquarters and everybody is reunited at last. Meanwhile Stea's leader, Miko, has stolen the Legendary O-Part, taken over Shin and is heading for Zenom Syndicate headquarters to wrest the Reverse Kabbalah from them. Jio and his friends pursue Miko, but as they enter the Zenom Syndicate's HQ they face various traps as well as the power of the Zenom Big Four!

O-Parts Hunter

18

Table of Contents

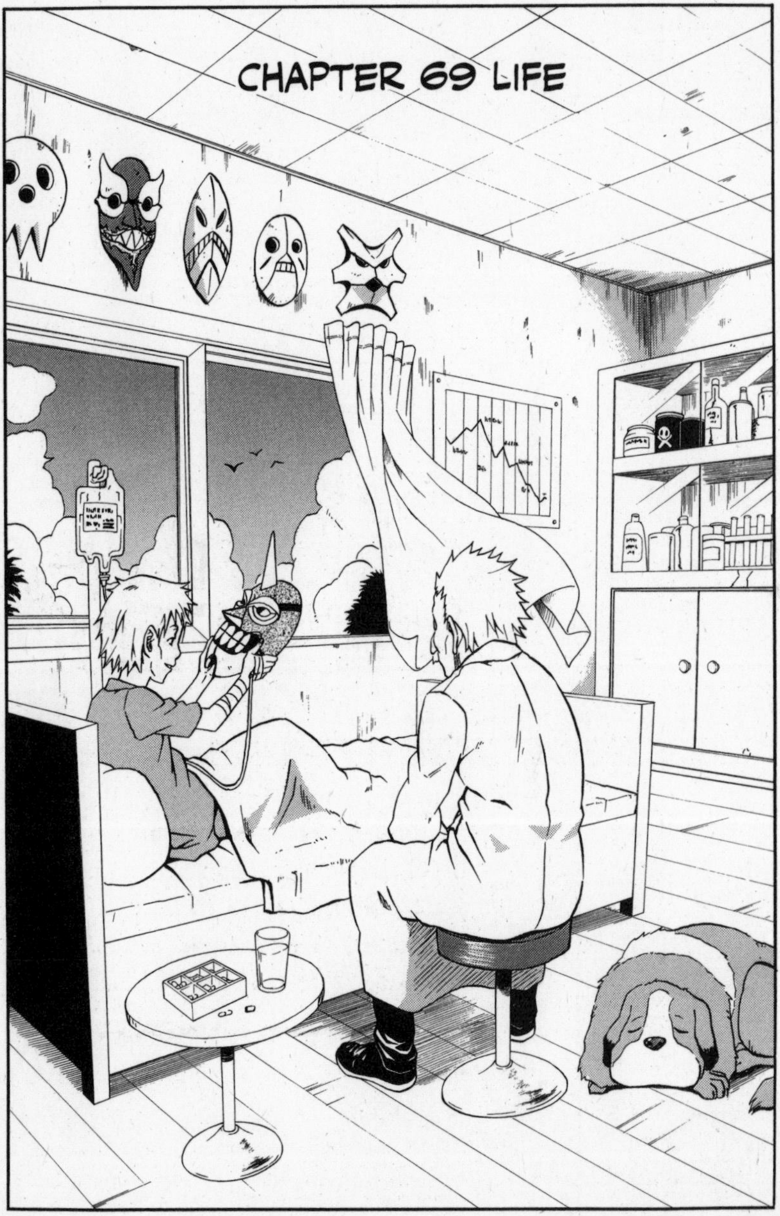
CHAPTER 69 LIFE

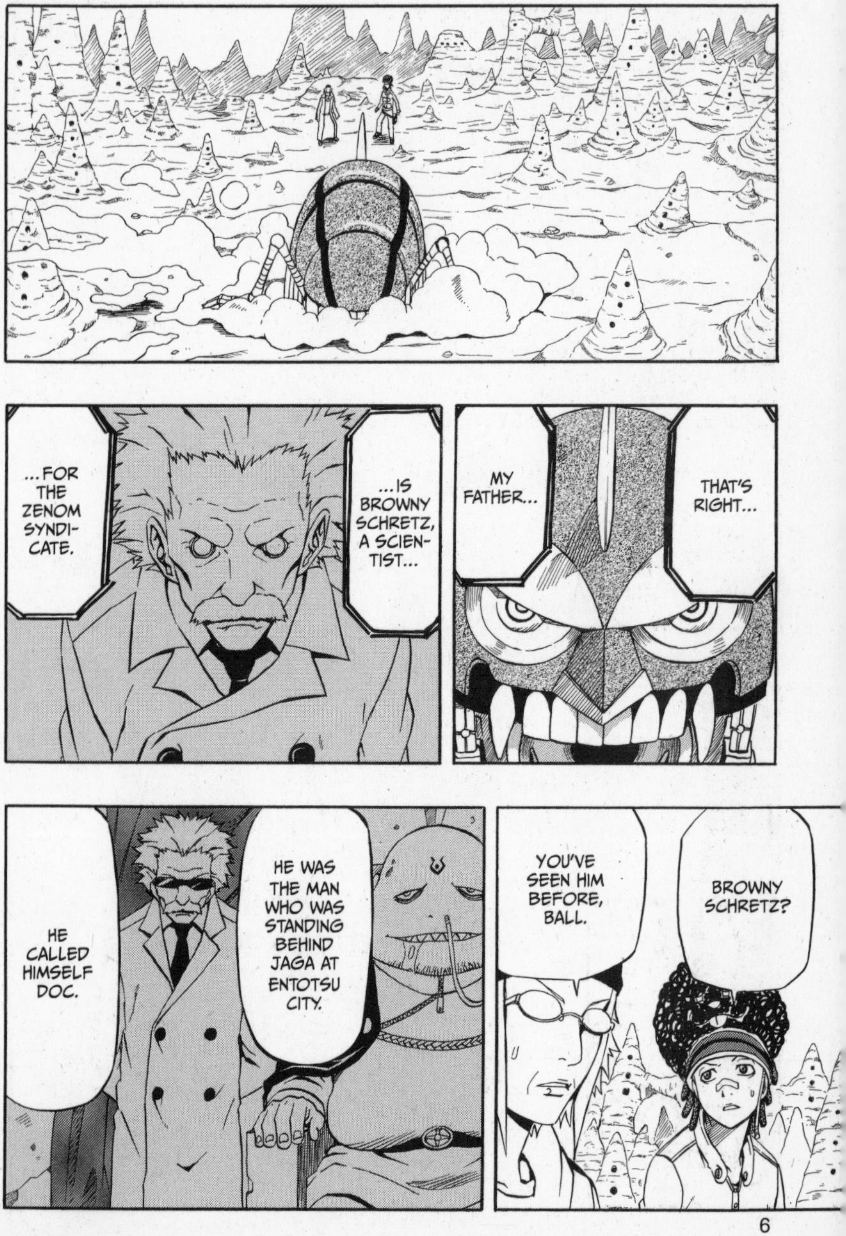
THAT'S RIGHT...
MY FATHER...
...IS BROWNY SCHRETZ, A SCIENTIST...
...FOR THE ZENOM SYNDICATE.
BROWNY SCHRETZ?
YOU'VE SEEN HIM BEFORE, BALL.
HE WAS THE MAN WHO WAS STANDING BEHIND JAGA AT ENTOTSU CITY.
HE CALLED HIMSELF DOC.

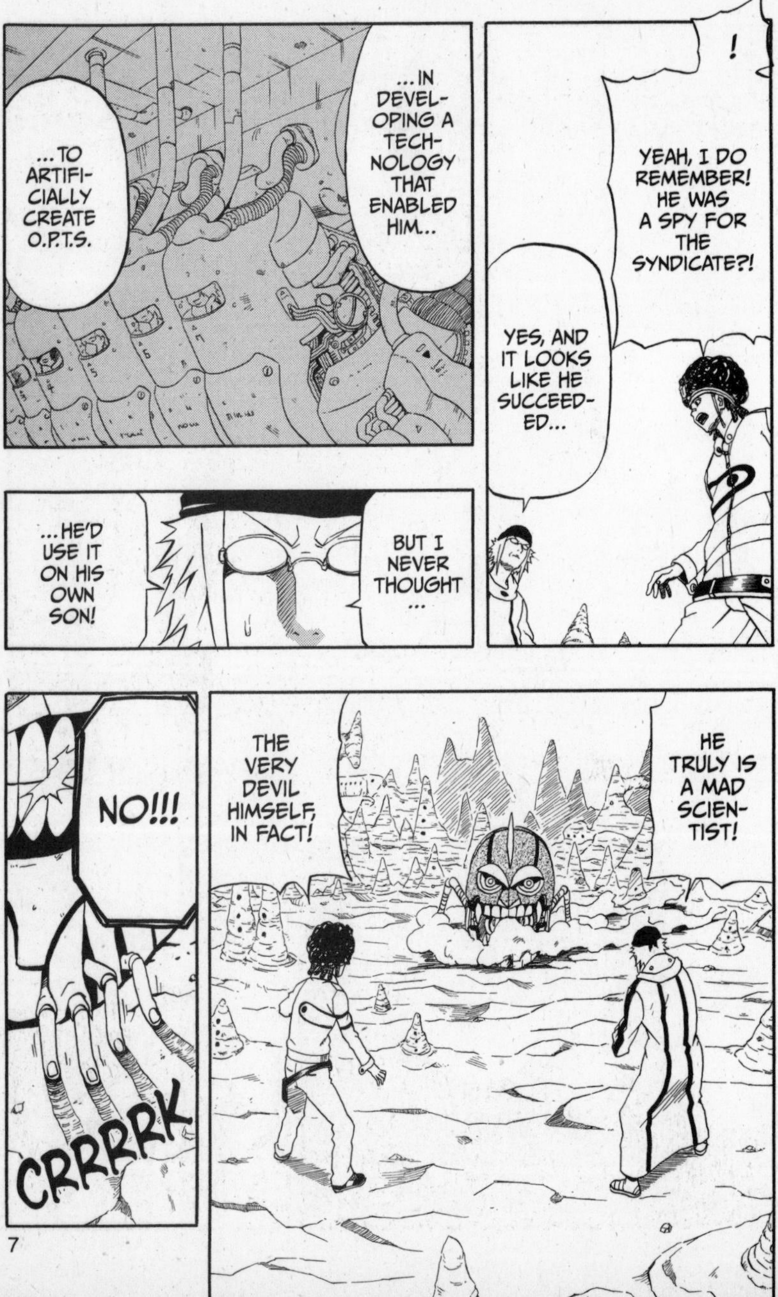
!
YEAH, I DO REMEMBER! HE WAS A SPY FOR THE SYNDICATE?!
YES, AND IT LOOKS LIKE HE SUCCEEDED...
...IN DEVELOPING A TECHNOLOGY THAT ENABLED HIM...
...TO ARTIFICIALLY CREATE O.P.T.S.
BUT I NEVER THOUGHT...
...HE'D USE IT ON HIS OWN SON!
HE TRULY IS A MAD SCIENTIST!
THE VERY DEVIL HIMSELF, IN FACT!
NO!!!
CRRRRK

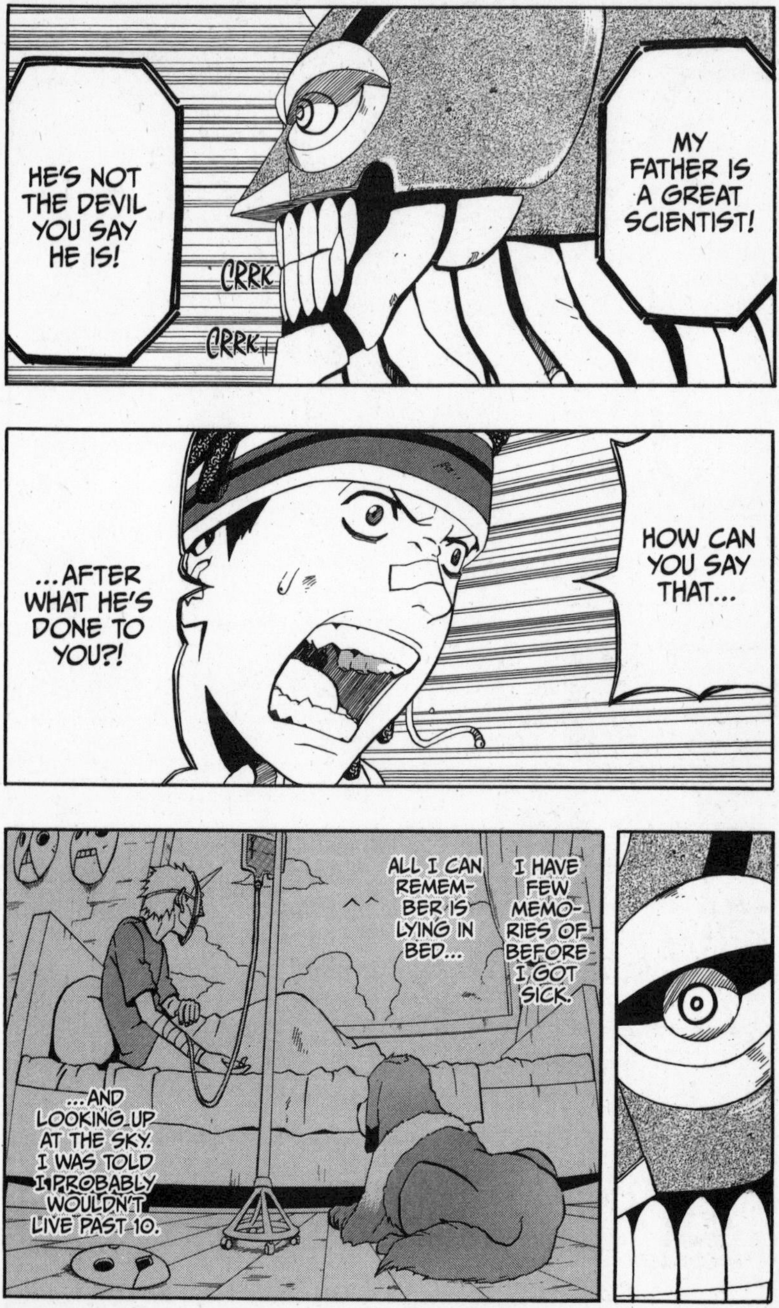
MY FATHER IS A GREAT SCIENTIST!
HE'S NOT THE DEVIL YOU SAY HE IS!
CRRK
CRRK
HOW CAN YOU SAY THAT...
...AFTER WHAT HE'S DONE TO YOU?!
I HAVE FEW MEMORIES OF BEFORE I GOT SICK.
ALL I CAN REMEMBER IS LYING IN BED...
...AND LOOKING UP AT THE SKY. I WAS TOLD I PROBABLY WOULDN'T LIVE PAST 10.

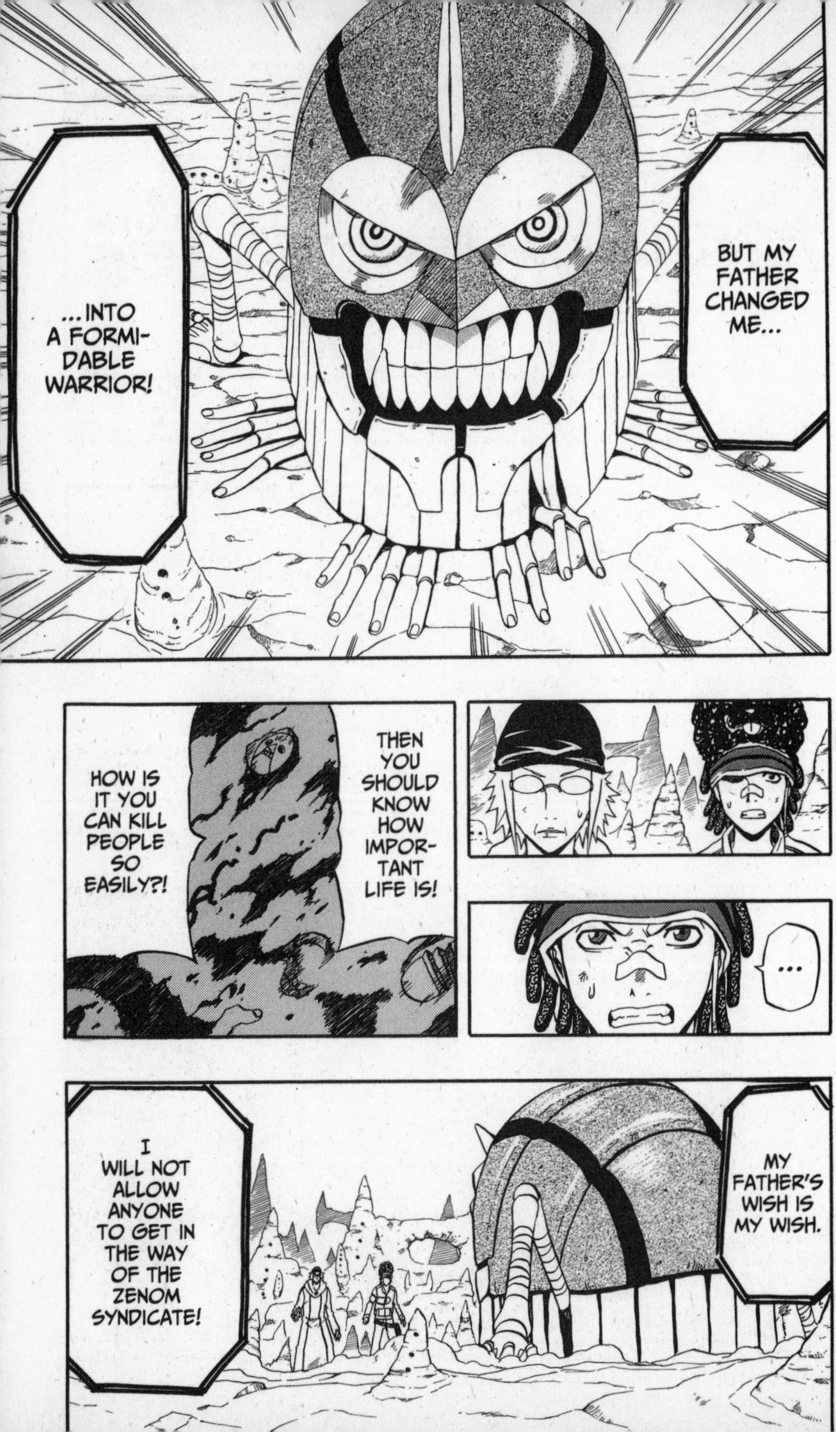
BUT MY FATHER CHANGED ME...
...INTO A FORMIDABLE WARRIOR!
...
THEN YOU SHOULD KNOW HOW IMPORTANT LIFE IS!
HOW IS IT YOU CAN KILL PEOPLE SO EASILY?!
MY FATHER'S WISH IS MY WISH.
I WILL NOT ALLOW ANYONE TO GET IN THE WAY OF THE ZENOM SYNDICATE!

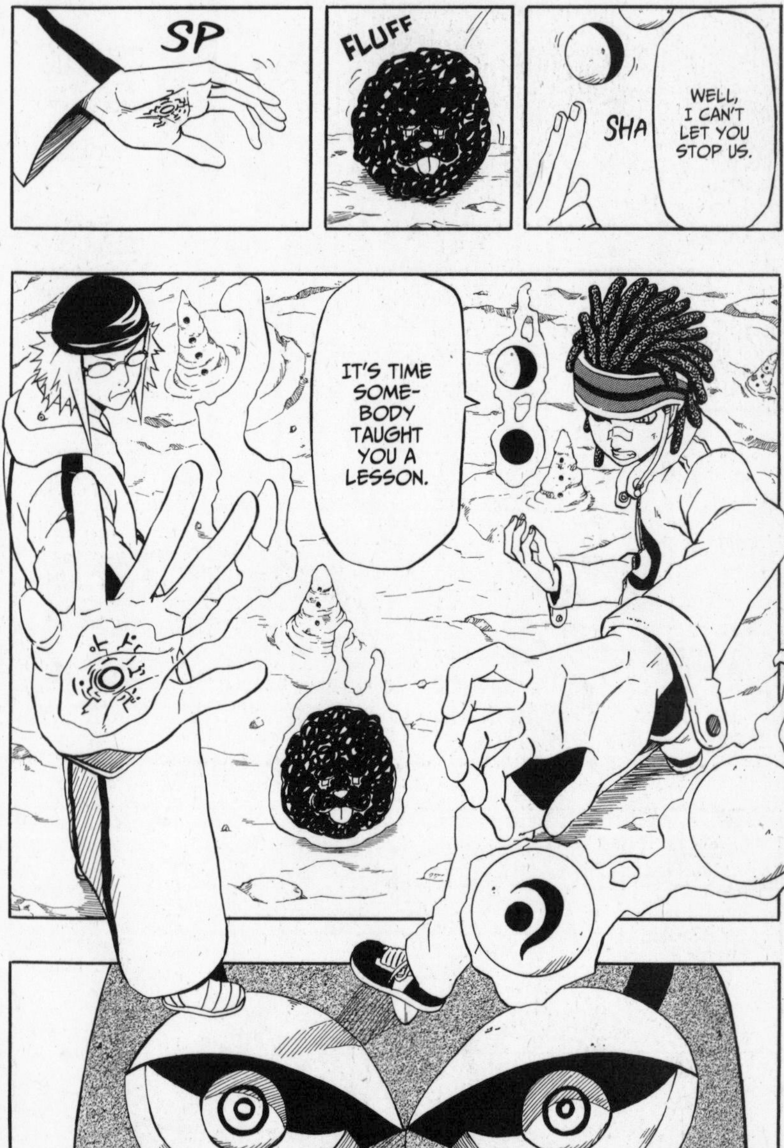
WELL, I CAN'T LET YOU STOP US.
SHA
FLUFF
SP
IT'S TIME SOMEBODY TAUGHT YOU A LESSON.

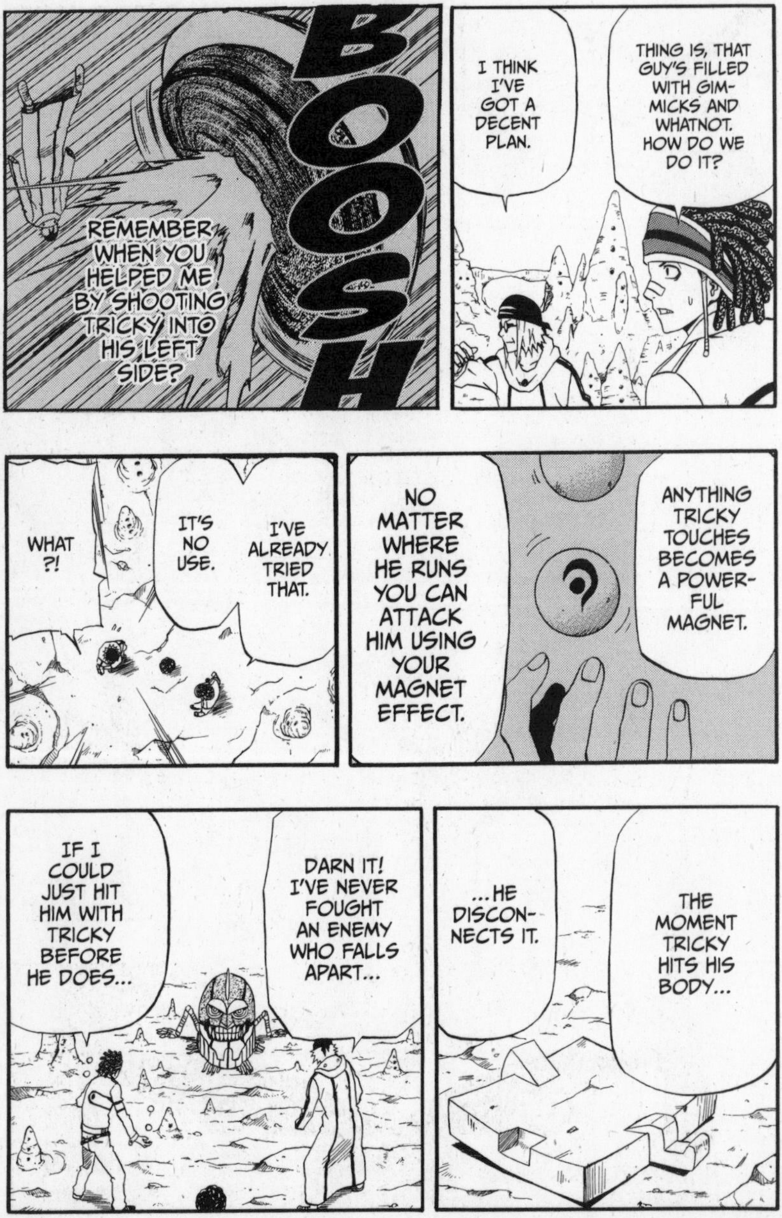
THING IS, THAT GUY'S FILLED WITH GIM-MICKS AND WHATNOT. HOW DO WE DO IT?
I THINK I'VE GOT A DECENT PLAN.
BOOSH
REMEMBER WHEN YOU HELPED ME BY SHOOTING TRICKY INTO HIS LEFT SIDE?
ANYTHING TRICKY TOUCHES BECOMES A POWER-FUL MAGNET.
NO MATTER WHERE HE RUNS YOU CAN ATTACK HIM USING YOUR MAGNET EFFECT.
I'VE ALREADY TRIED THAT.
IT'S NO USE.
WHAT?!
THE MOMENT TRICKY HITS HIS BODY...
...HE DISCON-NECTS IT.
DARN IT! I'VE NEVER FOUGHT AN ENEMY WHO FALLS APART...
IF I COULD JUST HIT HIM WITH TRICKY BEFORE HE DOES...

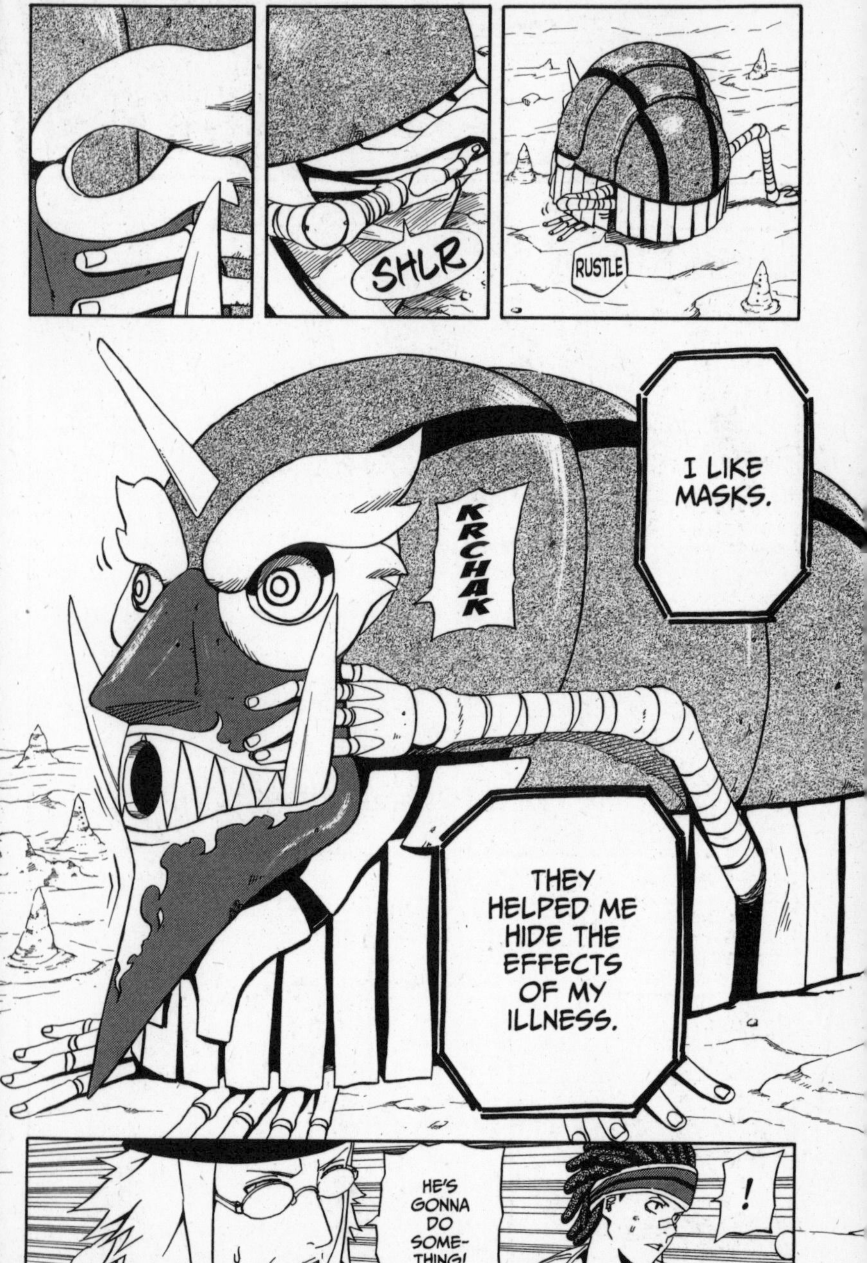
RUSTLE
SHLR
I LIKE MASKS.
KRCHAK
THEY HELPED ME HIDE THE EFFECTS OF MY ILLNESS.
!
HE'S GONNA DO SOME- THING!

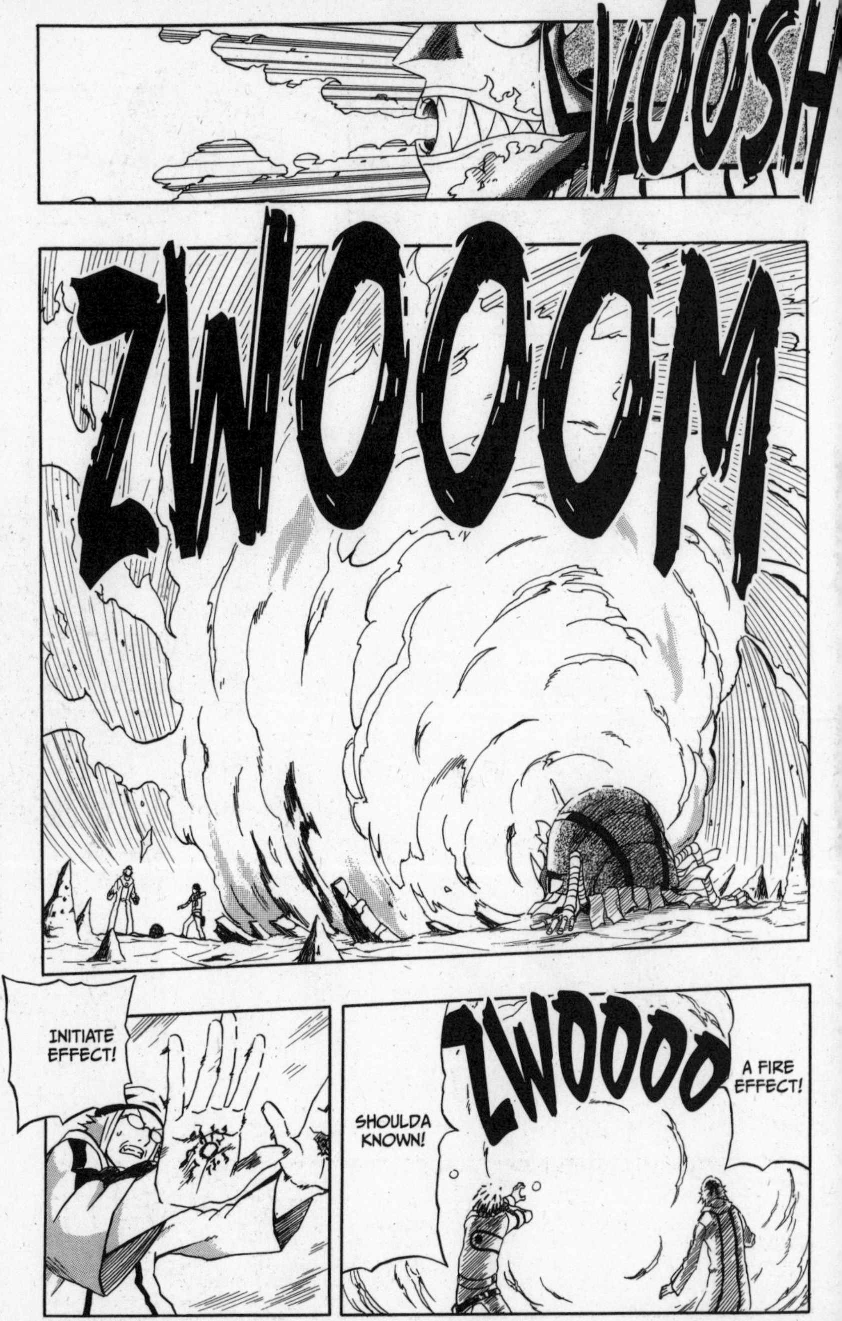
WOOSH
ZWOOOM
ZWOOOO
A FIRE EFFECT!
SHOULDA KNOWN!
INITIATE EFFECT!

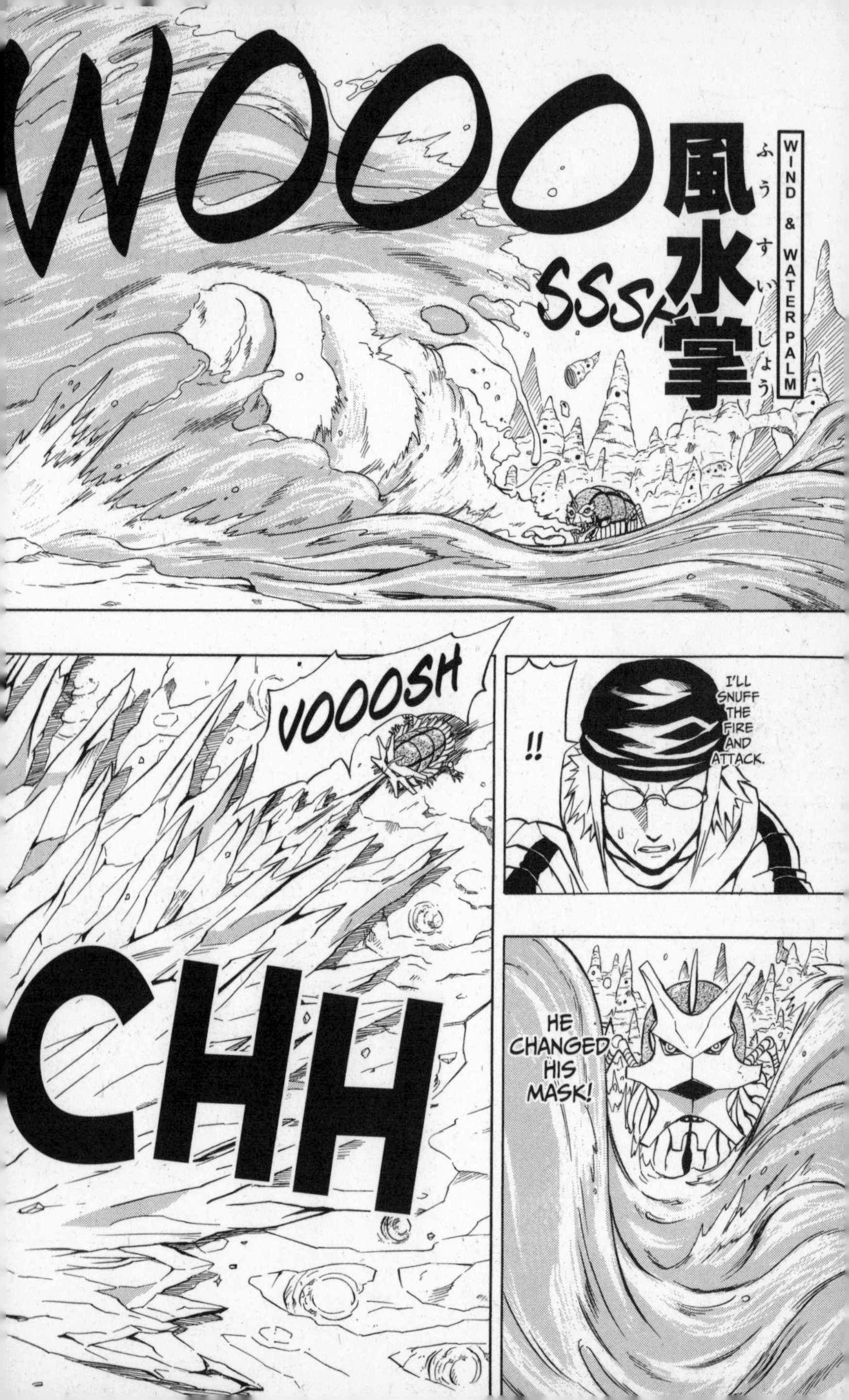
風水掌
ふうすいしょう
WIND & WATER PALM
SSSK
WOOOO
I'LL SNUFF THE FIRE AND ATTACK.
!!
HE CHANGED HIS MASK!
VOOOSH
CHH

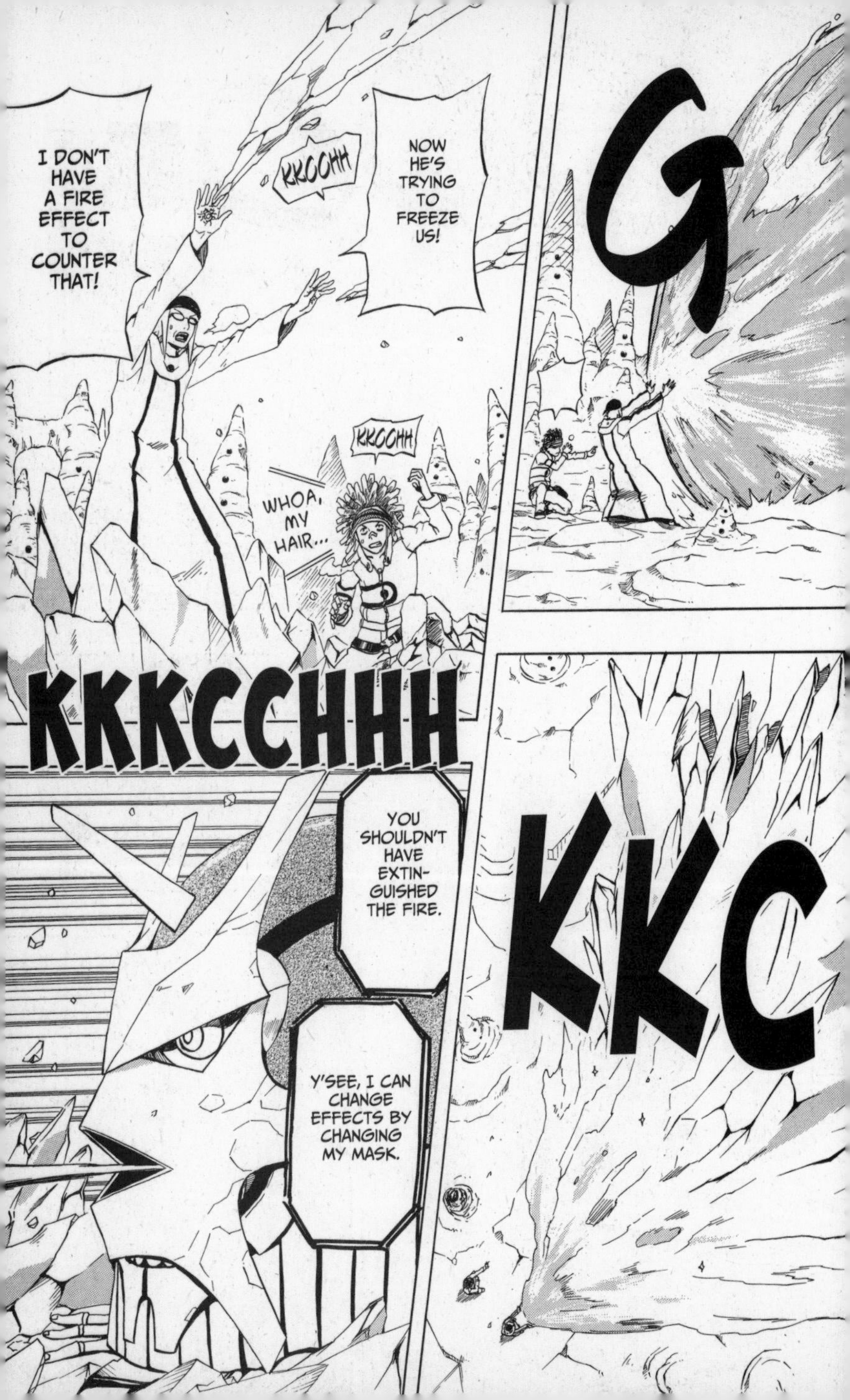
G
NOW HE'S TRYING TO FREEZE US!
KKOOHH
I DON'T HAVE A FIRE EFFECT TO COUNTER THAT!
KKOOHH
WHOA, MY HAIR...
KKKCCHHH
KKC
YOU SHOULDN'T HAVE EXTIN-GUISHED THE FIRE.
Y'SEE, I CAN CHANGE EFFECTS BY CHANGING MY MASK.

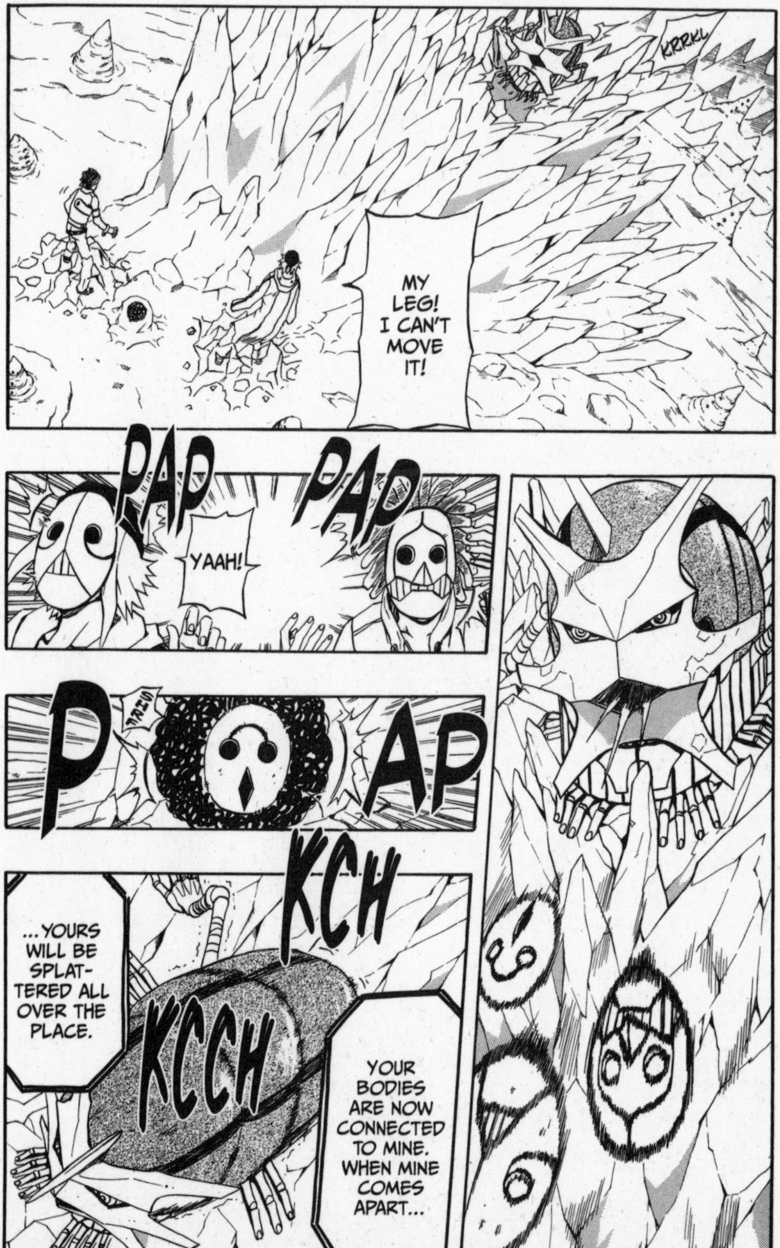

KRRKL
MY LEG! I CAN'T MOVE IT!
PAP
PAP
YAAH!
P
AP
KCH
KCCH
YOUR BODIES ARE NOW CONNECTED TO MINE. WHEN MINE COMES APART...
...YOURS WILL BE SPLAT-TERED ALL OVER THE PLACE.

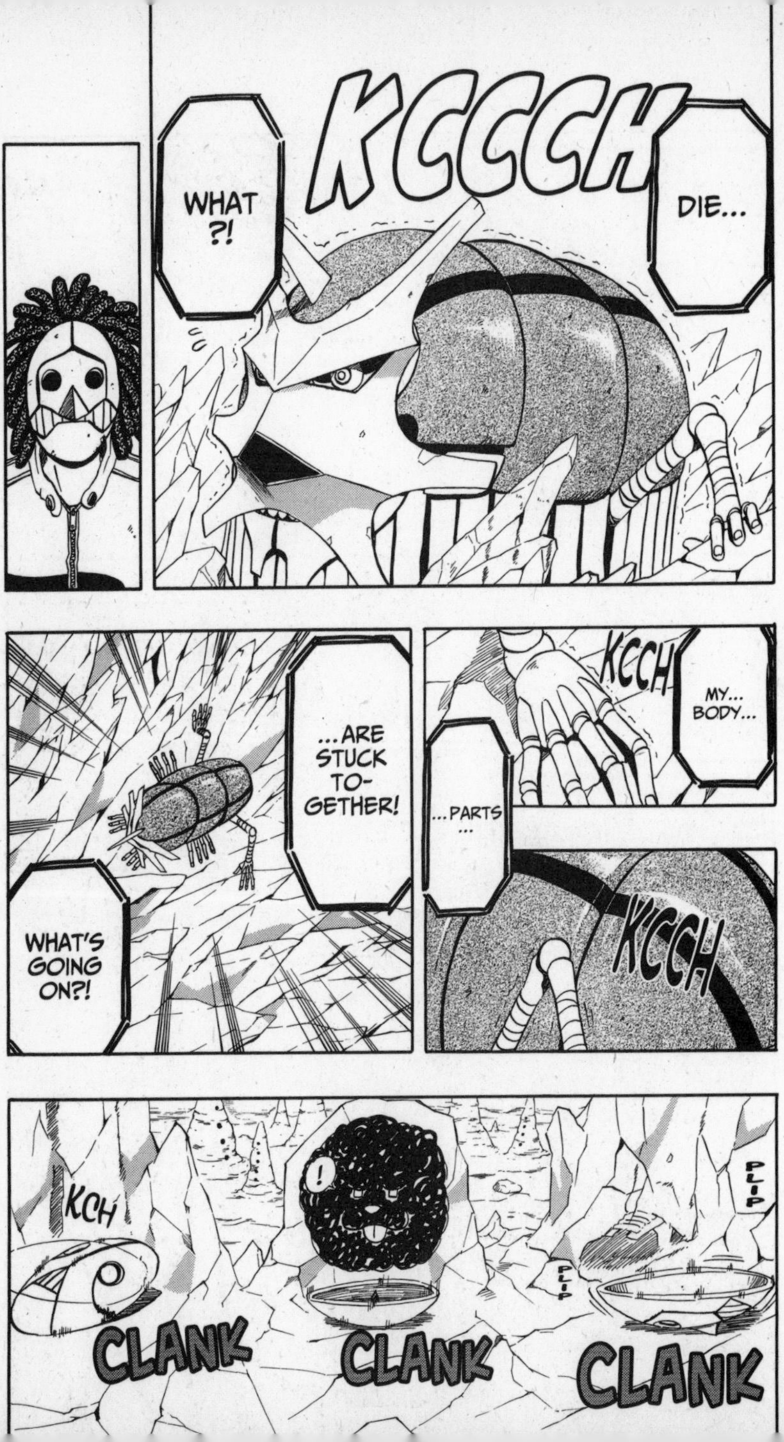
DIE...
KCCCH
WHAT ?!
KCCH
MY... BODY...
...PARTS ...
KCCH
...ARE STUCK TO-GETHER!
WHAT'S GOING ON?!
PLIP
PLIP
CLANK
!
CLANK
KCH
CLANK

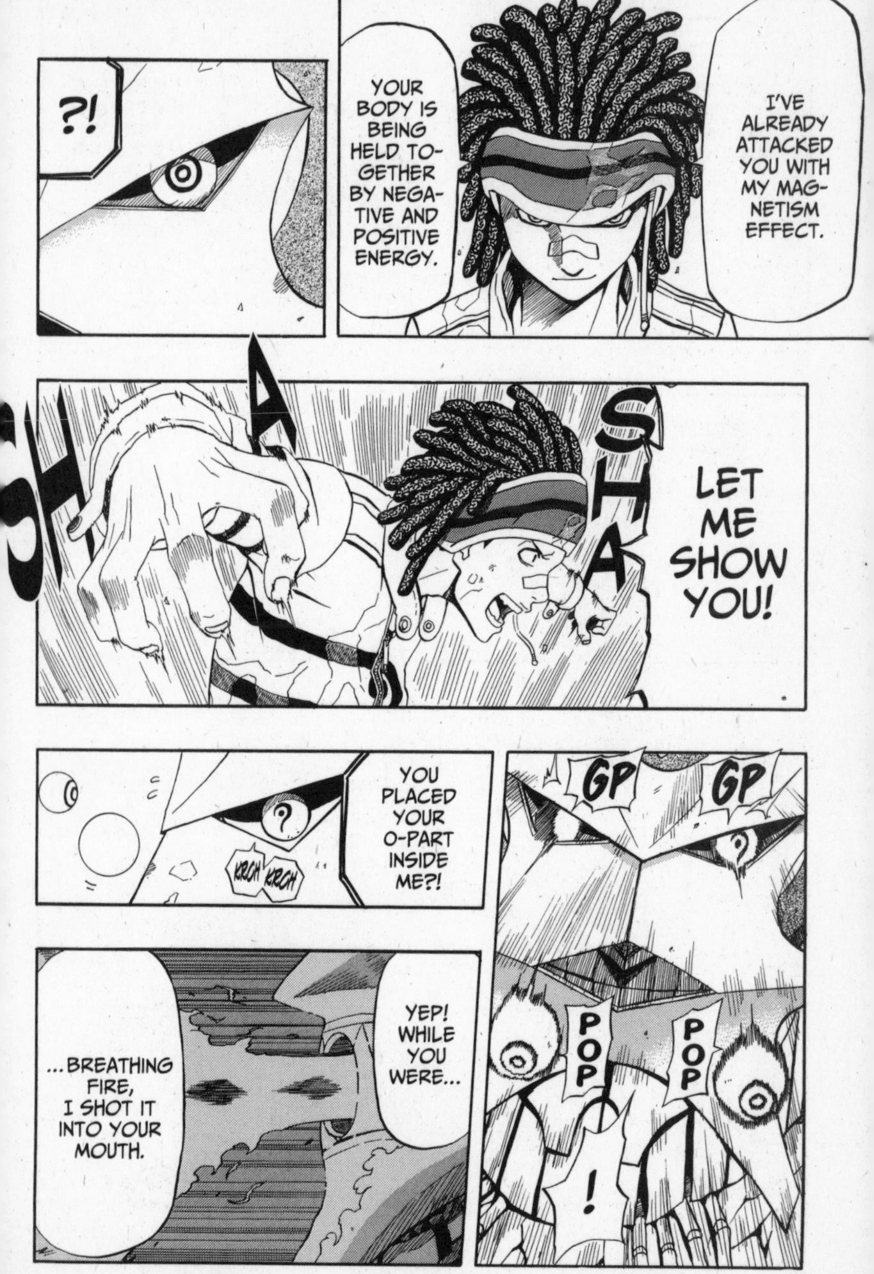
I'VE ALREADY ATTACKED YOU WITH MY MAG-NETISM EFFECT.
YOUR BODY IS BEING HELD TO-GETHER BY NEGA-TIVE AND POSITIVE ENERGY.
?!
SHA
LET ME SHOW YOU!
SHA
GP
GP
POP
POP
!
YOU PLACED YOUR O-PART INSIDE ME?!
KRCH KRCH
YEP! WHILE YOU WERE...
...BREATHING FIRE, I SHOT IT INTO YOUR MOUTH.

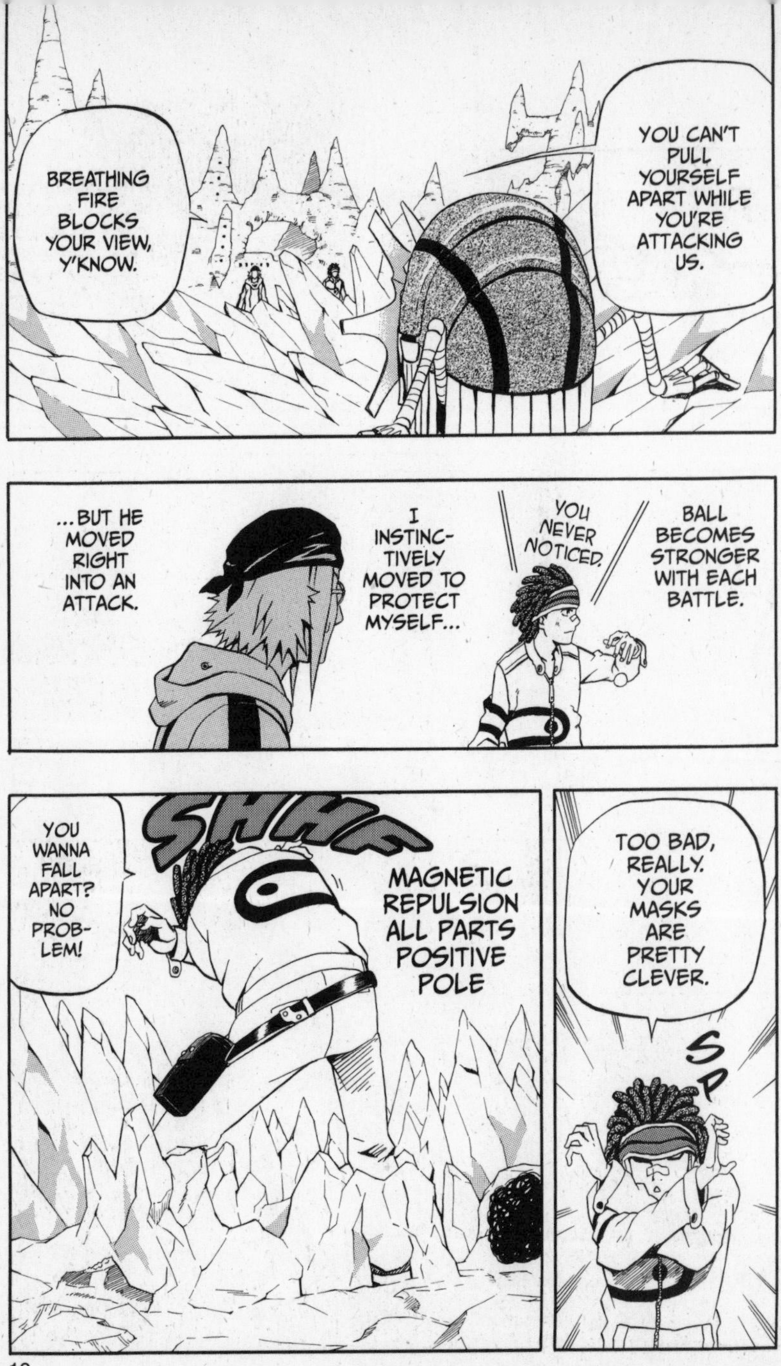
YOU CAN'T PULL YOURSELF APART WHILE YOU'RE ATTACKING US.
BREATHING FIRE BLOCKS YOUR VIEW, Y'KNOW.
BALL BECOMES STRONGER WITH EACH BATTLE.
YOU NEVER NOTICED.
I INSTINCTIVELY MOVED TO PROTECT MYSELF...
...BUT HE MOVED RIGHT INTO AN ATTACK.
TOO BAD, REALLY. YOUR MASKS ARE PRETTY CLEVER.
SP
SHHF
MAGNETIC REPULSION ALL PARTS POSITIVE POLE
YOU WANNA FALL APART? NO PROB-LEM!

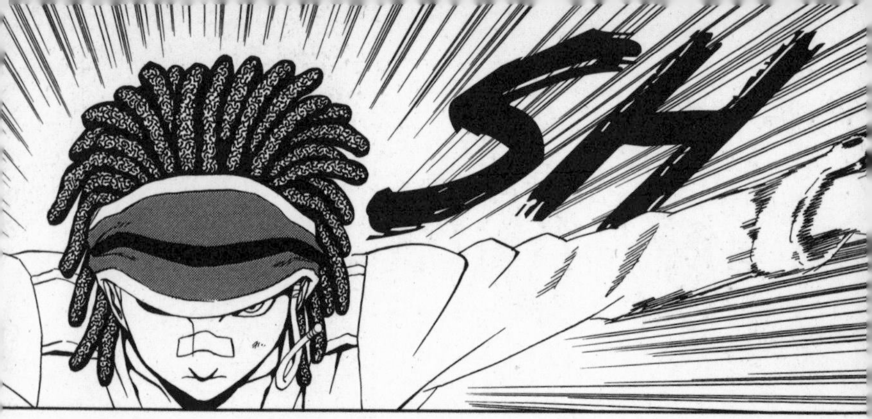
SH

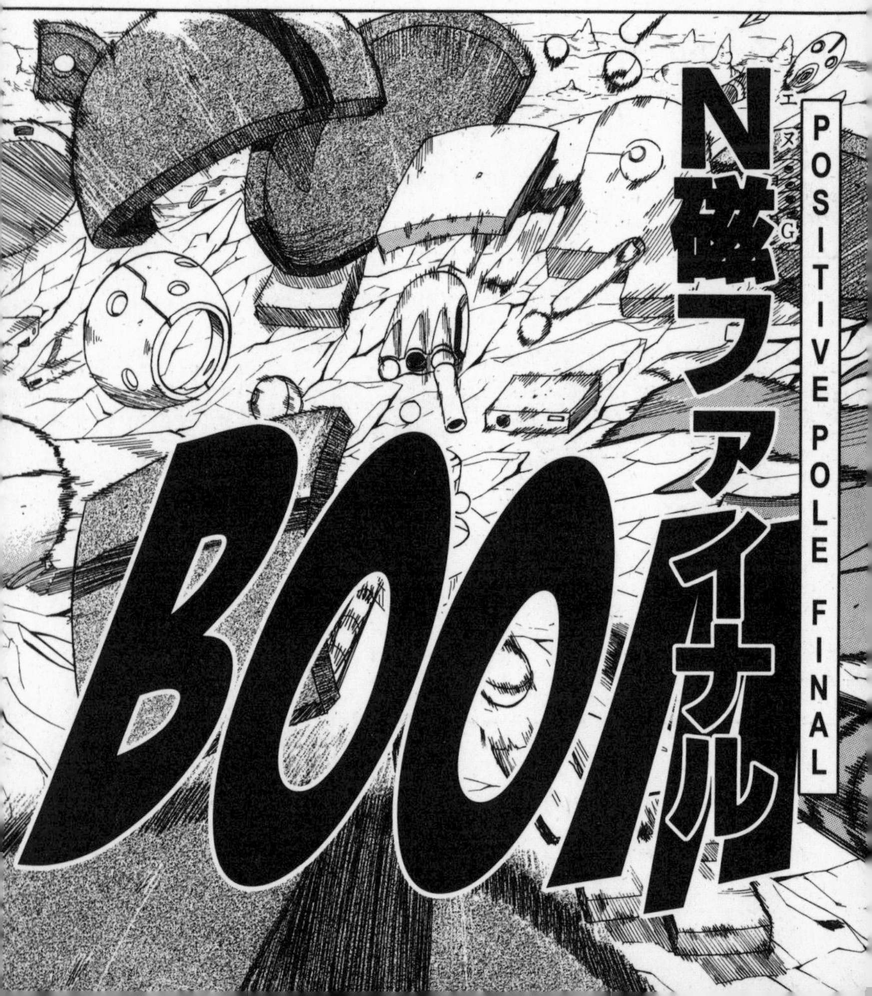
N磁ファイナル
POSITIVE POLE FINAL
BOOM

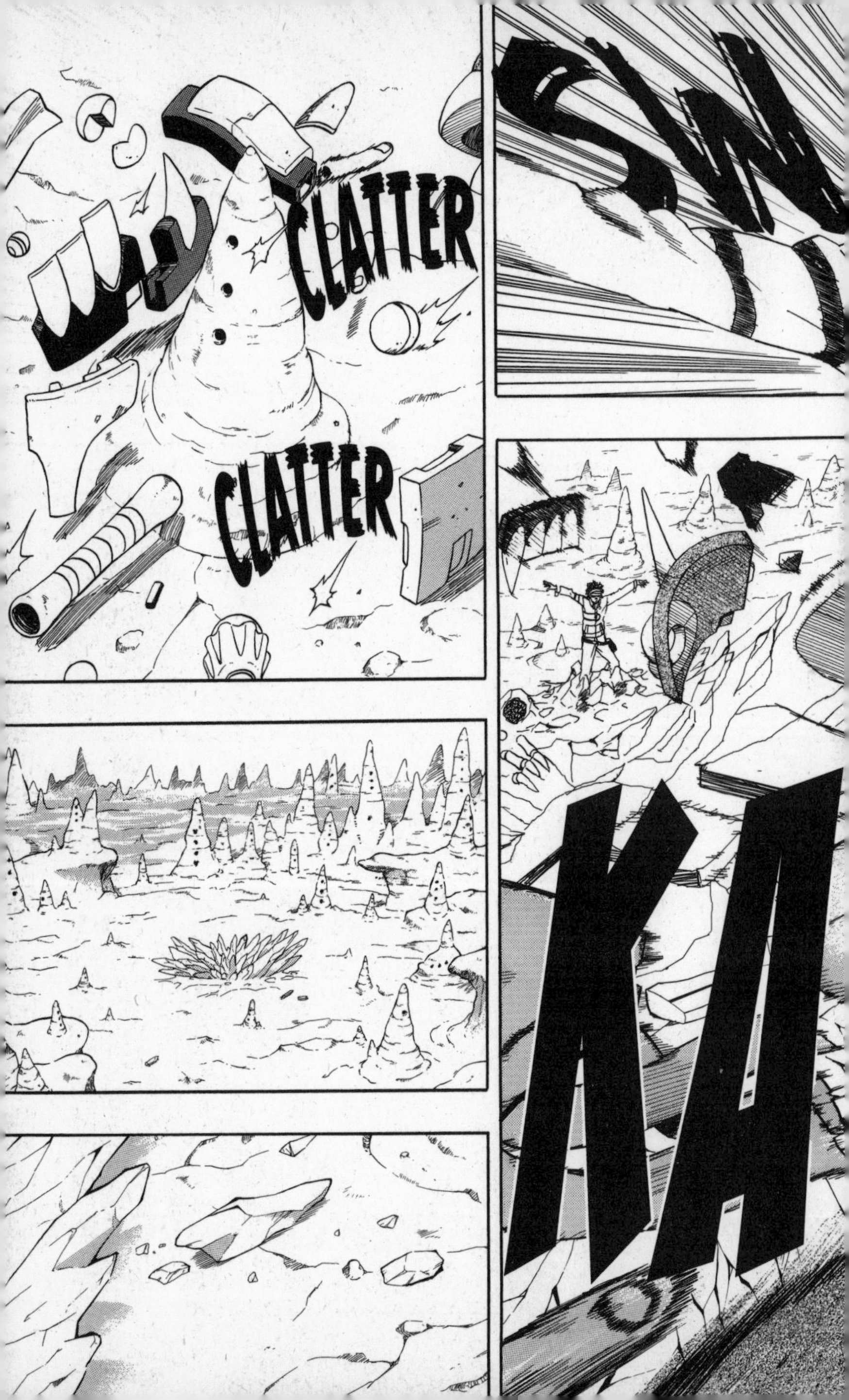
SWA
KA
CLATTER
CLATTER

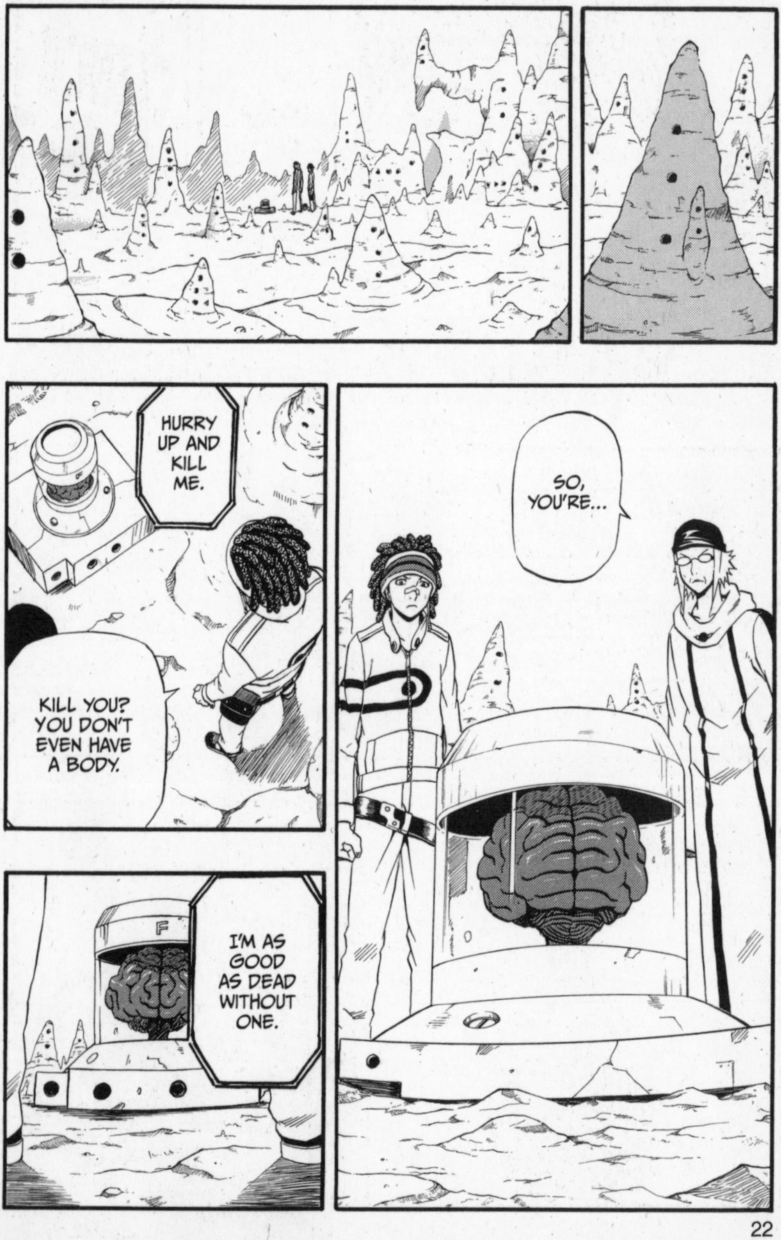
SO, YOU'RE...
HURRY UP AND KILL ME.
KILL YOU? YOU DON'T EVEN HAVE A BODY.
I'M AS GOOD AS DEAD WITHOUT ONE.

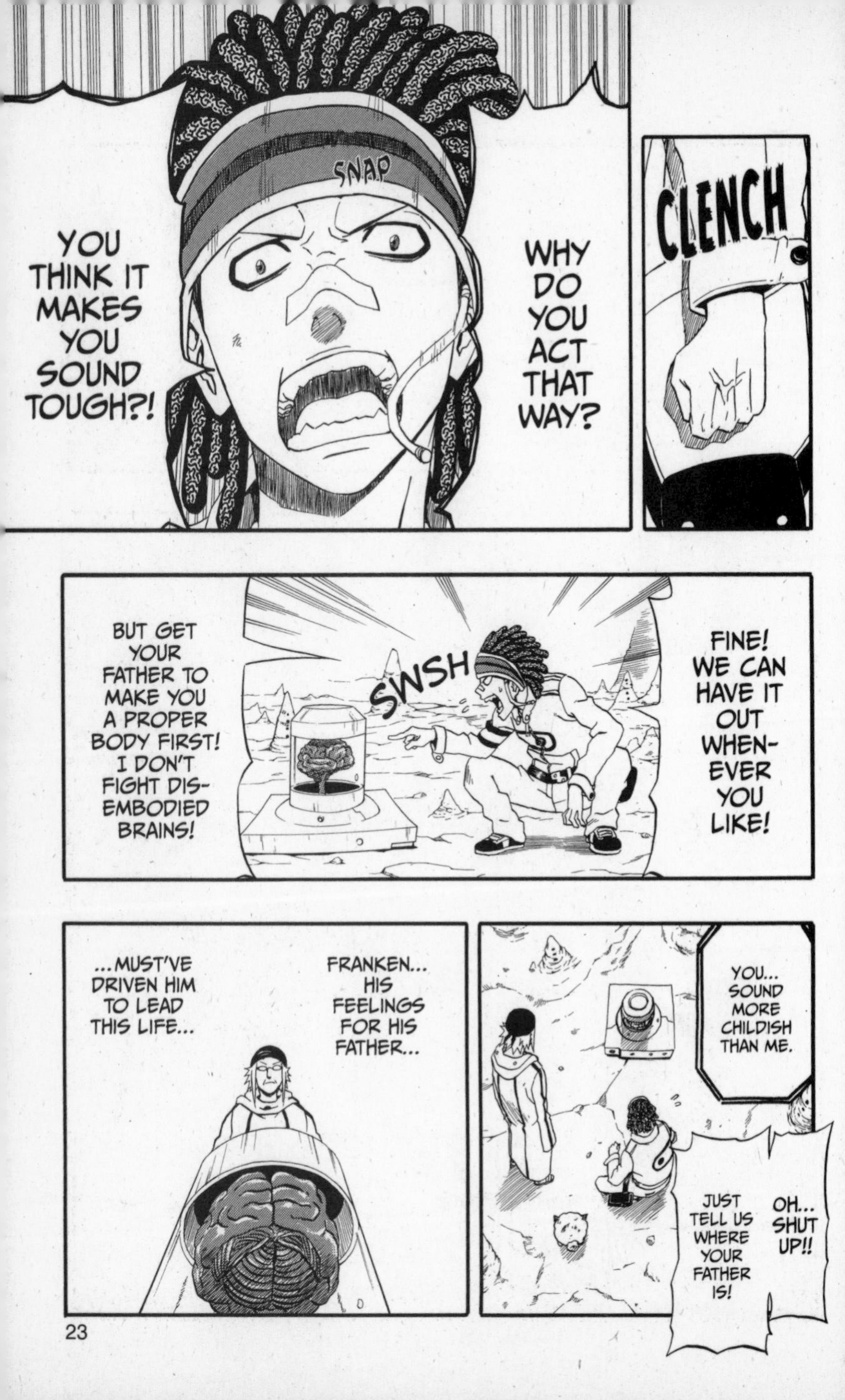
CLENCH
SNAP
WHY DO YOU ACT THAT WAY?
YOU THINK IT MAKES YOU SOUND TOUGH?!
FINE! WE CAN HAVE IT OUT WHEN-EVER YOU LIKE!
SWSH
BUT GET YOUR FATHER TO MAKE YOU A PROPER BODY FIRST! I DON'T FIGHT DIS-EMBODIED BRAINS!
YOU... SOUND MORE CHILDISH THAN ME.
OH... SHUT UP!!
JUST TELL US WHERE YOUR FATHER IS!
FRANKEN... HIS FEELINGS FOR HIS FATHER...
...MUST'VE DRIVEN HIM TO LEAD THIS LIFE...

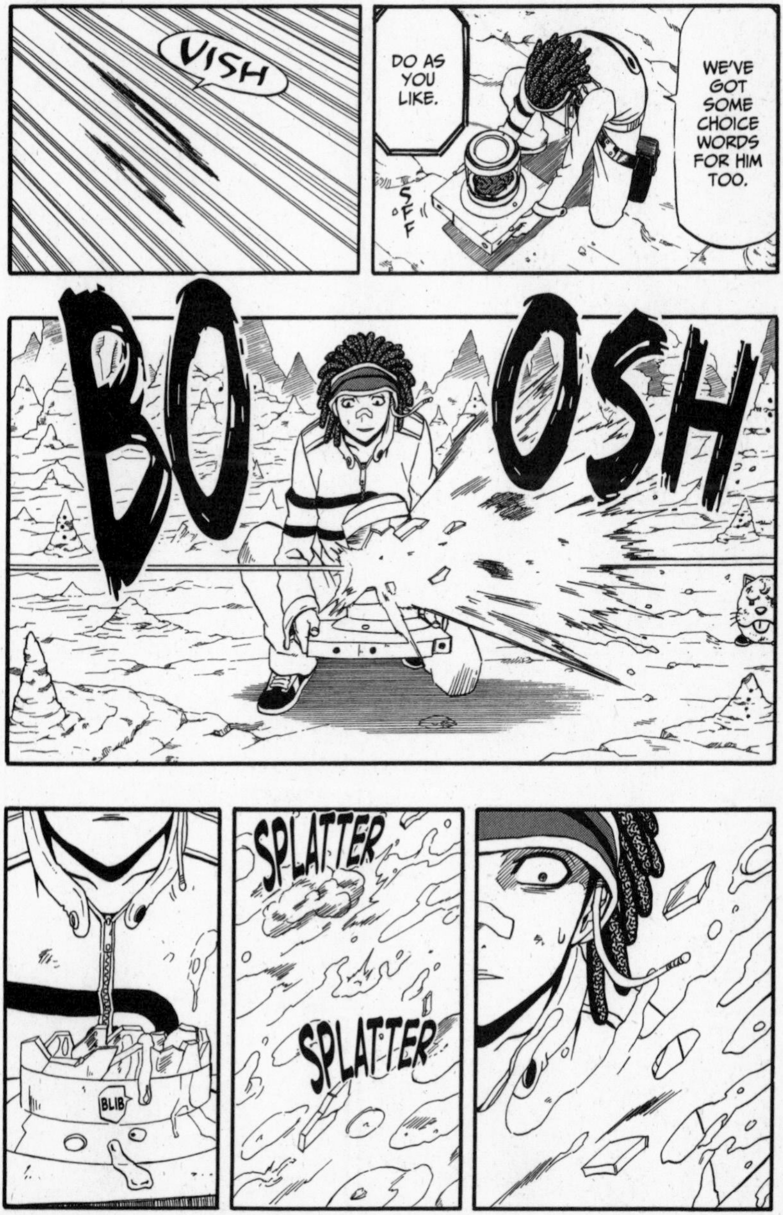
WE'VE GOT SOME CHOICE WORDS FOR HIM TOO.
DO AS YOU LIKE.
SFF
VISH
BO OSH
SPLATTER
SPLATTER
BLIB

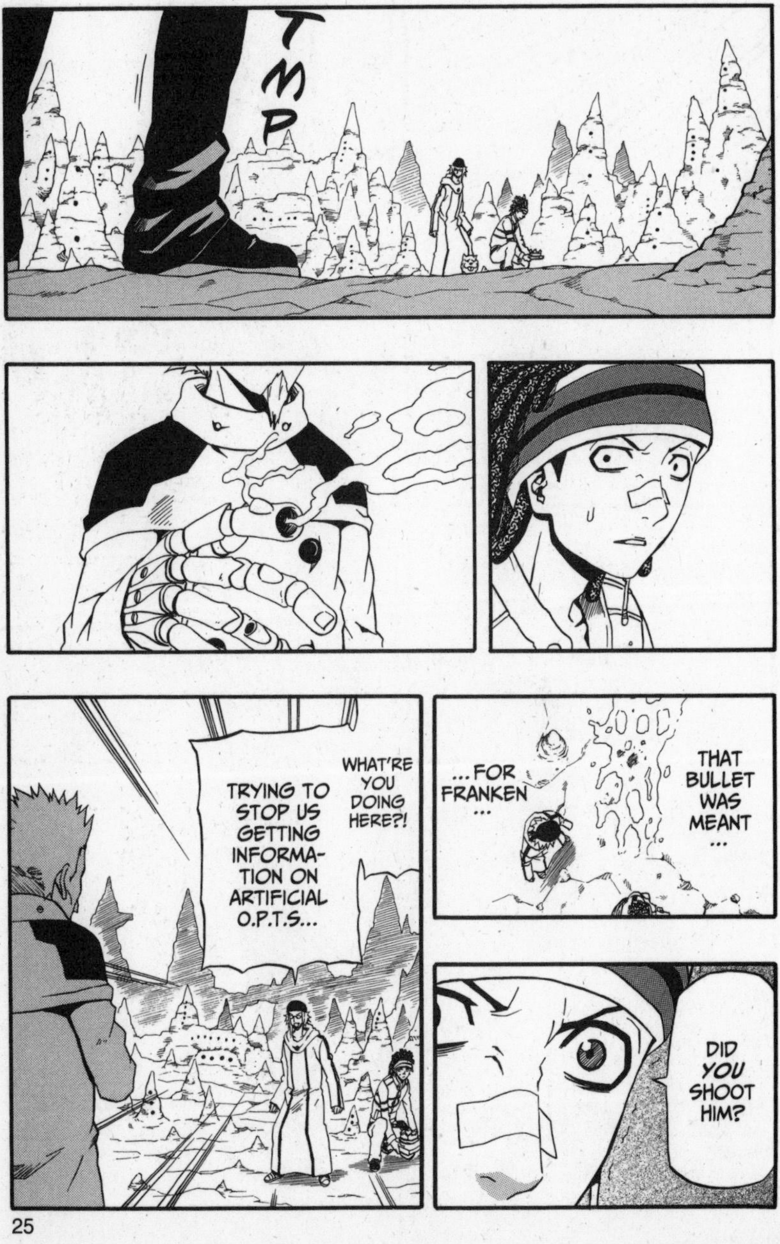
TMP
THAT BULLET WAS MEANT ...
...FOR FRANKEN ...
DID YOU SHOOT HIM?
WHAT'RE YOU DOING HERE?!
TRYING TO STOP US GETTING INFORMATION ON ARTIFICIAL O.P.T.S...

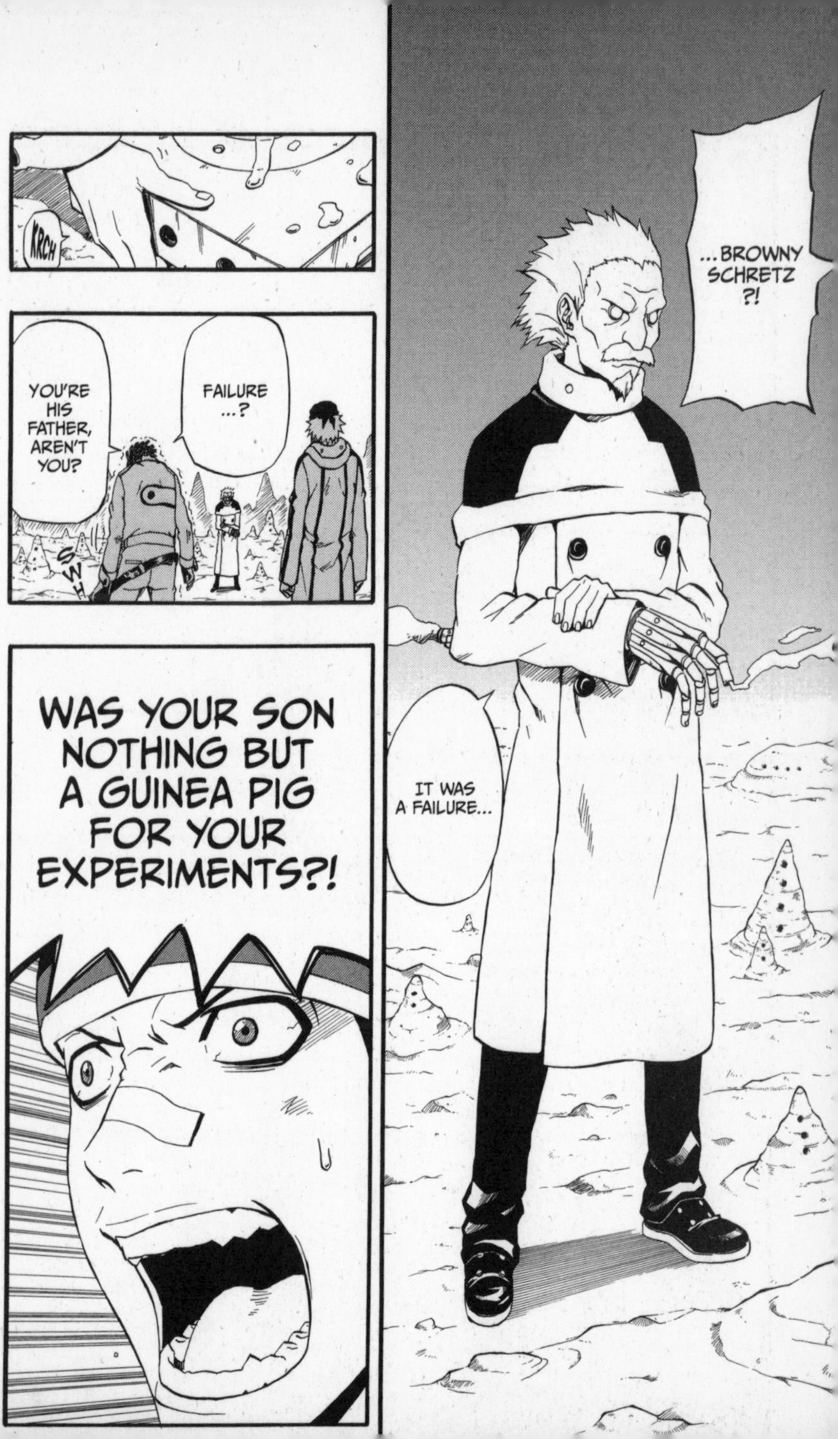
...BROWNY SCHRETZ ?!
IT WAS A FAILURE...
KRCH
FAILURE ...?
YOU'RE HIS FATHER, AREN'T YOU?
SWH
WAS YOUR SON NOTHING BUT A GUINEA PIG FOR YOUR EXPERIMENTS?!

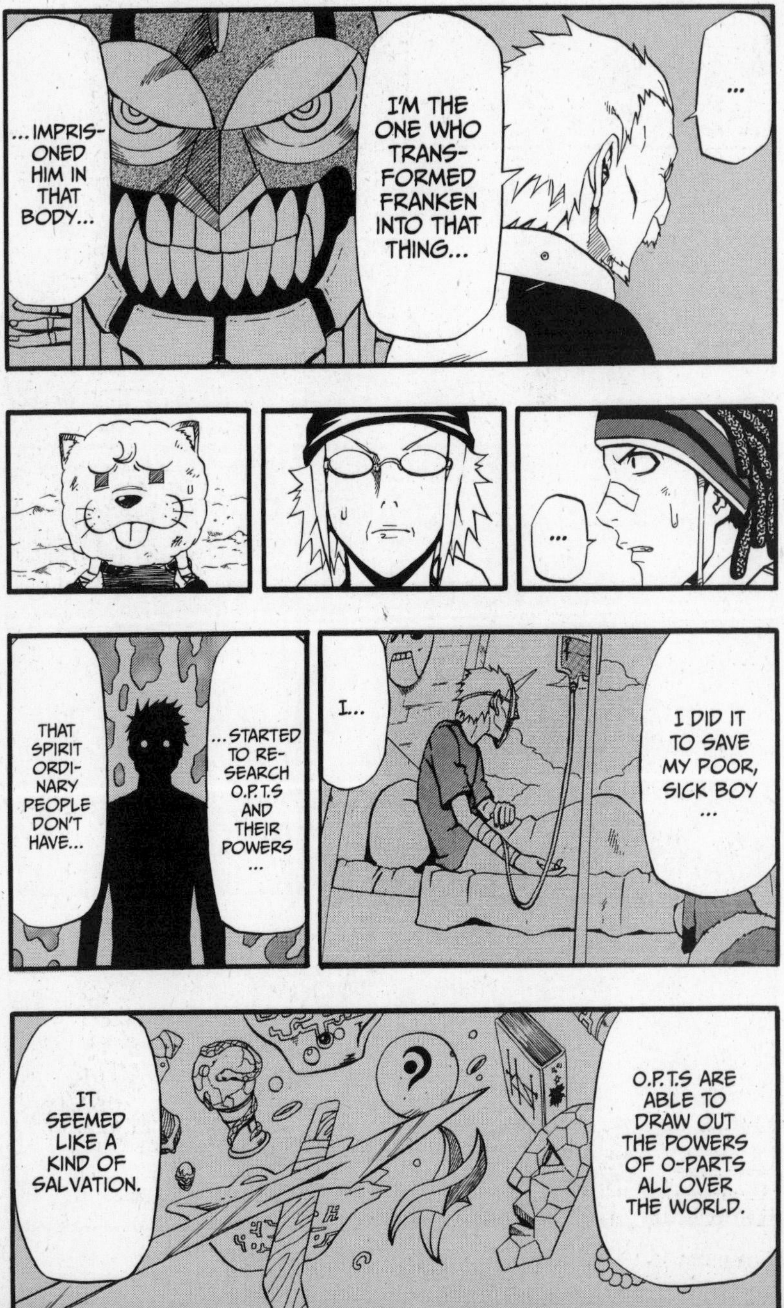
...
I'M THE ONE WHO TRANS-FORMED FRANKEN INTO THAT THING...
...IMPRIS-ONED HIM IN THAT BODY...
...
I DID IT TO SAVE MY POOR, SICK BOY ...
I...
...STARTED TO RE-SEARCH O.P.T.S AND THEIR POWERS ...
THAT SPIRIT ORDI-NARY PEOPLE DON'T HAVE...
O.P.T.S ARE ABLE TO DRAW OUT THE POWERS OF O-PARTS ALL OVER THE WORLD.
IT SEEMED LIKE A KIND OF SALVATION.

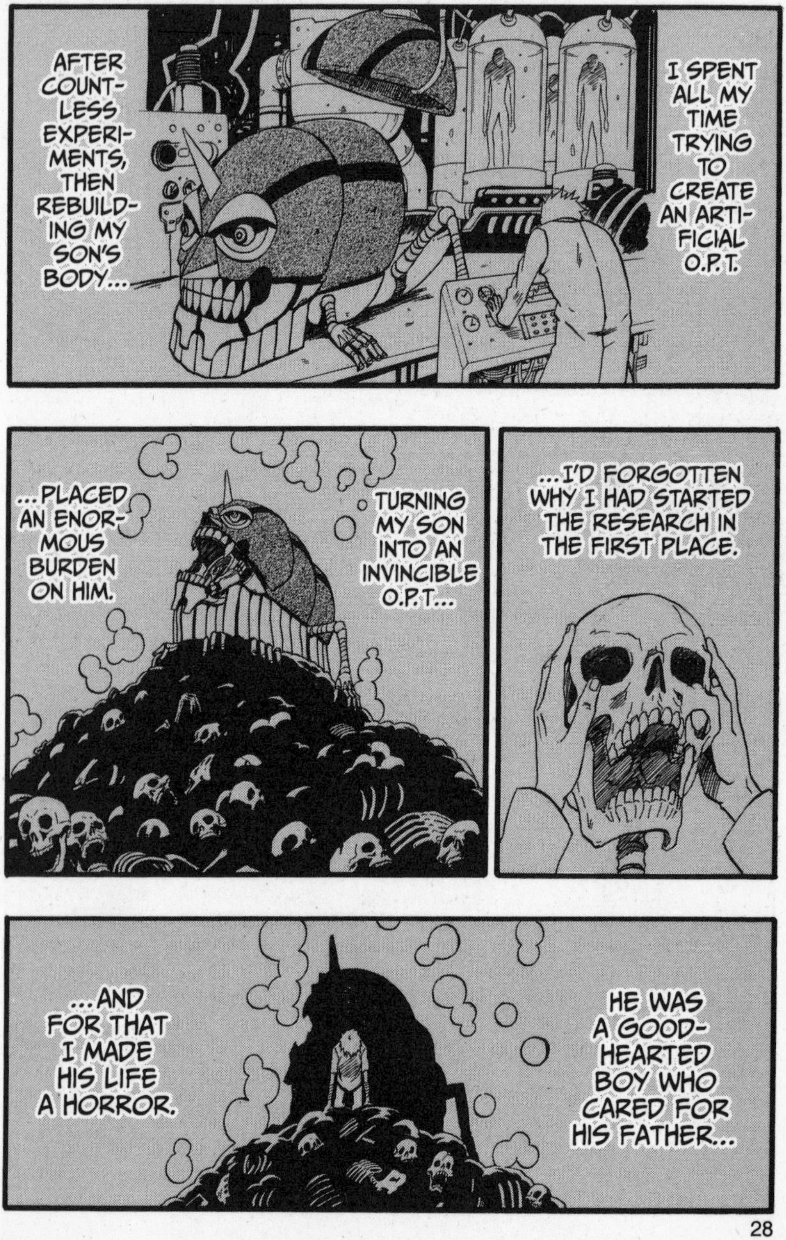
I SPENT ALL MY TIME TRYING TO CREATE AN ARTIFICIAL O.P.T.
AFTER COUNTLESS EXPERIMENTS, THEN REBUILDING MY SON'S BODY...
...I'D FORGOTTEN WHY I HAD STARTED THE RESEARCH IN THE FIRST PLACE.
TURNING MY SON INTO AN INVINCIBLE O.P.T...
...PLACED AN ENORMOUS BURDEN ON HIM.
HE WAS A GOOD-HEARTED BOY WHO CARED FOR HIS FATHER...
...AND FOR THAT I MADE HIS LIFE A HORROR.

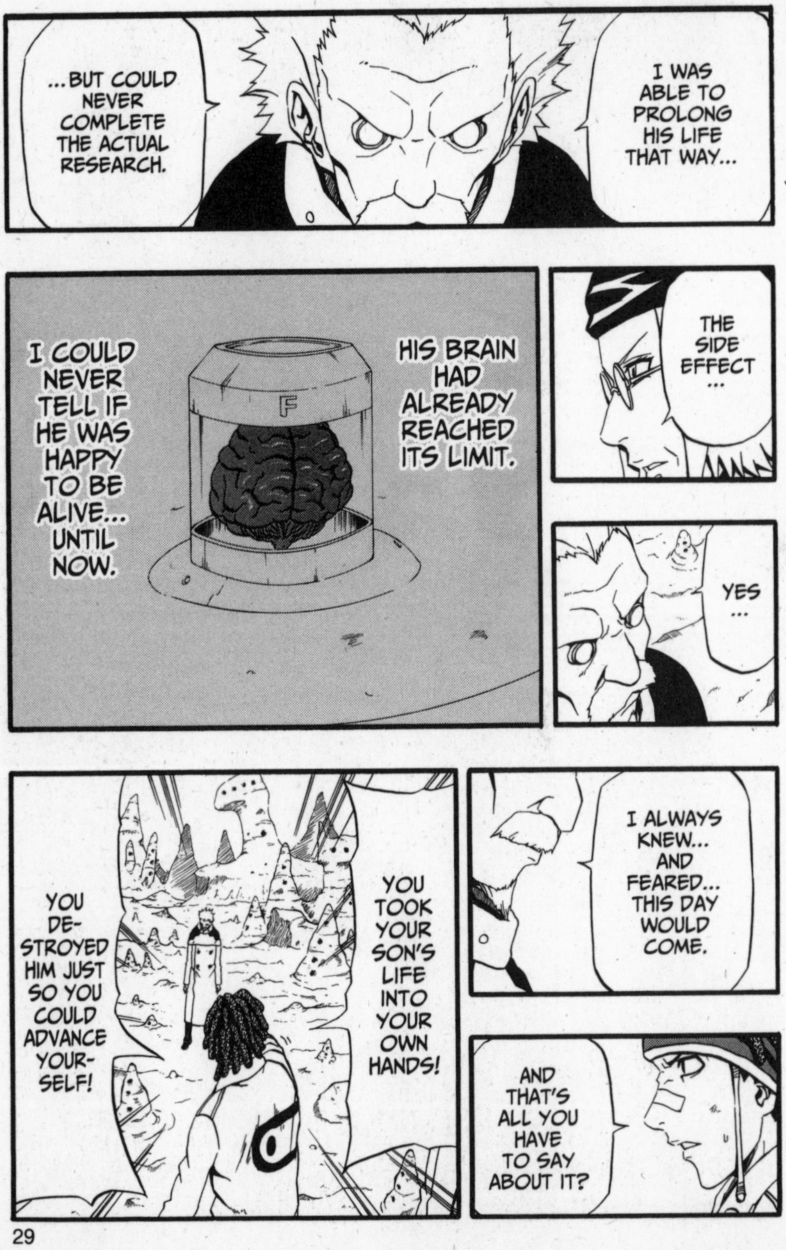
I WAS ABLE TO PROLONG HIS LIFE THAT WAY...
...BUT COULD NEVER COMPLETE THE ACTUAL RESEARCH.
THE SIDE EFFECT ...
YES ...
F
HIS BRAIN HAD ALREADY REACHED ITS LIMIT.
I COULD NEVER TELL IF HE WAS HAPPY TO BE ALIVE... UNTIL NOW.
I ALWAYS KNEW... AND FEARED... THIS DAY WOULD COME.
AND THAT'S ALL YOU HAVE TO SAY ABOUT IT?
YOU TOOK YOUR SON'S LIFE INTO YOUR OWN HANDS!
YOU DE-STROYED HIM JUST SO YOU COULD ADVANCE YOUR-SELF!

WHAT DO YOU KNOW ABOUT MY SON?!

YOU'RE AN OUTSIDER! WHAT DO YOU KNOW ABOUT ME?!

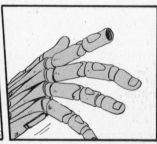

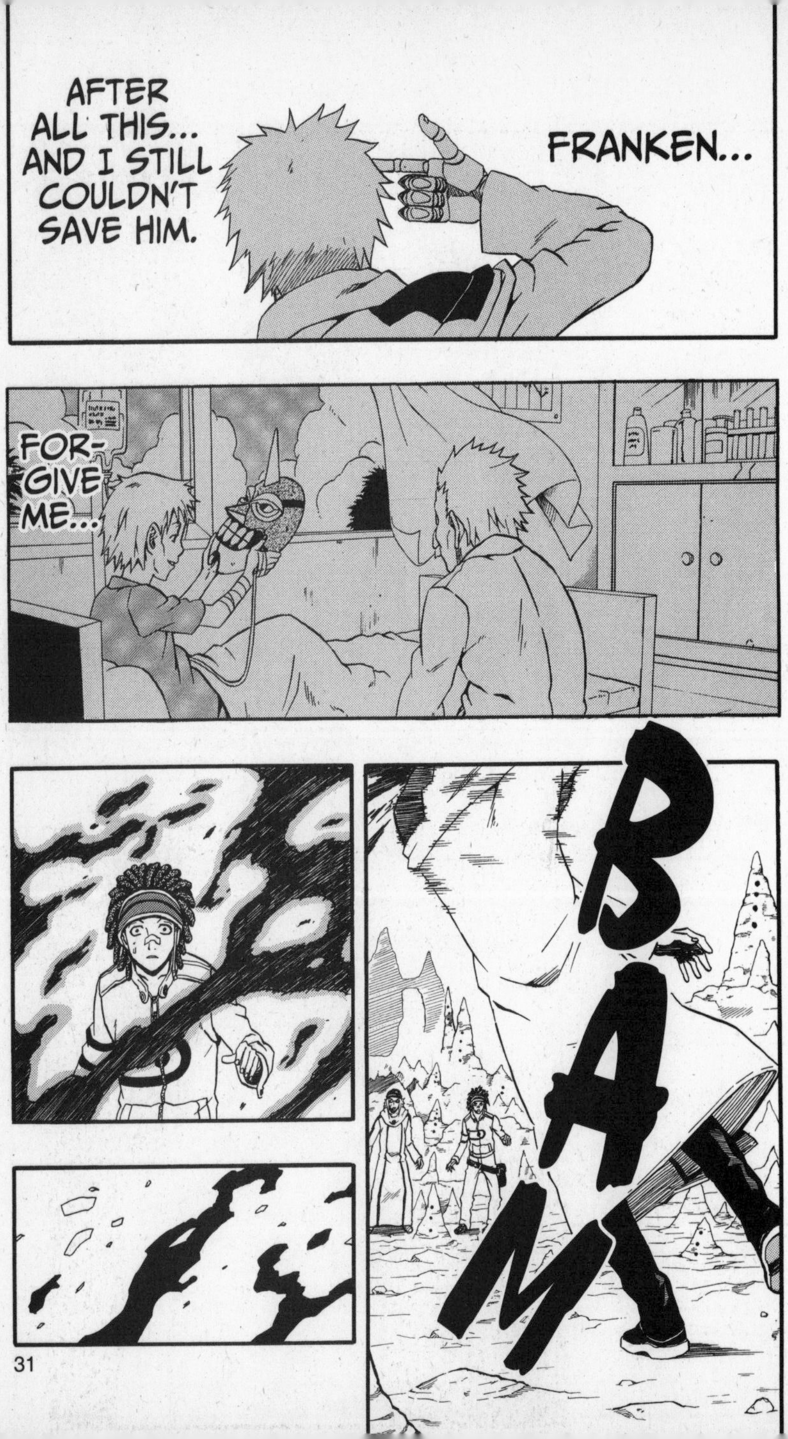
FRANKEN...
AFTER ALL THIS... AND I STILL COULDN'T SAVE HIM.
FOR-GIVE ME...
BAM

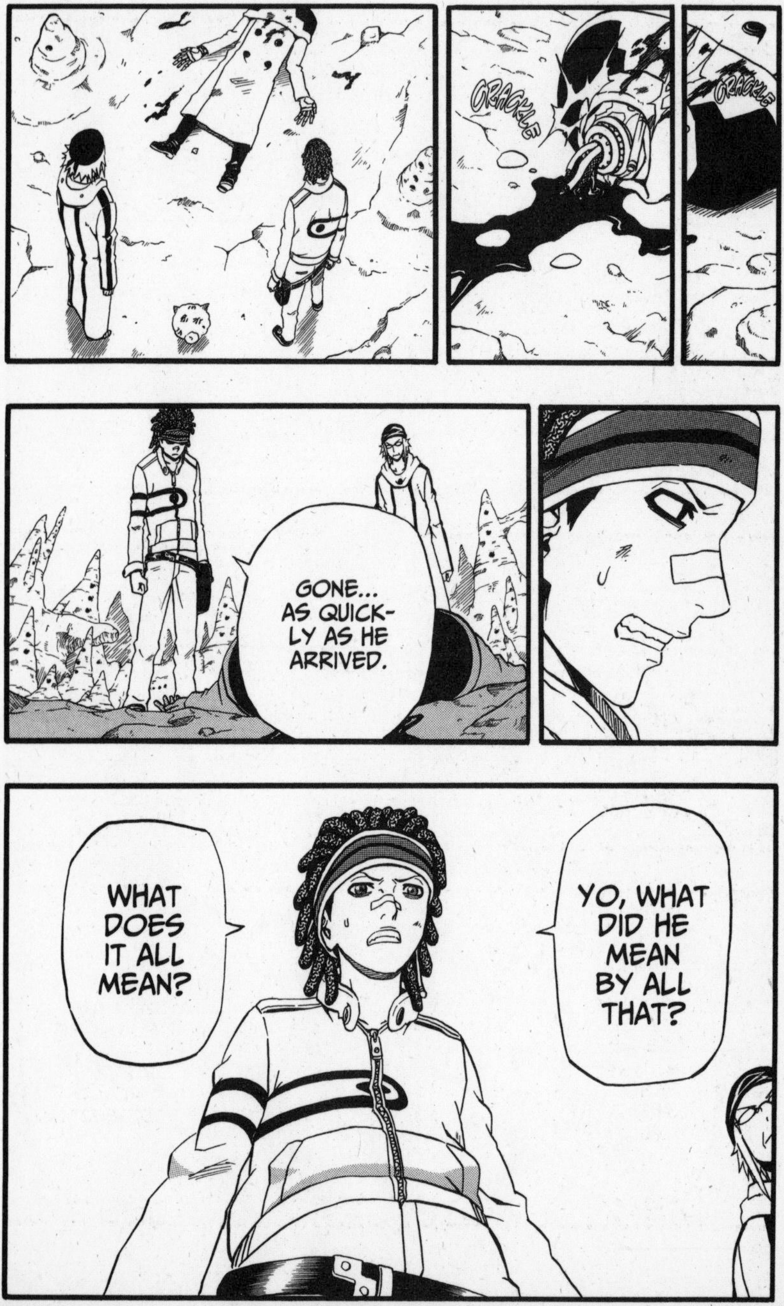
CRACKLE
CRACKLE
GONE... AS QUICKLY AS HE ARRIVED.
YO, WHAT DID HE MEAN BY ALL THAT?
WHAT DOES IT ALL MEAN?

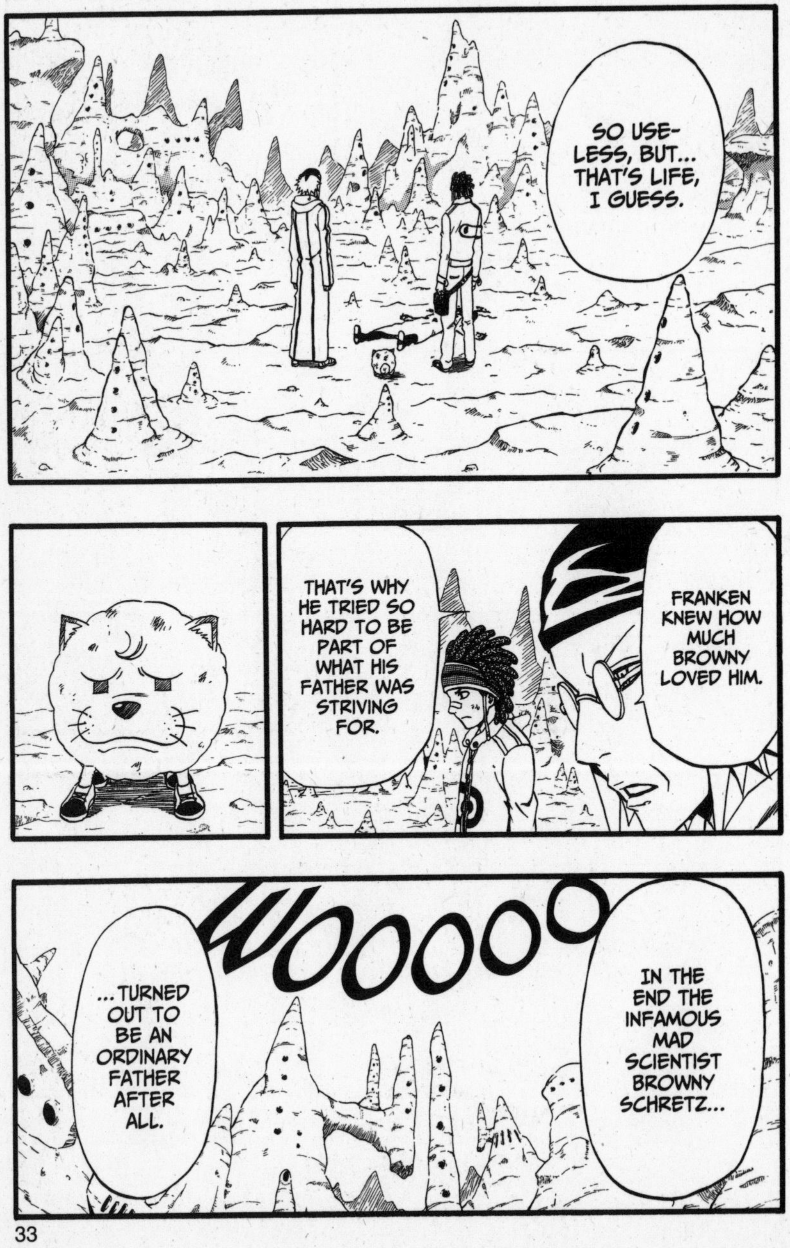
SO USE-LESS, BUT... THAT'S LIFE, I GUESS.
FRANKEN KNEW HOW MUCH BROWNY LOVED HIM.
THAT'S WHY HE TRIED SO HARD TO BE PART OF WHAT HIS FATHER WAS STRIVING FOR.
WOOOOO
IN THE END THE INFAMOUS MAD SCIENTIST BROWNY SCHRETZ...
...TURNED OUT TO BE AN ORDINARY FATHER AFTER ALL.

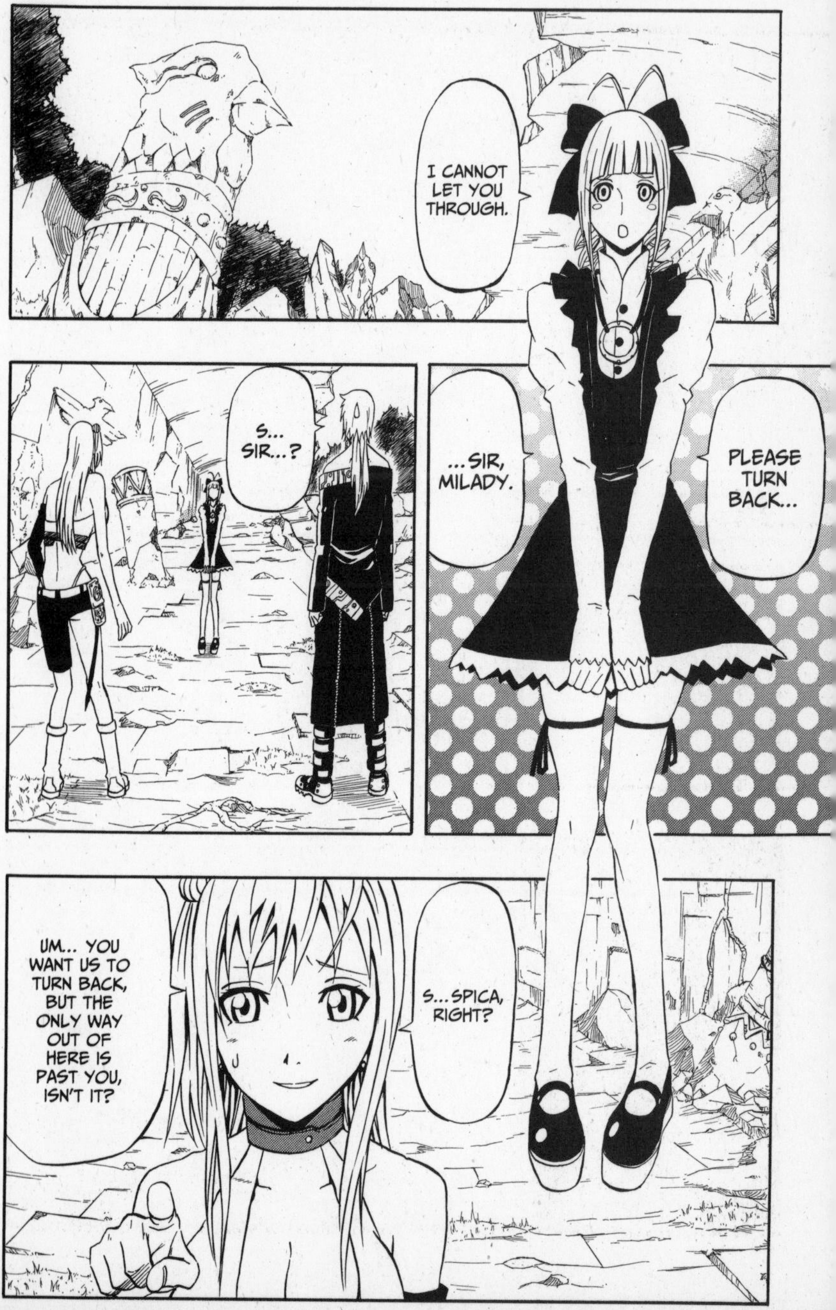
I CANNOT LET YOU THROUGH.
PLEASE TURN BACK...
...SIR, MILADY.
S... SIR...?
S...SPICA, RIGHT?
UM... YOU WANT US TO TURN BACK, BUT THE ONLY WAY OUT OF HERE IS PAST YOU, ISN'T IT?

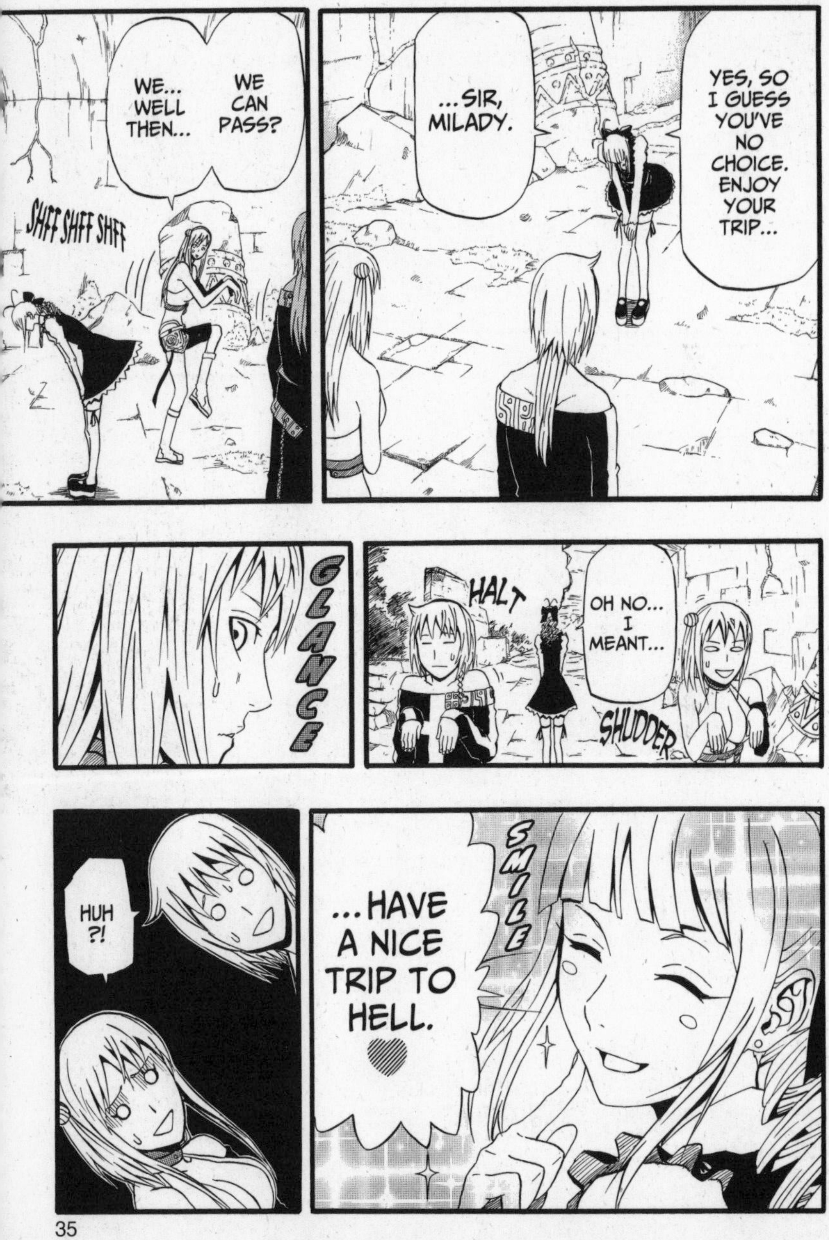
YES, SO I GUESS YOU'VE NO CHOICE. ENJOY YOUR TRIP...
...SIR, MILADY.
WE... WELL THEN... WE CAN PASS?
SHFF SHFF SHFF
OH NO... I MEANT...
HALT
SHUDDER
GLANCE
SMILE
...HAVE A NICE TRIP TO HELL.
HUH ?!

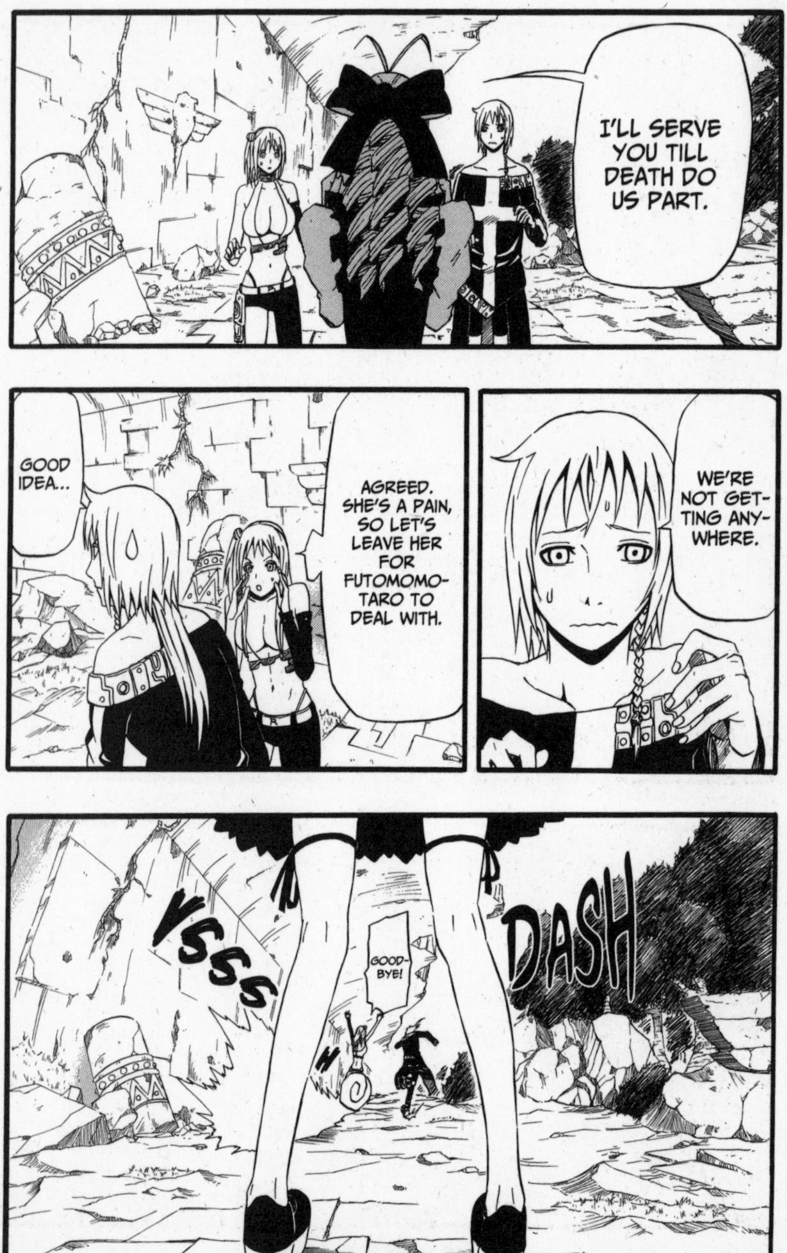
I'LL SERVE YOU TILL DEATH DO US PART.
WE'RE NOT GETTING ANYWHERE.
AGREED. SHE'S A PAIN, SO LET'S LEAVE HER FOR FUTOMOMOTARO TO DEAL WITH.
GOOD IDEA...
DASH
GOOD-BYE!
VSSS

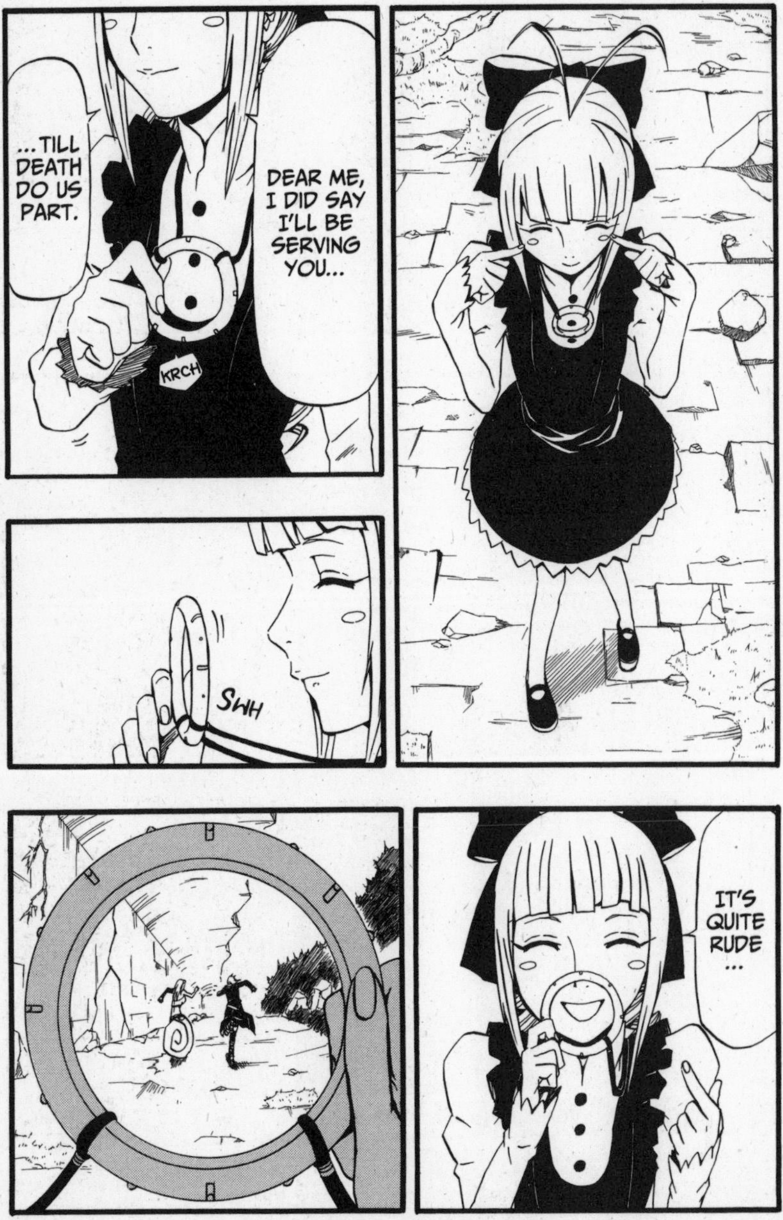
DEAR ME, I DID SAY I'LL BE SERVING YOU...
...TILL DEATH DO US PART.
KRCH
SWH
IT'S QUITE RUDE ...

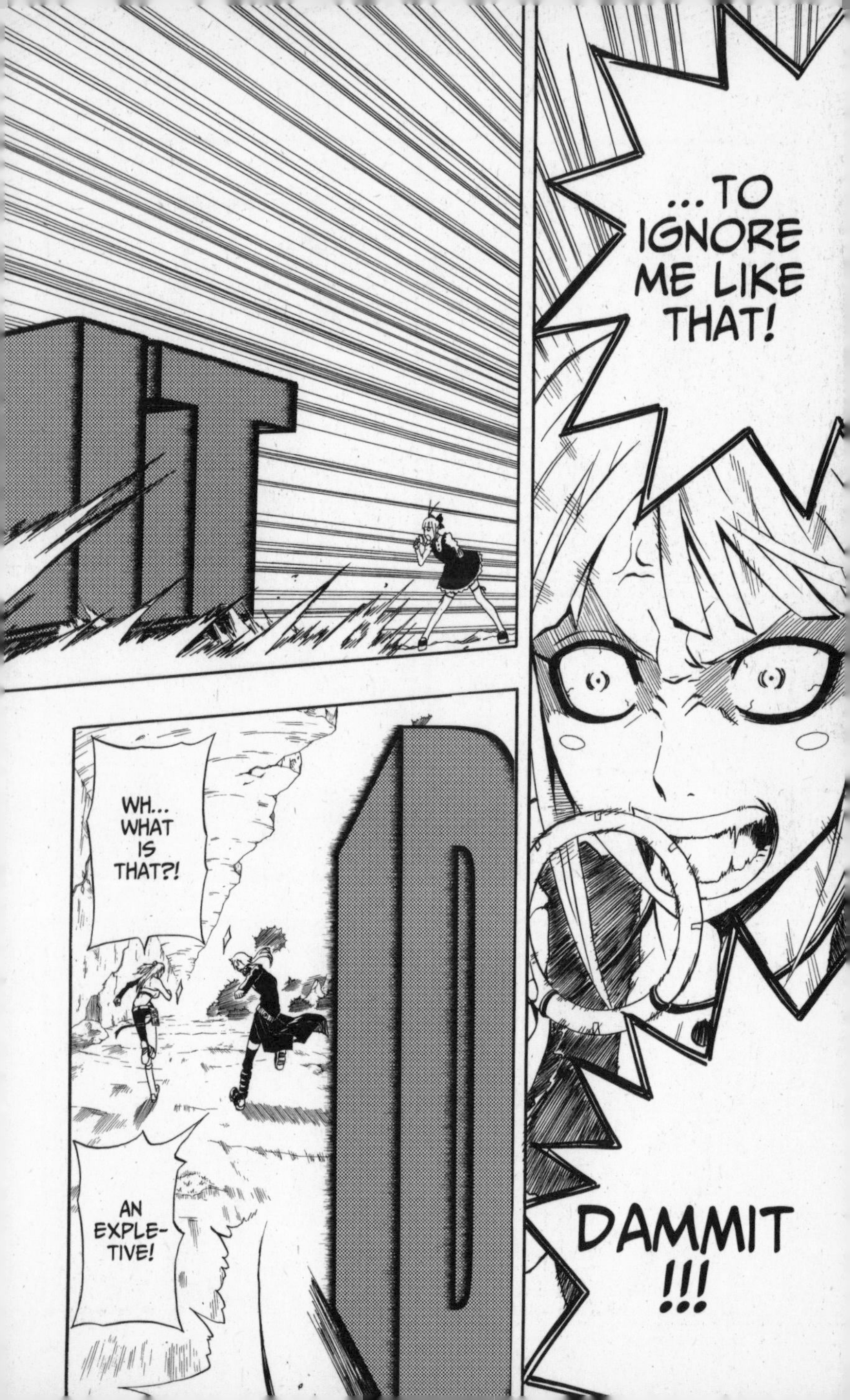
... TO IGNORE ME LIKE THAT!
DAMMIT !!!
WH... WHAT IS THAT?!
AN EXPLE-TIVE!

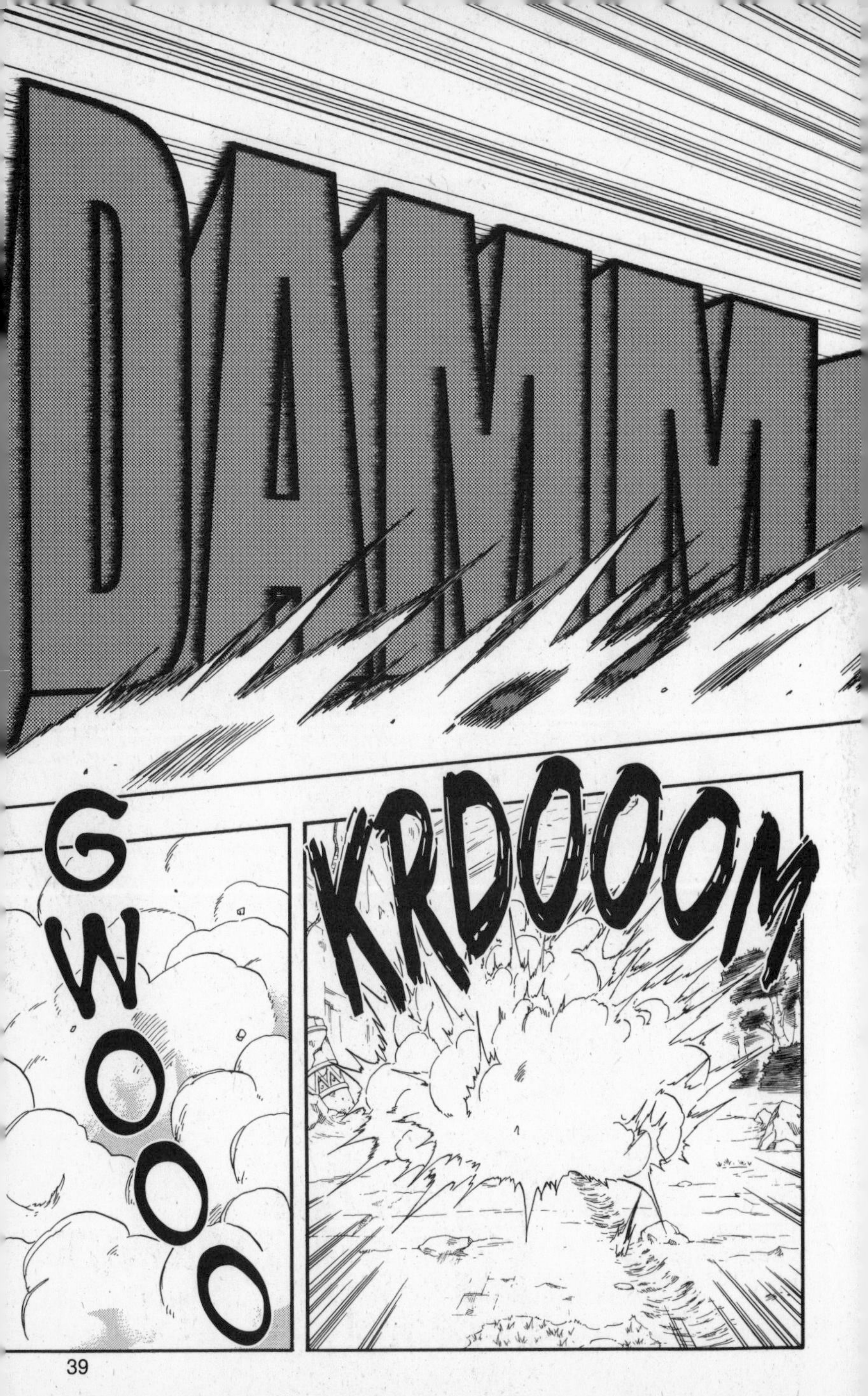
DAMM
KRDOOOM
GWOOOO

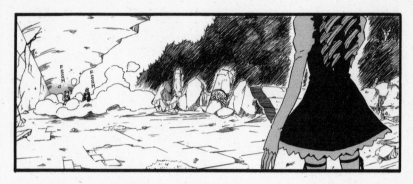

FSSH
FSSH
I SURE WASN'T EXPECTING ANYTHING LIKE THAT.
IT'S PROBABLY...
...THAT PENDANT.
TSK
IT MUST BE AN O-PART THAT CAN...
...TURN SOUND WAVES INTO SOLID MATERIALIZATIONS.
666
666
I'M GUESSING IT'S A B RANK O-PART.
DON'T MESS WITH ME...
SHE'S SUPPOSED TO BE ONE OF THE ZENOM BIG FOUR... AND NOW I BELIEVE IT!

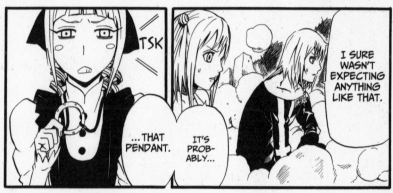

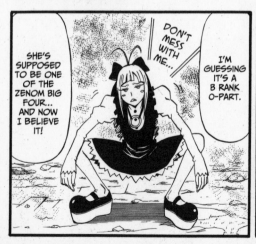

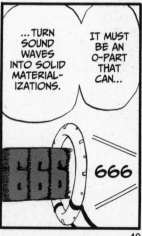

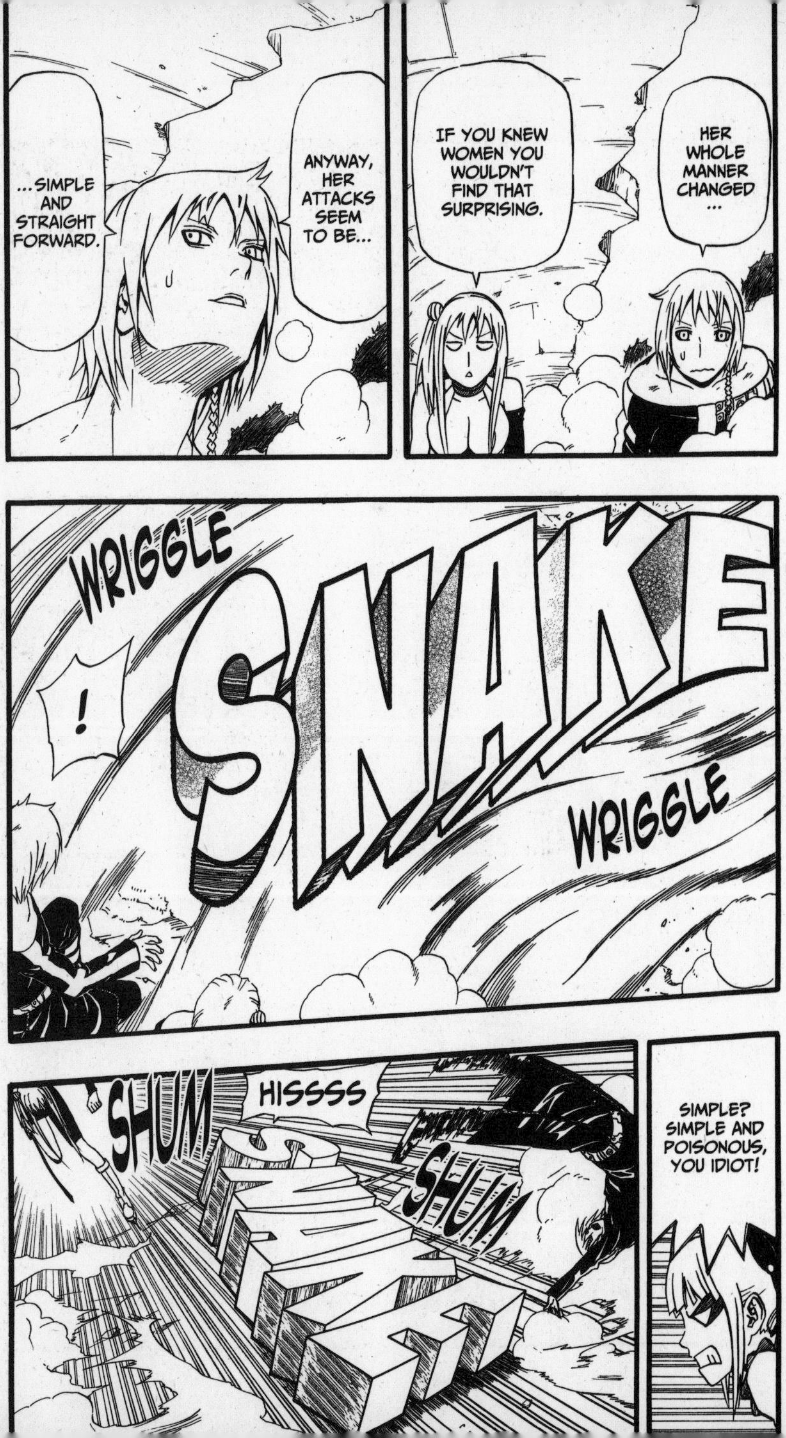
HER WHOLE MANNER CHANGED ...
IF YOU KNEW WOMEN YOU WOULDN'T FIND THAT SURPRISING.
ANYWAY, HER ATTACKS SEEM TO BE...
...SIMPLE AND STRAIGHT FORWARD.
WRIGGLE
SNAKE
!
WRIGGLE
SIMPLE? SIMPLE AND POISONOUS, YOU IDIOT!
SHUM
HISSSS
SHUM
SHUM

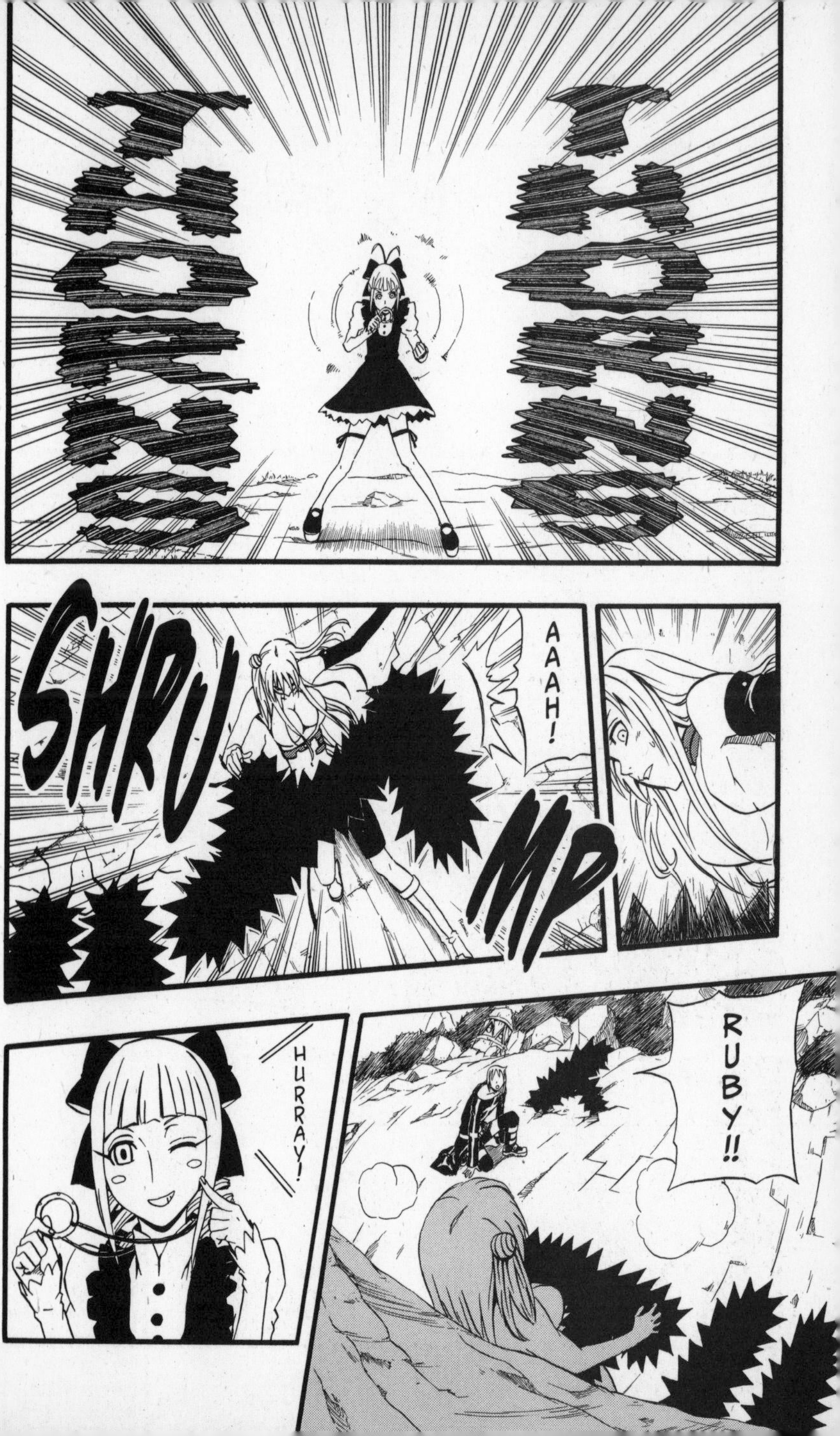
AAAH!
SHRUMP
RUBY!!
HURRAY!

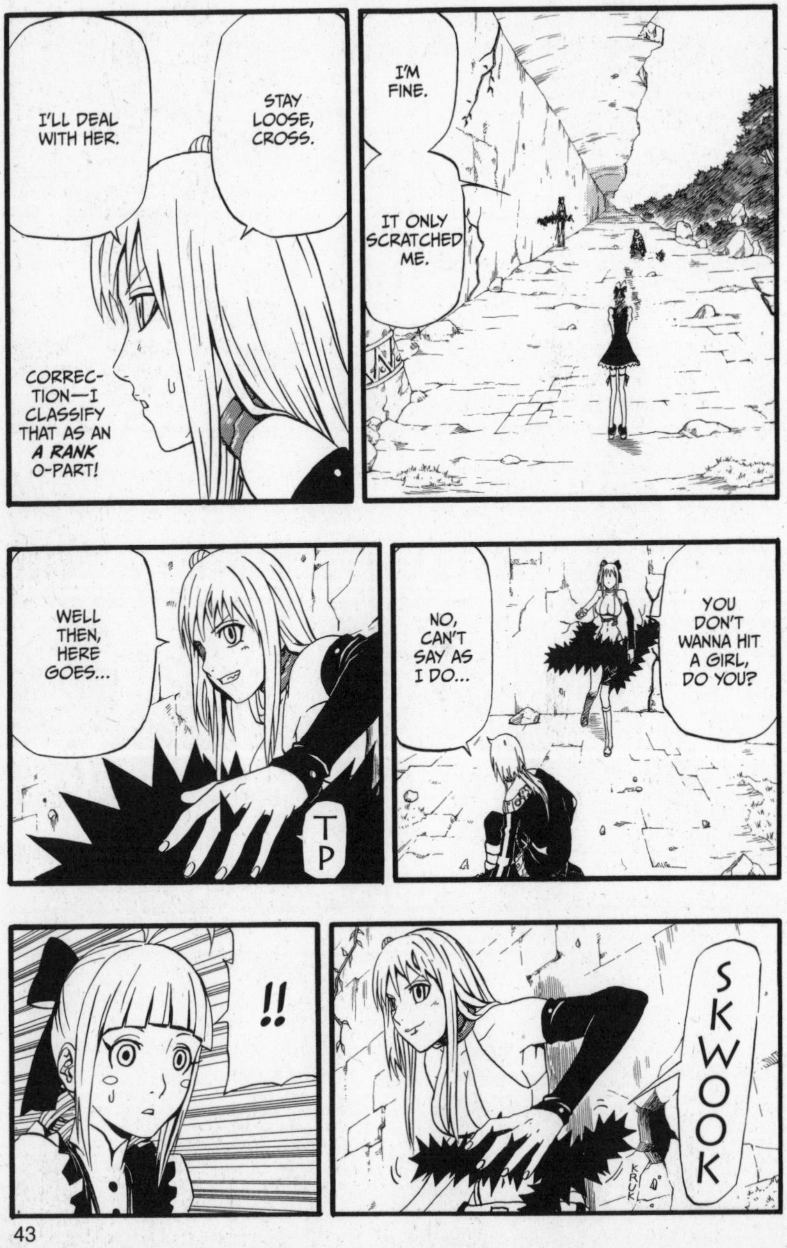
I'M FINE.
IT ONLY SCRATCHED ME.
STAY LOOSE, CROSS.
I'LL DEAL WITH HER.
CORRECTION—I CLASSIFY THAT AS AN *A RANK* O-PART!
YOU DON'T WANNA HIT A GIRL, DO YOU?
NO, CAN'T SAY AS I DO...
WELL THEN, HERE GOES...
TP
SKWOOK
KRUK
!!

GET READY!

THE PRICKLE'S GRADUALLY SHRINKING.

SWN

SWNNNN

SHE SHRANK! I CAN'T SEE HER! NO FAIR!

SHUP

BOOSH

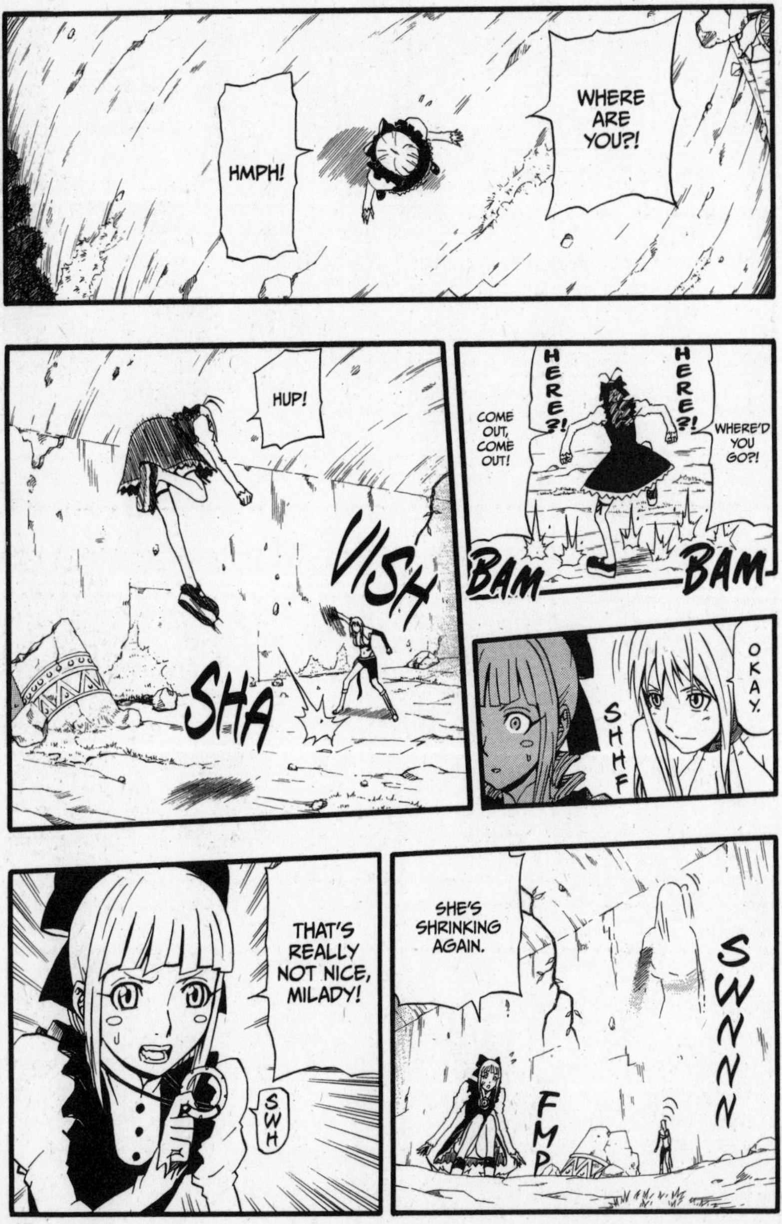
WHERE ARE YOU?!
HMPH!
WHERE'D YOU GO?!
HERE?!
HERE?!
COME OUT, COME OUT!
BAM
BAM
OKAY.
SHHF
HUP!
VISH
SHA
SWNNN
SHE'S SHRINKING AGAIN.
FMP
THAT'S REALLY NOT NICE, MILADY!
SWH

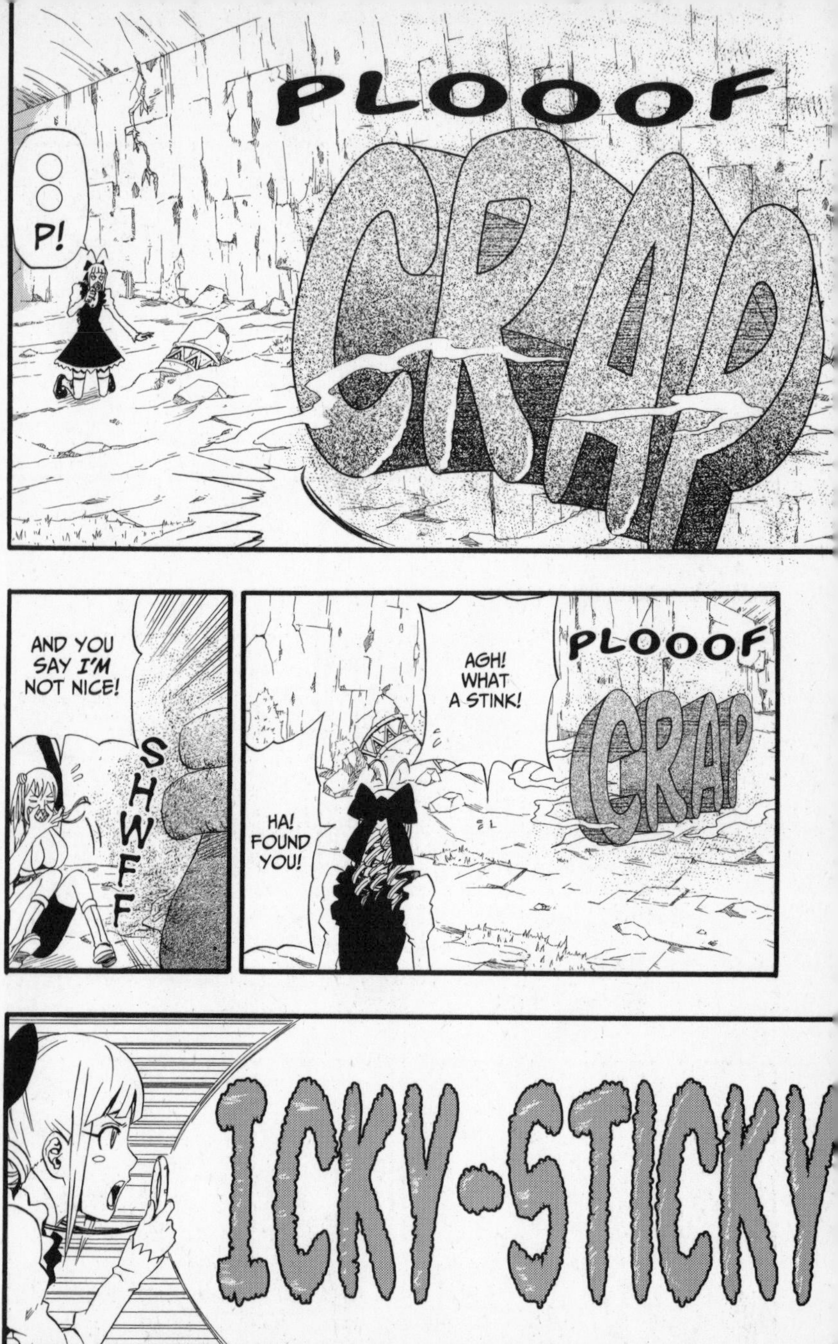
PLOOOF
CRAP
OOP!
PLOOOF
CRAP
AGH! WHAT A STINK!
HA! FOUND YOU!
SHWFF
AND YOU SAY *I'M* NOT NICE!
ICKY-STICKY

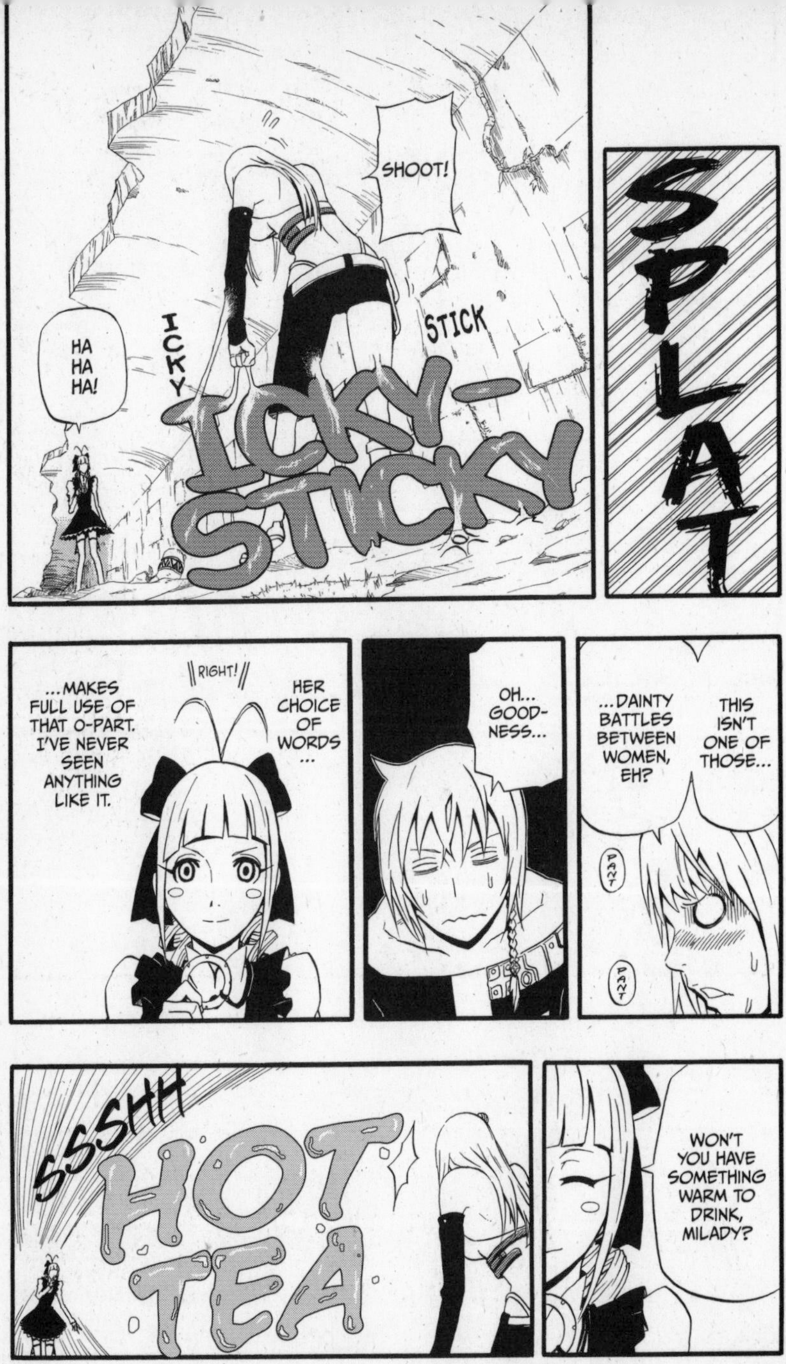
SPLAT
SHOOT!
STICK
ICKY
ICKY-STICKY
HA HA HA!
THIS ISN'T ONE OF THOSE...
...DAINTY BATTLES BETWEEN WOMEN, EH?
PANT
PANT
OH... GOODNESS...
HER CHOICE OF WORDS...
RIGHT!
...MAKES FULL USE OF THAT O-PART. I'VE NEVER SEEN ANYTHING LIKE IT.
WON'T YOU HAVE SOMETHING WARM TO DRINK, MILADY?
SSSHH
HOT TEA

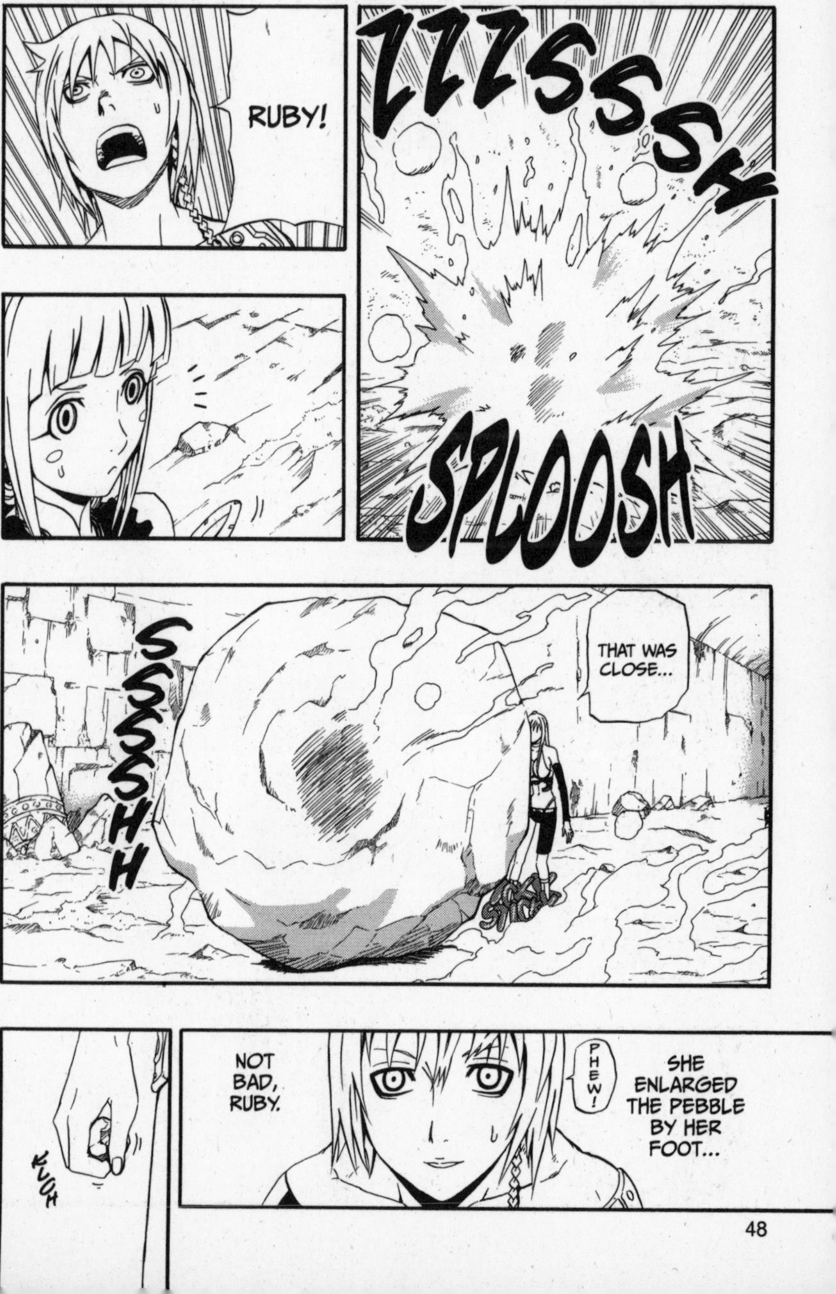
ZZZSSSH
SPLOOSH
RUBY!
SSSSHH
THAT WAS CLOSE...
SHE ENLARGED THE PEBBLE BY HER FOOT...
PHEW!
NOT BAD, RUBY.

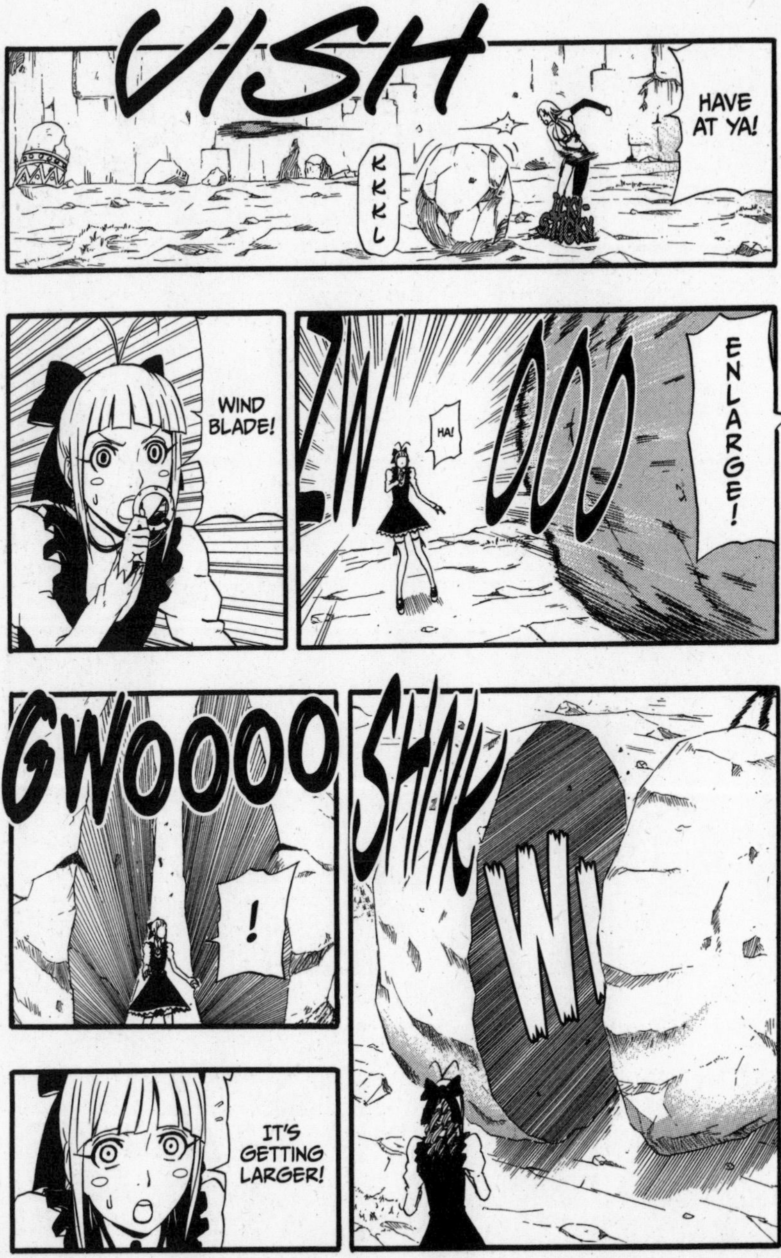
VISH
HAVE AT YA!
ICKY-STICKY!
KKKL
ENLARGE!
ZW OOO
HA!
WIND BLADE!
SHINK
GWOOOO
!
IT'S GETTING LARGER!

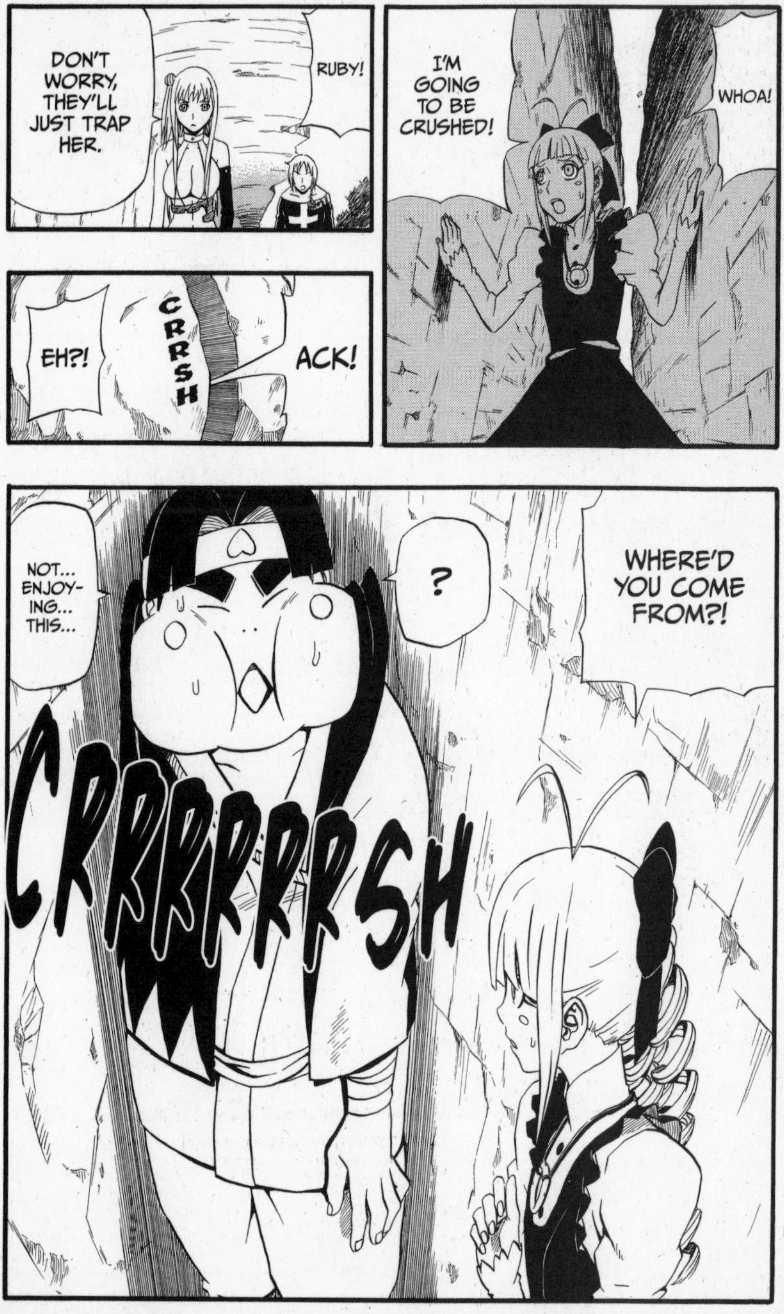
WHOA!
I'M GOING TO BE CRUSHED!
RUBY!
DON'T WORRY, THEY'LL JUST TRAP HER.
ACK!
CRRSH
EH?!
WHERE'D YOU COME FROM?!
?
NOT... ENJOY-ING... THIS...
CRRRRRRSH

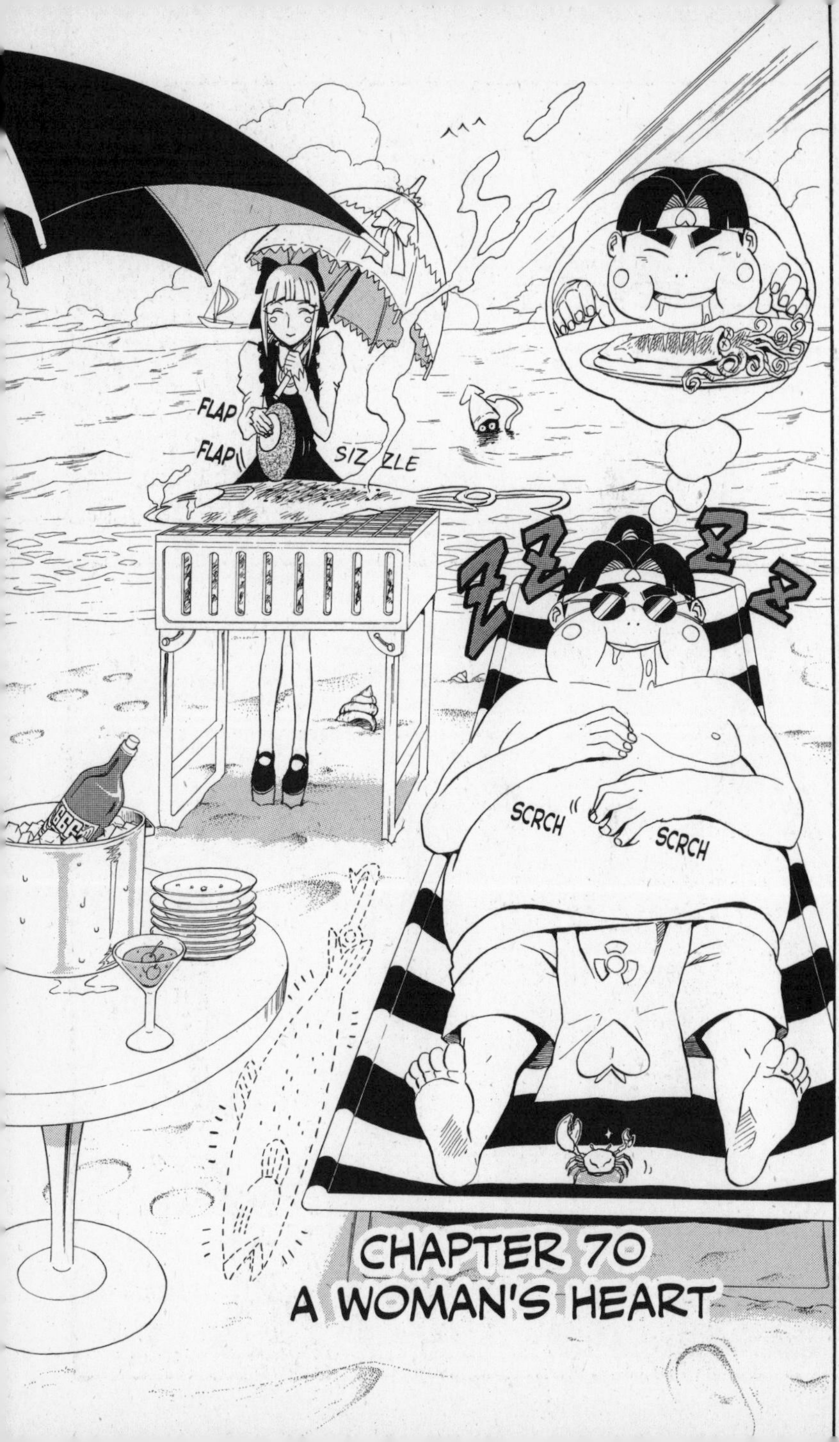
ZZZZ
SCRCH
SCRCH
FLAP
FLAP
SIZZLE

CHAPTER 70
A WOMAN'S HEART

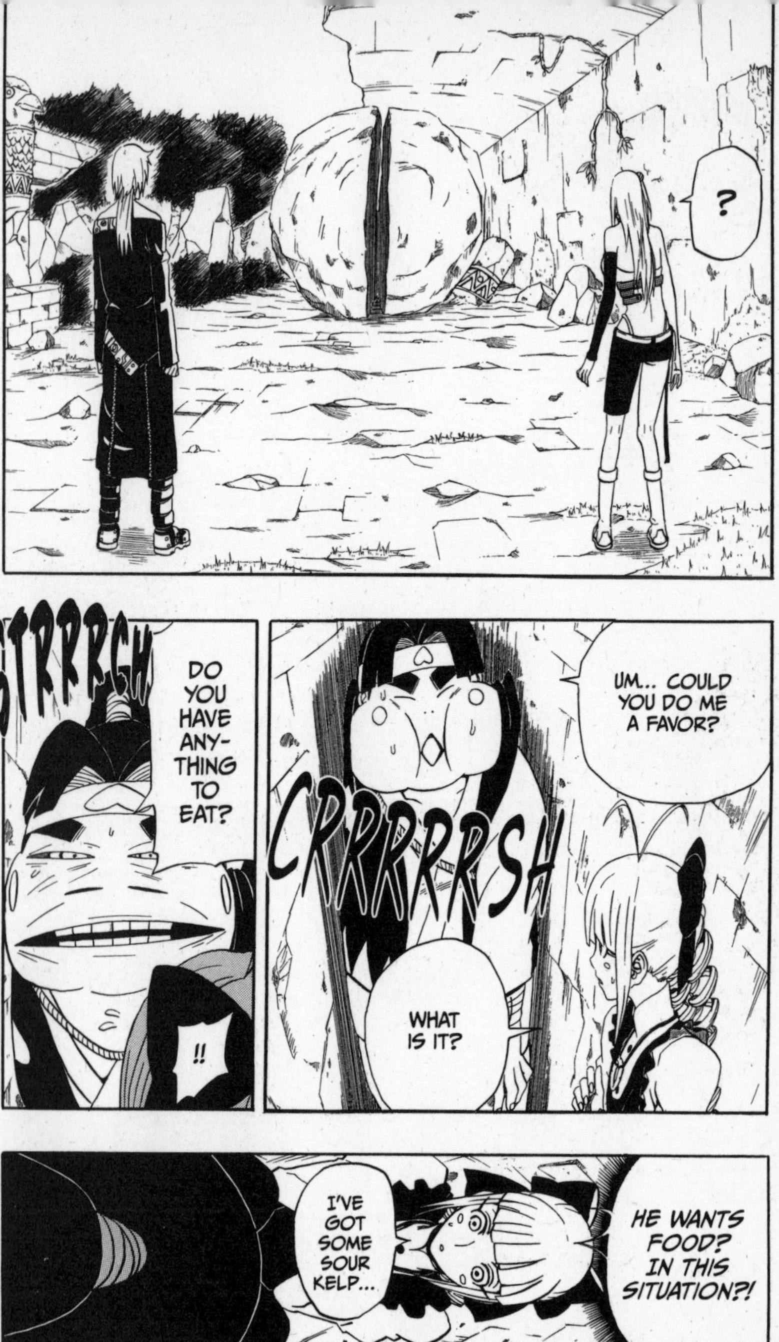
?
UM... COULD YOU DO ME A FAVOR?
CRRRRRSH
WHAT IS IT?
STRRRCH
DO YOU HAVE ANY-THING TO EAT?
!!
HE WANTS FOOD? IN THIS SITUATION?!
I'VE GOT SOME SOUR KELP...

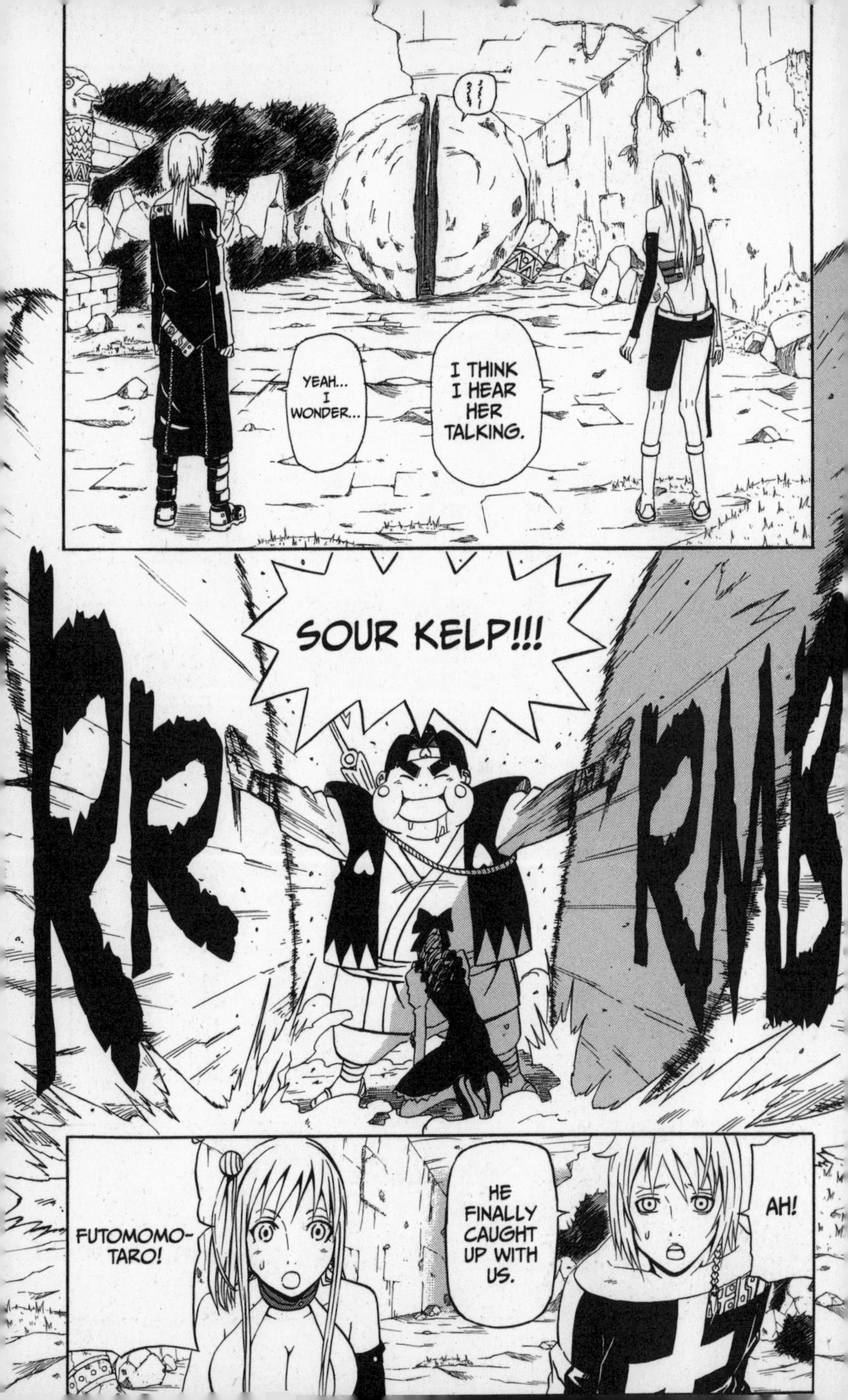
I THINK I HEAR HER TALKING.
YEAH... I WONDER...
SOUR KELP!!!
RR
RMB
AH!
HE FINALLY CAUGHT UP WITH US.
FUTOMOMO-TARO!

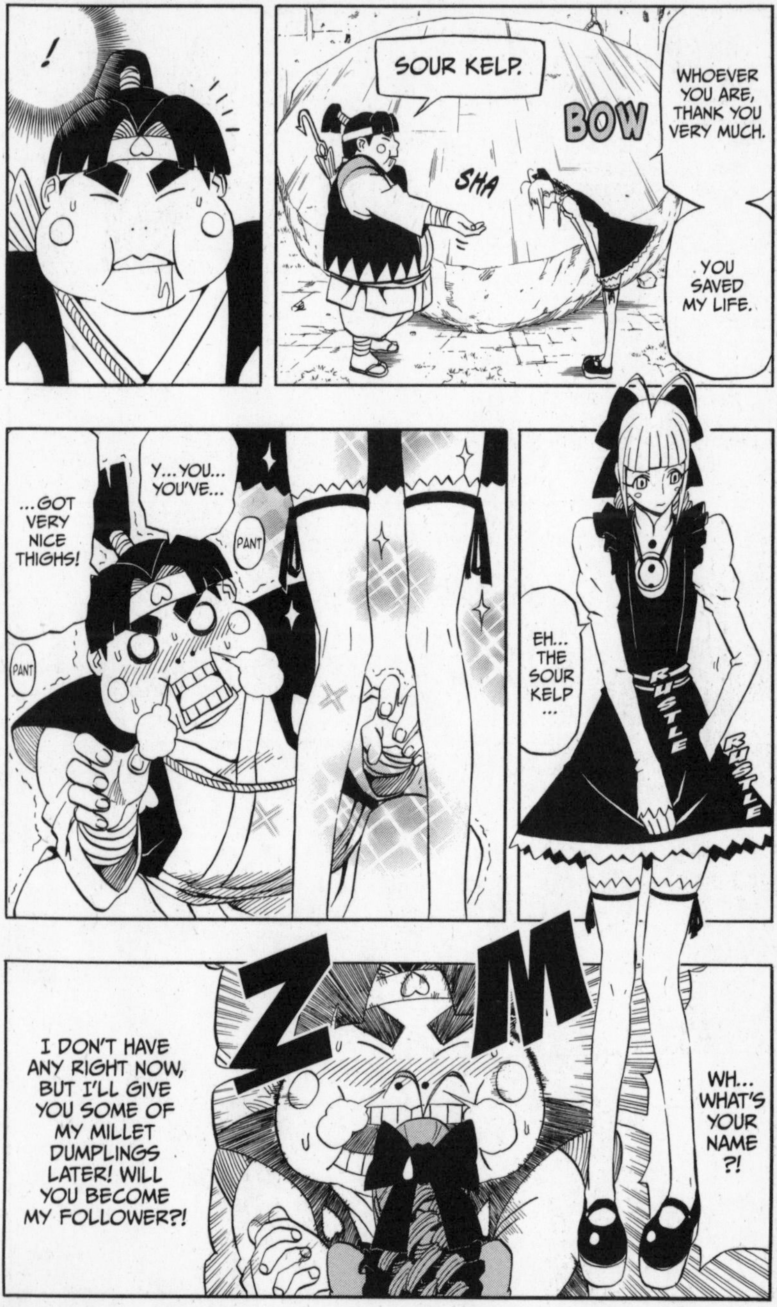
WHOEVER YOU ARE, THANK YOU VERY MUCH.
BOW
YOU SAVED MY LIFE.
SOUR KELP.
SHA
!
EH... THE SOUR KELP ...
RUSTLE
RUSTLE
Y... YOU... YOU'VE...
...GOT VERY NICE THIGHS!
PANT
PANT
WH... WHAT'S YOUR NAME ?!
Z M
I DON'T HAVE ANY RIGHT NOW, BUT I'LL GIVE YOU SOME OF MY MILLET DUMPLINGS LATER! WILL YOU BECOME MY FOLLOWER?!

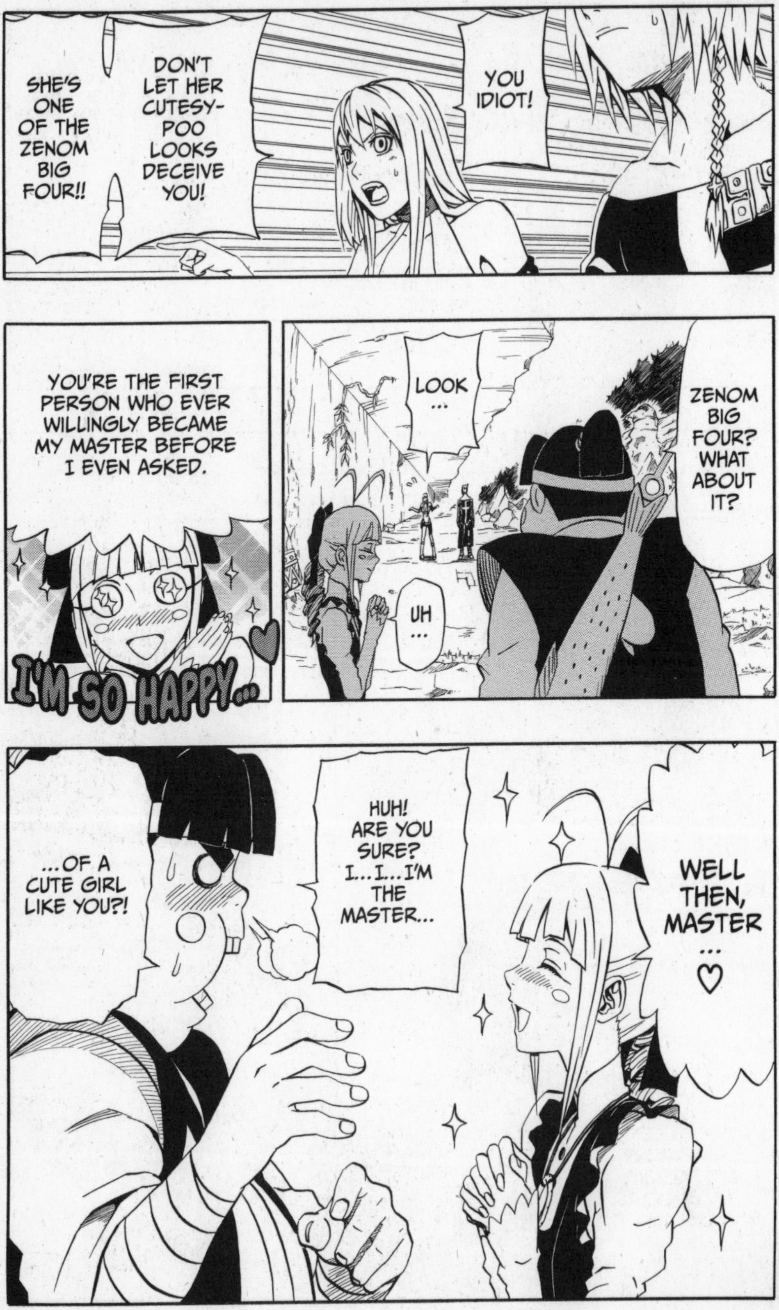
YOU IDIOT!
DON'T LET HER CUTESY-POO LOOKS DECEIVE YOU!
SHE'S ONE OF THE ZENOM BIG FOUR!!
ZENOM BIG FOUR? WHAT ABOUT IT?
LOOK ...
UH ...
YOU'RE THE FIRST PERSON WHO EVER WILLINGLY BECAME MY MASTER BEFORE I EVEN ASKED.
I'M SO HAPPY...
WELL THEN, MASTER ... ♡
HUH! ARE YOU SURE? I...I...I'M THE MASTER...
...OF A CUTE GIRL LIKE YOU?!

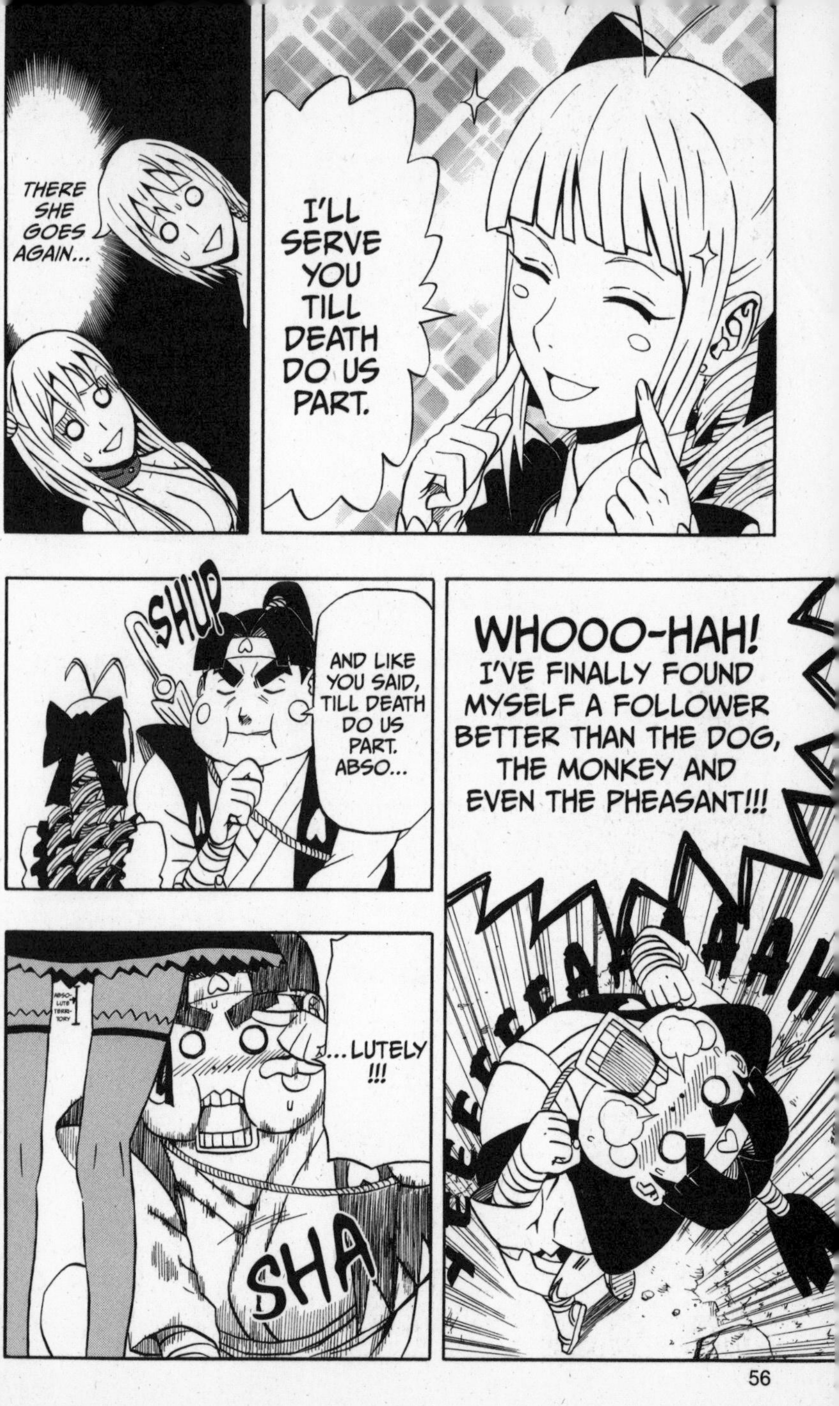
I'LL SERVE YOU TILL DEATH DO US PART.
THERE SHE GOES AGAIN...
WHOOO-HAH!
I'VE FINALLY FOUND MYSELF A FOLLOWER BETTER THAN THE DOG, THE MONKEY AND EVEN THE PHEASANT!!!
AND LIKE YOU SAID, TILL DEATH DO US PART. ABSO...
SHUP
ABSOLUTE TERRITORY
...LUTELY !!!
SHA

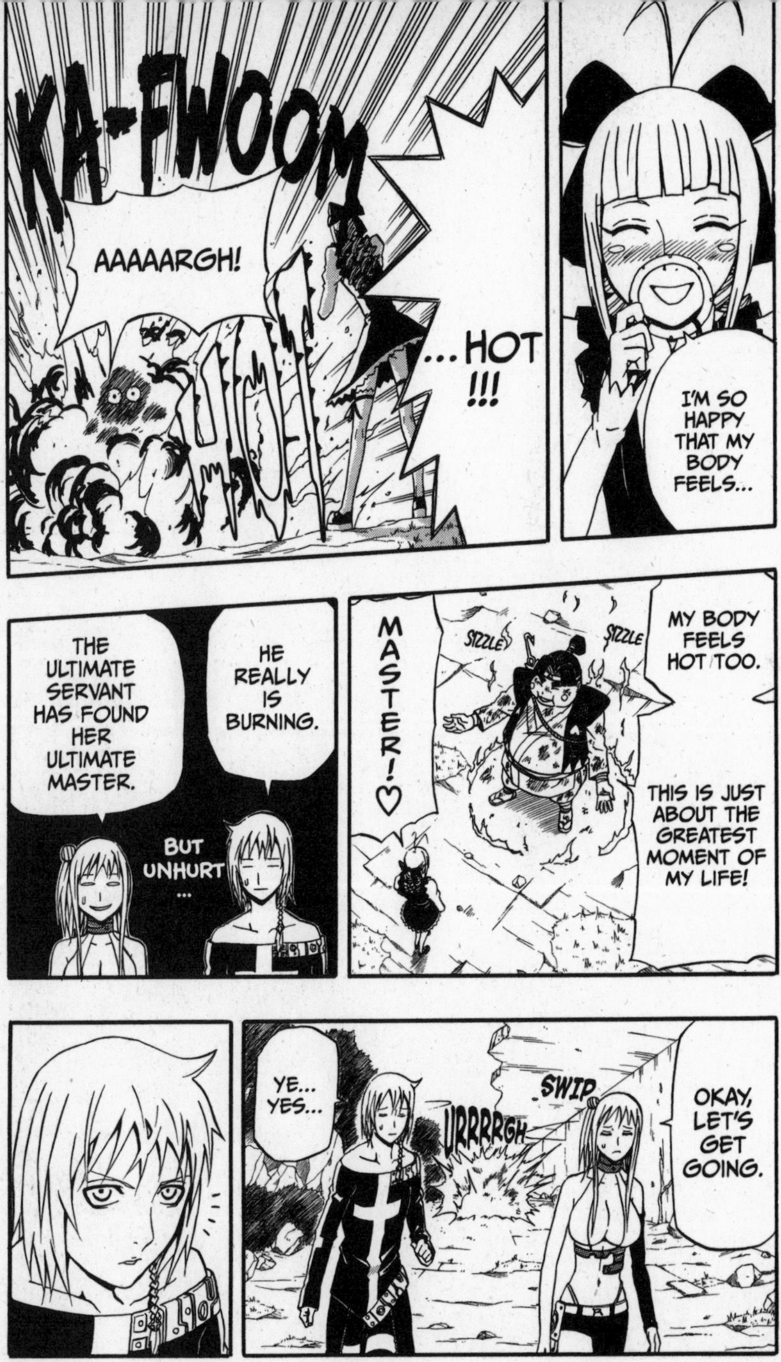
I'M SO HAPPY THAT MY BODY FEELS...
KA-FWOOM
...HOT !!!
AAAAARGH!
HOT
MY BODY FEELS HOT TOO.
SIZZLE
SIZZLE
MASTER!♡
THIS IS JUST ABOUT THE GREATEST MOMENT OF MY LIFE!
HE REALLY IS BURNING.
THE ULTIMATE SERVANT HAS FOUND HER ULTIMATE MASTER.
BUT UNHURT ...
OKAY, LET'S GET GOING.
SWIP
URRRRGH
YE... YES...

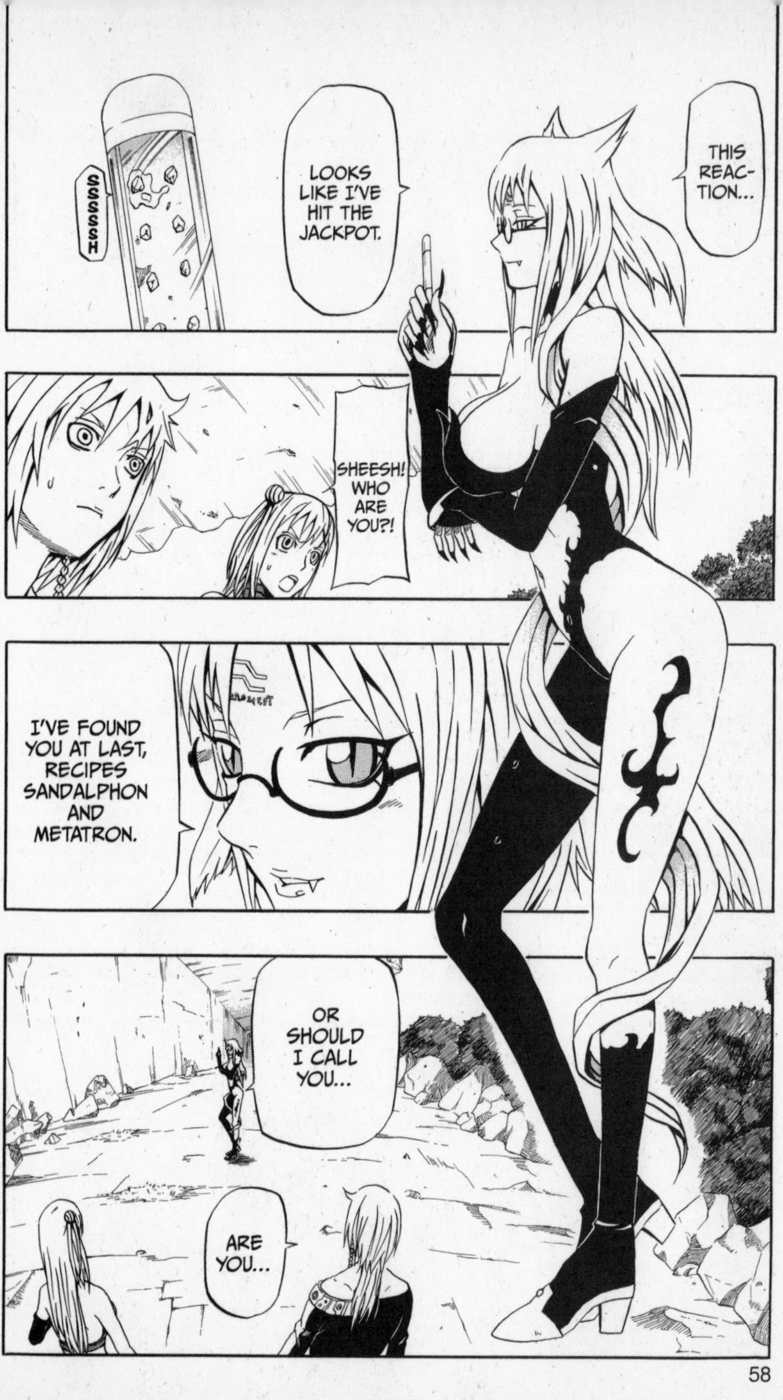
THIS REACTION...
LOOKS LIKE I'VE HIT THE JACKPOT.
SSSSSH
SHEESH! WHO ARE YOU?!
I'VE FOUND YOU AT LAST, RECIPES SANDALPHON AND METATRON.
OR SHOULD I CALL YOU...
ARE YOU...

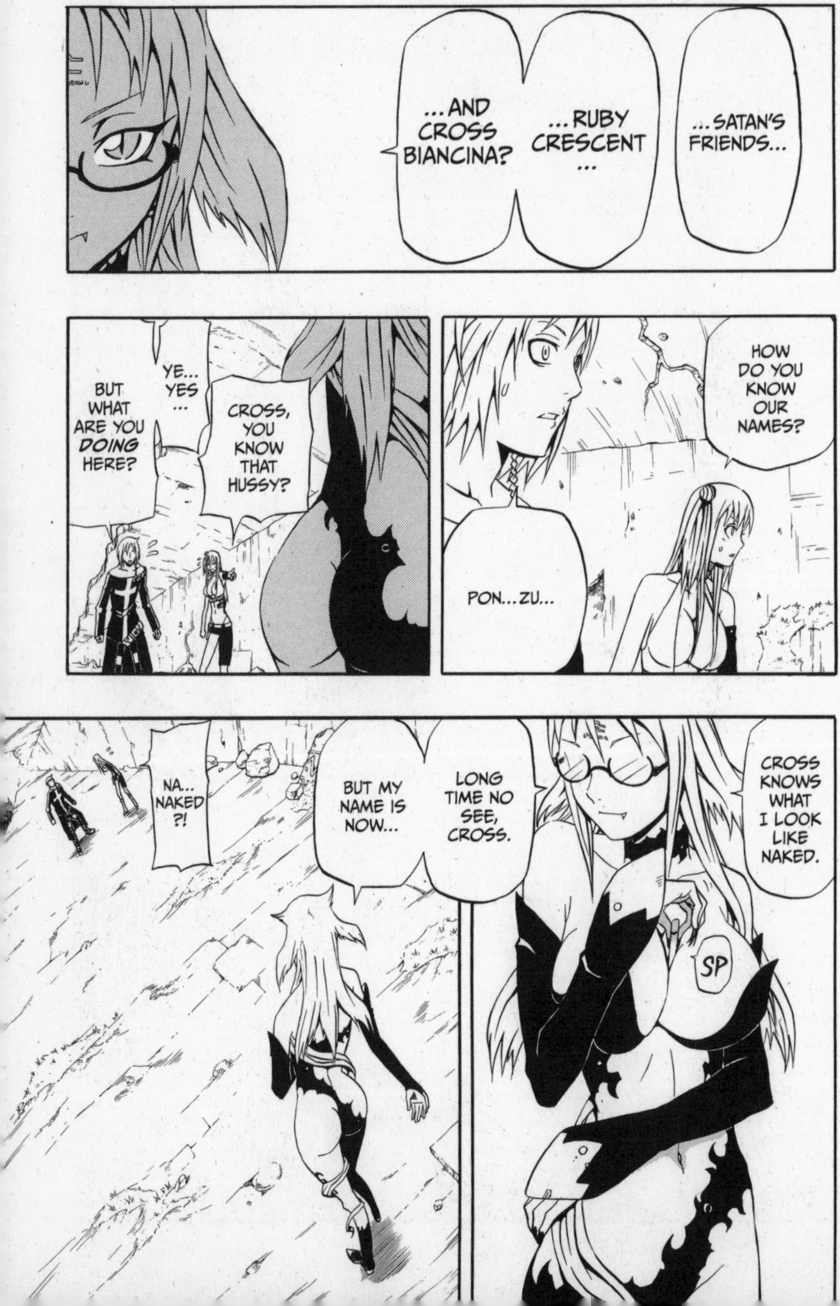
...SATAN'S FRIENDS...
...RUBY CRESCENT ...
...AND CROSS BIANCINA?
HOW DO YOU KNOW OUR NAMES?
PON...ZU...
CROSS, YOU KNOW THAT HUSSY?
YE... YES ...
BUT WHAT ARE YOU *DOING* HERE?
CROSS KNOWS WHAT I LOOK LIKE NAKED.
SP
LONG TIME NO SEE, CROSS.
BUT MY NAME IS NOW...
NA... NAKED ?!

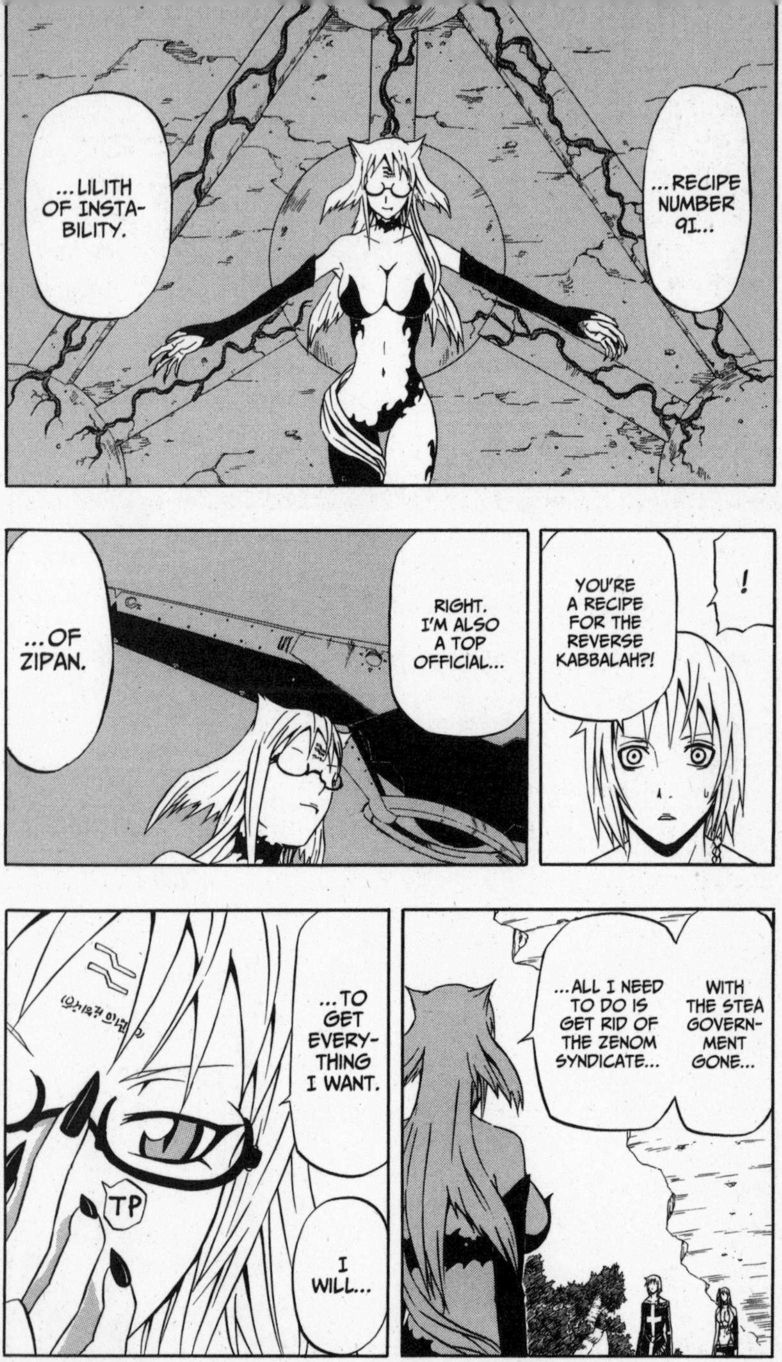
...RECIPE NUMBER 91...
...LILITH OF INSTA-BILITY.
!
YOU'RE A RECIPE FOR THE REVERSE KABBALAH?!
RIGHT. I'M ALSO A TOP OFFICIAL...
...OF ZIPAN.
WITH THE STEA GOVERN-MENT GONE...
...ALL I NEED TO DO IS GET RID OF THE ZENOM SYNDICATE...
...TO GET EVERY-THING I WANT.
I WILL...
TP

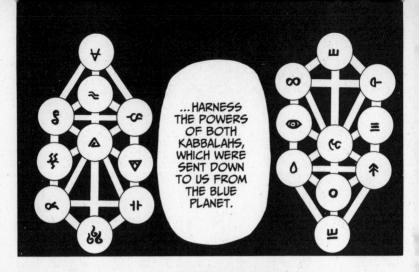

...HARNESS THE POWERS OF BOTH KABBALAHS, WHICH WERE SENT DOWN TO US FROM THE BLUE PLANET.
REMEM-BER HOW I ONCE TOLD YOU HUMANS...
...HAVE AN UN-CONSCIOUS URGE TO BECOME HIGHER ORGANIC ENTITIES?
AS IF WE'VE...
...BEEN PRO-GRAMMED FOR IT?
THAT'S WHY, WHEN ZIPAN FOUND ME, THEY EMBEDDED THE NUMBER 91 IN MY BODY.
WH...WHAT IS SHE SAYING?
CROSS ...

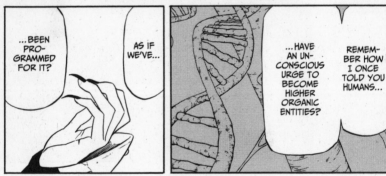

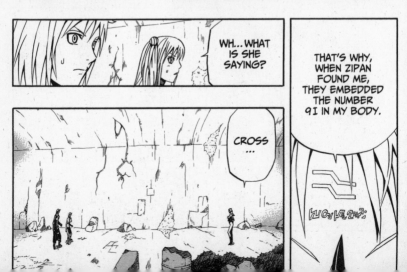

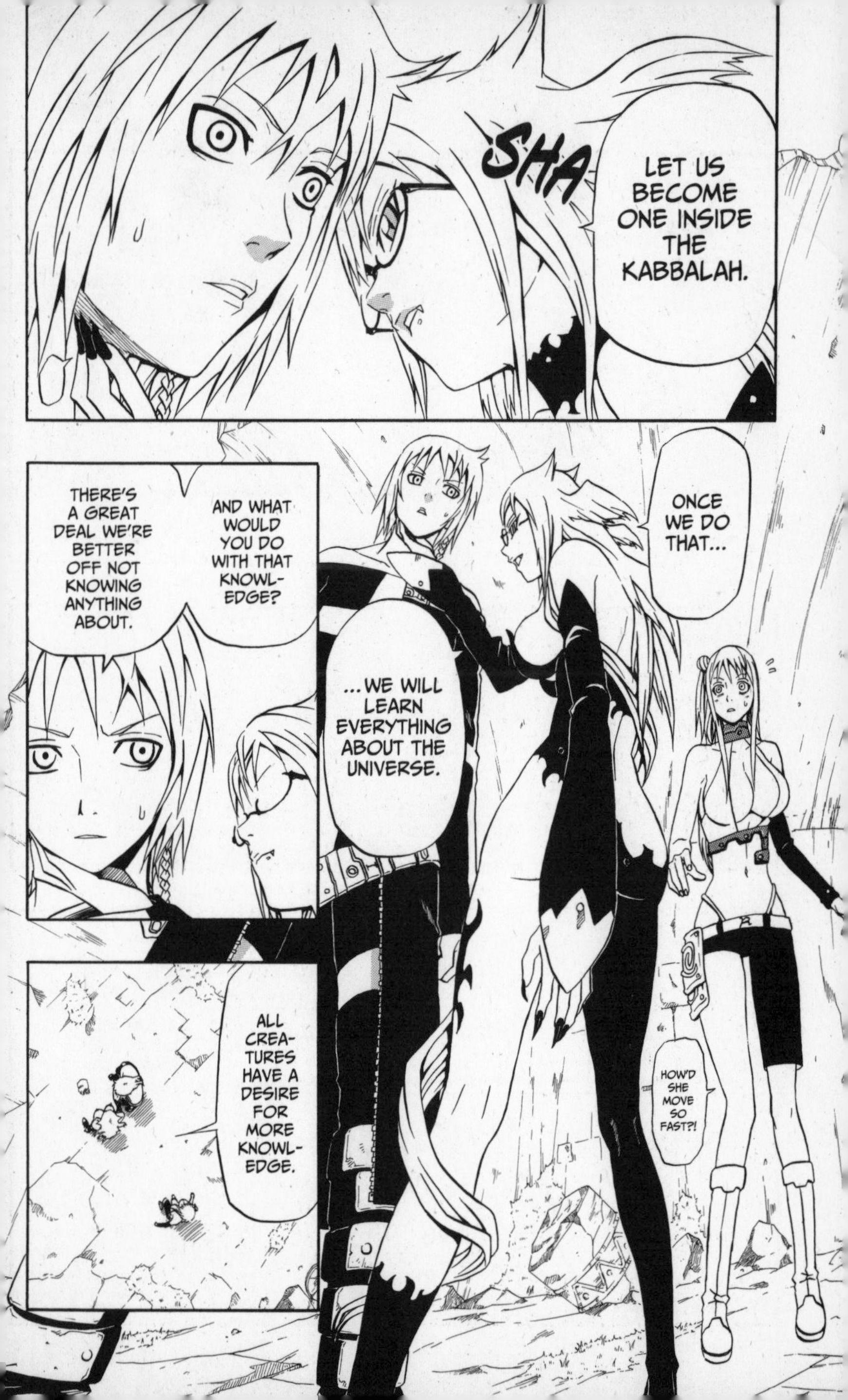
SHA
LET US BECOME ONE INSIDE THE KABBALAH.
ONCE WE DO THAT...
...WE WILL LEARN EVERYTHING ABOUT THE UNIVERSE.
HOW'D SHE MOVE SO FAST?!
AND WHAT WOULD YOU DO WITH THAT KNOWL-EDGE?
THERE'S A GREAT DEAL WE'RE BETTER OFF NOT KNOWING ANYTHING ABOUT.
ALL CREA-TURES HAVE A DESIRE FOR MORE KNOWL-EDGE.

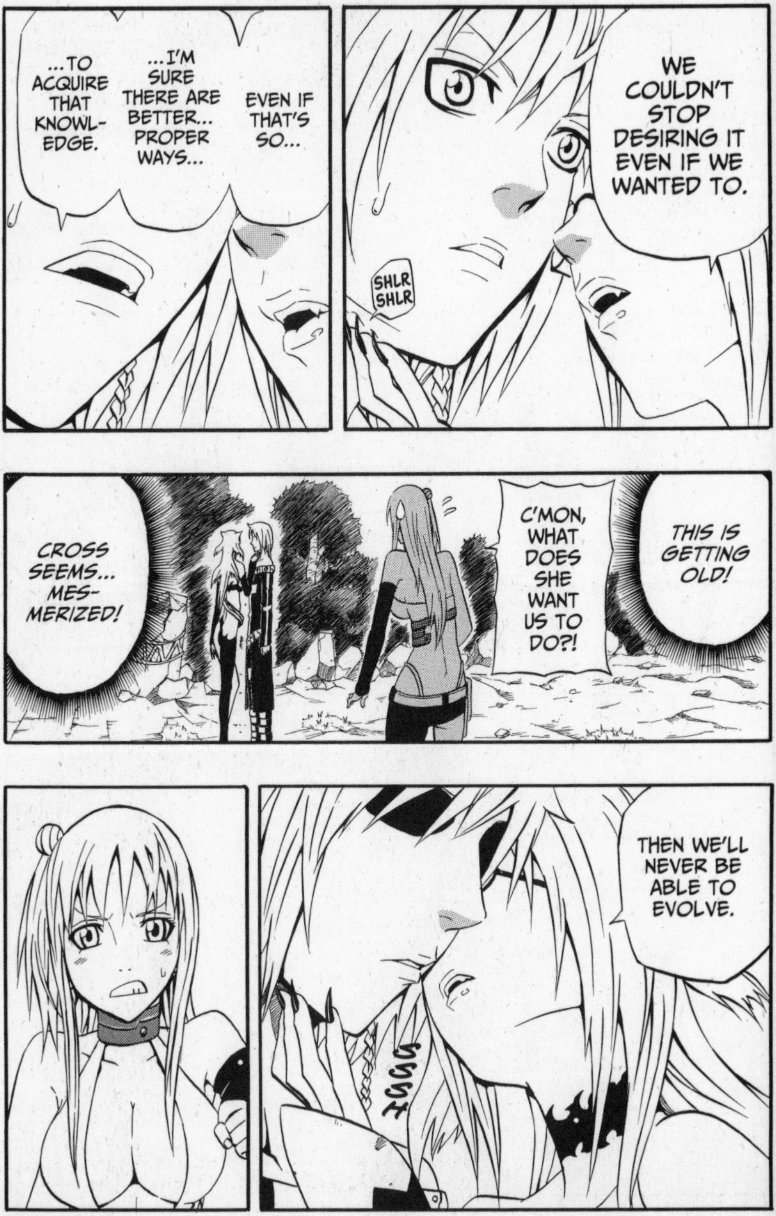
WE COULDN'T STOP DESIRING IT EVEN IF WE WANTED TO.
SHLR SHLR
EVEN IF THAT'S SO...
...I'M SURE THERE ARE BETTER... PROPER WAYS...
...TO ACQUIRE THAT KNOWL-EDGE.
THIS IS GETTING OLD!
C'MON, WHAT DOES SHE WANT US TO DO?!
CROSS SEEMS... MES-MERIZED!
THEN WE'LL NEVER BE ABLE TO EVOLVE.
SSSH

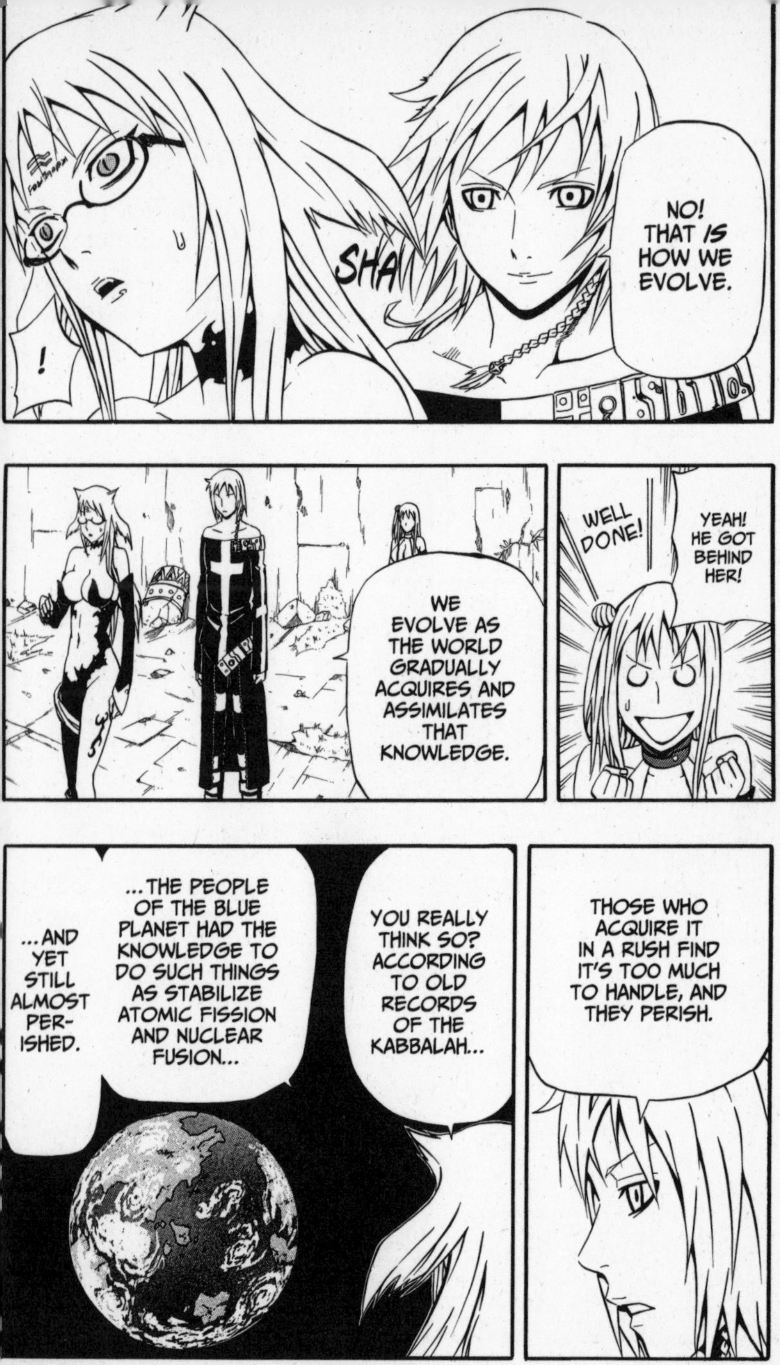
NO! THAT IS HOW WE EVOLVE.
SHA
!
YEAH! HE GOT BEHIND HER!
WELL DONE!
WE EVOLVE AS THE WORLD GRADUALLY ACQUIRES AND ASSIMILATES THAT KNOWLEDGE.
THOSE WHO ACQUIRE IT IN A RUSH FIND IT'S TOO MUCH TO HANDLE, AND THEY PERISH.
YOU REALLY THINK SO? ACCORDING TO OLD RECORDS OF THE KABBALAH...
...THE PEOPLE OF THE BLUE PLANET HAD THE KNOWLEDGE TO DO SUCH THINGS AS STABILIZE ATOMIC FISSION AND NUCLEAR FUSION...
...AND YET STILL ALMOST PER-ISHED.

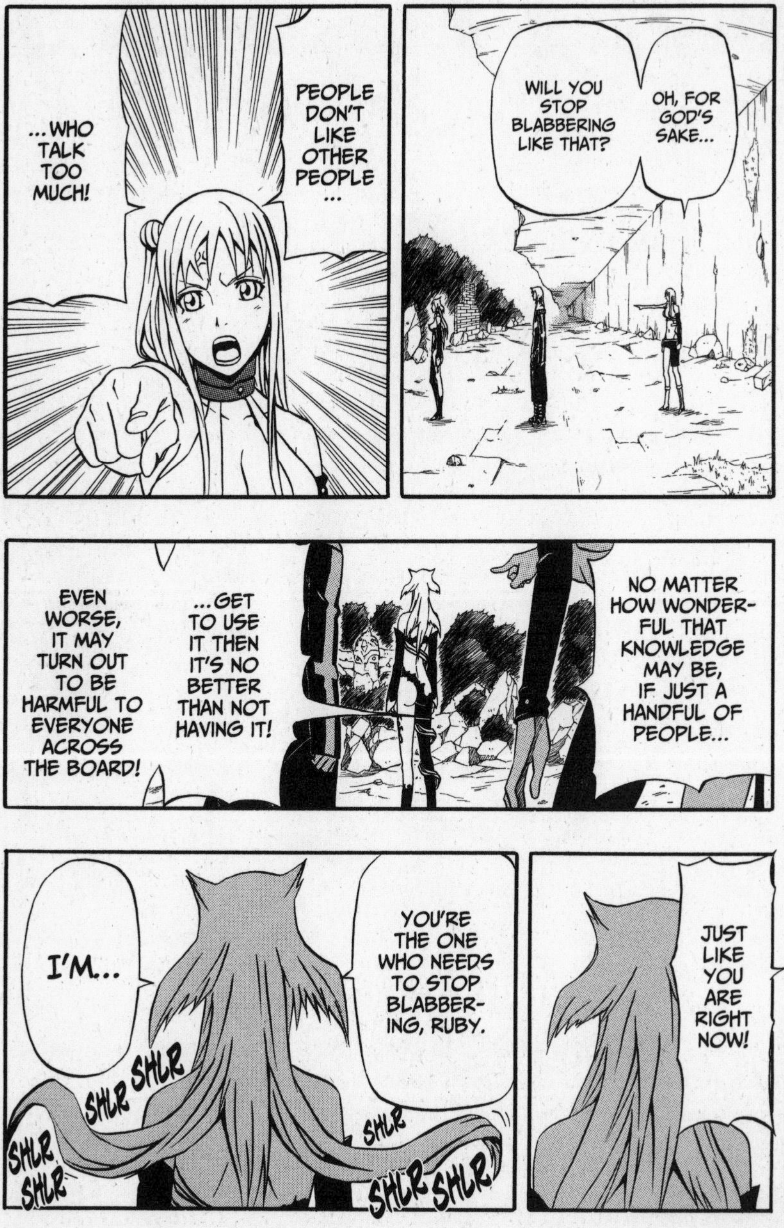
OH, FOR GOD'S SAKE...
WILL YOU STOP BLABBERING LIKE THAT?
PEOPLE DON'T LIKE OTHER PEOPLE...
...WHO TALK TOO MUCH!
NO MATTER HOW WONDER-FUL THAT KNOWLEDGE MAY BE, IF JUST A HANDFUL OF PEOPLE...
...GET TO USE IT THEN IT'S NO BETTER THAN NOT HAVING IT!
EVEN WORSE, IT MAY TURN OUT TO BE HARMFUL TO EVERYONE ACROSS THE BOARD!
JUST LIKE YOU ARE RIGHT NOW!
YOU'RE THE ONE WHO NEEDS TO STOP BLABBER-ING, RUBY.
SHLR
SHLR SHLR
I'M...
SHLR SHLR
SHLR SHLR
SHLR SHLR

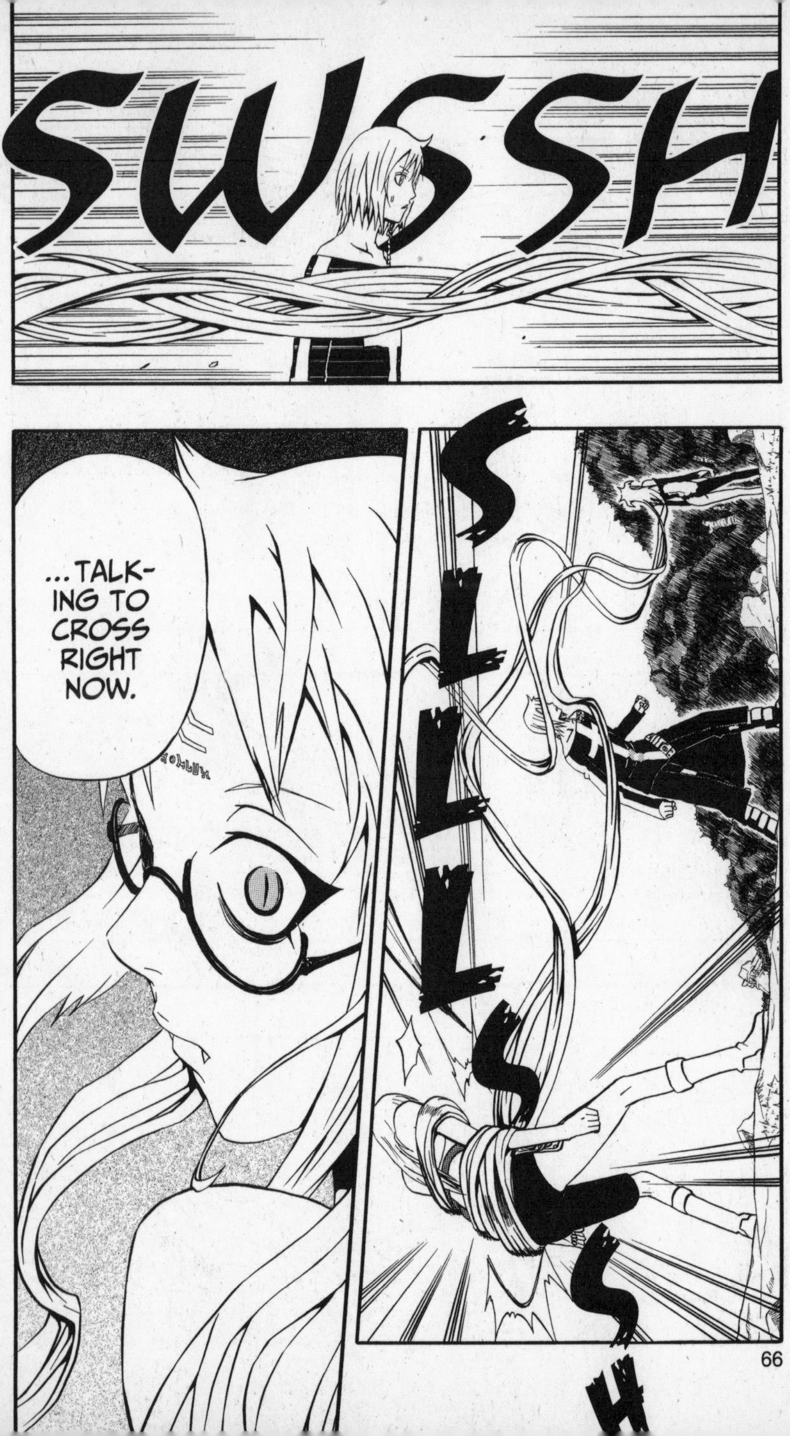
...TALKING TO CROSS RIGHT NOW.

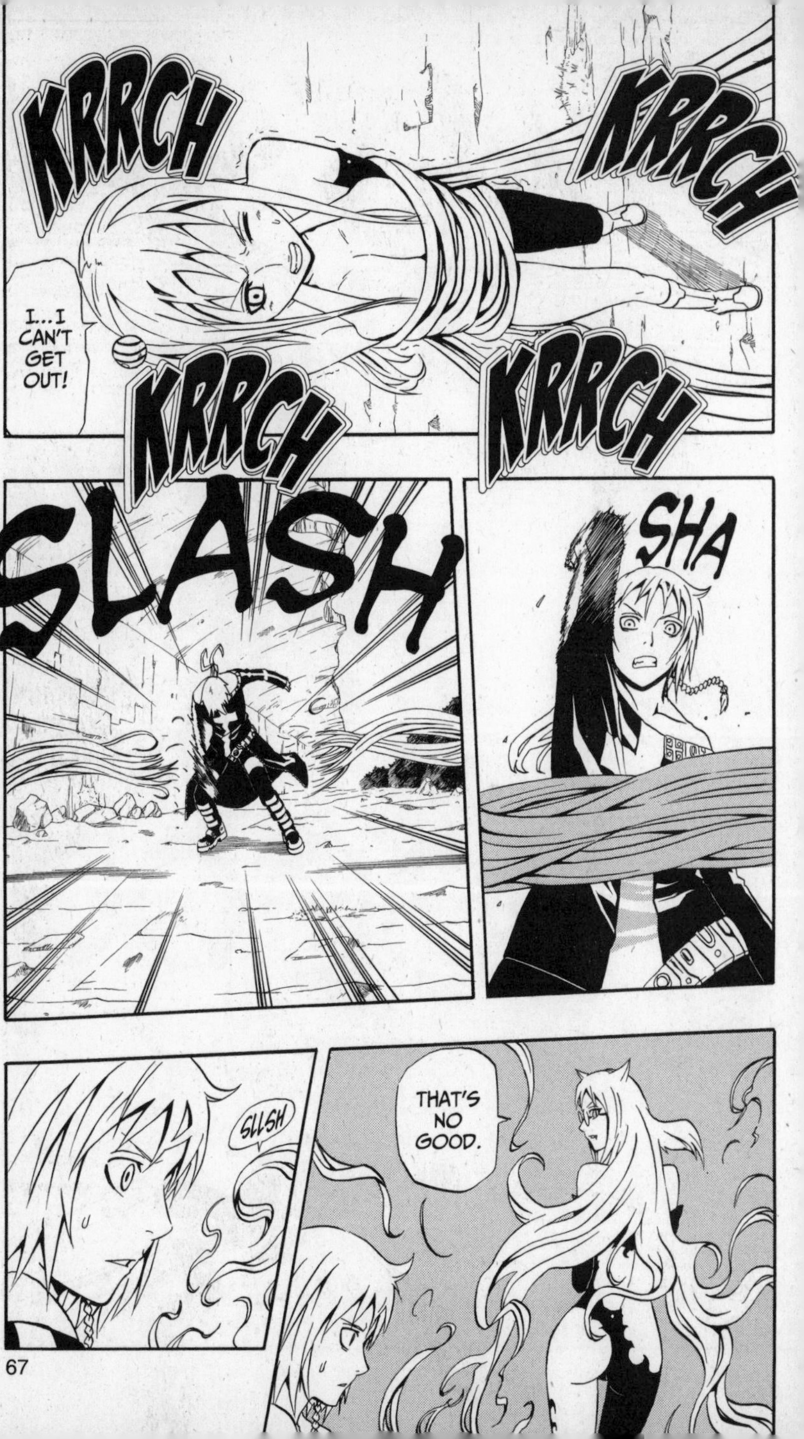
KRRCH
KRRCH
I...I CAN'T GET OUT!
KRRCH
KRRCH
SHA
SLASH
THAT'S NO GOOD.
SLLSH

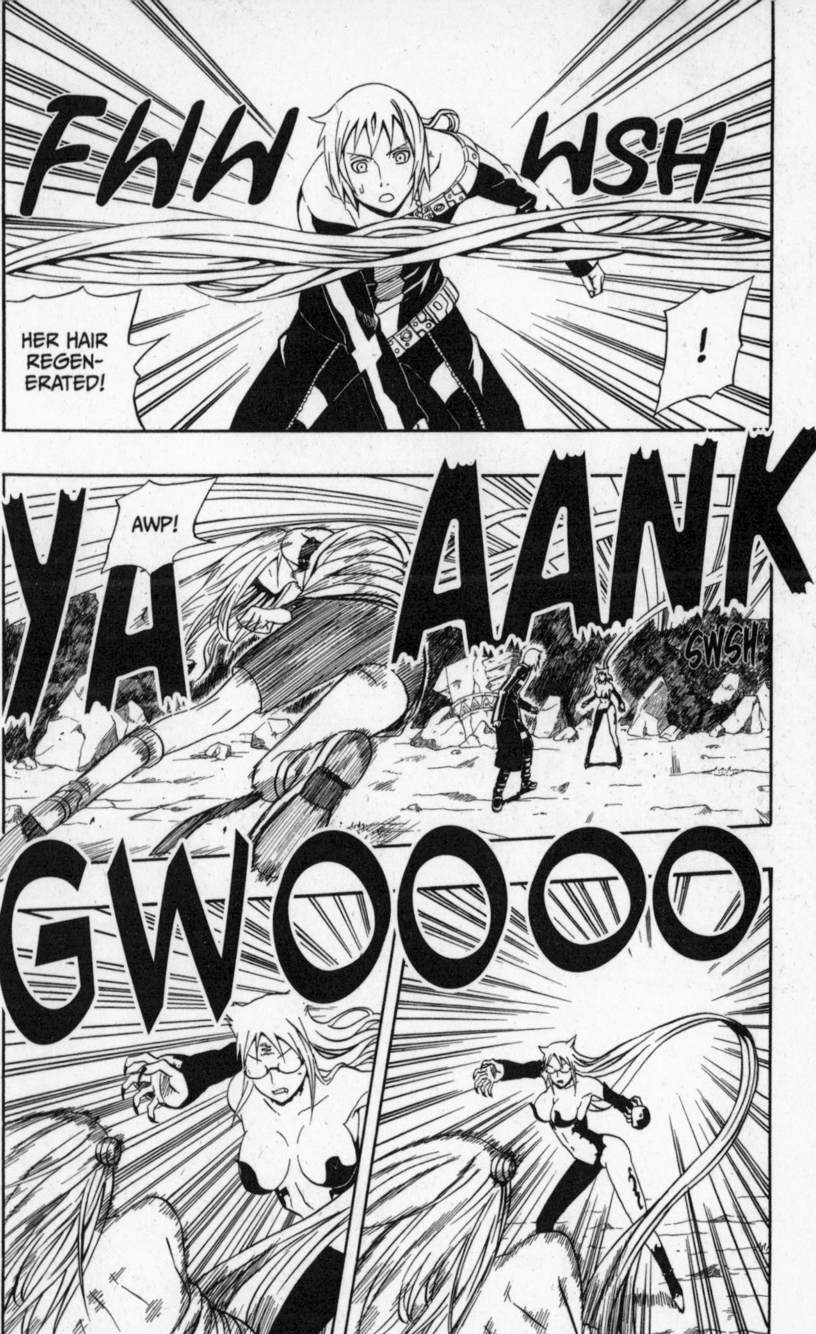
FWW WSH
!
HER HAIR REGEN-ERATED!
YAAANK
AWP!
SWSH
GWOOOO

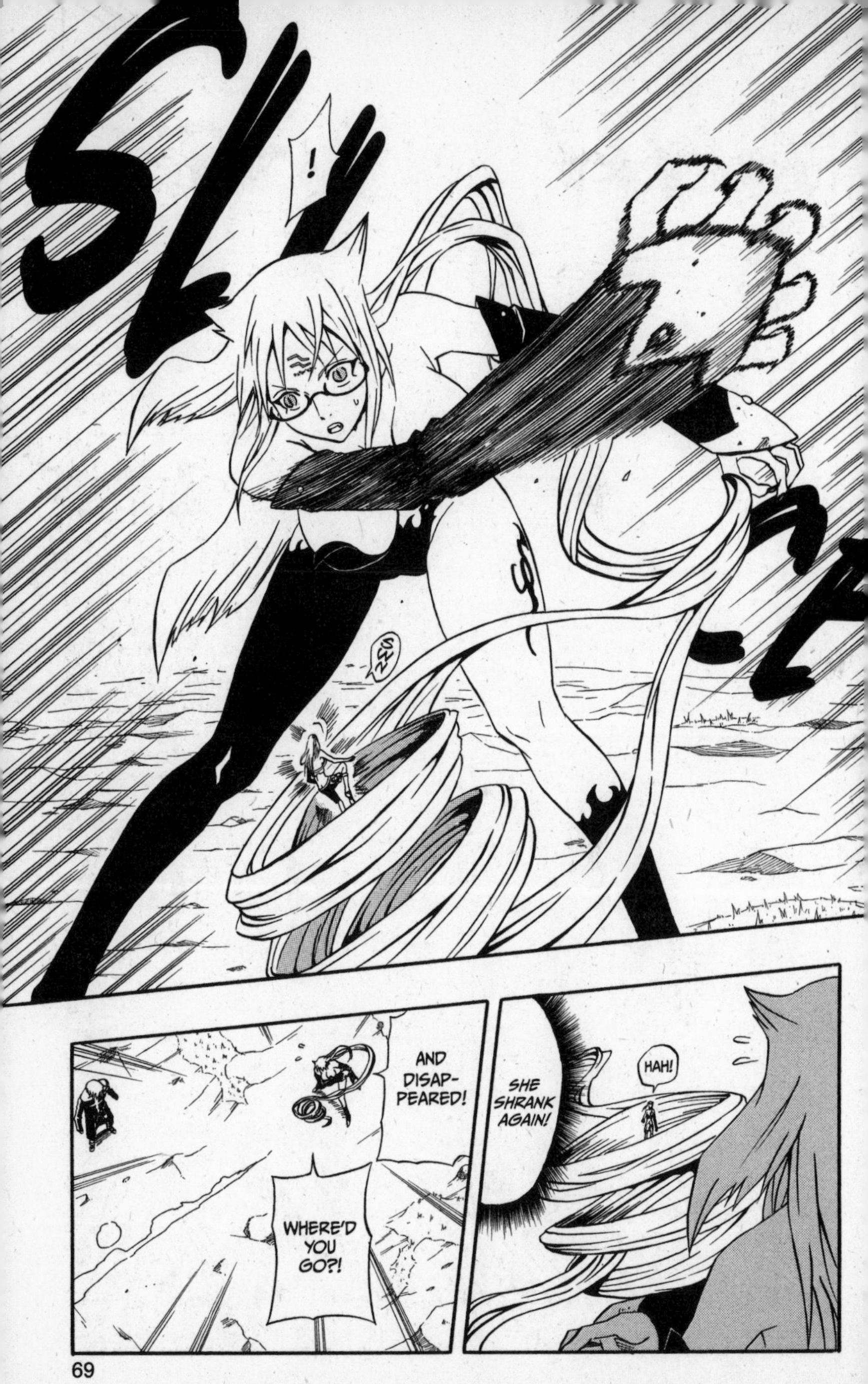
!
HAH!
SHE SHRANK AGAIN!
AND DISAP-PEARED!
WHERE'D YOU GO?!

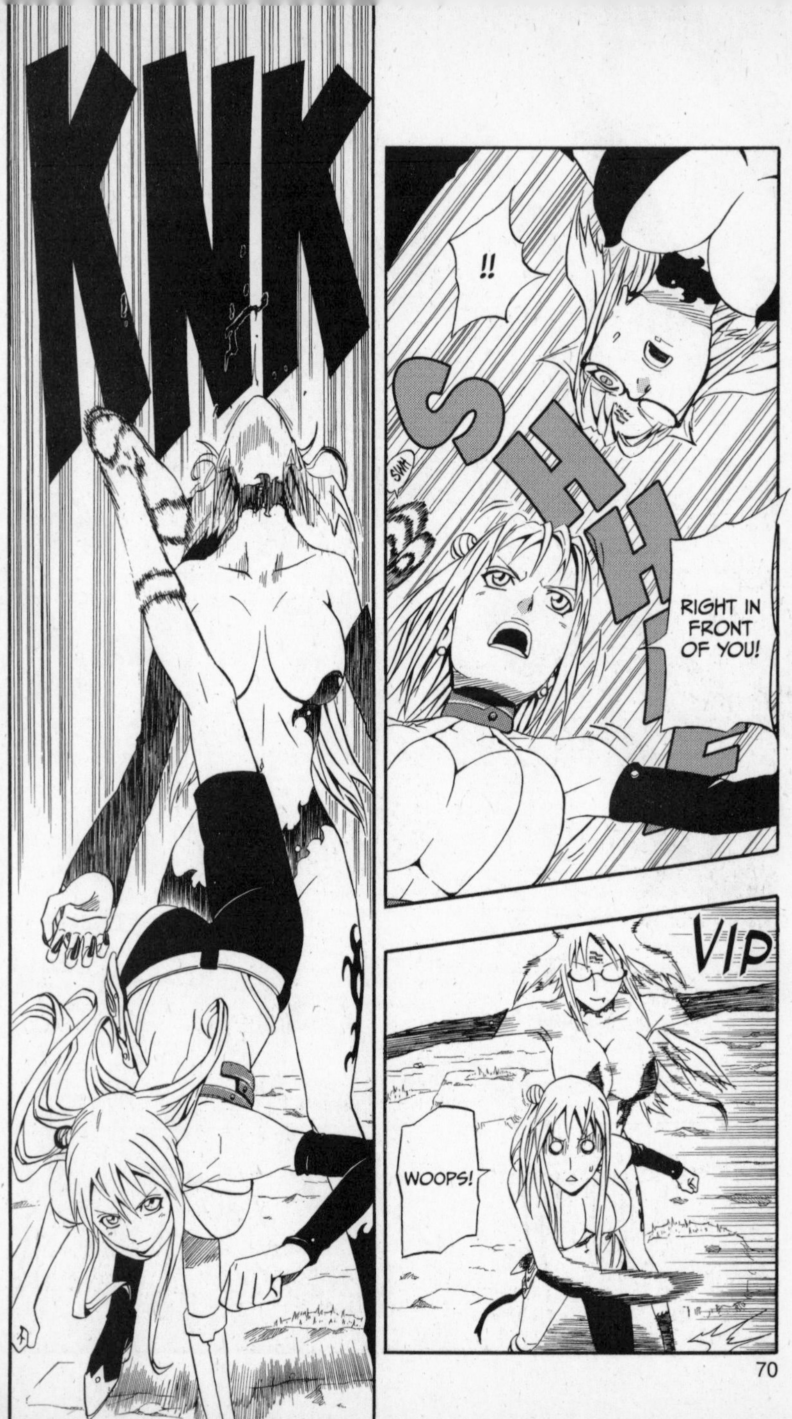
!!
SHH
SWM
RIGHT IN FRONT OF YOU!
VIP
WOOPS!
KNK

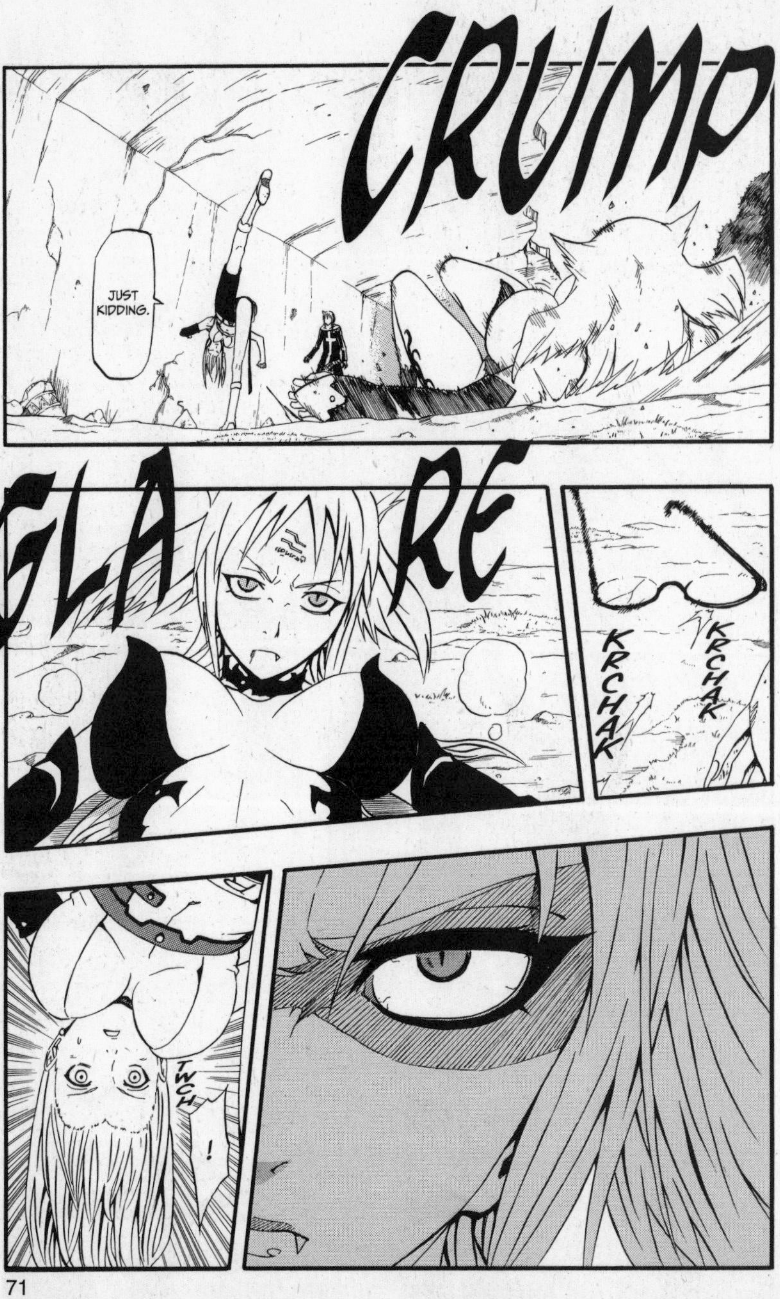
CRUMP
JUST KIDDING.
KRCHAK
KRCHAK
GLARE
TWCH
!

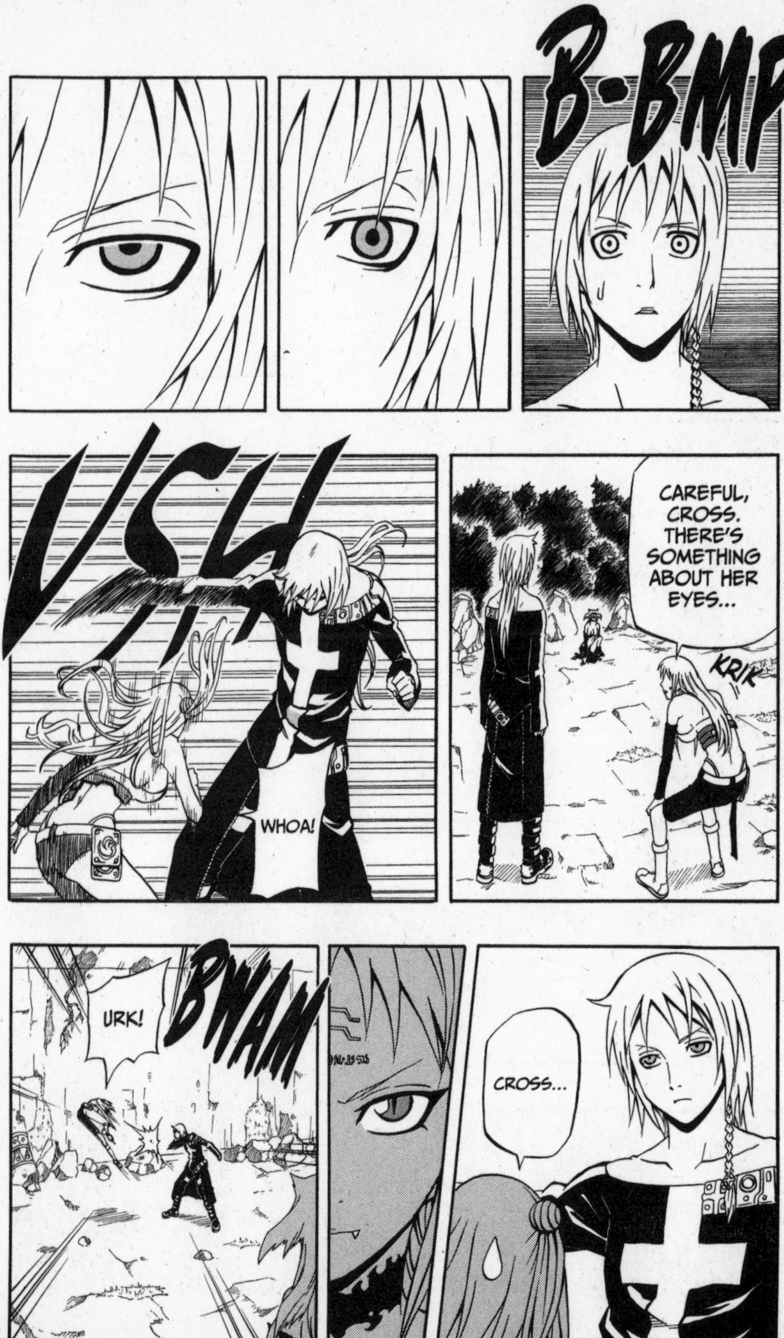
B-BMP
CAREFUL, CROSS. THERE'S SOMETHING ABOUT HER EYES...
KRIK
VSH
WHOA!
CROSS...
BWAM
URK!

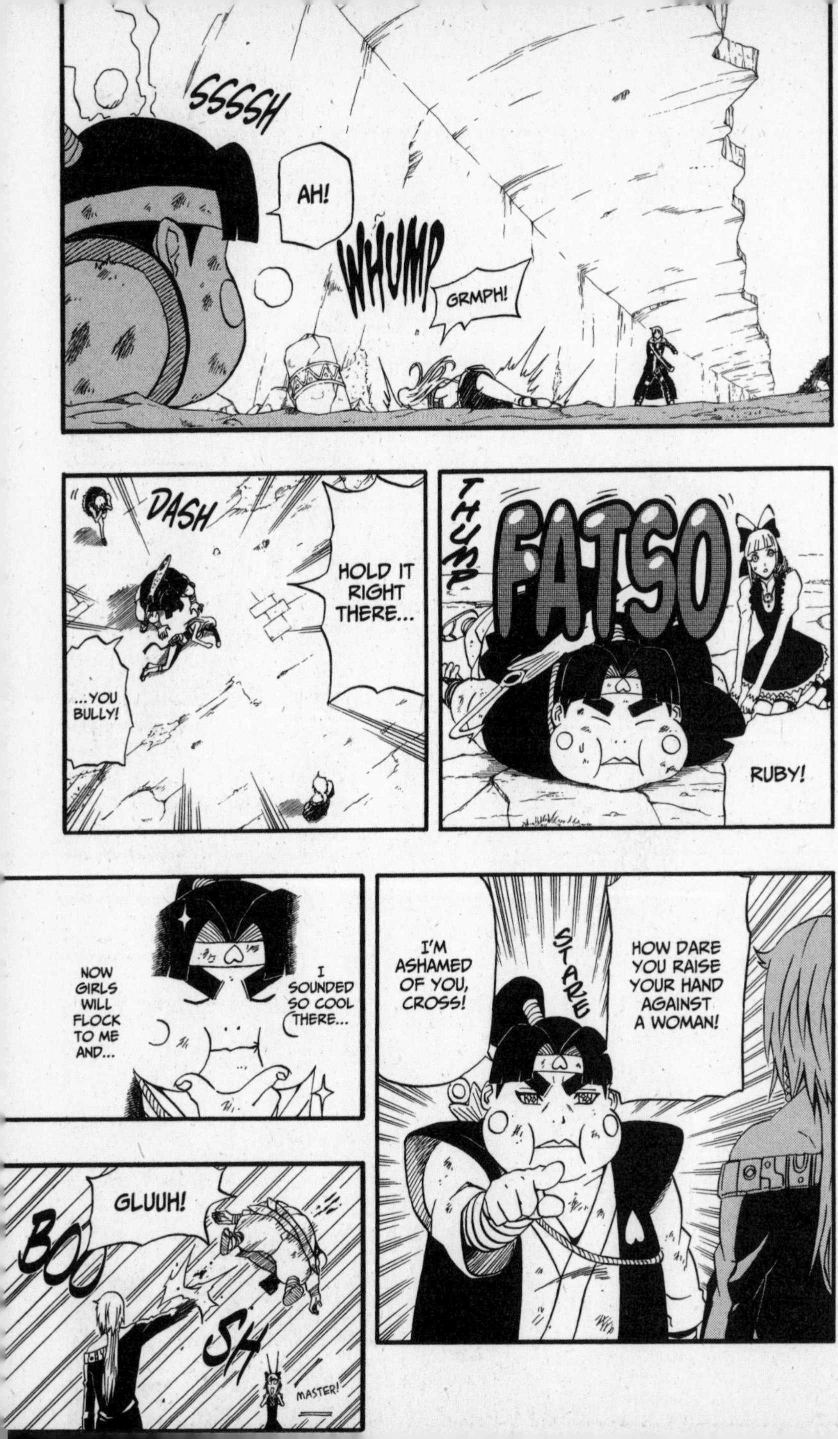
SSSSH
AH!
WHUMP
GRMPH!
THUMP
FATSO
RUBY!
DASH
HOLD IT RIGHT THERE...
...YOU BULLY!
HOW DARE YOU RAISE YOUR HAND AGAINST A WOMAN!
STARE
I'M ASHAMED OF YOU, CROSS!
I SOUNDED SO COOL THERE...
NOW GIRLS WILL FLOCK TO ME AND...
GLUUH!
BOOSH
MASTER!

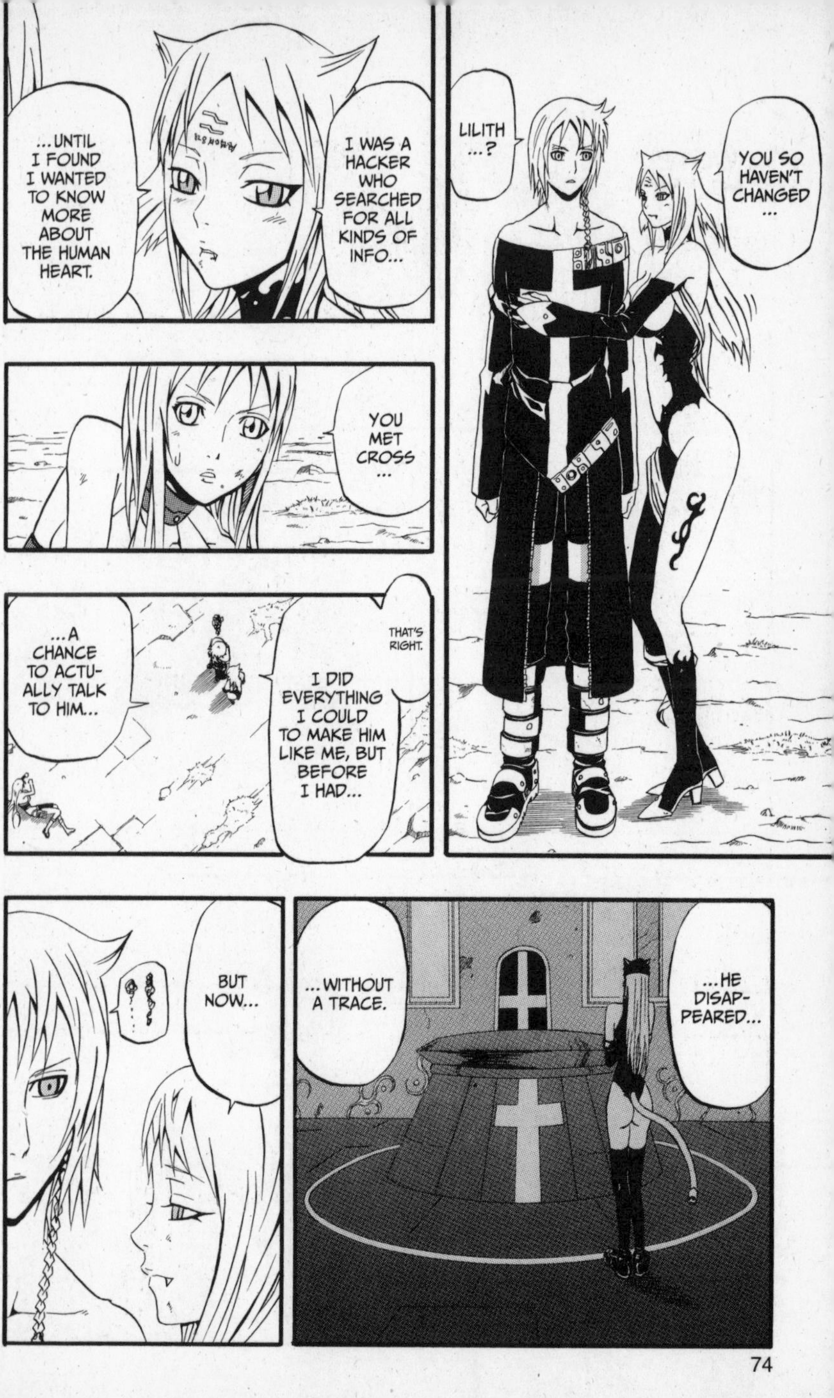
YOU SO HAVEN'T CHANGED...
LILITH...?
I WAS A HACKER WHO SEARCHED FOR ALL KINDS OF INFO...
...UNTIL I FOUND I WANTED TO KNOW MORE ABOUT THE HUMAN HEART.
YOU MET CROSS...
THAT'S RIGHT.
I DID EVERYTHING I COULD TO MAKE HIM LIKE ME, BUT BEFORE I HAD...
...A CHANCE TO ACTU-ALLY TALK TO HIM...
...HE DISAP-PEARED...
...WITHOUT A TRACE.
BUT NOW...

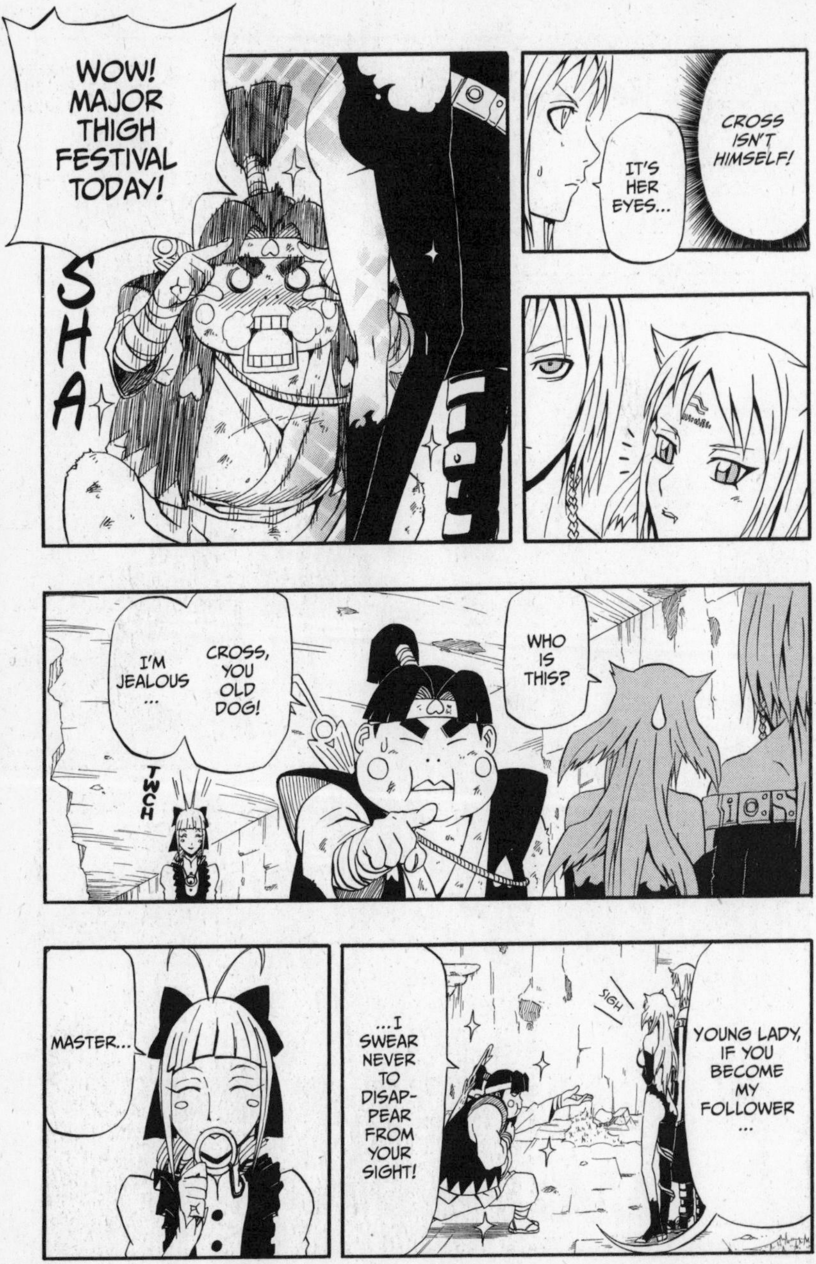
CROSS ISN'T HIMSELF!
IT'S HER EYES...
WOW! MAJOR THIGH FESTIVAL TODAY!
SHA
WHO IS THIS?
CROSS, YOU OLD DOG!
I'M JEALOUS ...
TWCH
SIGH
YOUNG LADY, IF YOU BECOME MY FOLLOWER ...
...I SWEAR NEVER TO DISAP-PEAR FROM YOUR SIGHT!
MASTER...

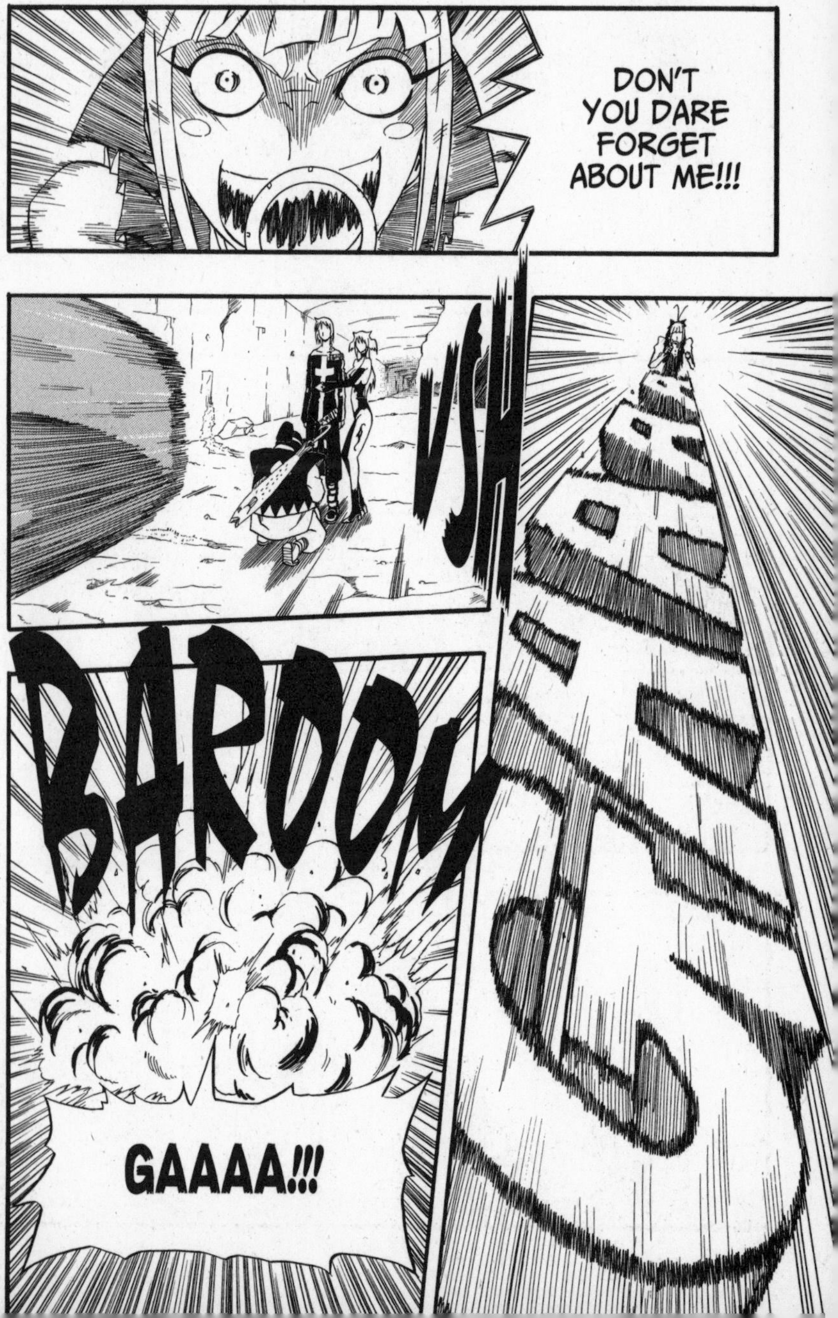
DON'T YOU DARE FORGET ABOUT ME!!!
VSH
BAROOM
GAAAA!!!

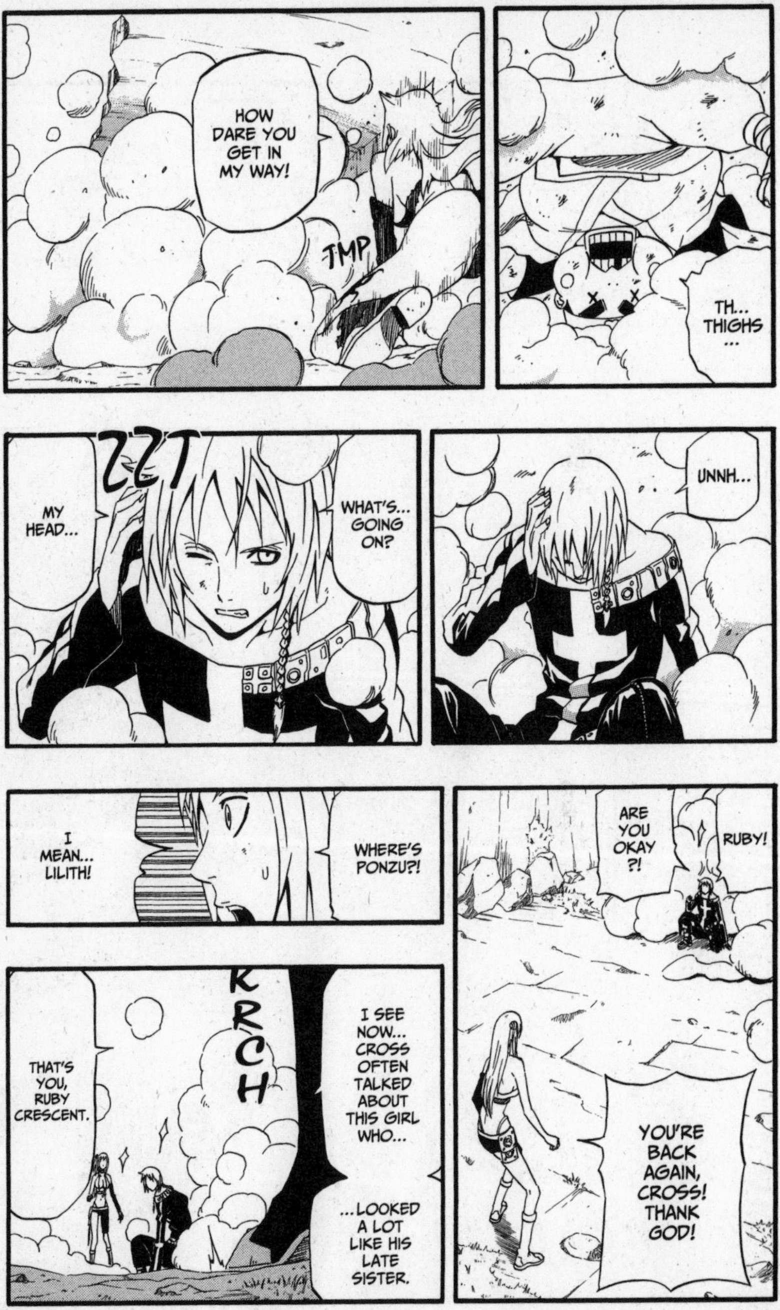
TH... THIGHS ...
HOW DARE YOU GET IN MY WAY!
TMP
UNNH...
ZZT
WHAT'S... GOING ON?
MY HEAD...
RUBY!
ARE YOU OKAY ?!
YOU'RE BACK AGAIN, CROSS! THANK GOD!
WHERE'S PONZU?!
I MEAN... LILITH!
KRCH
I SEE NOW... CROSS OFTEN TALKED ABOUT THIS GIRL WHO...
...LOOKED A LOT LIKE HIS LATE SISTER.
THAT'S YOU, RUBY CRESCENT.

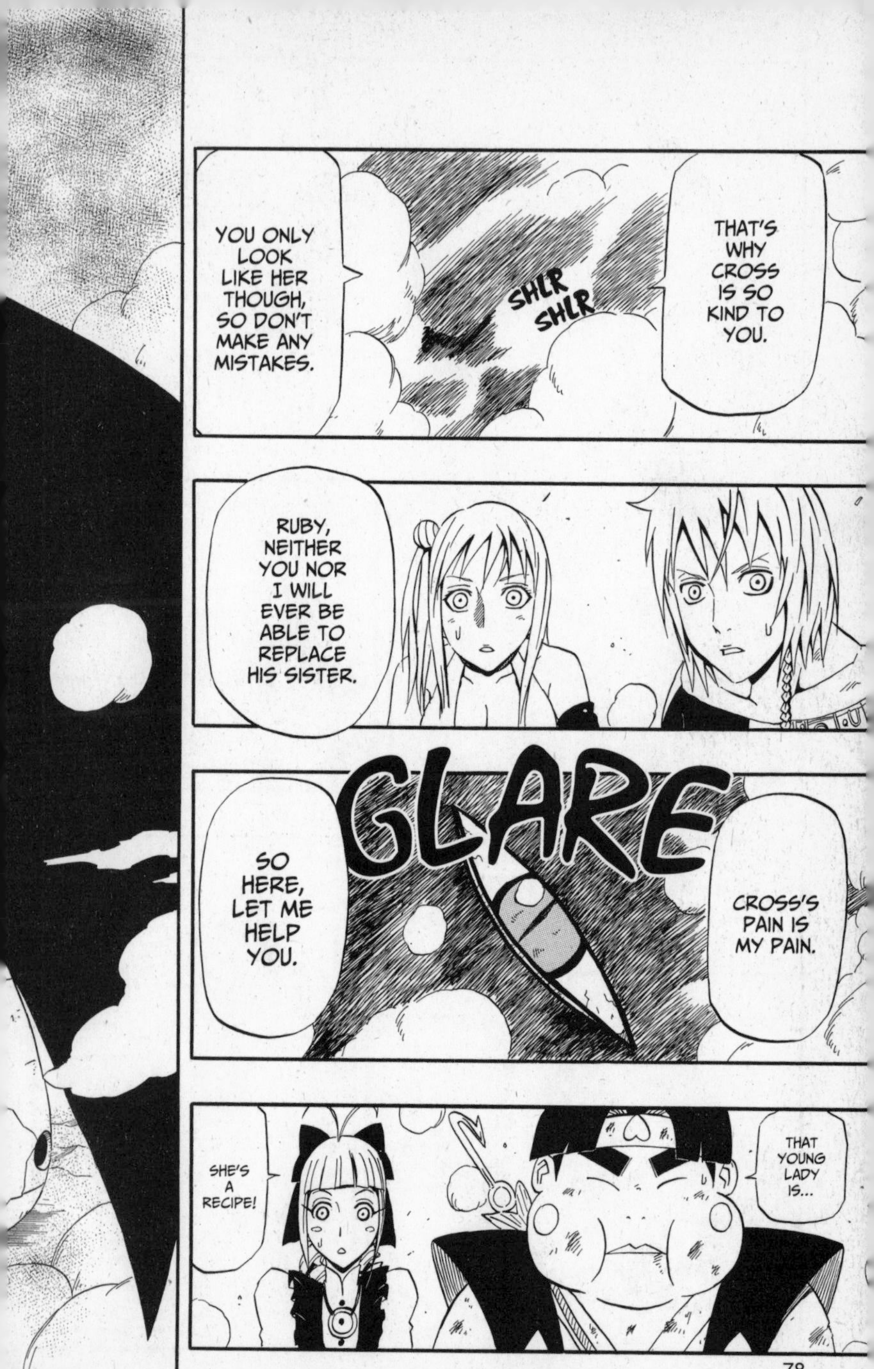
THAT'S WHY CROSS IS SO KIND TO YOU.
SHLR SHLR
YOU ONLY LOOK LIKE HER THOUGH, SO DON'T MAKE ANY MISTAKES.
RUBY, NEITHER YOU NOR I WILL EVER BE ABLE TO REPLACE HIS SISTER.
CROSS'S PAIN IS MY PAIN.
GLARE
SO HERE, LET ME HELP YOU.
THAT YOUNG LADY IS...
SHE'S A RECIPE!

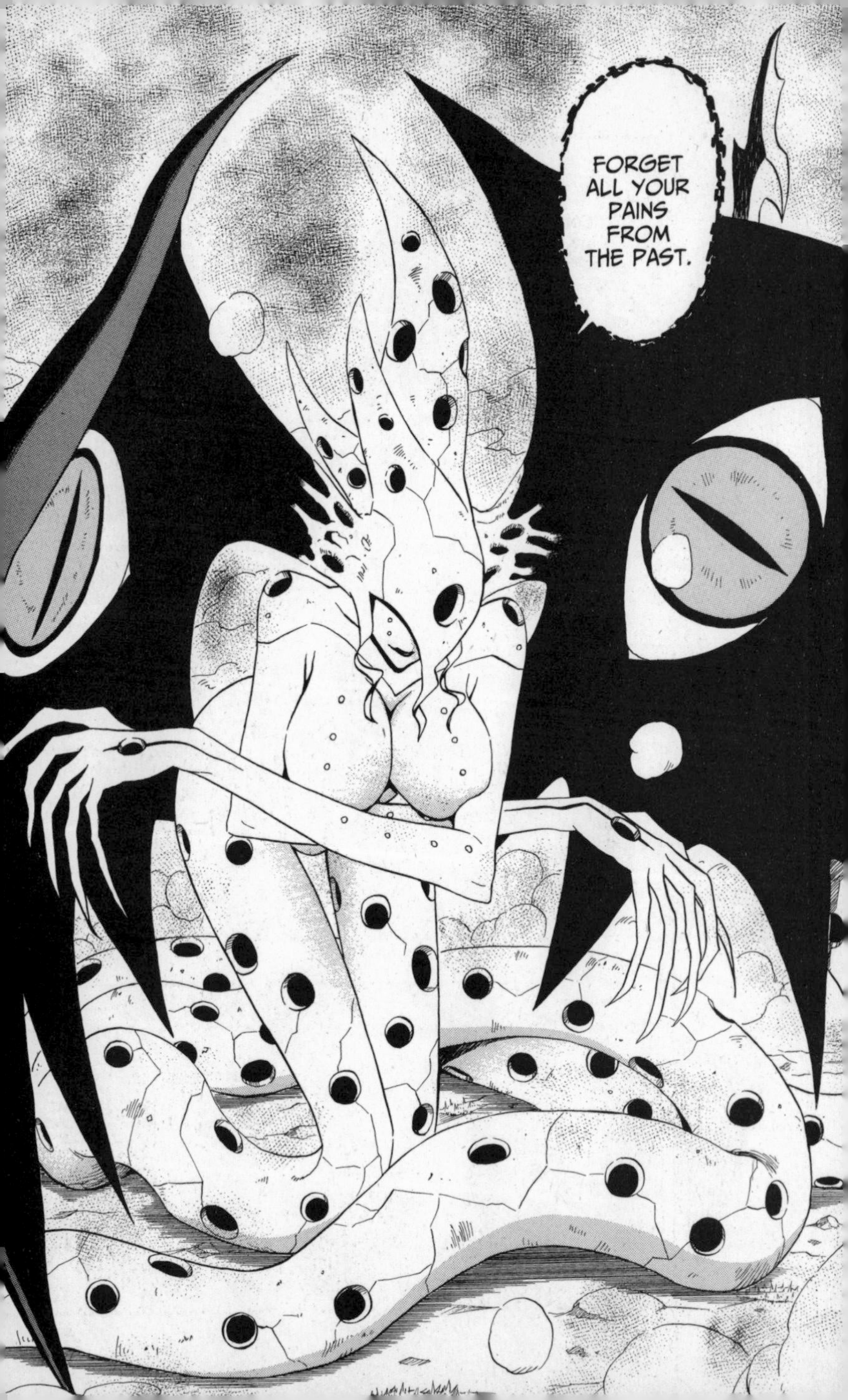
FORGET ALL YOUR PAINS FROM THE PAST.

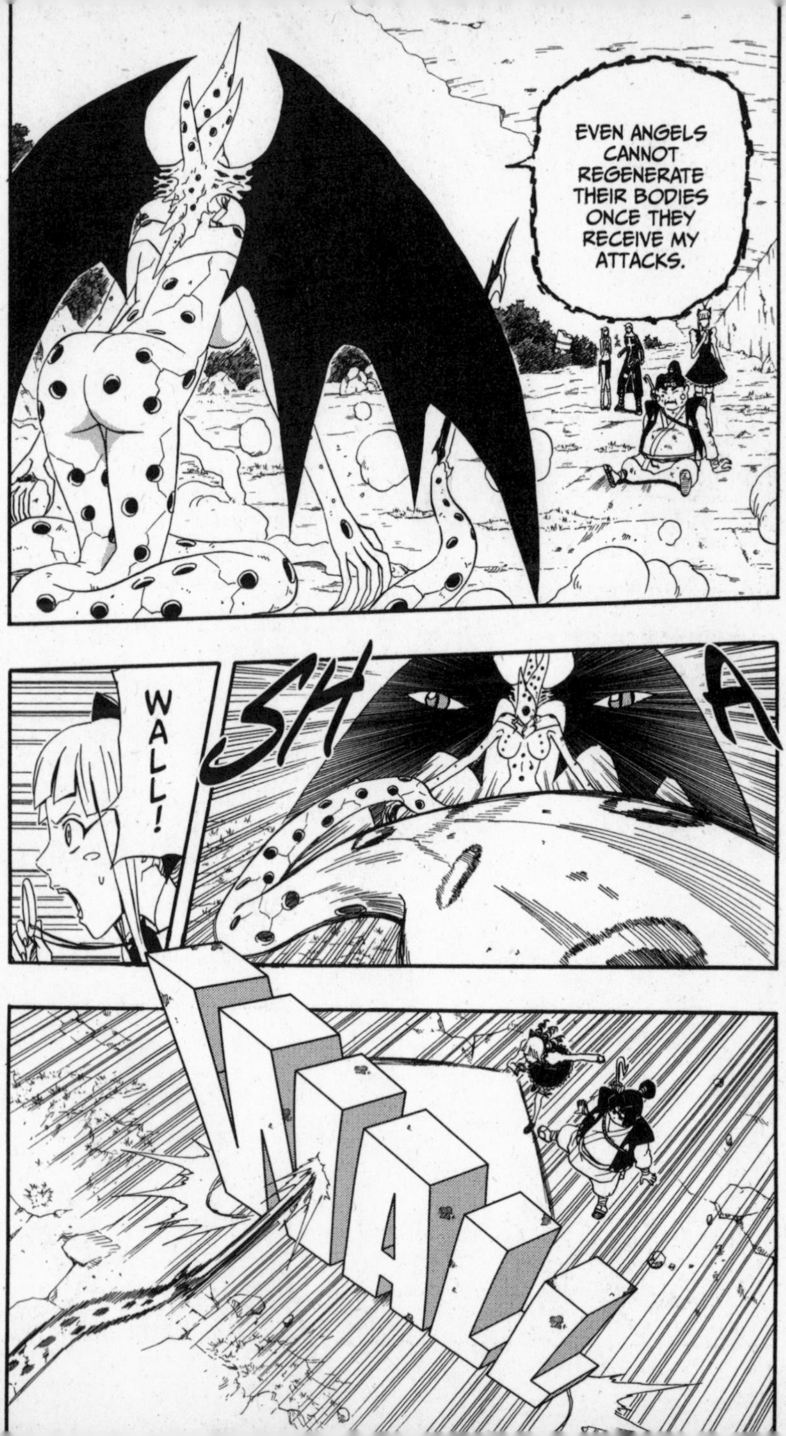
EVEN ANGELS CANNOT REGENERATE THEIR BODIES ONCE THEY RECEIVE MY ATTACKS.
SHA
WALL!
WALL

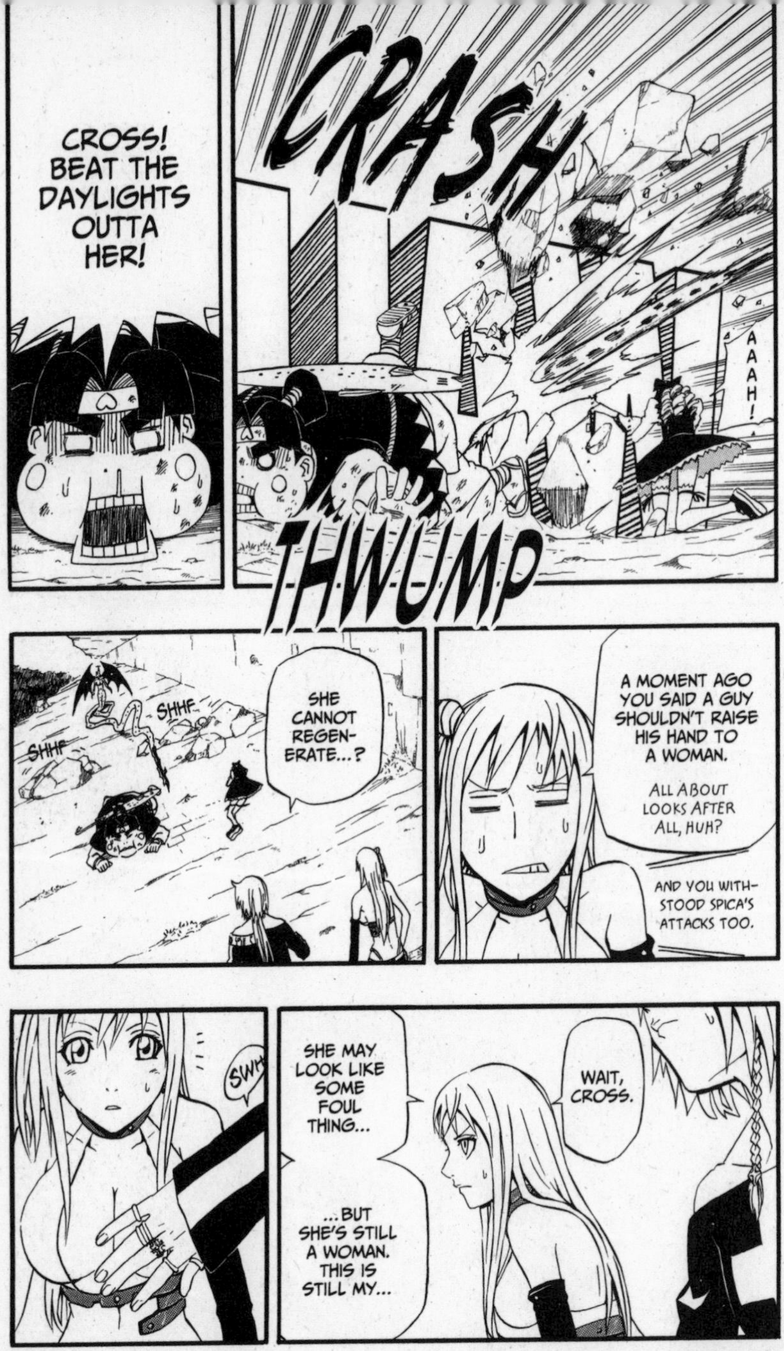
CRASH
AAAH!
THWUMP
CROSS! BEAT THE DAYLIGHTS OUTTA HER!
A MOMENT AGO YOU SAID A GUY SHOULDN'T RAISE HIS HAND TO A WOMAN.
ALL ABOUT LOOKS AFTER ALL, HUH?
AND YOU WITH-STOOD SPICA'S ATTACKS TOO.
SHE CANNOT REGEN-ERATE...?
SHHF
SHHF
WAIT, CROSS.
SHE MAY LOOK LIKE SOME FOUL THING...
...BUT SHE'S STILL A WOMAN. THIS IS STILL MY...
SWH

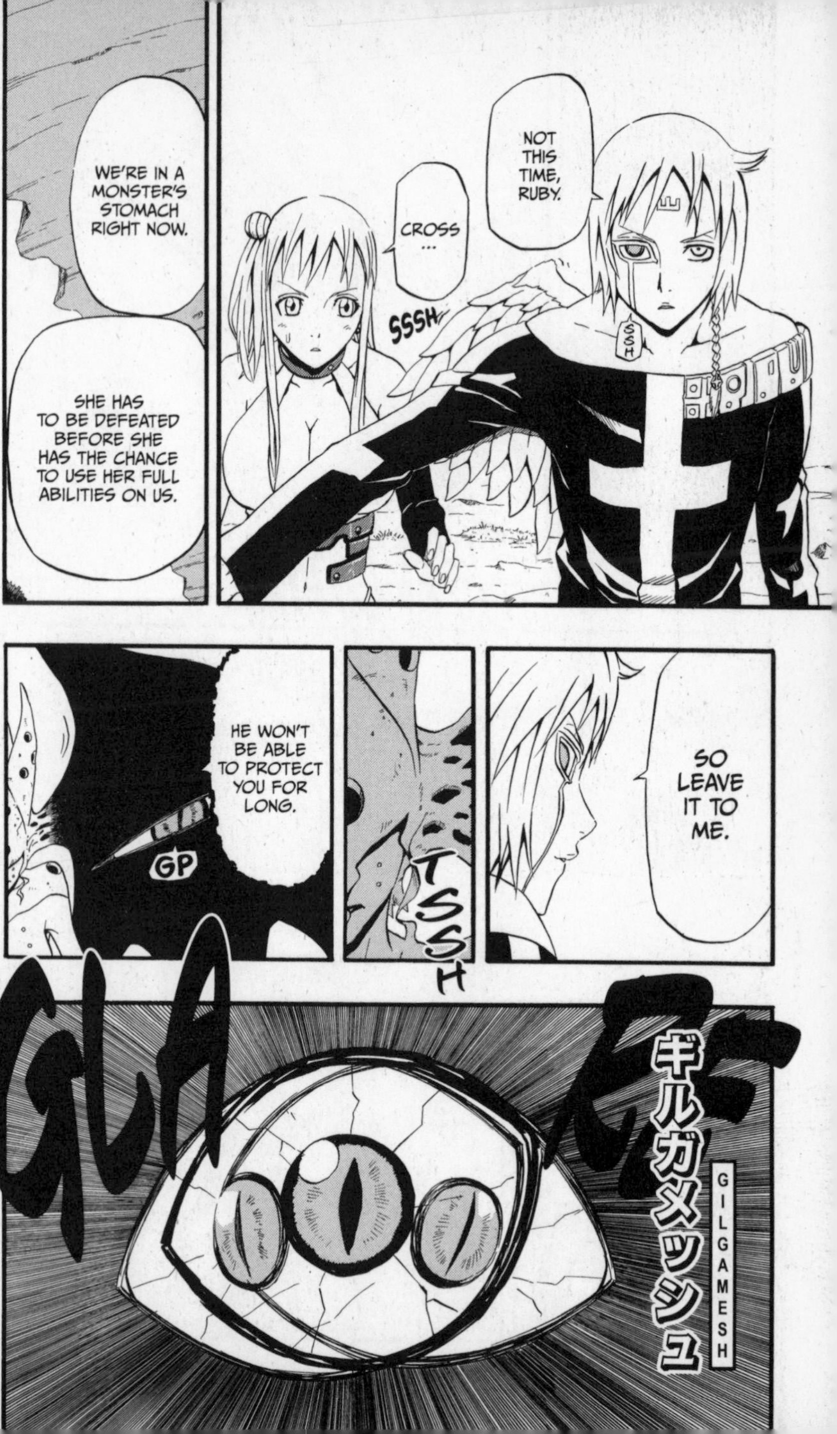
NOT THIS TIME, RUBY.
CROSS ...
SSH
SSSH
WE'RE IN A MONSTER'S STOMACH RIGHT NOW.
SHE HAS TO BE DEFEATED BEFORE SHE HAS THE CHANCE TO USE HER FULL ABILITIES ON US.
SO LEAVE IT TO ME.
TSSSH
HE WON'T BE ABLE TO PROTECT YOU FOR LONG.
GP
GLARE
ギルガメッシュ
GILGAMESH

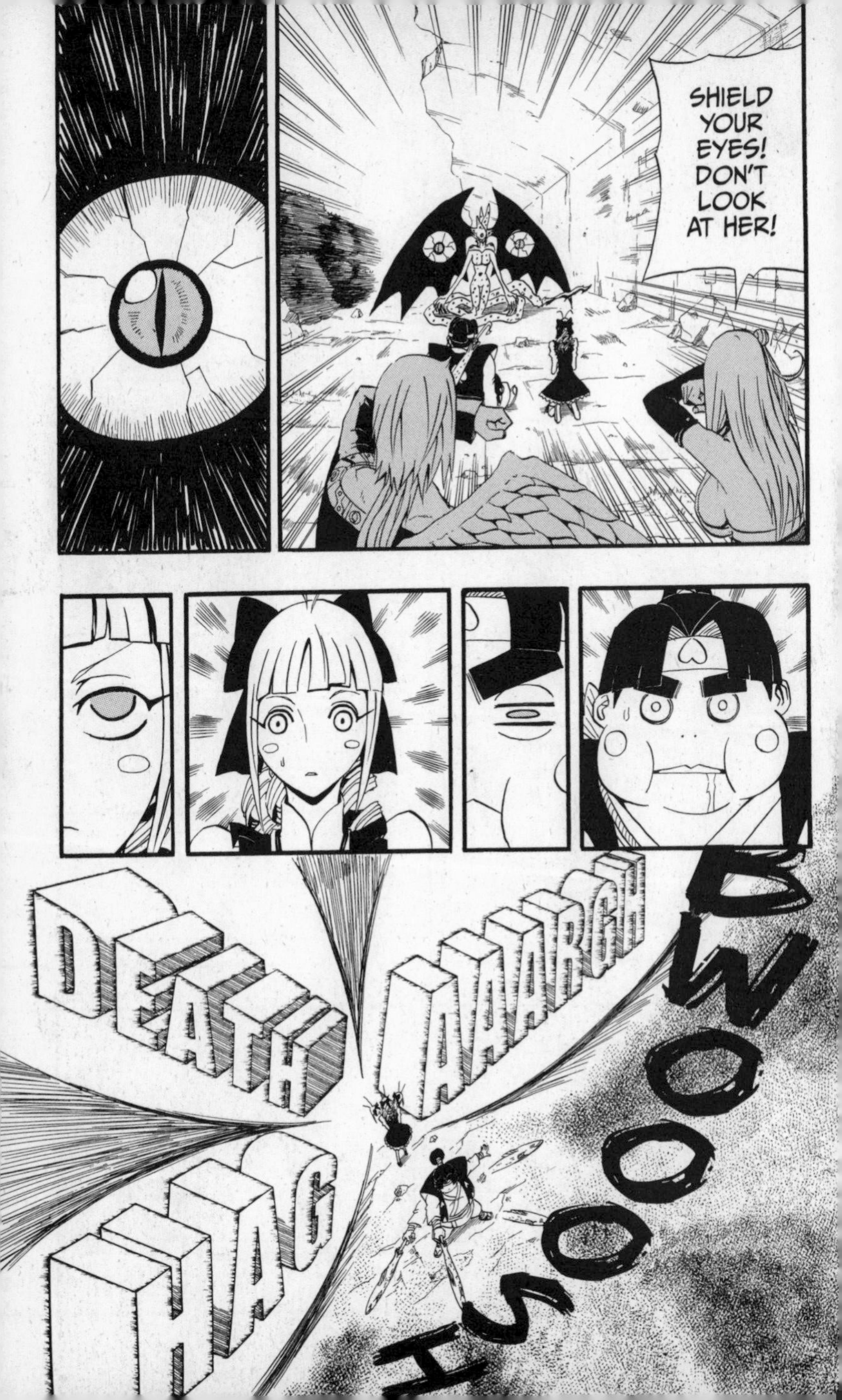

SHIELD YOUR EYES! DON'T LOOK AT HER!
BWOOOOSH
AAARGH
DEATH
HAG

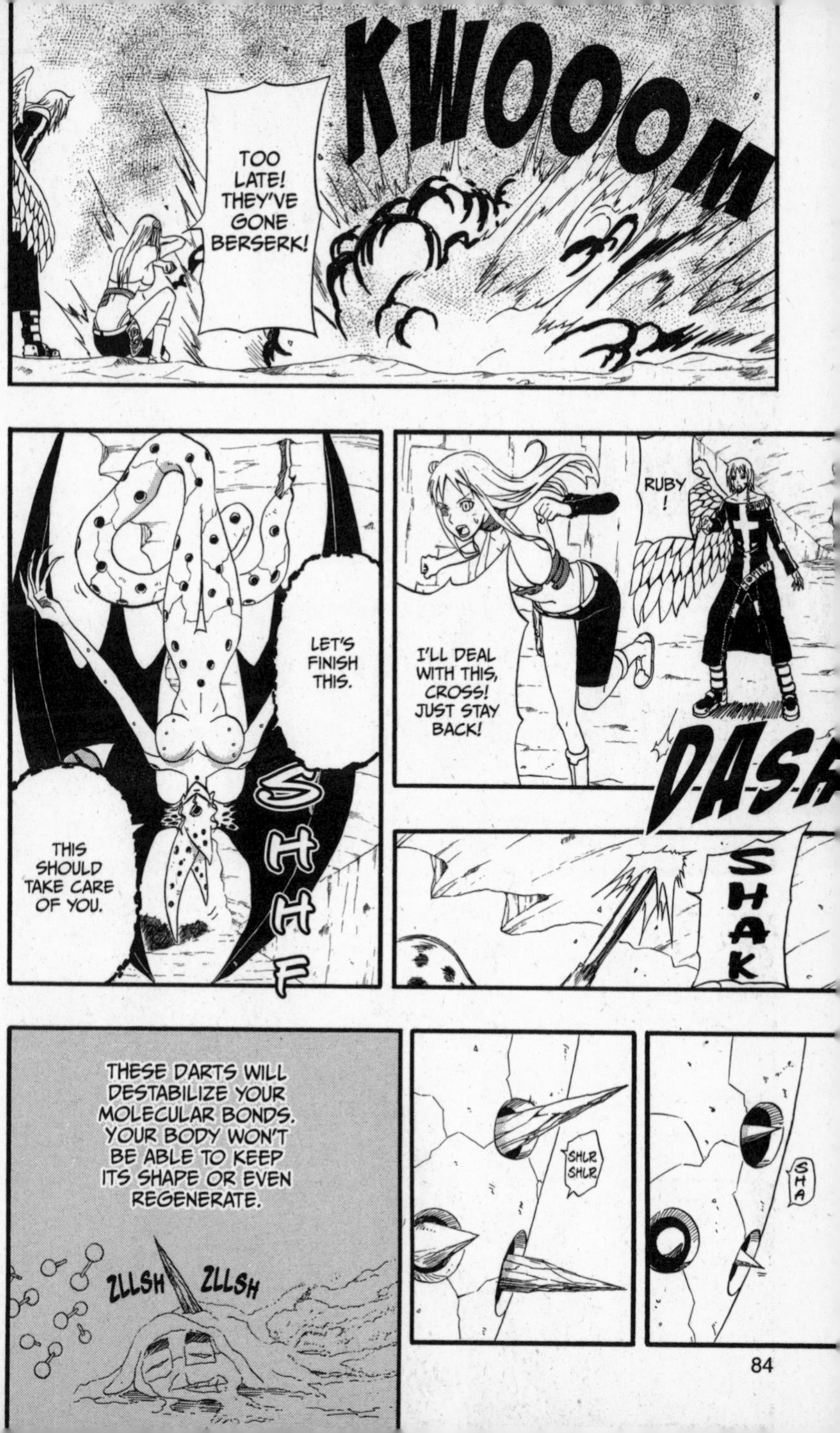
KWOOOOM
TOO LATE! THEY'VE GONE BERSERK!
RUBY!
I'LL DEAL WITH THIS, CROSS! JUST STAY BACK!
DASH
SHAK
LET'S FINISH THIS.
SHHF
THIS SHOULD TAKE CARE OF YOU.
SHA
SHLR SHLR
THESE DARTS WILL DESTABILIZE YOUR MOLECULAR BONDS. YOUR BODY WON'T BE ABLE TO KEEP ITS SHAPE OR EVEN REGENERATE.
ZLLSH ZLLSH

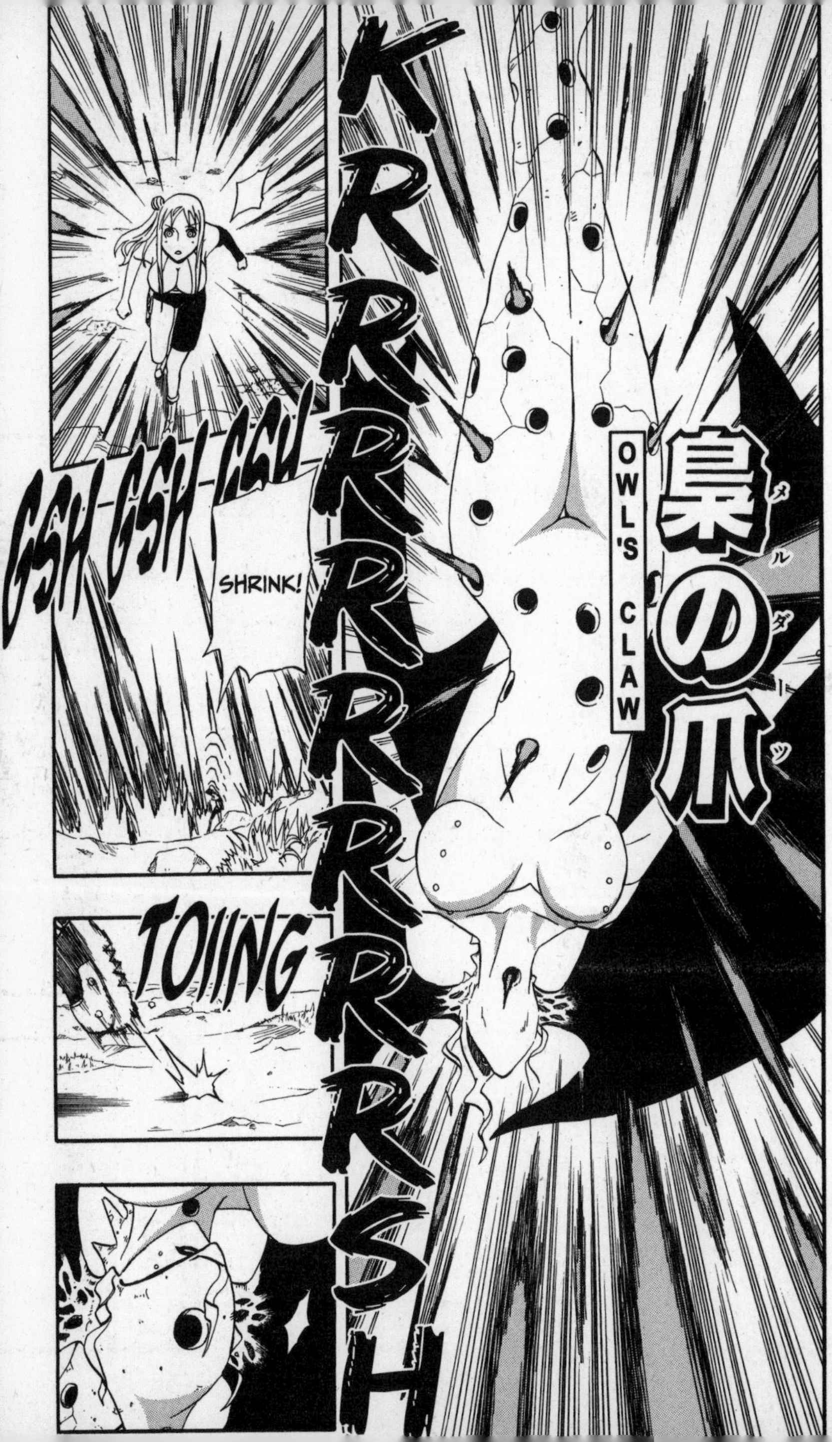
梟の爪(メルダーツ)
OWL'S CLAW
KRRRRRRRRRRRSH
GSH GSH GSU
SHRINK!
TOIING

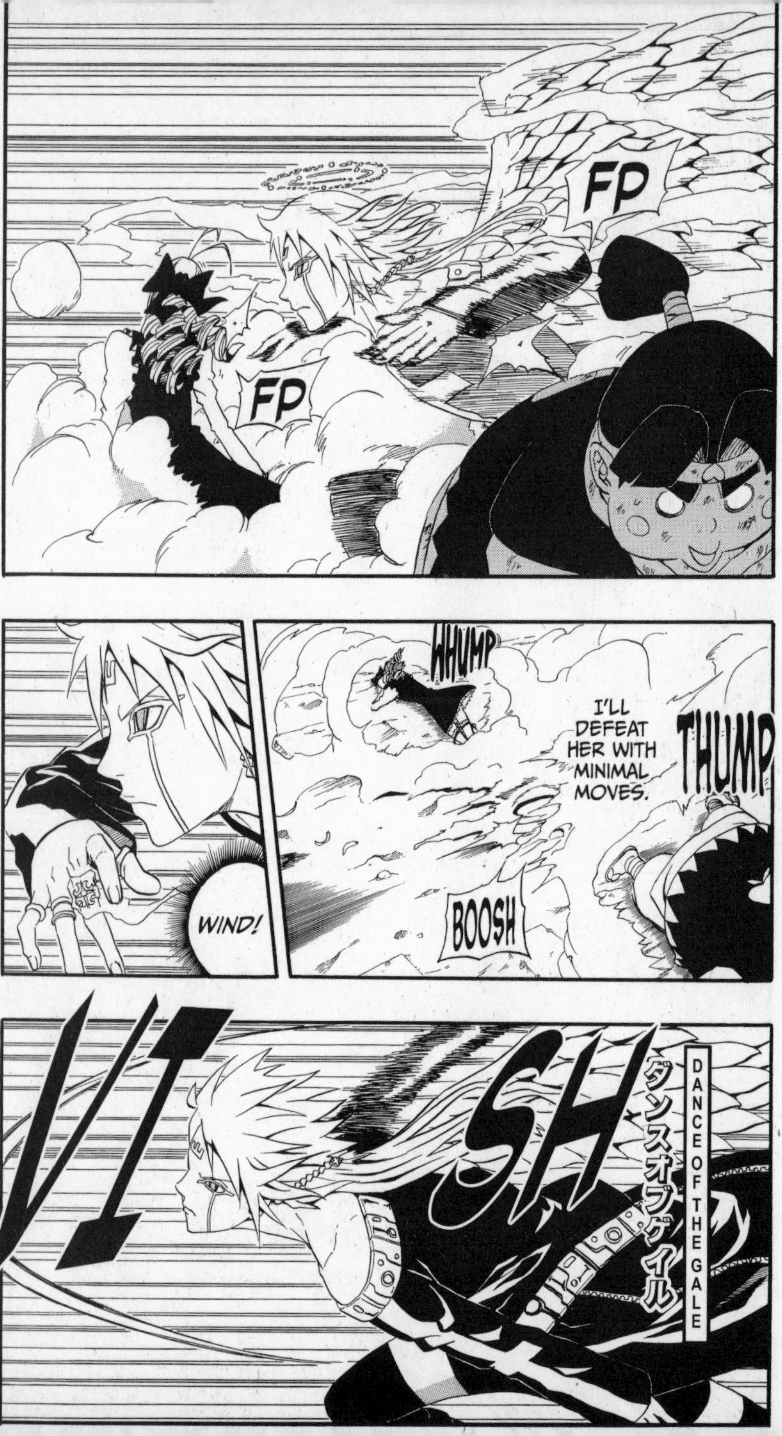
FP
FP
THUMP
I'LL DEFEAT HER WITH MINIMAL MOVES.
WHUMP
BOOSH
WIND!
DANCE OF THE GALE
ダンスオブゲイル
VISH

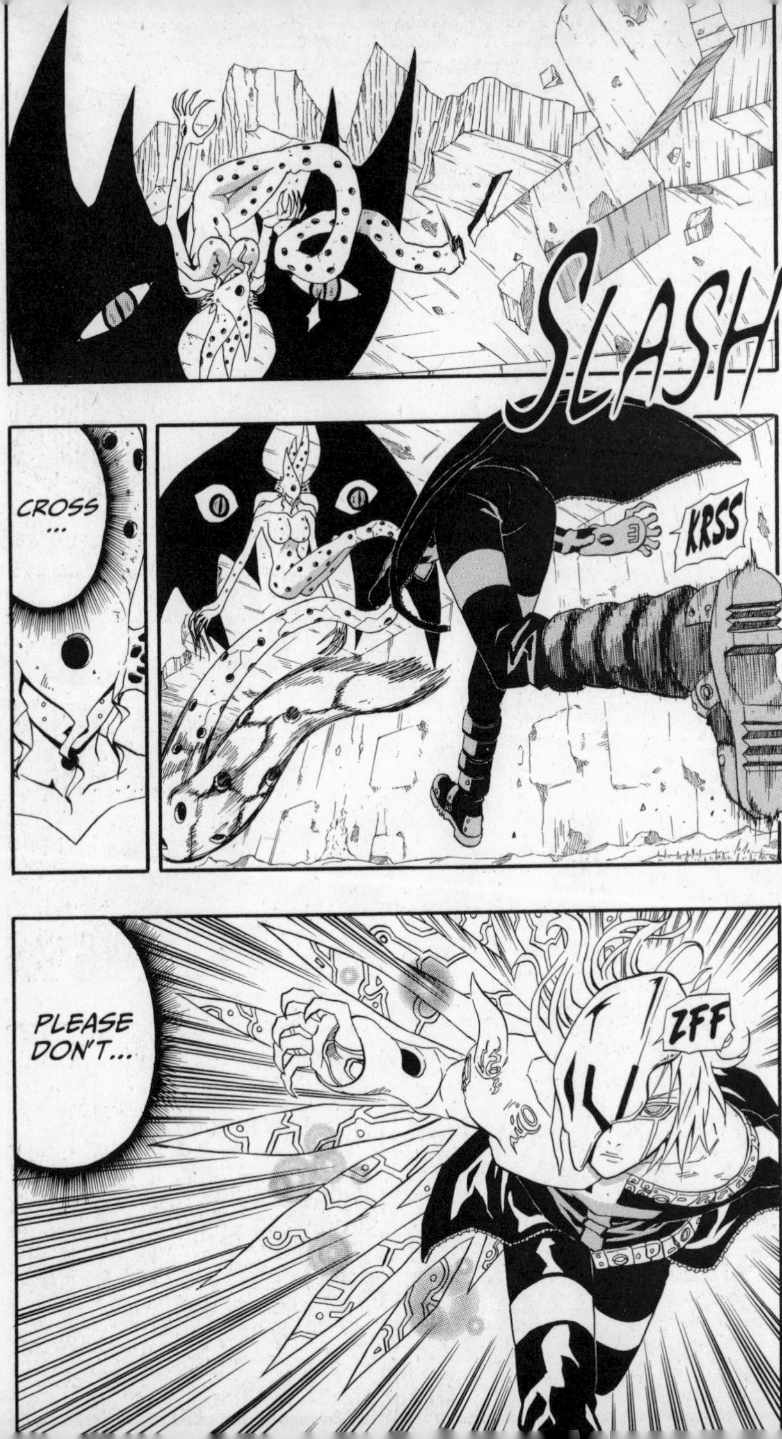
SLASH
KRSS
CROSS
...
ZFF
PLEASE
DON'T...

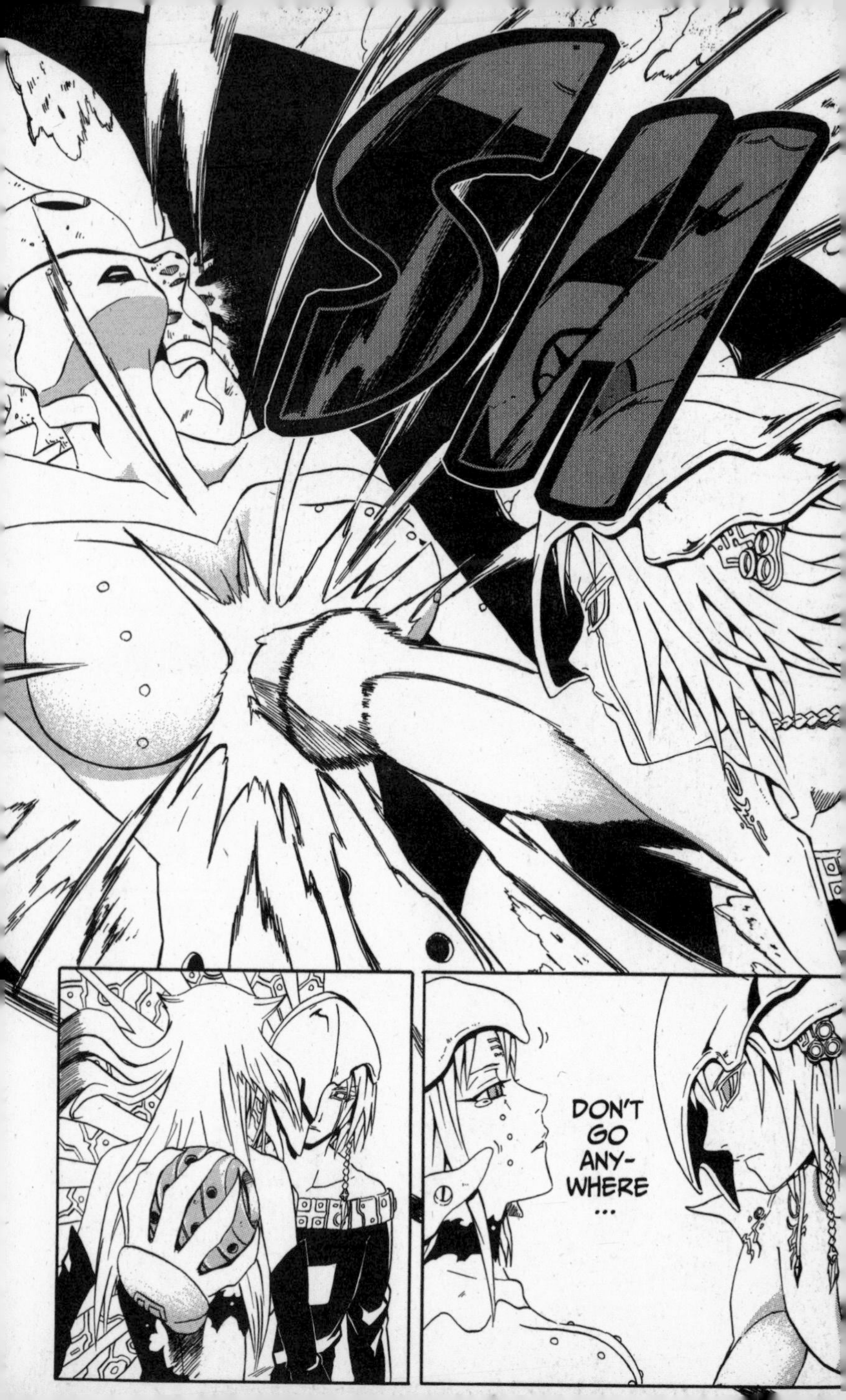
SCH
DON'T GO ANY-WHERE ...

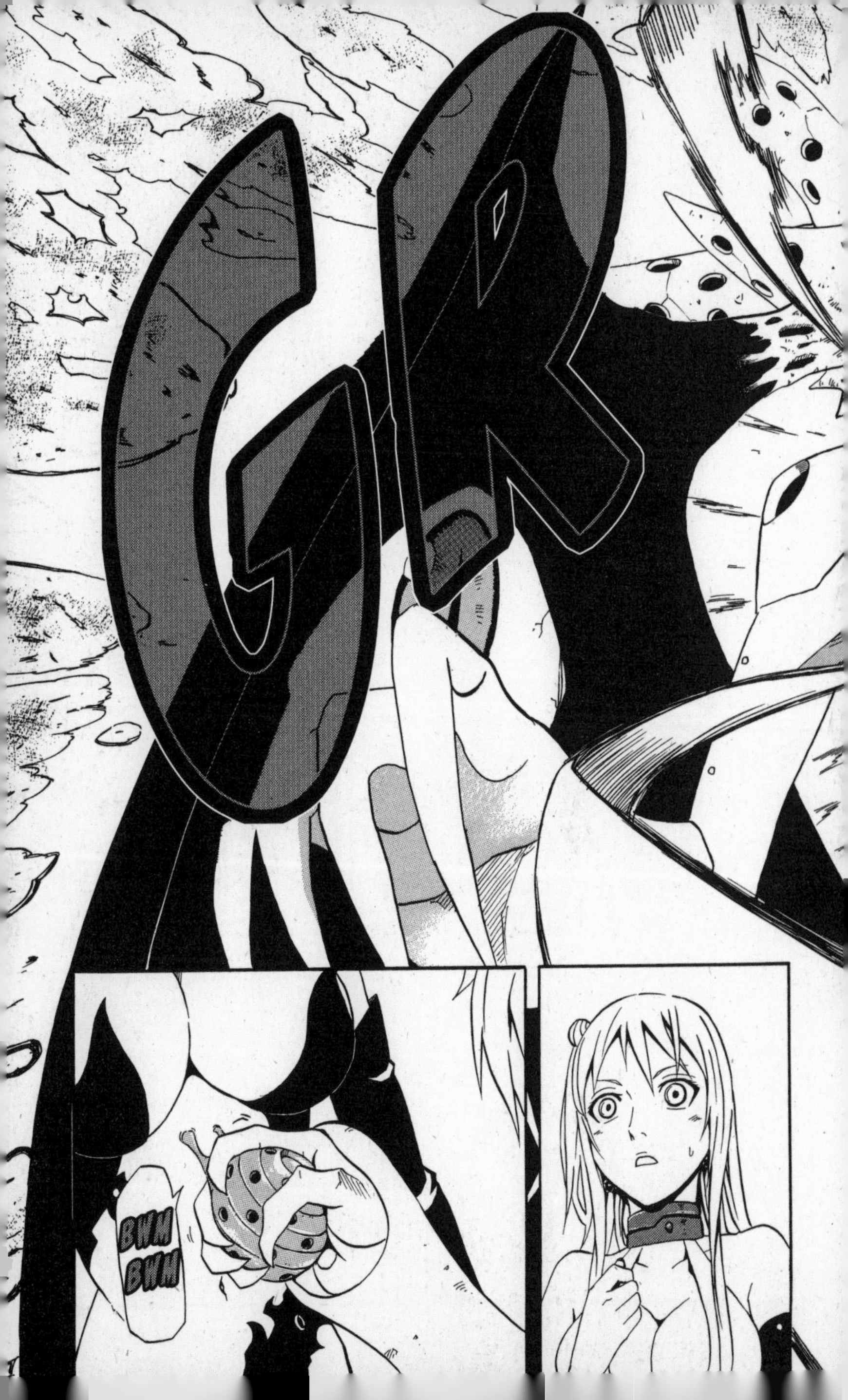
GR
BWM BWM

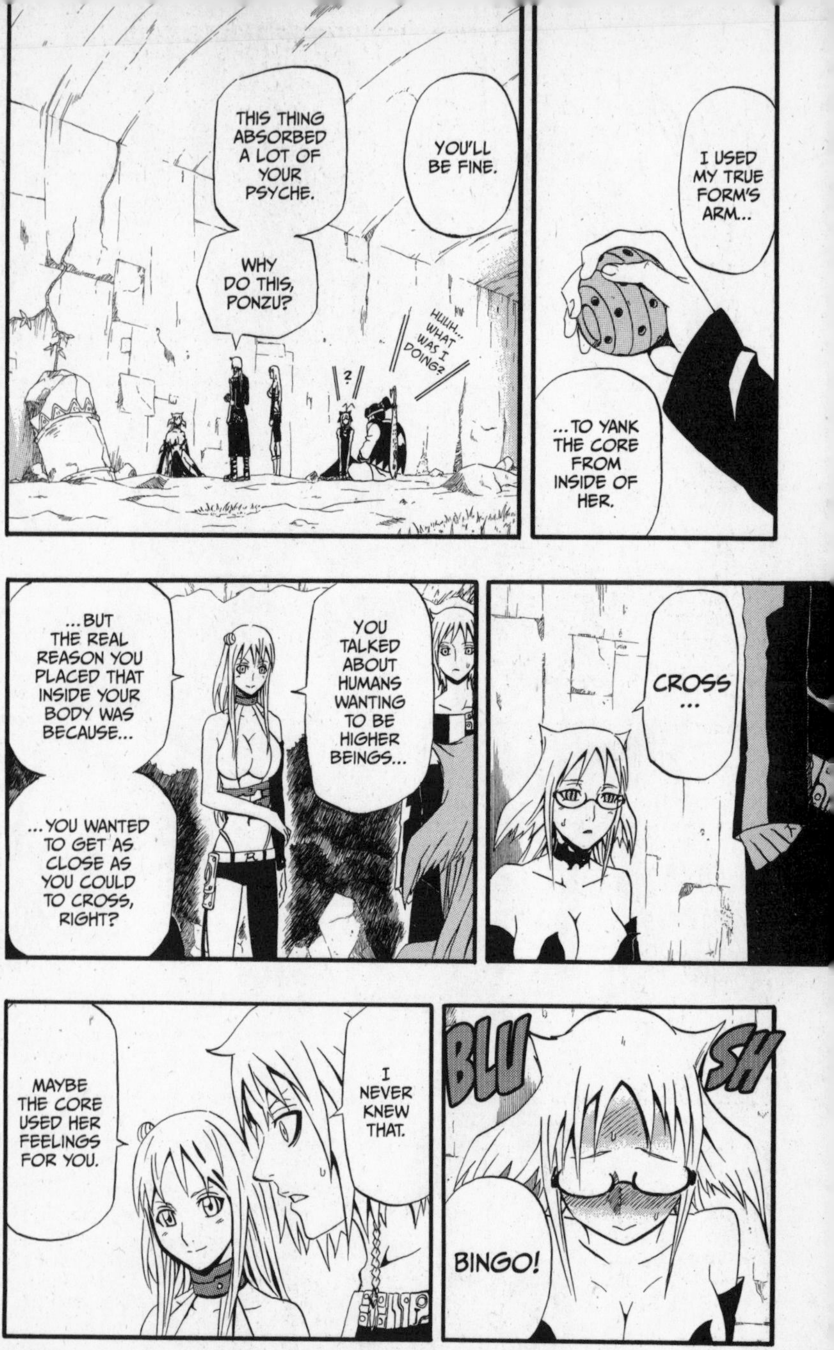
I USED MY TRUE FORM'S ARM...
...TO YANK THE CORE FROM INSIDE OF HER.
YOU'LL BE FINE.
THIS THING ABSORBED A LOT OF YOUR PSYCHE.
HUUH... WHAT WAS I DOING?
WHY DO THIS, PONZU?
CROSS ...
YOU TALKED ABOUT HUMANS WANTING TO BE HIGHER BEINGS...
...BUT THE REAL REASON YOU PLACED THAT INSIDE YOUR BODY WAS BECAUSE...
...YOU WANTED TO GET AS CLOSE AS YOU COULD TO CROSS, RIGHT?
BLUSH
BINGO!
I NEVER KNEW THAT.
MAYBE THE CORE USED HER FEELINGS FOR YOU.

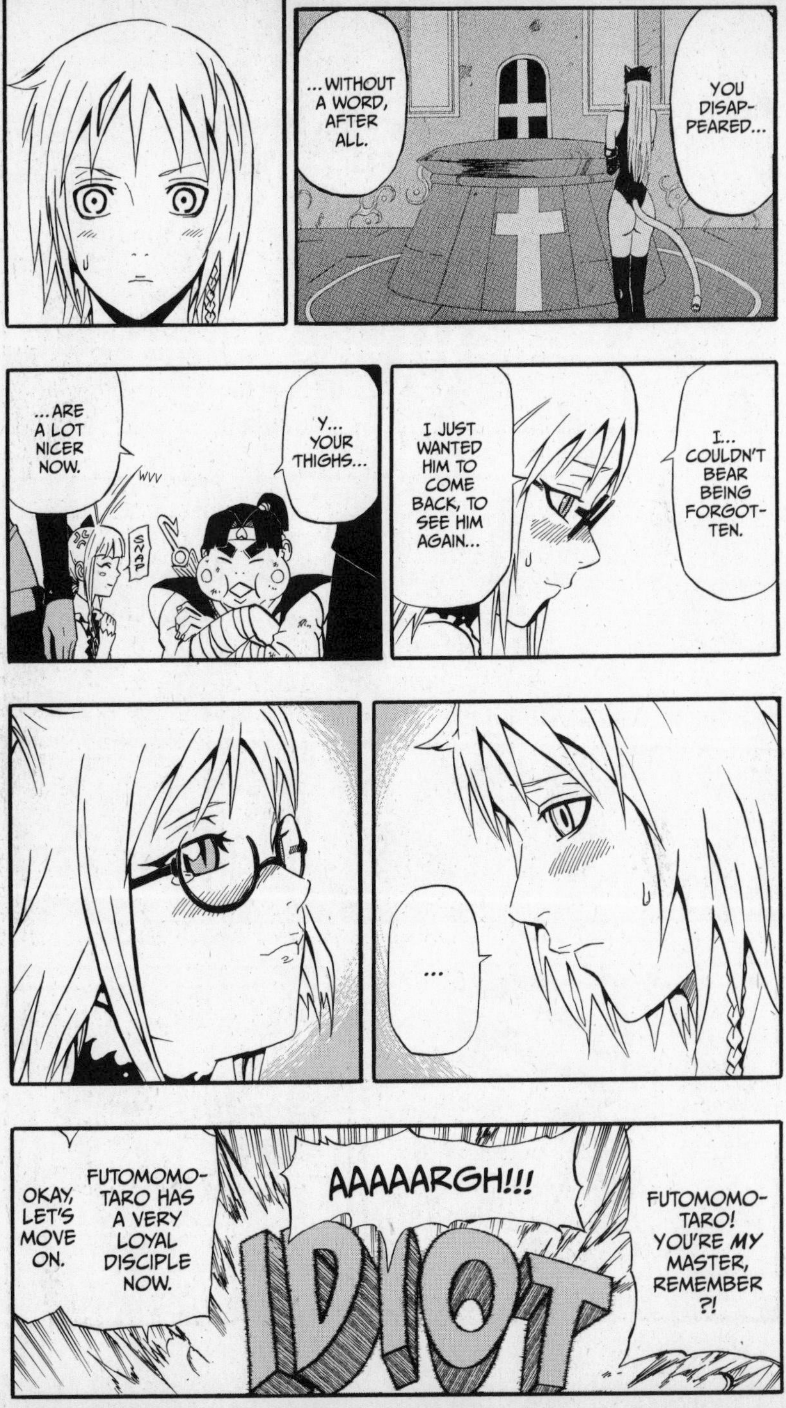
YOU DISAP-PEARED...
...WITHOUT A WORD, AFTER ALL.
I... COULDN'T BEAR BEING FORGOT-TEN.
I JUST WANTED HIM TO COME BACK, TO SEE HIM AGAIN...
Y... YOUR THIGHS...
...ARE A LOT NICER NOW.
WVV
SNAP
...
FUTOMOMO-TARO! YOU'RE MY MASTER, REMEMBER?!
AAAAARGH!!!
IDIOT
FUTOMOMO-TARO HAS A VERY LOYAL DISCIPLE NOW.
OKAY, LET'S MOVE ON.

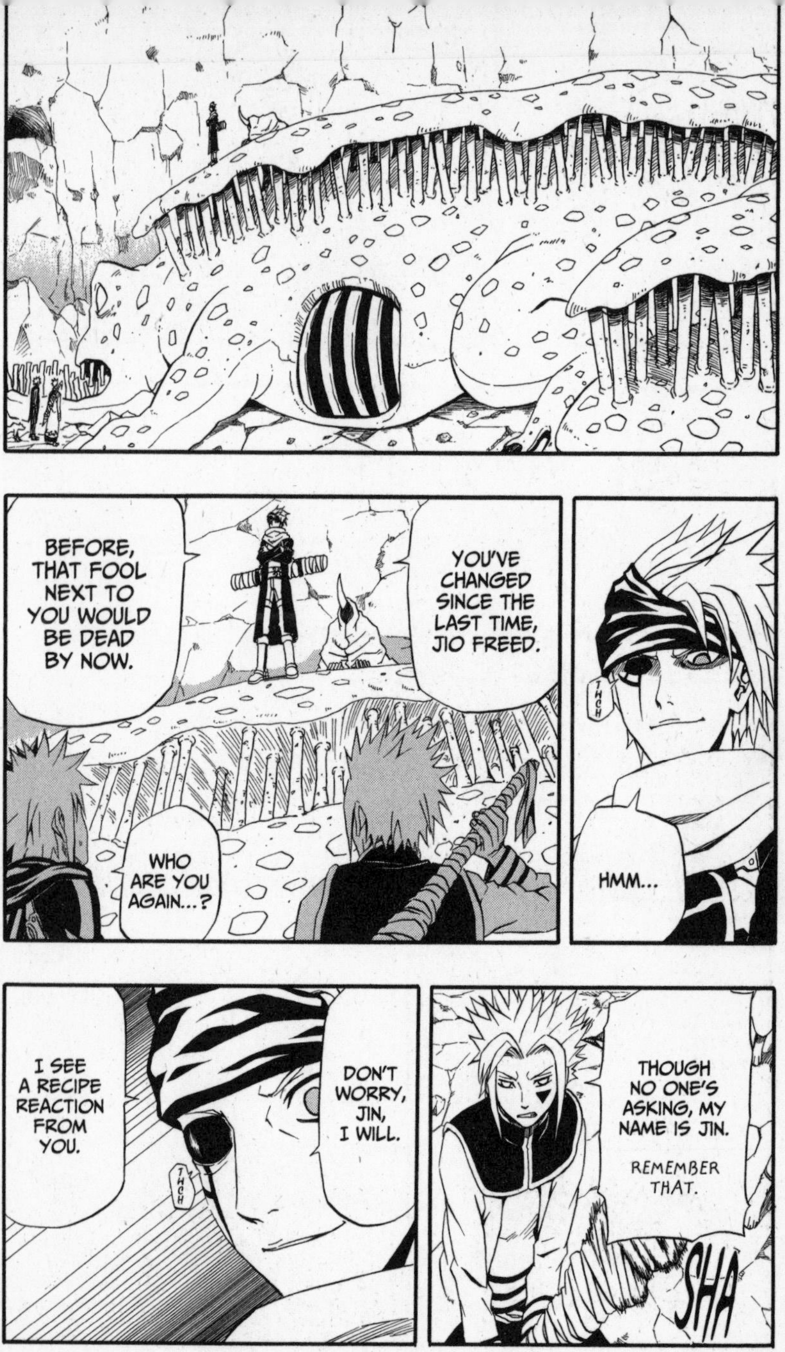

HMM...
THCH
YOU'VE CHANGED SINCE THE LAST TIME, JIO FREED.
BEFORE, THAT FOOL NEXT TO YOU WOULD BE DEAD BY NOW.
WHO ARE YOU AGAIN...?
THOUGH NO ONE'S ASKING, MY NAME IS JIN.
REMEMBER THAT.
SHA
DON'T WORRY, JIN, I WILL.
I SEE A RECIPE REACTION FROM YOU.
THCH

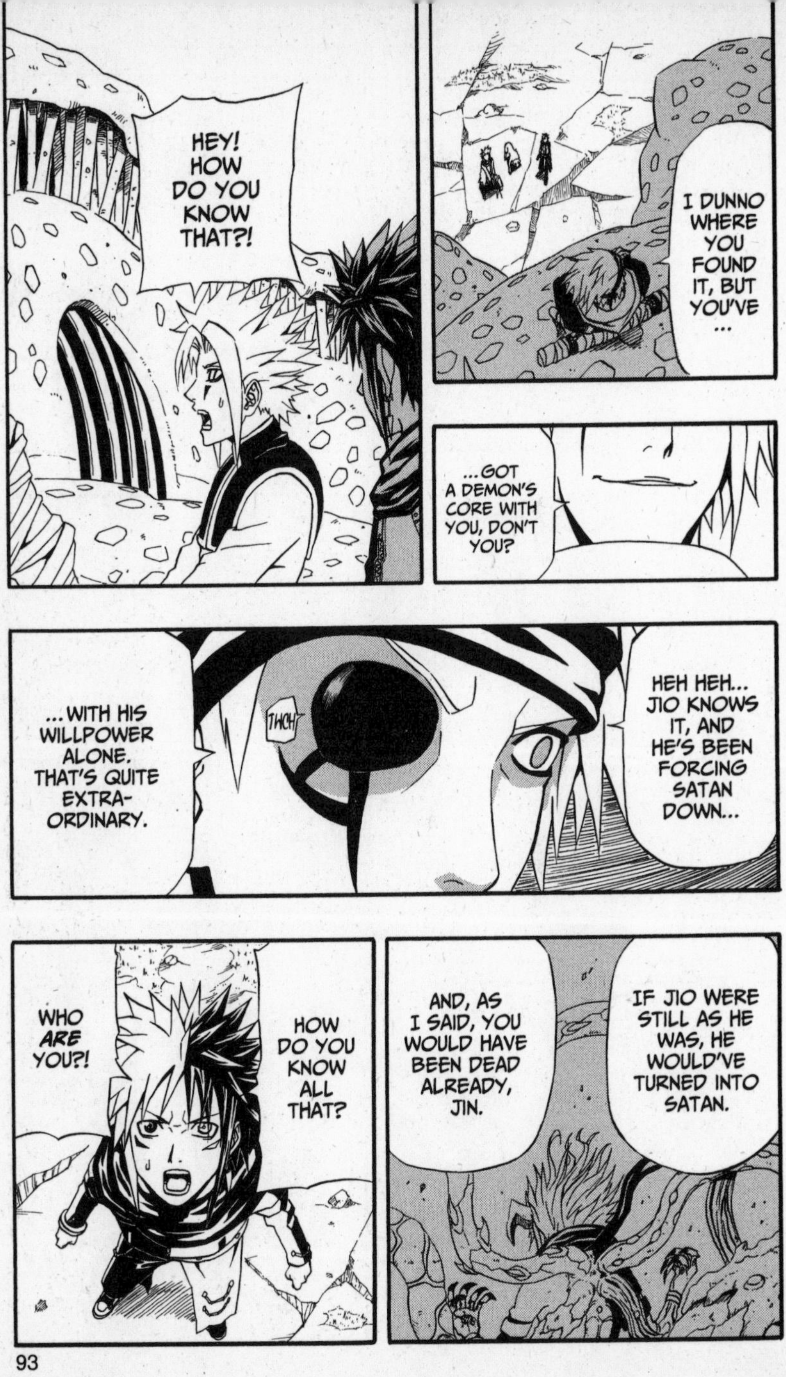
I DUNNO WHERE YOU FOUND IT, BUT YOU'VE ...
...GOT A DEMON'S CORE WITH YOU, DON'T YOU?
HEY! HOW DO YOU KNOW THAT?!
HEH HEH... JIO KNOWS IT, AND HE'S BEEN FORCING SATAN DOWN...
TWCH
...WITH HIS WILLPOWER ALONE. THAT'S QUITE EXTRA-ORDINARY.
IF JIO WERE STILL AS HE WAS, HE WOULD'VE TURNED INTO SATAN.
AND, AS I SAID, YOU WOULD HAVE BEEN DEAD ALREADY, JIN.
HOW DO YOU KNOW ALL THAT?
WHO *ARE* YOU?!

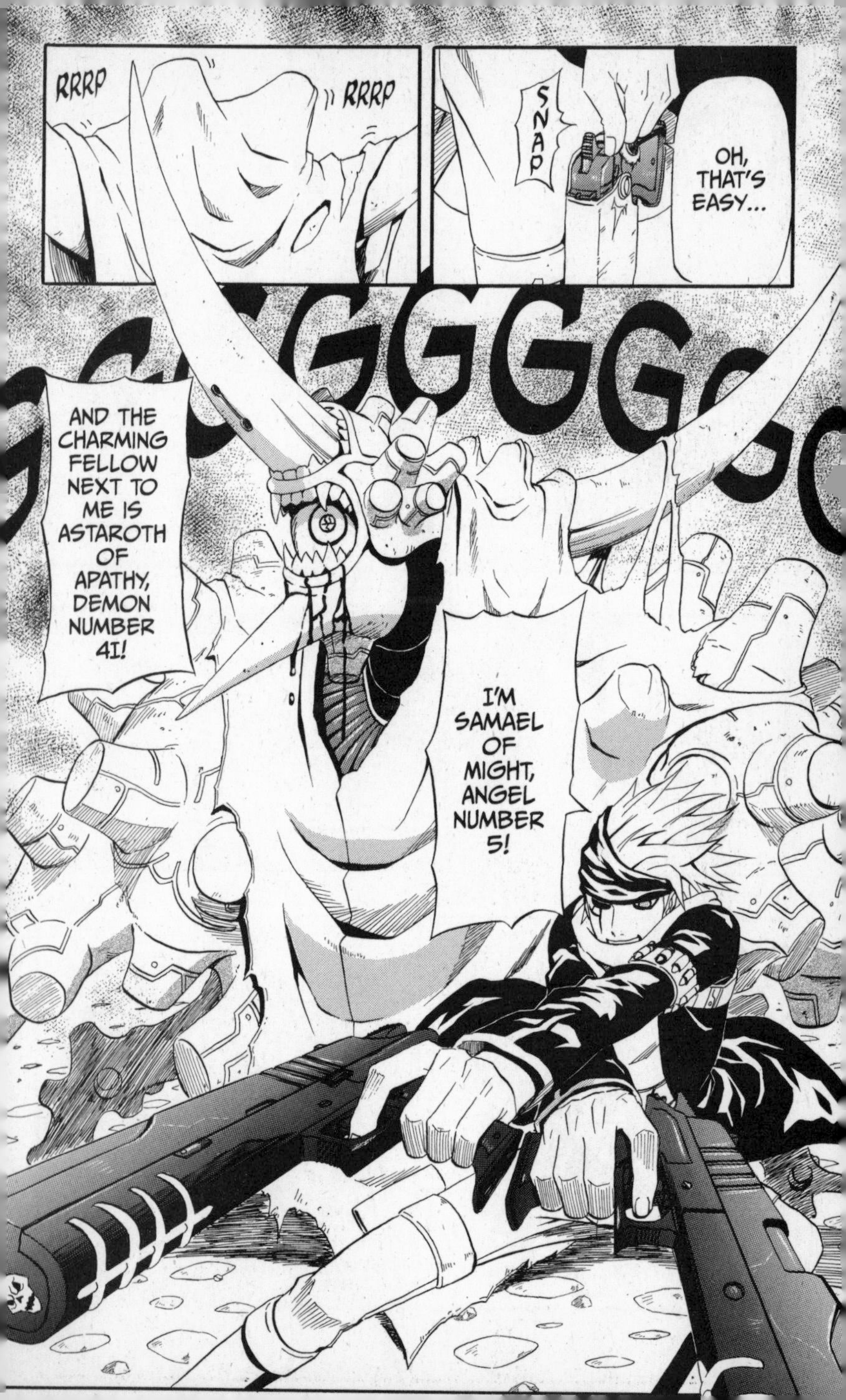
SNAP
OH, THAT'S EASY...
RRRP
RRRP
GGGGG
I'M SAMAEL OF MIGHT, ANGEL NUMBER 5!
AND THE CHARMING FELLOW NEXT TO ME IS ASTAROTH OF APATHY, DEMON NUMBER 41!

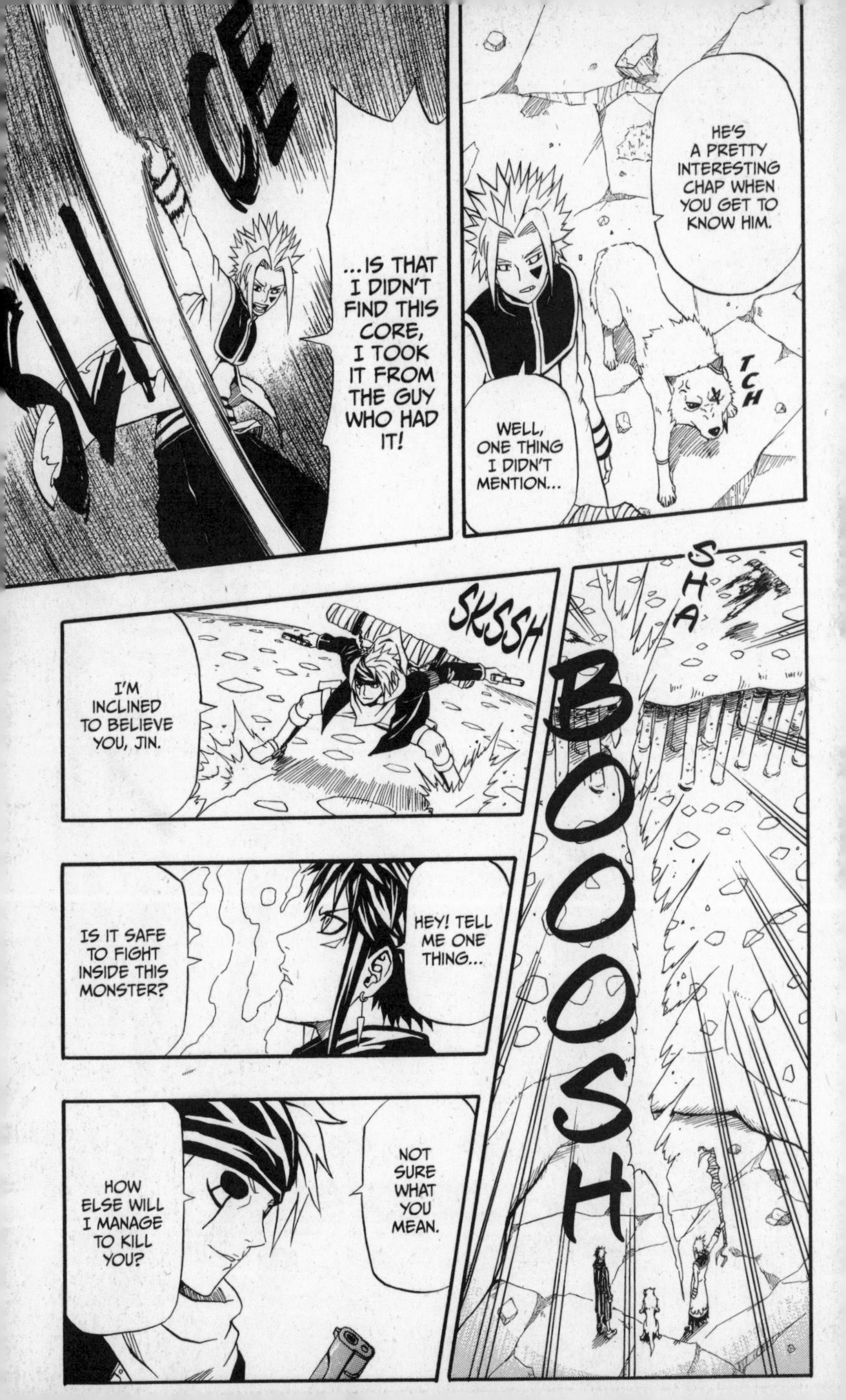

HE'S A PRETTY INTERESTING CHAP WHEN YOU GET TO KNOW HIM.
TCH
WELL, ONE THING I DIDN'T MENTION...
...IS THAT I DIDN'T FIND THIS CORE, I TOOK IT FROM THE GUY WHO HAD IT!
SLICE
SHA
BOOOOSH
SKSSH
I'M INCLINED TO BELIEVE YOU, JIN.
HEY! TELL ME ONE THING...
IS IT SAFE TO FIGHT INSIDE THIS MONSTER?
NOT SURE WHAT YOU MEAN.
HOW ELSE WILL I MANAGE TO KILL YOU?

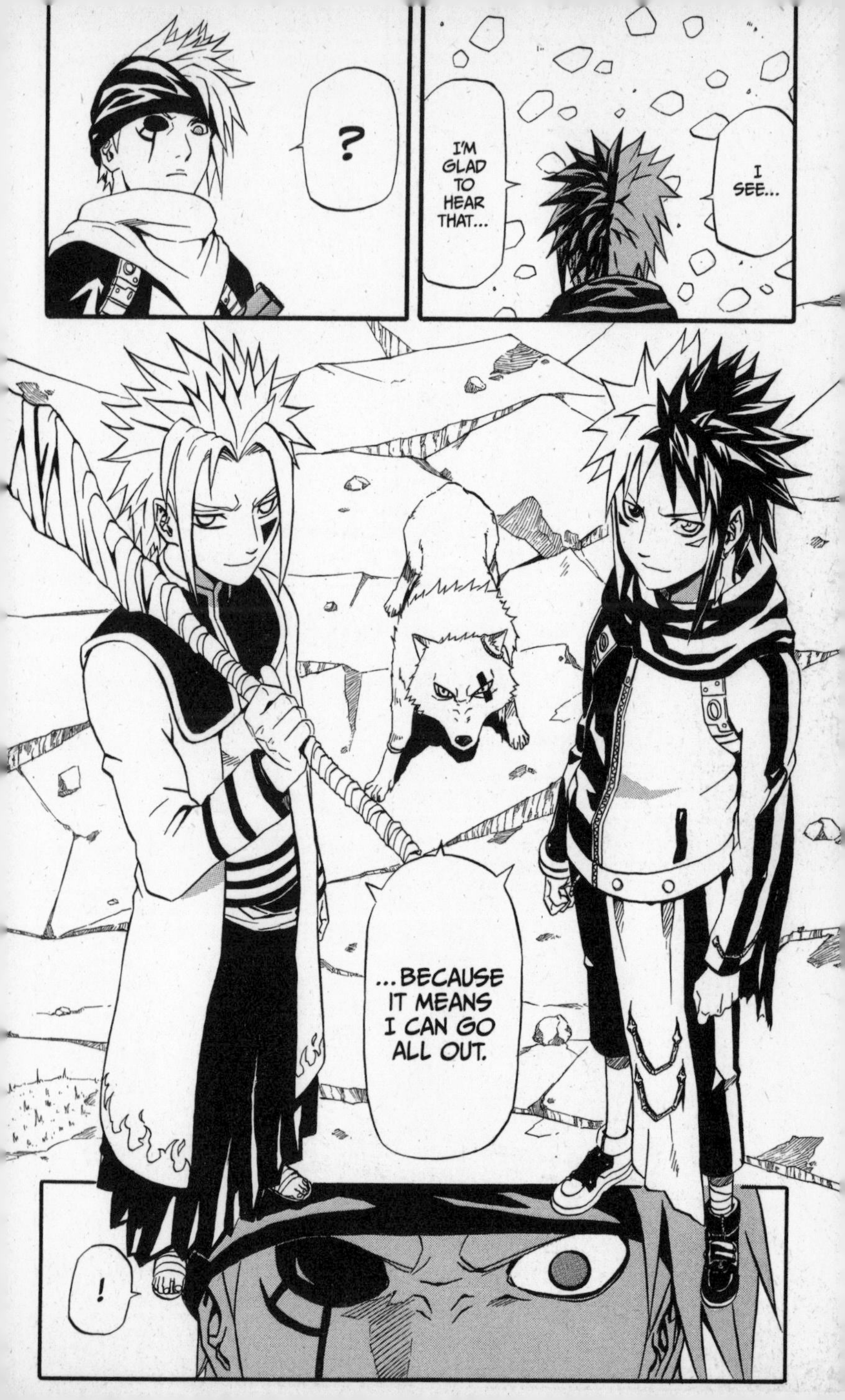
I SEE...
I'M GLAD TO HEAR THAT...
?
...BECAUSE IT MEANS I CAN GO ALL OUT.
!

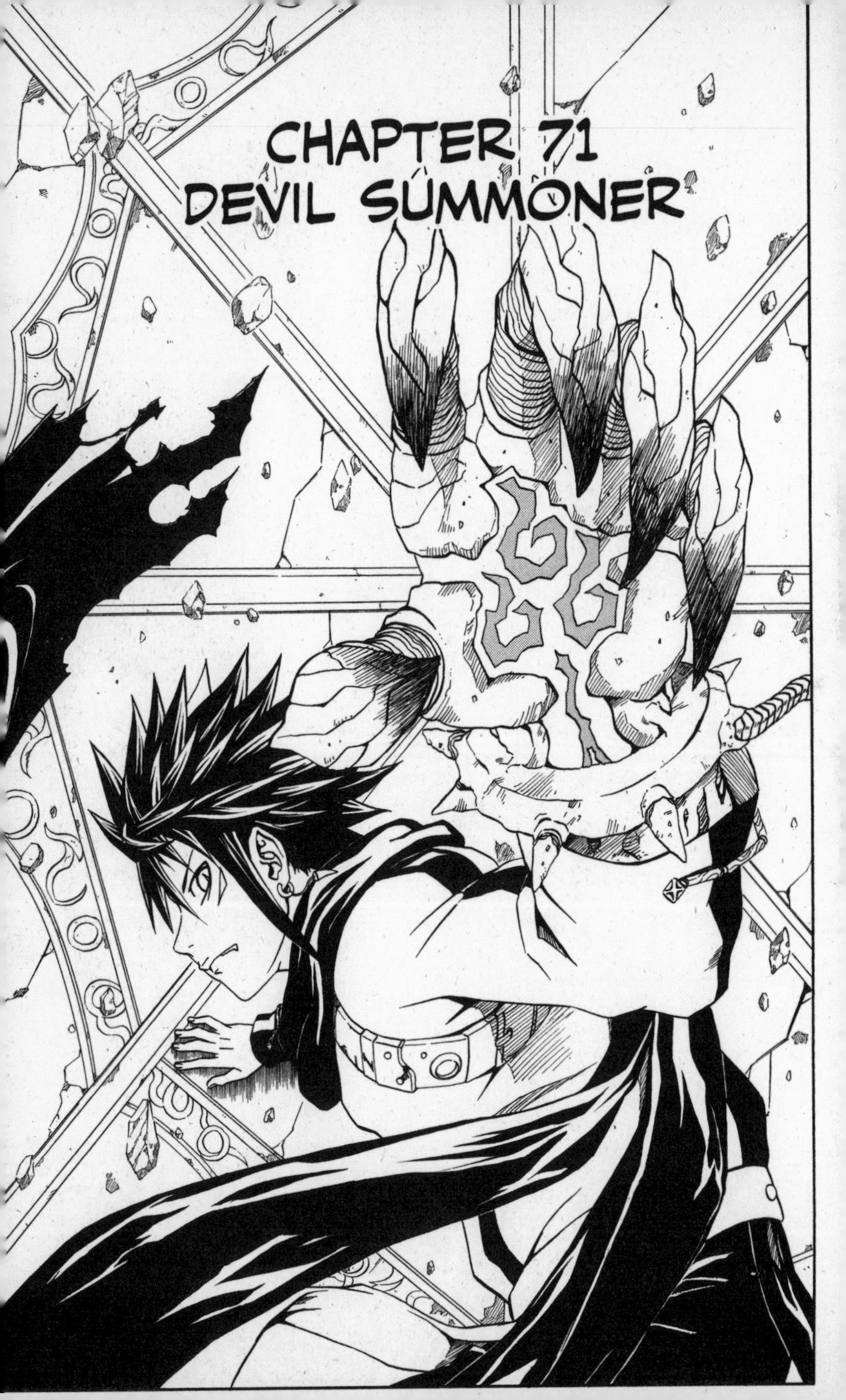
CHAPTER 71
DEVIL SUMMONER

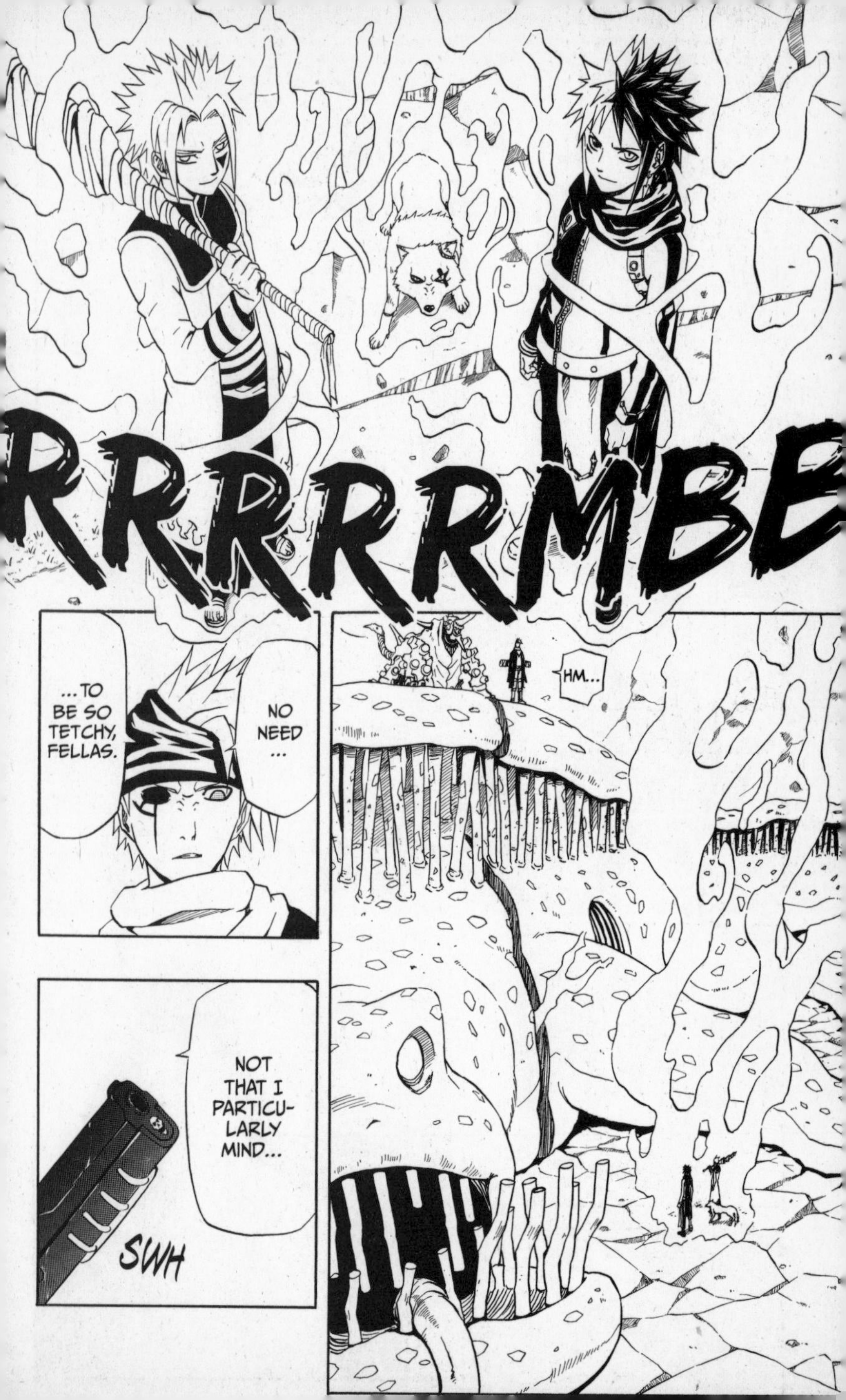
RRRRRMBB
HM...
NO NEED...
...TO BE SO TETCHY, FELLAS.
NOT THAT I PARTICU-LARLY MIND...
SWH

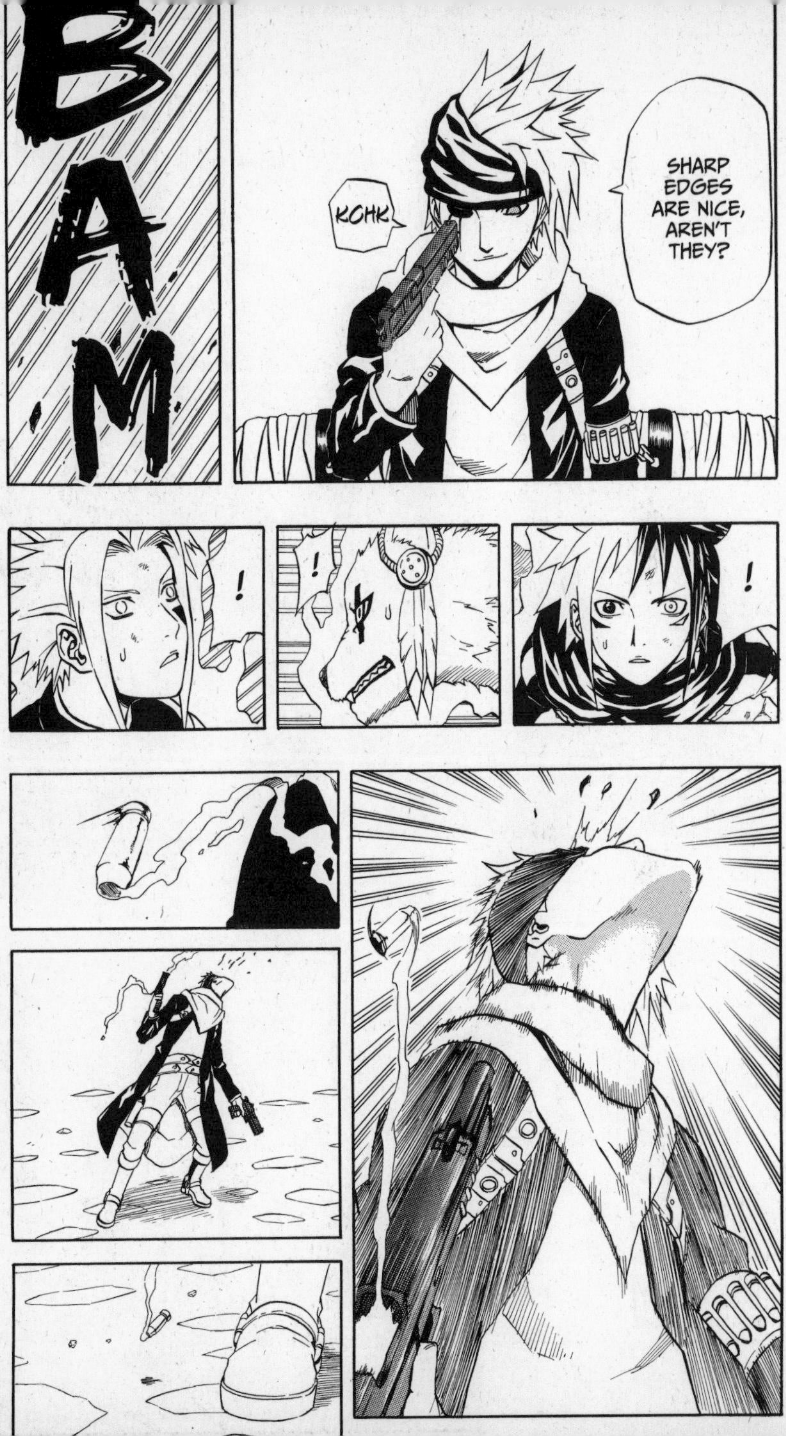
SHARP EDGES ARE NICE, AREN'T THEY?
KOHK
BAM
!
!
!

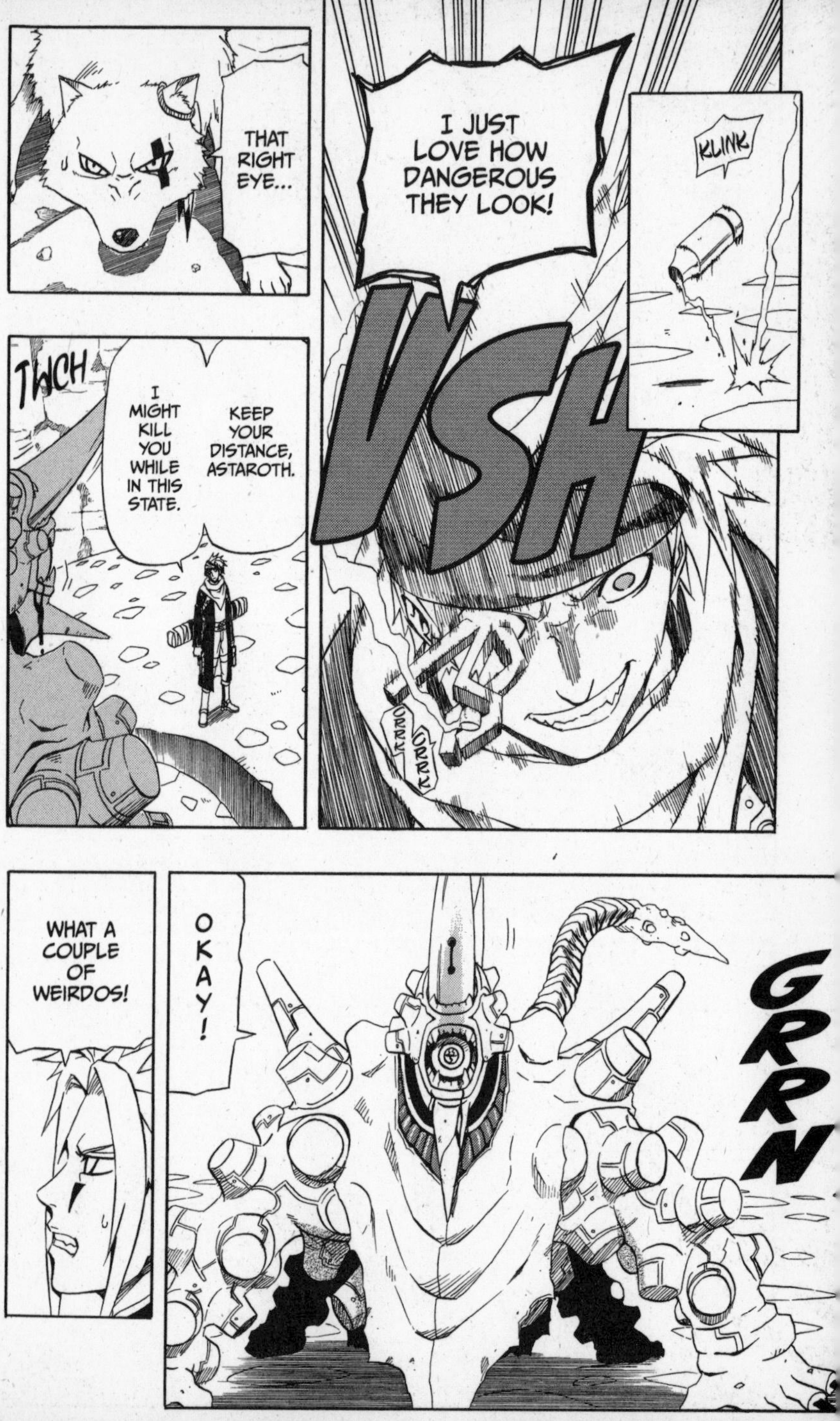

KLINK
I JUST LOVE HOW DANGEROUS THEY LOOK!
VSH
CRRK
CRRK
THAT RIGHT EYE...
TWCH
KEEP YOUR DISTANCE, ASTAROTH.
I MIGHT KILL YOU WHILE IN THIS STATE.
GRRN
OKAY!
WHAT A COUPLE OF WEIRDOS!

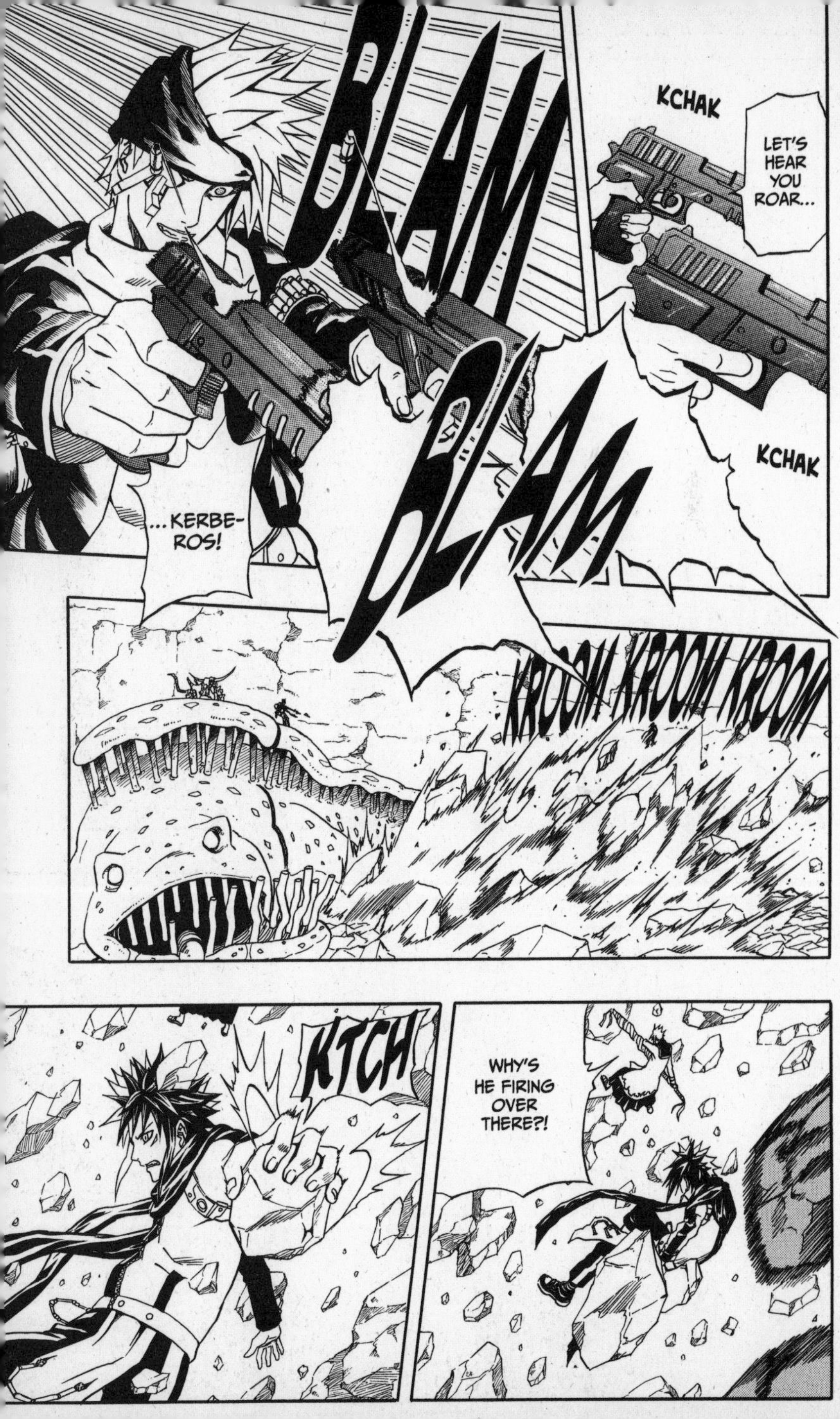
KCHAK
LET'S HEAR YOU ROAR...
KCHAK
BLAM
BLAM
...KERBE-ROS!
KROOM KROOM KROOM
WHY'S HE FIRING OVER THERE?!
KTCH

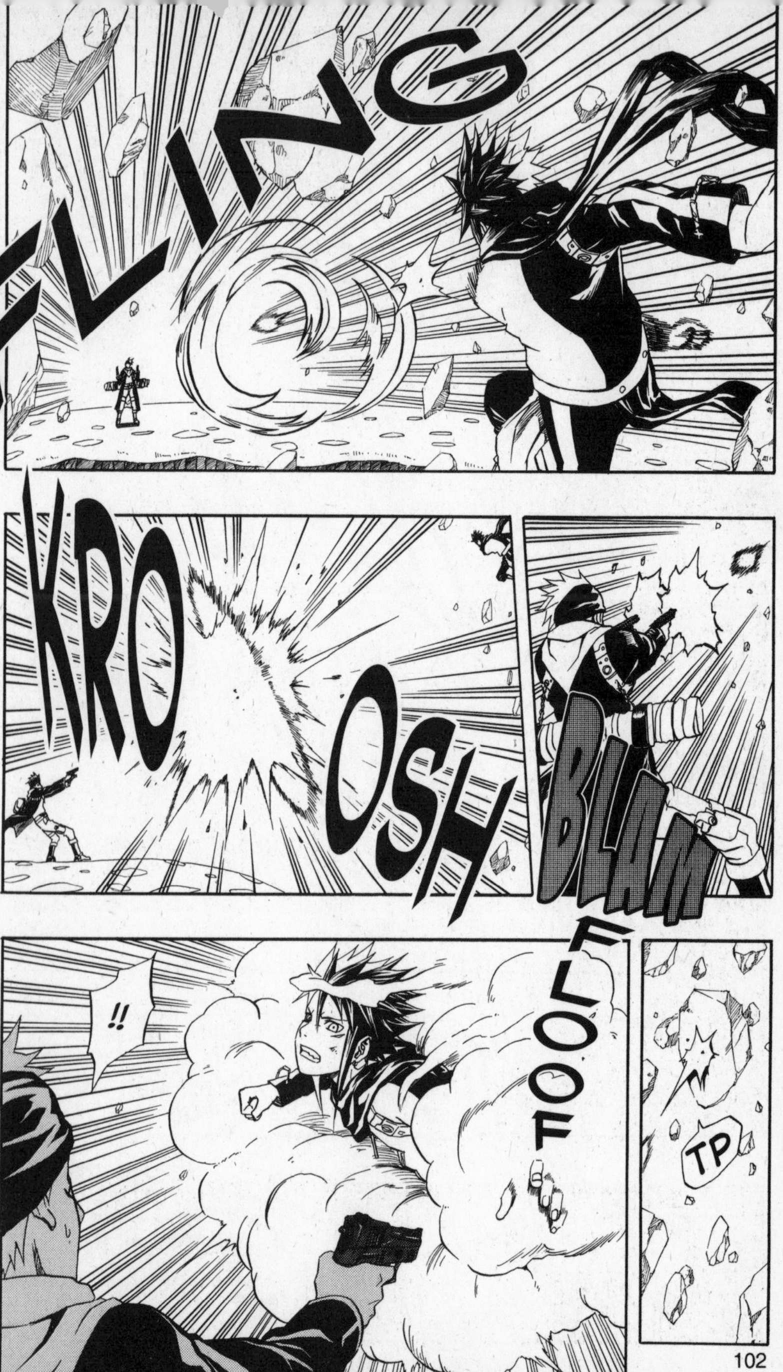
FLING
BLAM
KROOSH
TP
FLOOF
!!

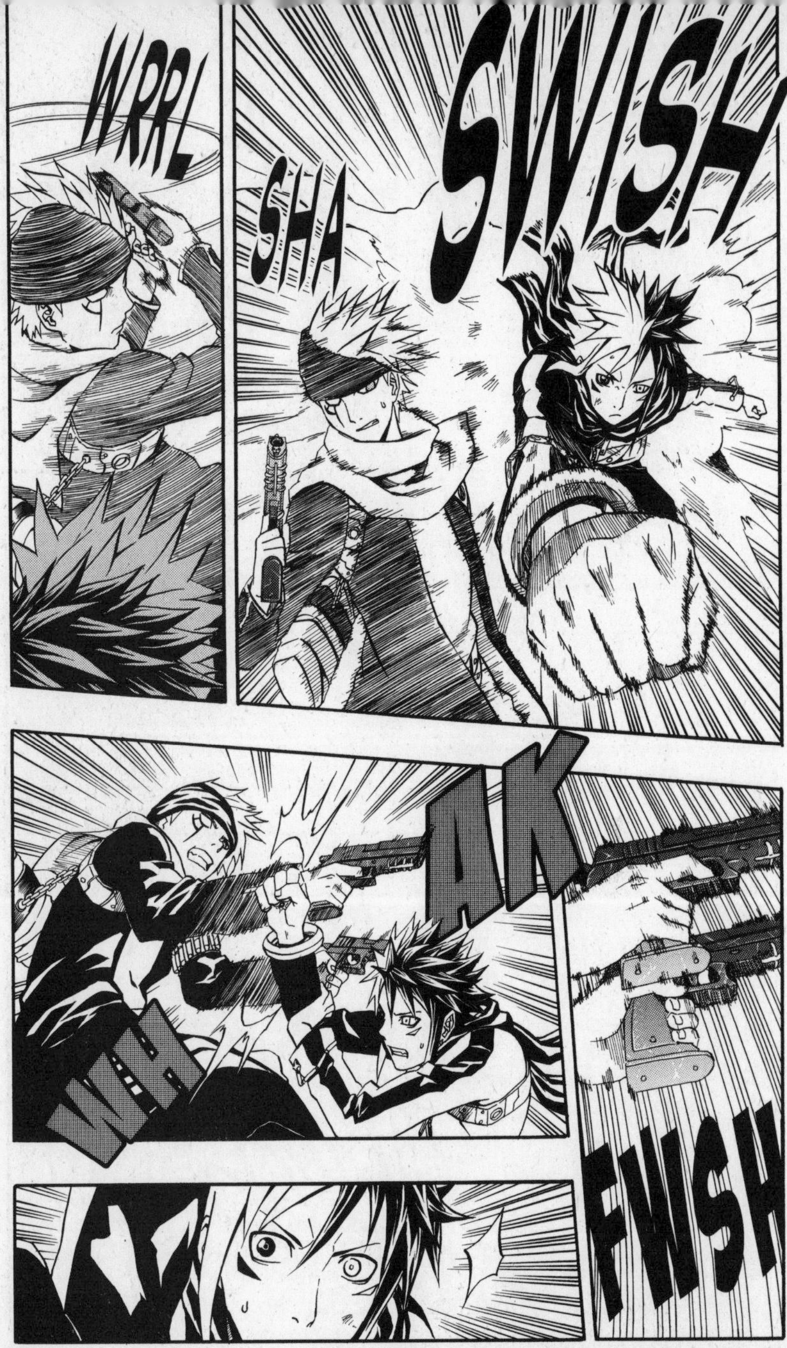
SWISH
SHA
WRRL
AK
WHA
FWSH

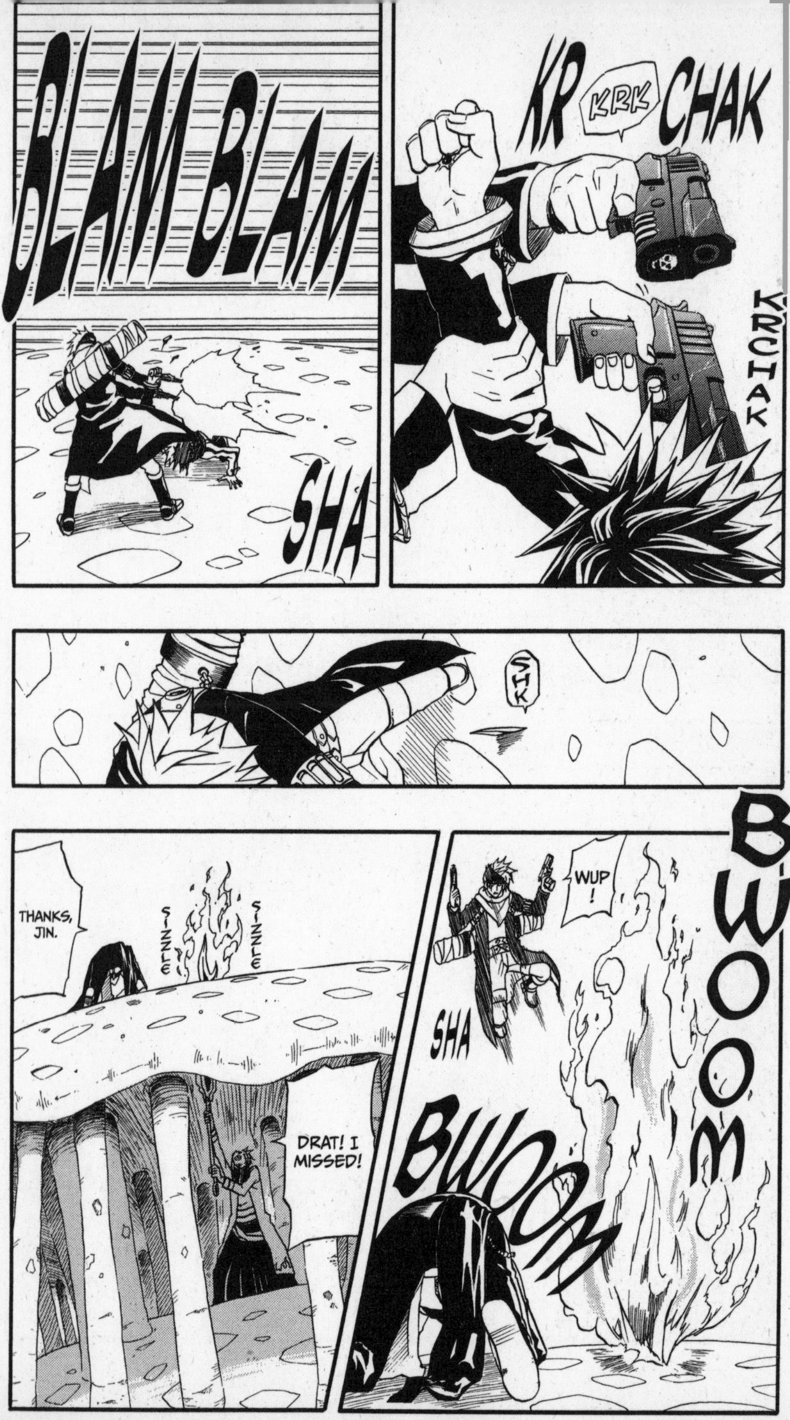
KR
KRK
CHAK
KRCHAK
BLAM BLAM
SHA
SHK
BWOOOM
WUP!
SHA
BWOOM
THANKS, JIN.
SIZZLE
SIZZLE
DRAT! I MISSED!

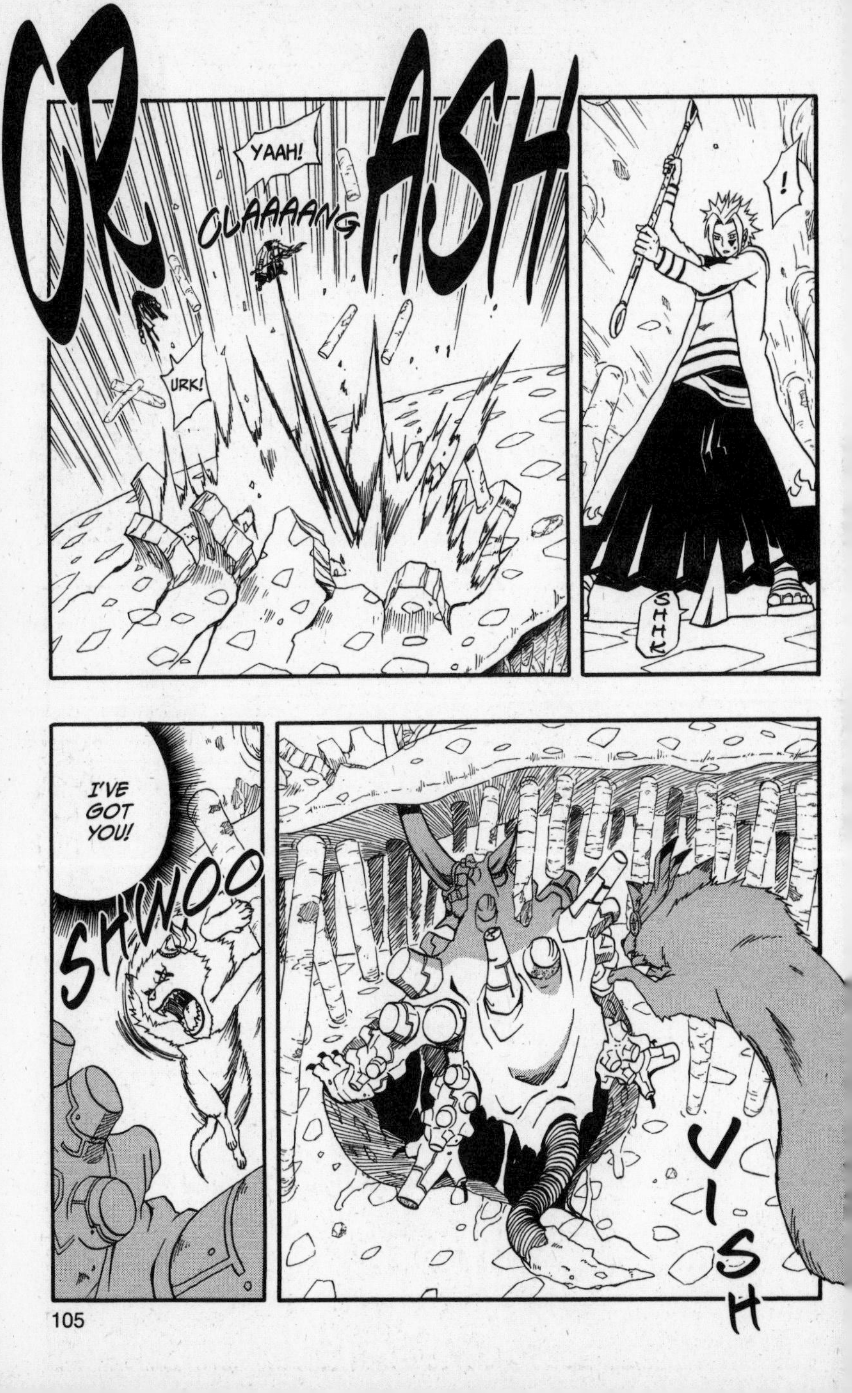
!
SHHK
CRASH
YAAH!
CLAAAANG
URK!
VISH
I'VE GOT YOU!
SHWOO

HE HASN'T USED ANY SPECIAL ABILITIES YET...

I CAN'T TELL HOW THAT GUY'S GOING TO ATTACK.

TSK!!

TMP

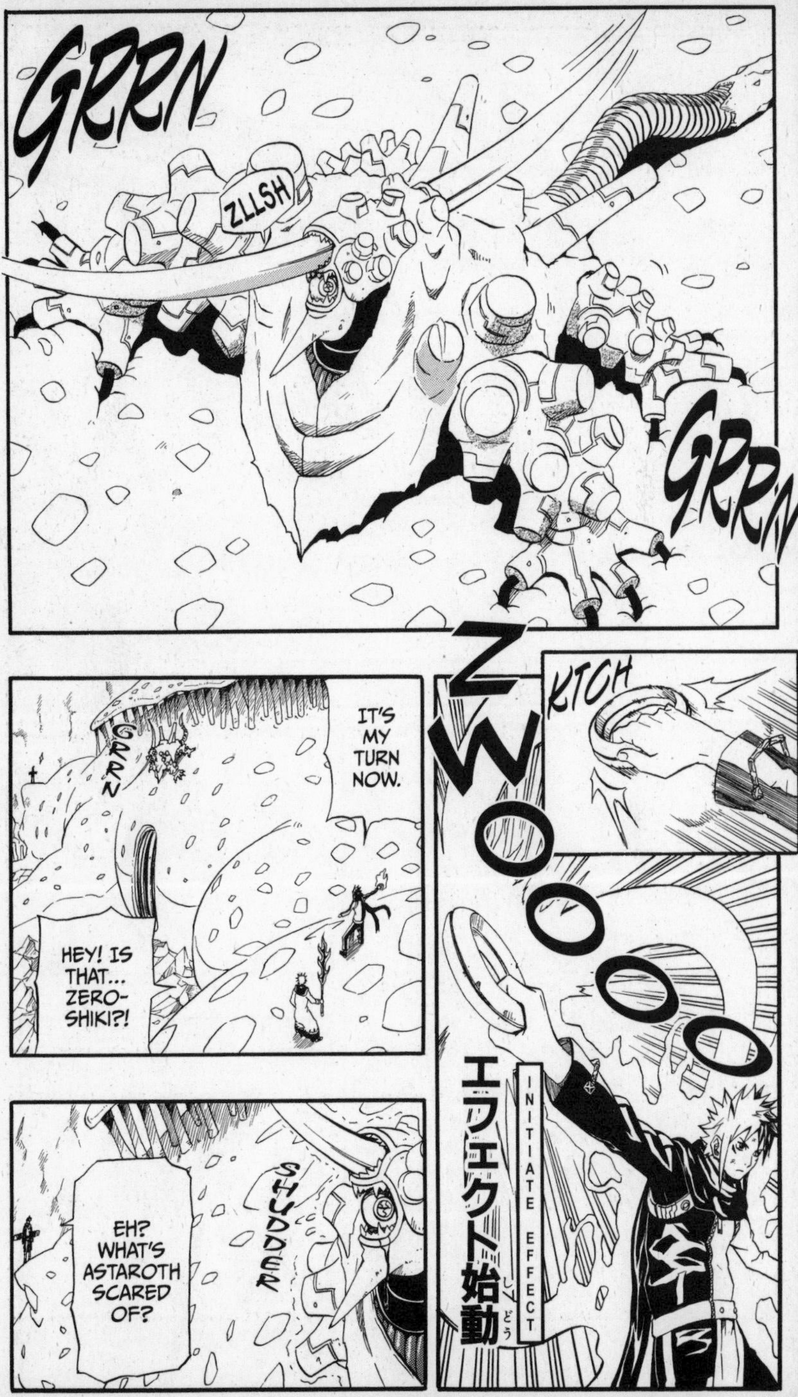
GRRN
ZLLSH
GRRN
KTCH
ZWOOOOO
INITIATE EFFECT
エフェクト始動
GRRN
IT'S MY TURN NOW.
HEY! IS THAT... ZERO-SHIKI?!
SHUDDER
EH? WHAT'S ASTAROTH SCARED OF?

ONLY HE CAN TELL US THAT.

TAKE THIS, ASTA-ROTH!

I DON'T SEE ANY-THING.

WHAT'S GOING ON?

?

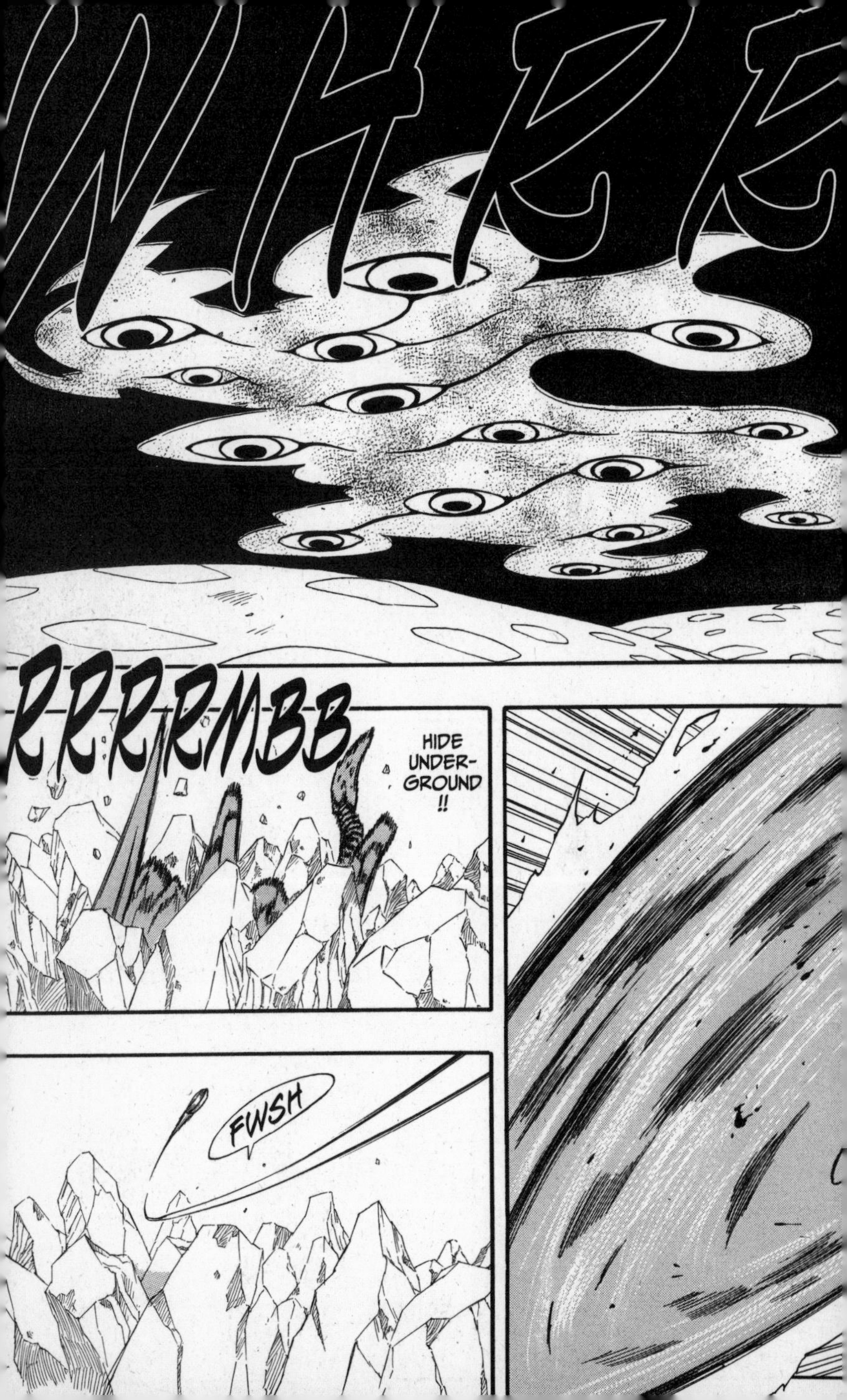
WHRRR
RRRRMBB
HIDE UNDER-GROUND !!
FWSH

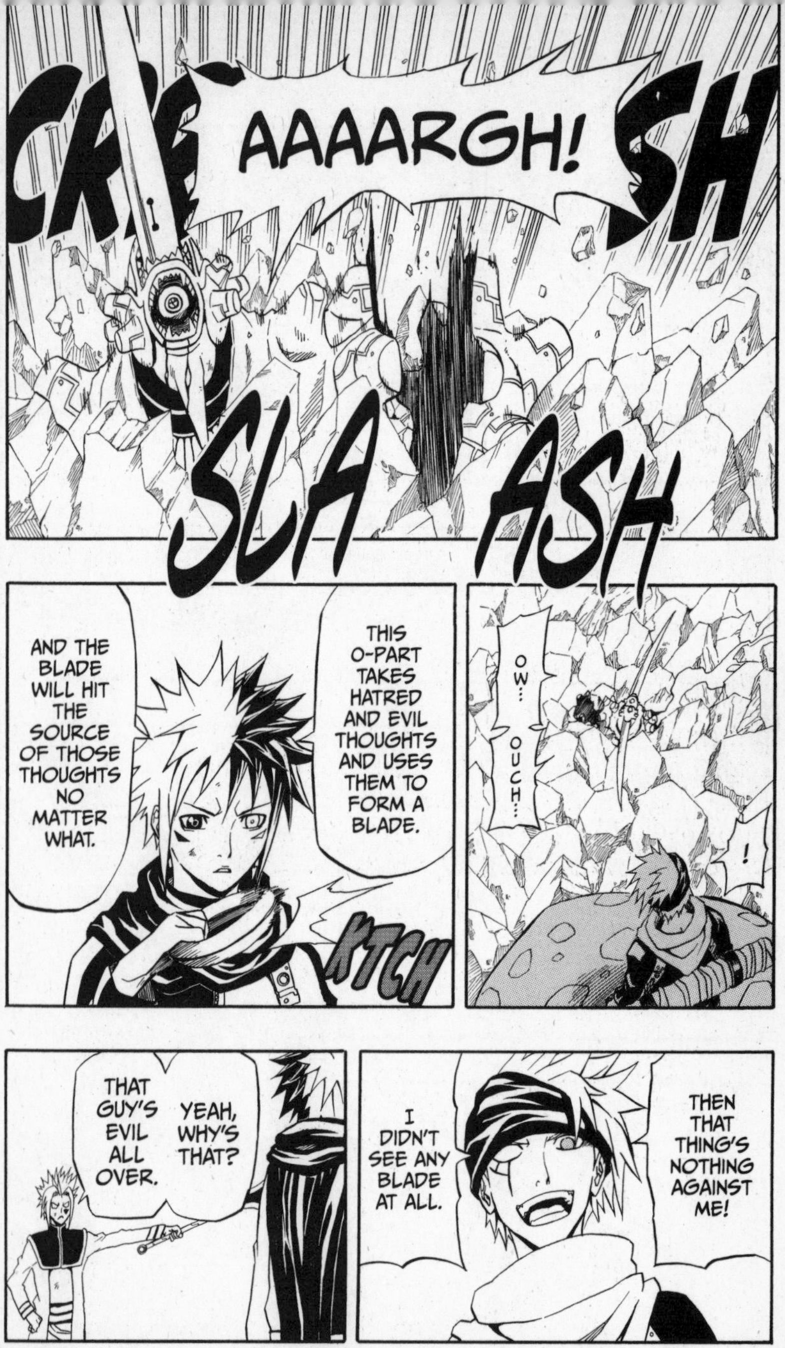
CRA
AAAARGH!
SH
SLA ASH
OW... OUCH...
!
THIS O-PART TAKES HATRED AND EVIL THOUGHTS AND USES THEM TO FORM A BLADE.
AND THE BLADE WILL HIT THE SOURCE OF THOSE THOUGHTS NO MATTER WHAT.
KTCH
THEN THAT THING'S NOTHING AGAINST ME!
I DIDN'T SEE ANY BLADE AT ALL.
YEAH, WHY'S THAT?
THAT GUY'S EVIL ALL OVER.

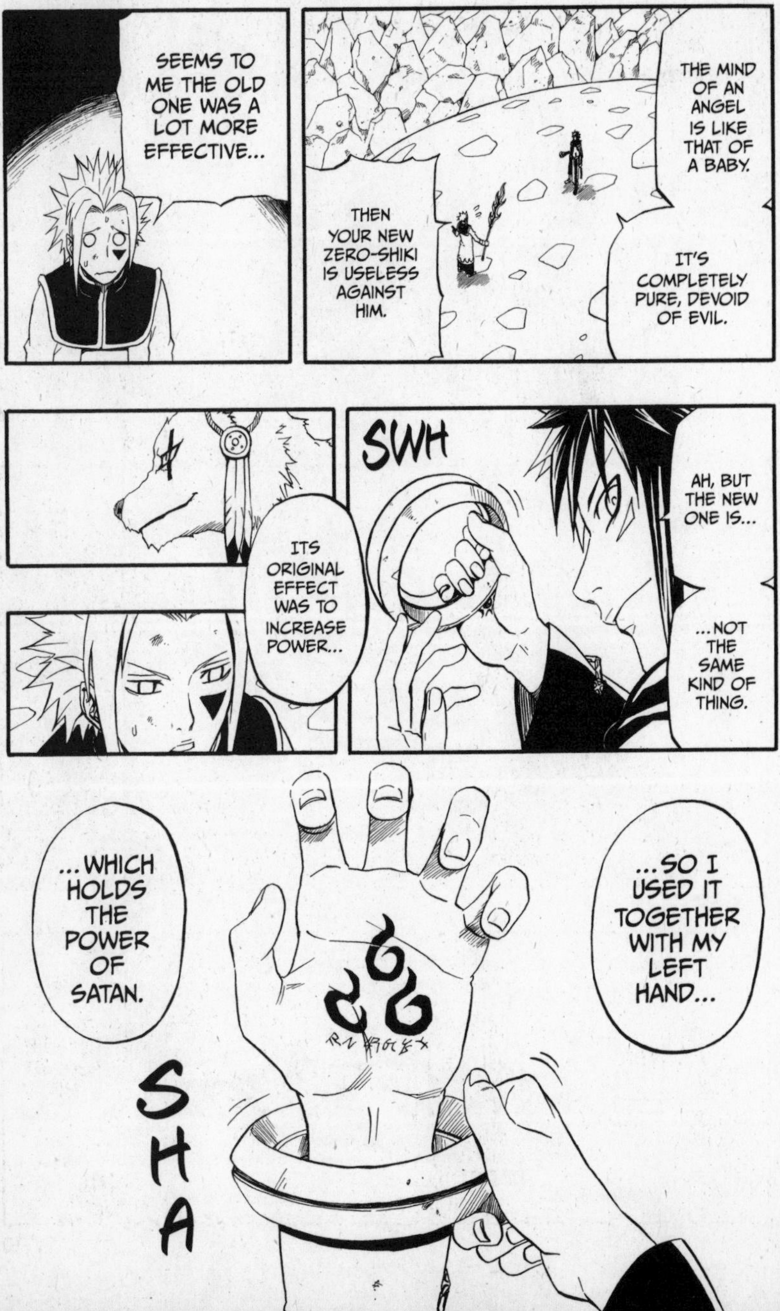
THE MIND OF AN ANGEL IS LIKE THAT OF A BABY.
IT'S COMPLETELY PURE, DEVOID OF EVIL.
THEN YOUR NEW ZERO-SHIKI IS USELESS AGAINST HIM.
SEEMS TO ME THE OLD ONE WAS A LOT MORE EFFECTIVE...
SWH
AH, BUT THE NEW ONE IS...
...NOT THE SAME KIND OF THING.
ITS ORIGINAL EFFECT WAS TO INCREASE POWER...
...SO I USED IT TOGETHER WITH MY LEFT HAND...
...WHICH HOLDS THE POWER OF SATAN.
SHA

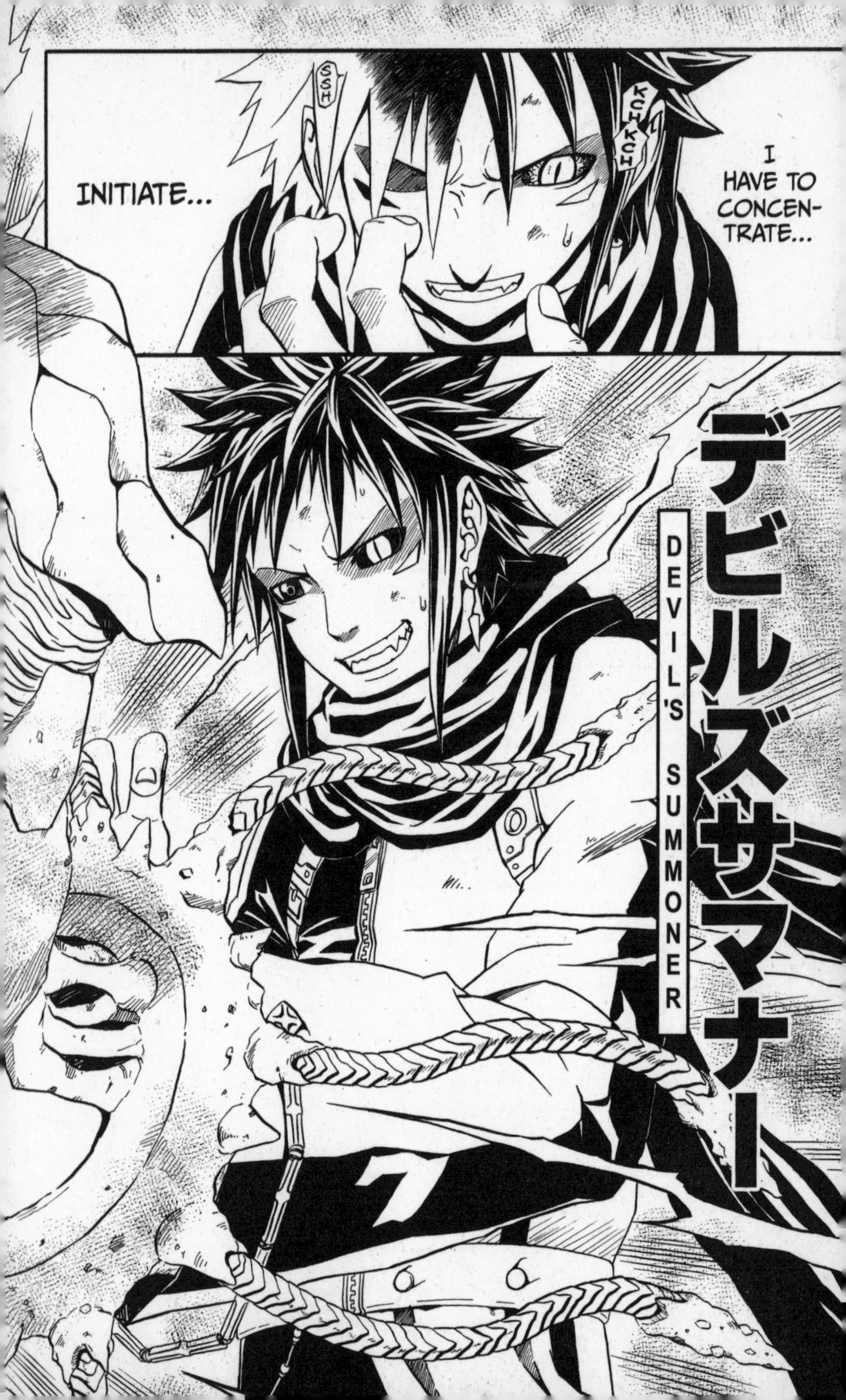
I HAVE TO CONCENTRATE...
KCH KCH
SSH
INITIATE...
デビルズサマナー
DEVIL'S SUMMONER

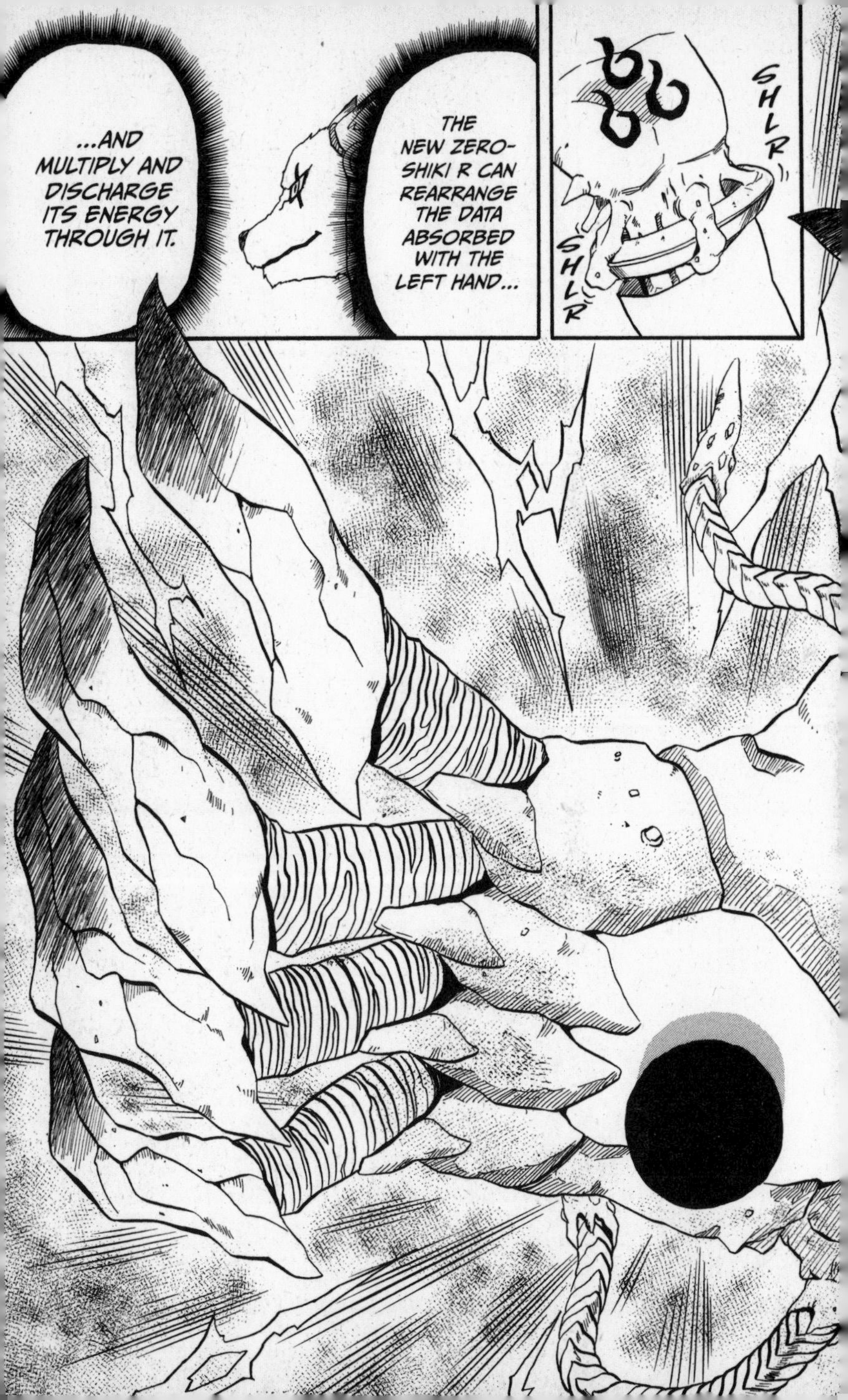
SHLR
SHLR
THE NEW ZERO-SHIKI R CAN REARRANGE THE DATA ABSORBED WITH THE LEFT HAND...
...AND MULTIPLY AND DISCHARGE ITS ENERGY THROUGH IT.

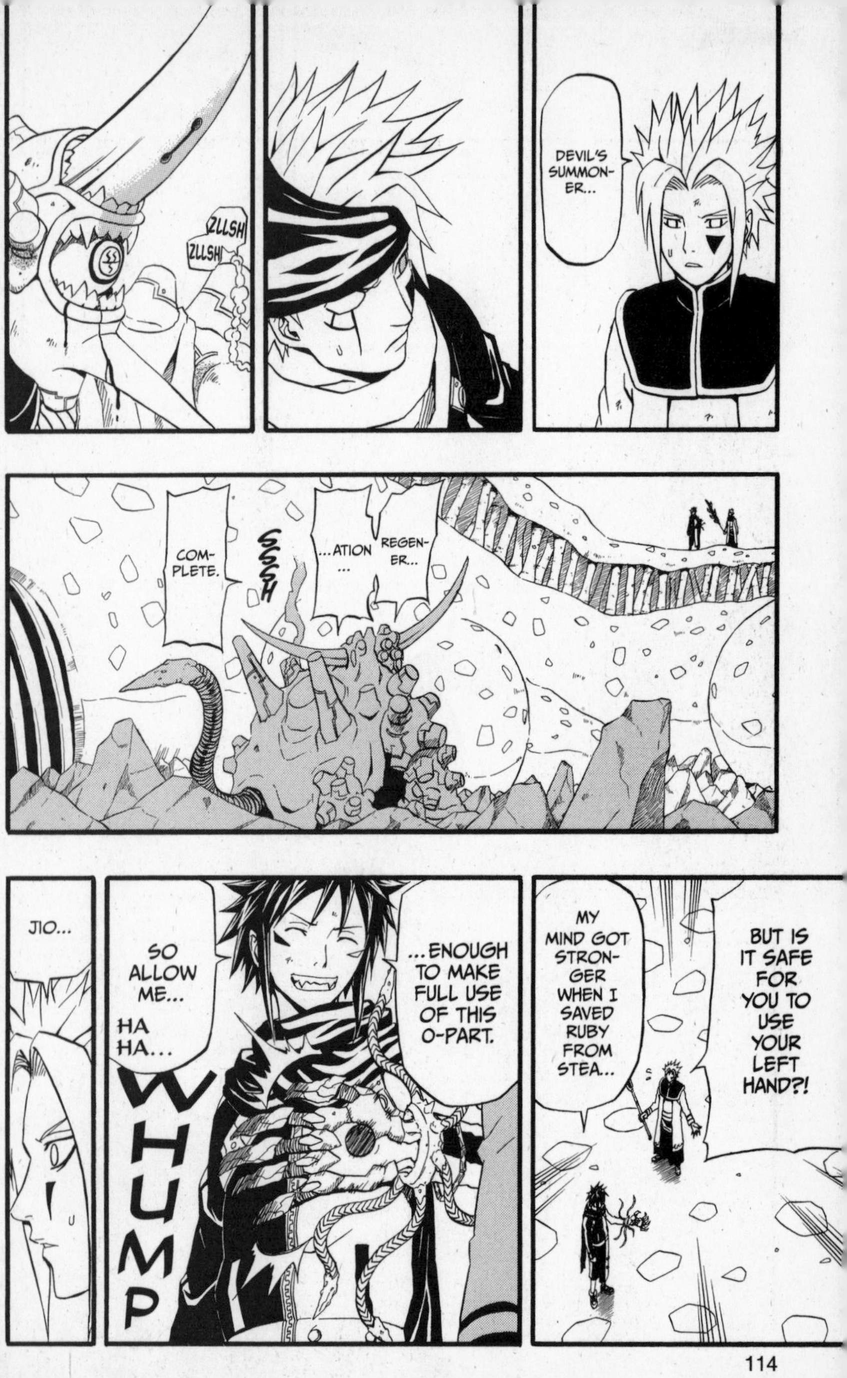
DEVIL'S SUMMONER...
ZLLSH
ZLLSH
REGENER...
...ATION...
SSGH
COMPLETE.
BUT IS IT SAFE FOR YOU TO USE YOUR LEFT HAND?!
MY MIND GOT STRONGER WHEN I SAVED RUBY FROM STEA...
...ENOUGH TO MAKE FULL USE OF THIS O-PART.
SO ALLOW ME...
HA HA...
WHUMP
JIO...

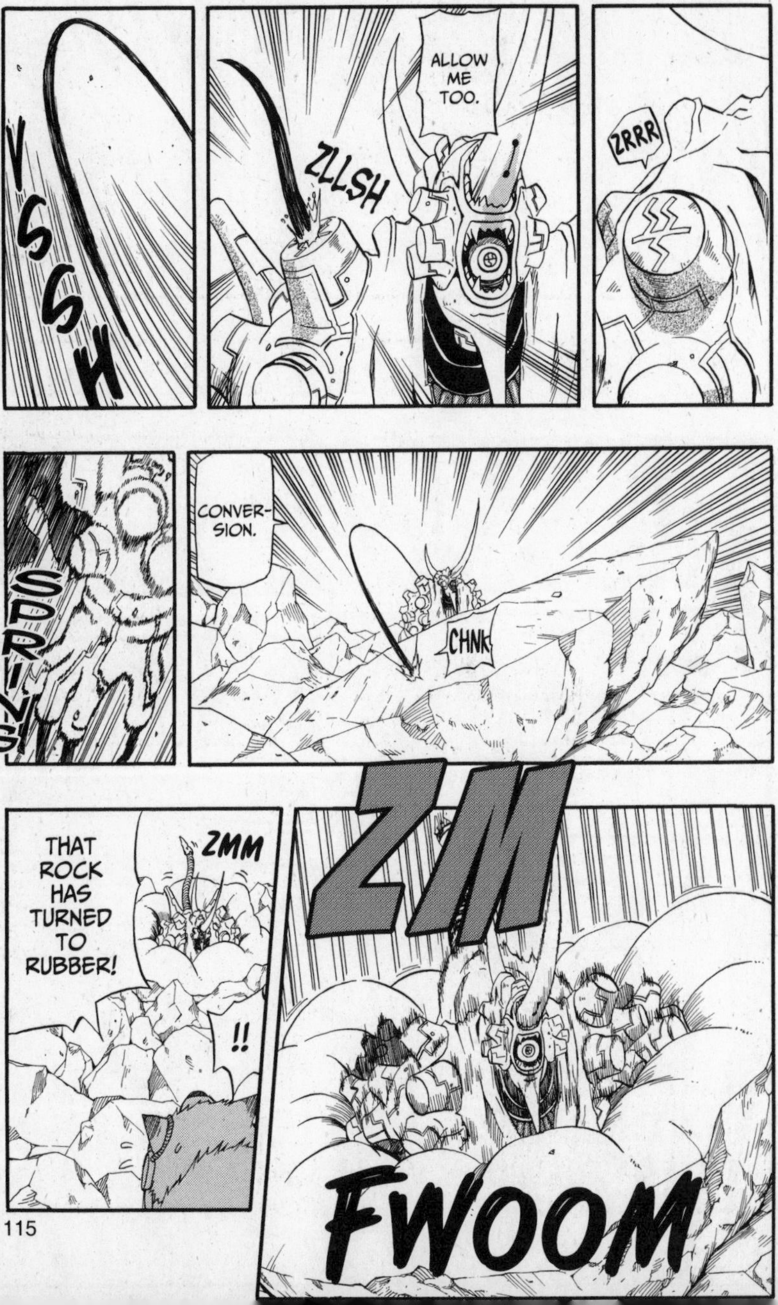
ZRRR
ALLOW ME TOO.
ZLLSH
VSSH
CONVERSION.
CHNK
SPRING
ZM
FWOOM
THAT ROCK HAS TURNED TO RUBBER!
ZMM
!!

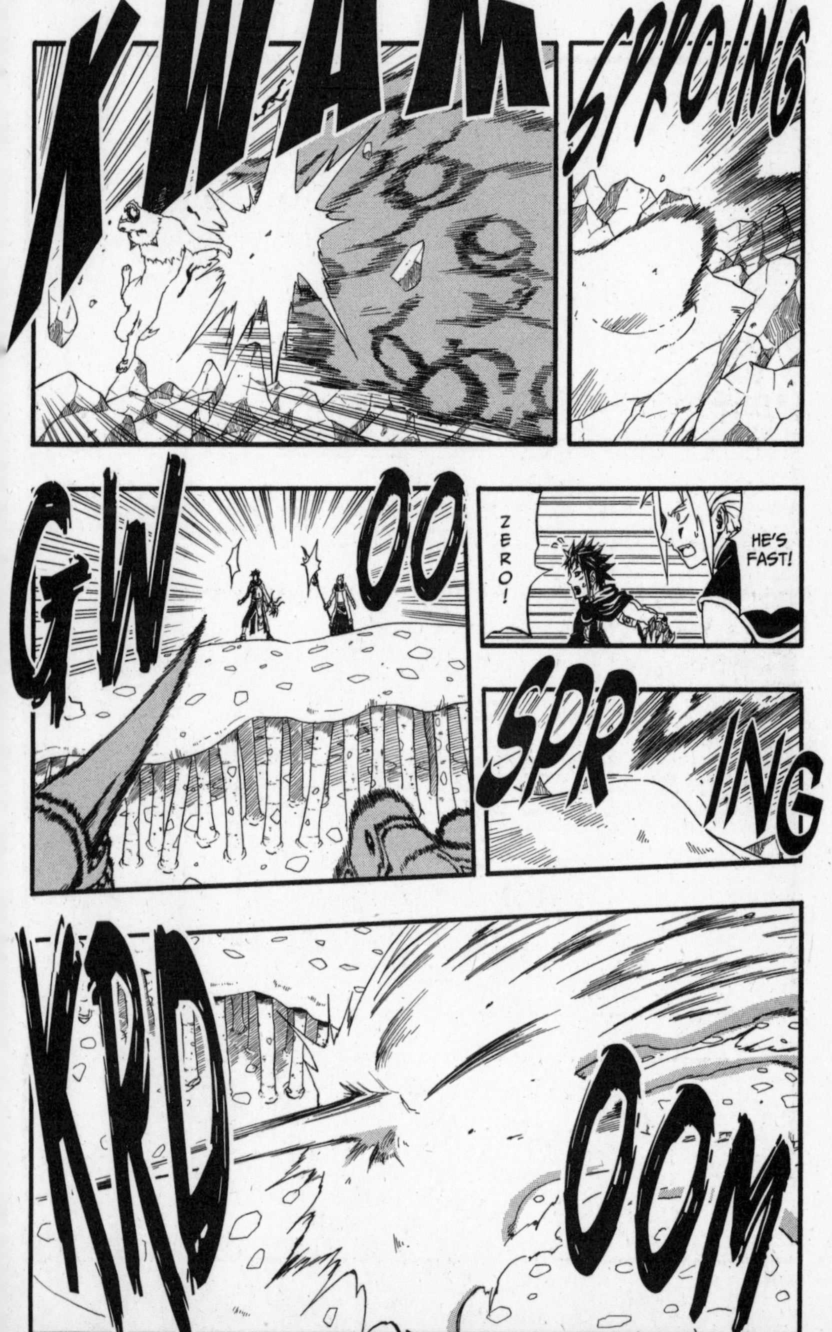
SPROING
KWAM
HE'S FAST!
ZERO!
SPRING
GWOO
KRDOOM

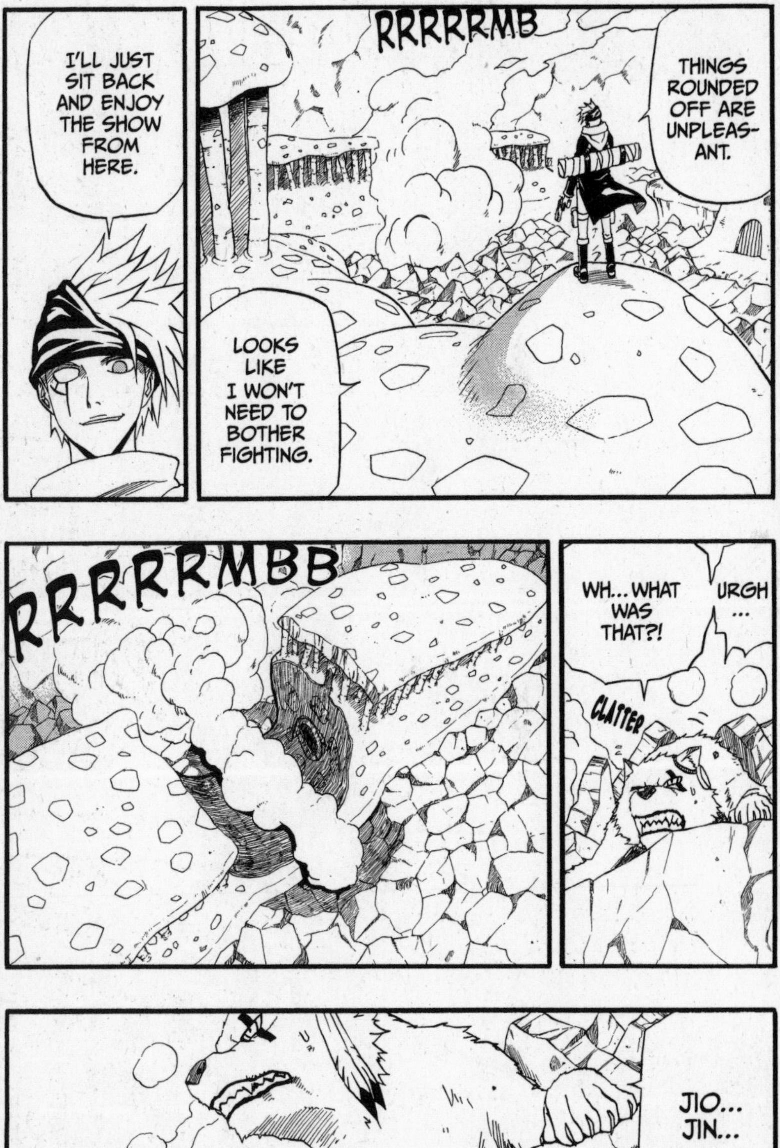
THINGS ROUNDED OFF ARE UNPLEASANT.
RRRRRMB
LOOKS LIKE I WON'T NEED TO BOTHER FIGHTING.
I'LL JUST SIT BACK AND ENJOY THE SHOW FROM HERE.
URGH...
WH... WHAT WAS THAT?!
CLATTER
RRRRRRMBB
JIO... JIN...

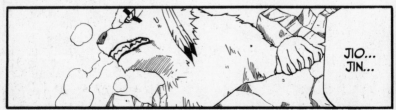

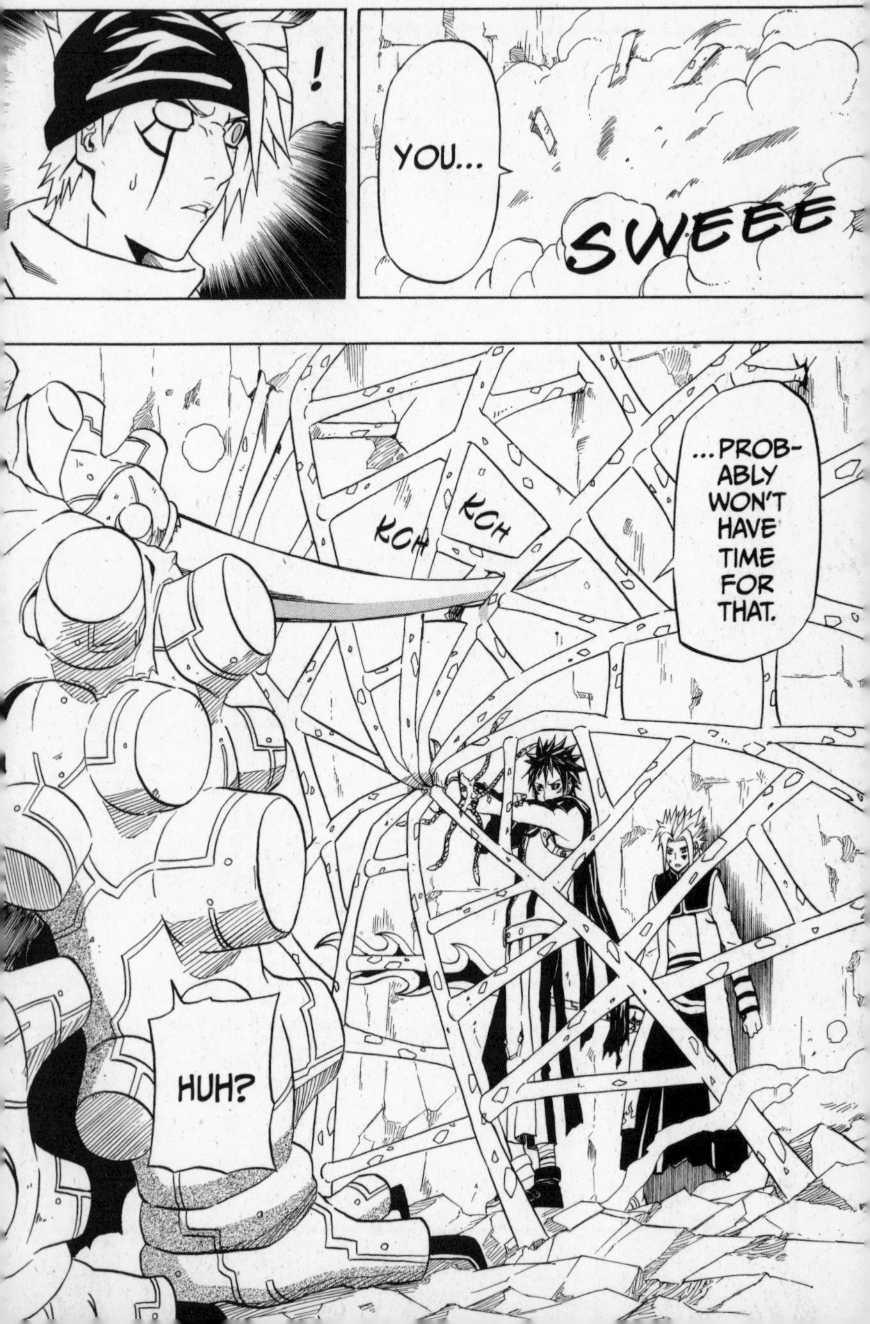
YOU...
SWEEE
!
...PROB-
ABLY
WON'T
HAVE
TIME
FOR
THAT.
KOH
KOH
HUH?

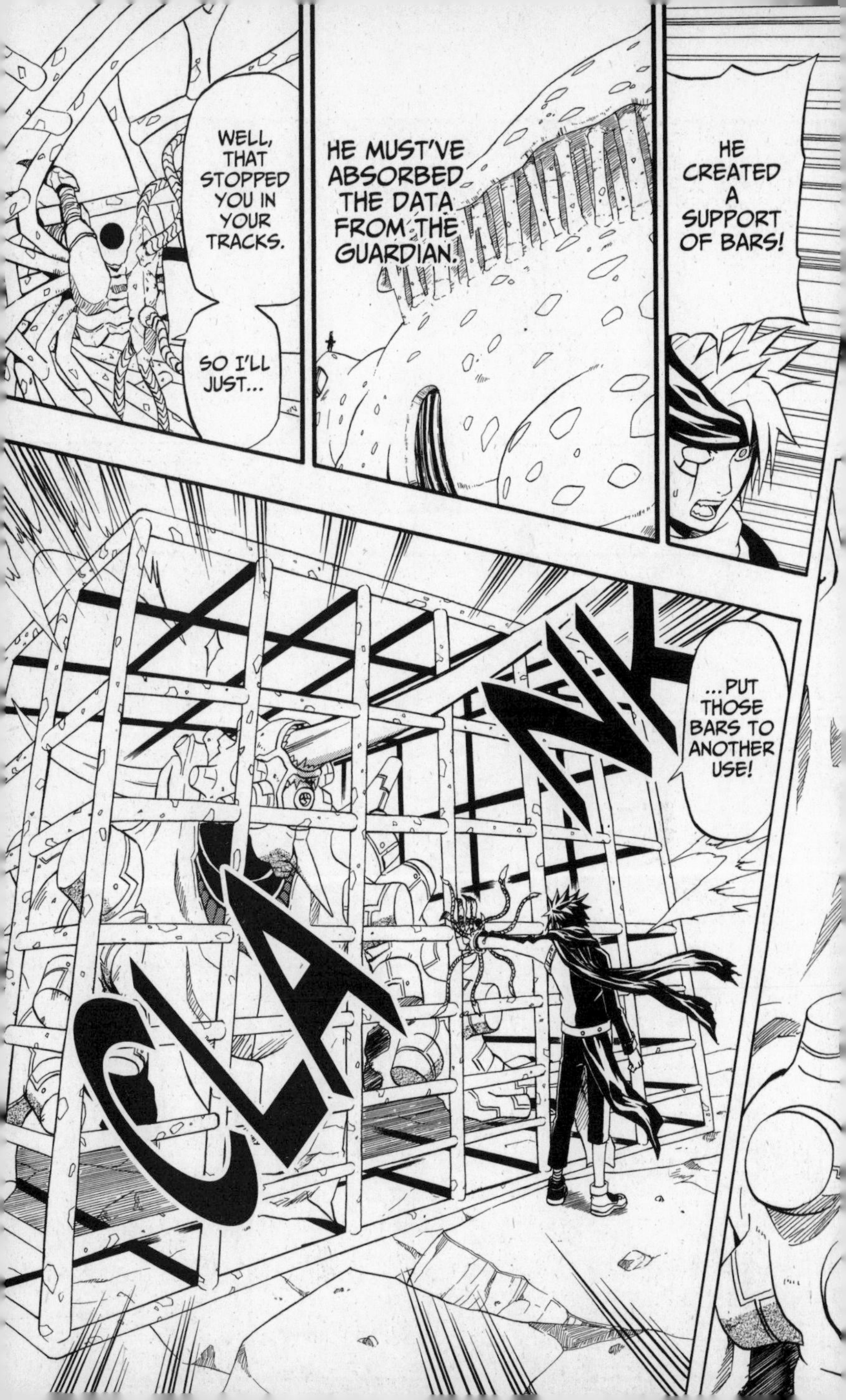
HE CREATED A SUPPORT OF BARS!
HE MUST'VE ABSORBED THE DATA FROM THE GUARDIAN.
WELL, THAT STOPPED YOU IN YOUR TRACKS.
SO I'LL JUST...
...PUT THOSE BARS TO ANOTHER USE!
CLANK

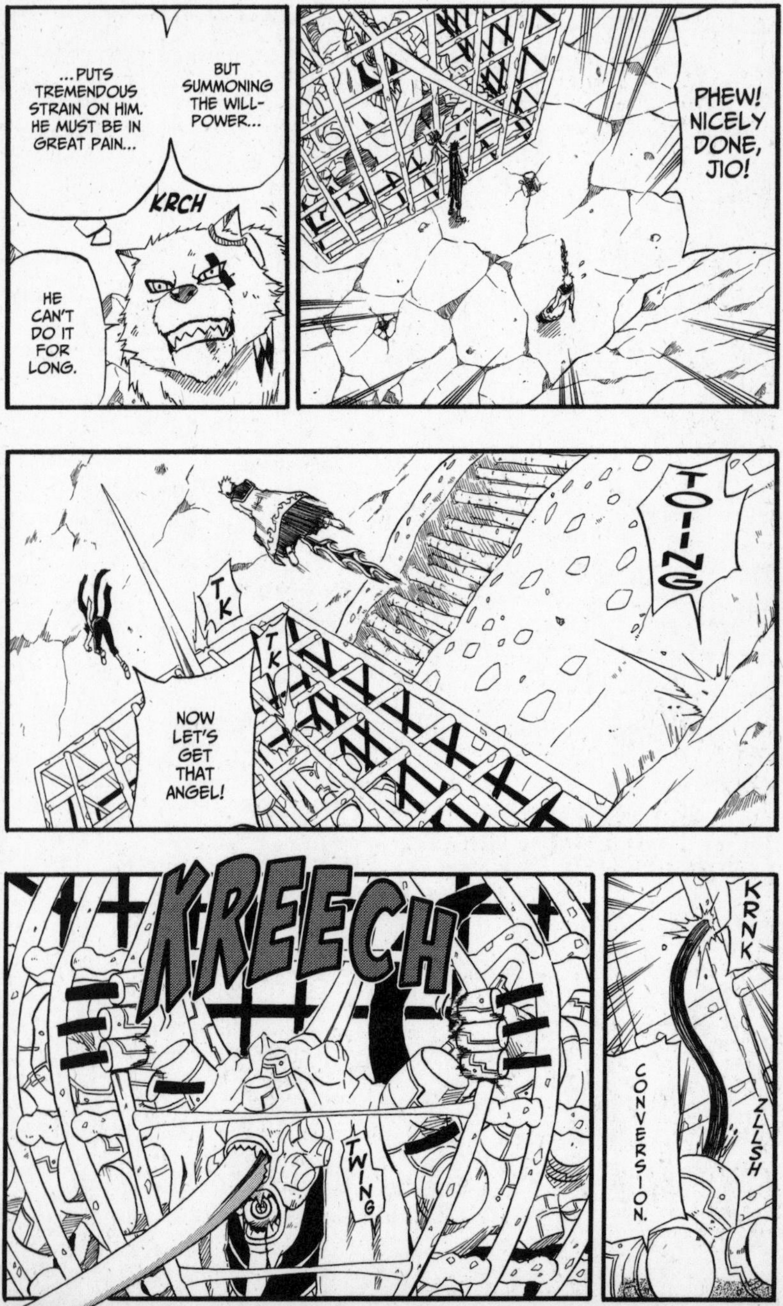
PHEW! NICELY DONE, JIO!
BUT SUMMONING THE WILL-POWER...
...PUTS TREMENDOUS STRAIN ON HIM. HE MUST BE IN GREAT PAIN...
KRCH
HE CAN'T DO IT FOR LONG.
TOING
TK
TK
NOW LET'S GET THAT ANGEL!
KRNK
ZLLSH
CONVERSION.
KREECH
TWING

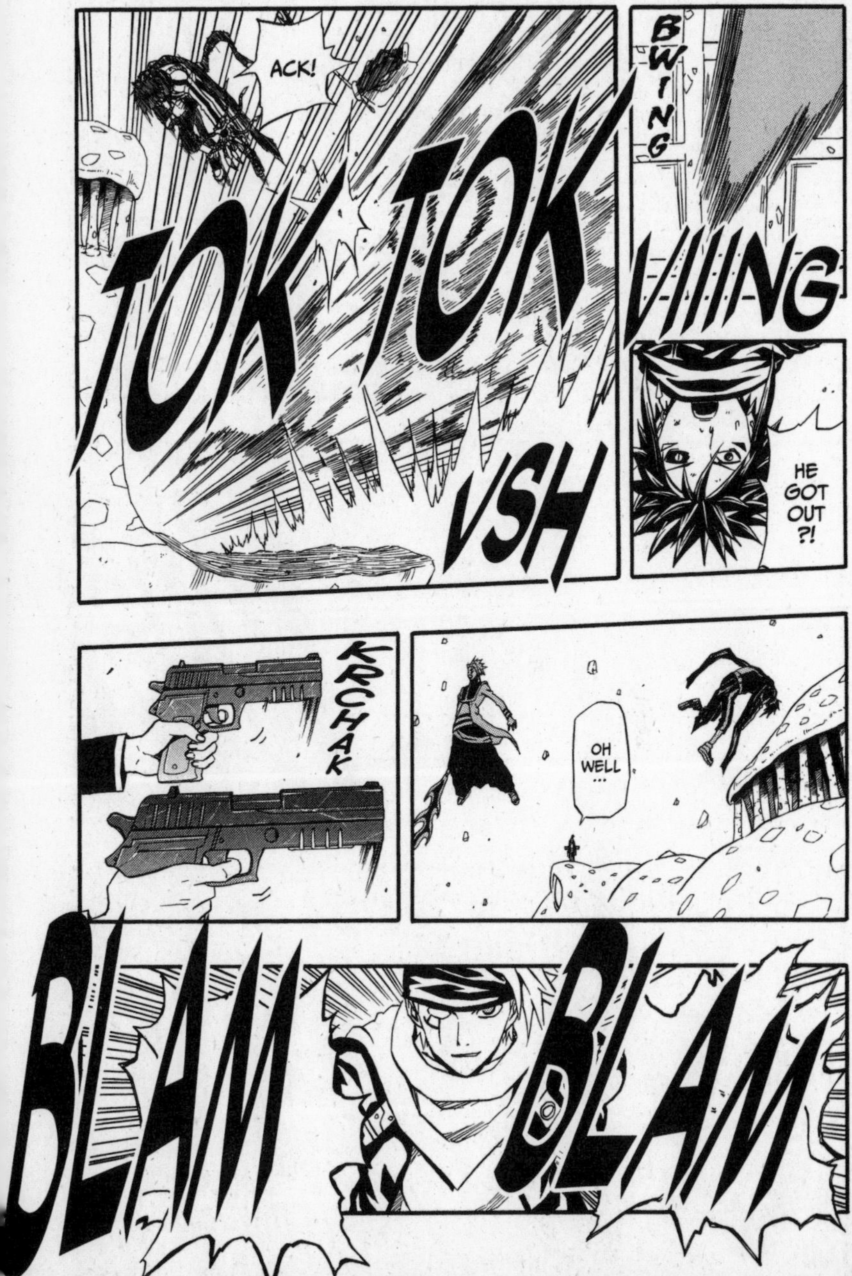
BWING
VIIING
HE GOT OUT ?!
ACK!
TOK TOK
VSH
OH WELL ...
KRCHAK
BLAM BLAM

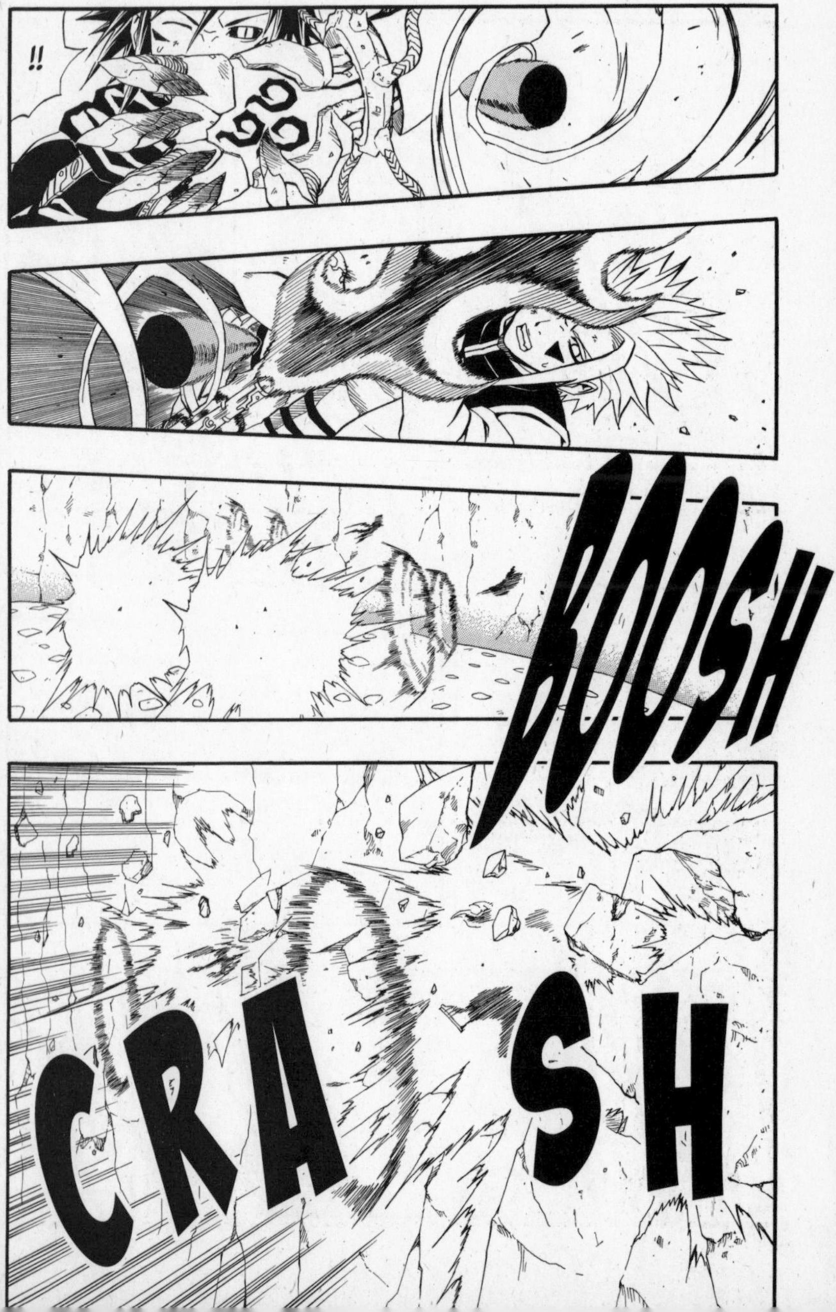
!!
BOOSH
CRA SH

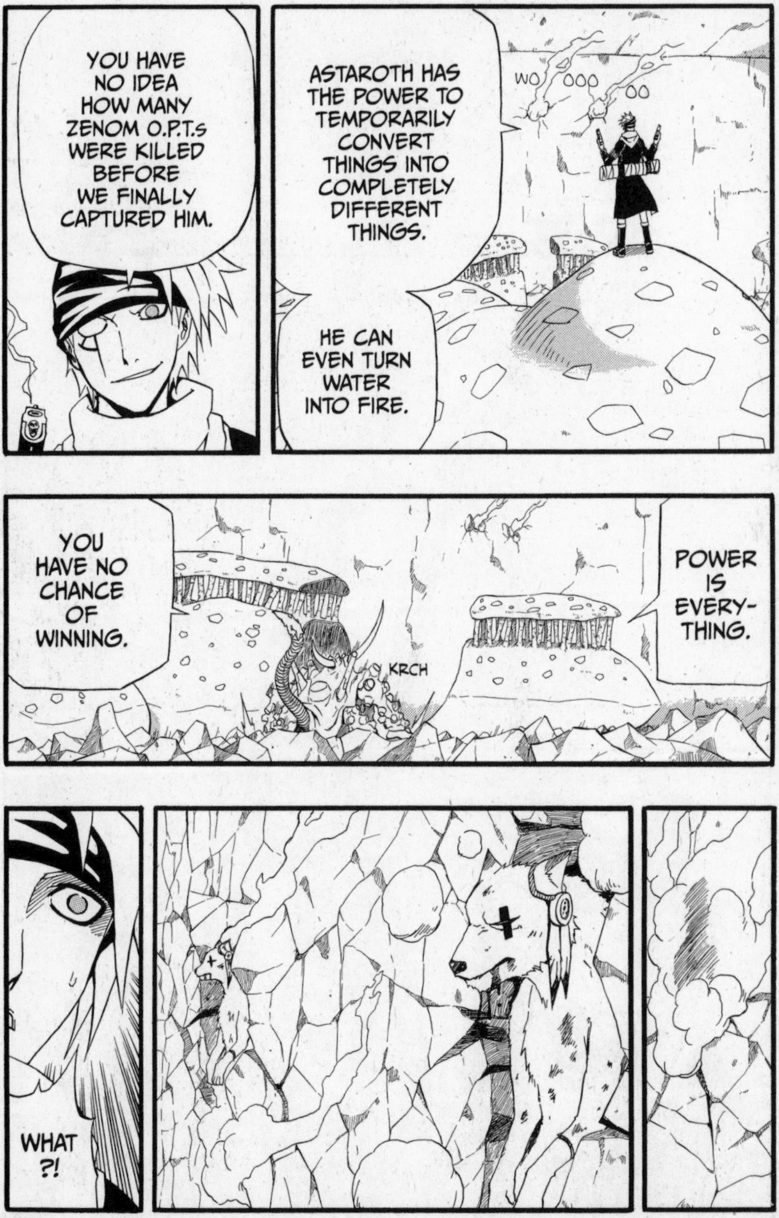
WO OOO OO
ASTAROTH HAS THE POWER TO TEMPORARILY CONVERT THINGS INTO COMPLETELY DIFFERENT THINGS.
HE CAN EVEN TURN WATER INTO FIRE.
YOU HAVE NO IDEA HOW MANY ZENOM O.P.T.s WERE KILLED BEFORE WE FINALLY CAPTURED HIM.
POWER IS EVERY-THING.
KRCH
YOU HAVE NO CHANCE OF WINNING.
WHAT ?!

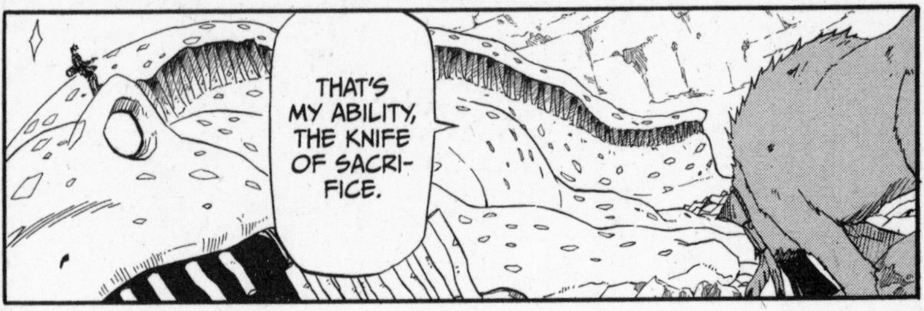
THAT'S MY ABILITY, THE KNIFE OF SACRI- FICE.

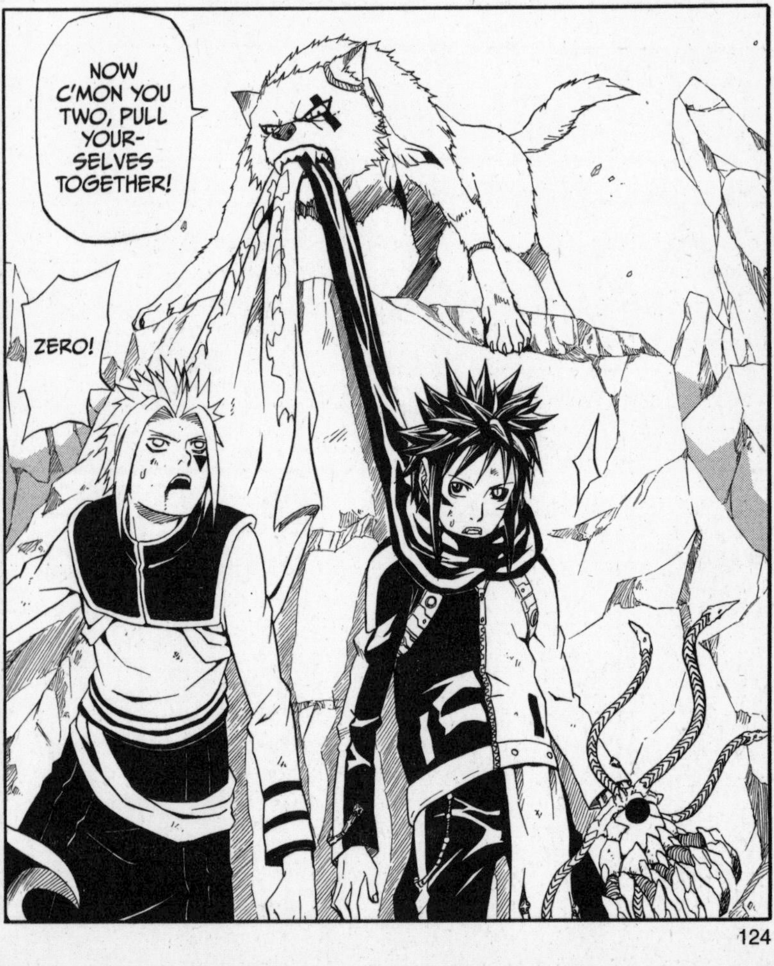
NOW C'MON YOU TWO, PULL YOUR- SELVES TOGETHER!
ZERO!

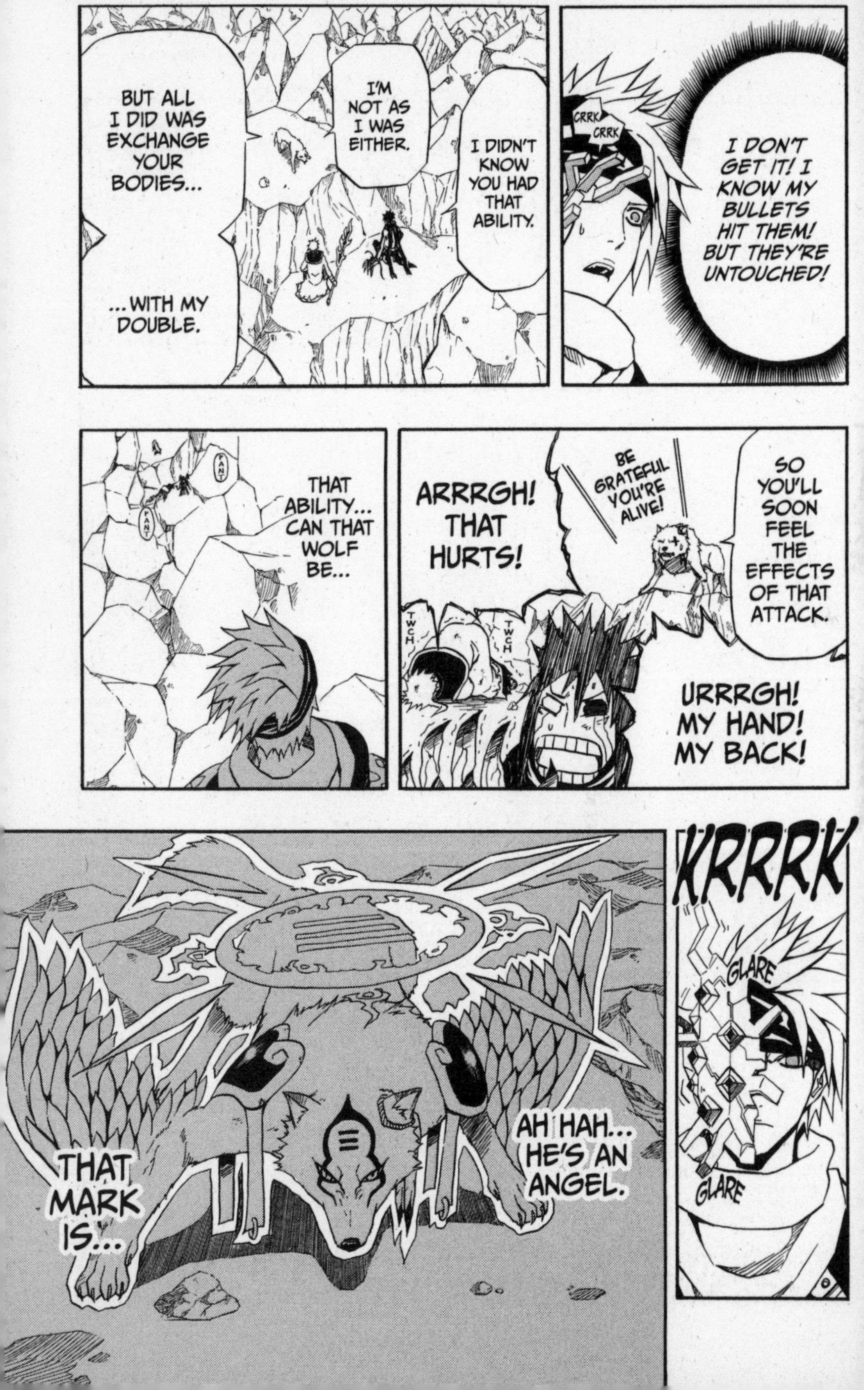
CRRK
CRRK
I DON'T GET IT! I KNOW MY BULLETS HIT THEM! BUT THEY'RE UNTOUCHED!
I DIDN'T KNOW YOU HAD THAT ABILITY.
I'M NOT AS I WAS EITHER.
BUT ALL I DID WAS EXCHANGE YOUR BODIES...
...WITH MY DOUBLE.
SO YOU'LL SOON FEEL THE EFFECTS OF THAT ATTACK.
BE GRATEFUL YOU'RE ALIVE!
ARRRGH! THAT HURTS!
TWCH
TWCH
URRRGH! MY HAND! MY BACK!
FANT
FANT
THAT ABILITY... CAN THAT WOLF BE...
KRRRK
GLARE
GLARE
AH HAH... HE'S AN ANGEL.
THAT MARK IS...

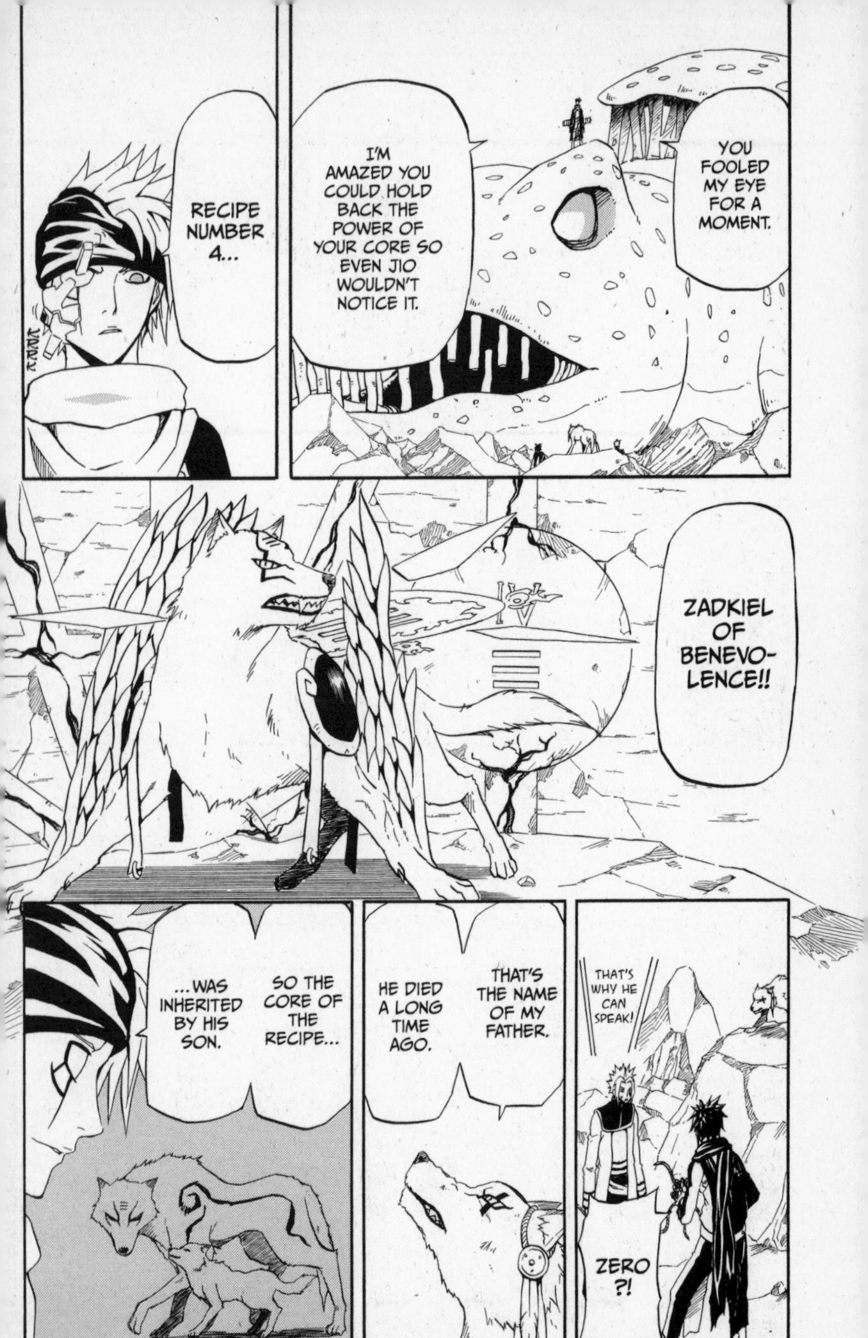
YOU FOOLED MY EYE FOR A MOMENT.
I'M AMAZED YOU COULD HOLD BACK THE POWER OF YOUR CORE SO EVEN JIO WOULDN'T NOTICE IT.
RECIPE NUMBER 4...
ZADKIEL OF BENEVOLENCE!!
THAT'S WHY HE CAN SPEAK!
ZERO?!
THAT'S THE NAME OF MY FATHER.
HE DIED A LONG TIME AGO.
SO THE CORE OF THE RECIPE...
...WAS INHERITED BY HIS SON.

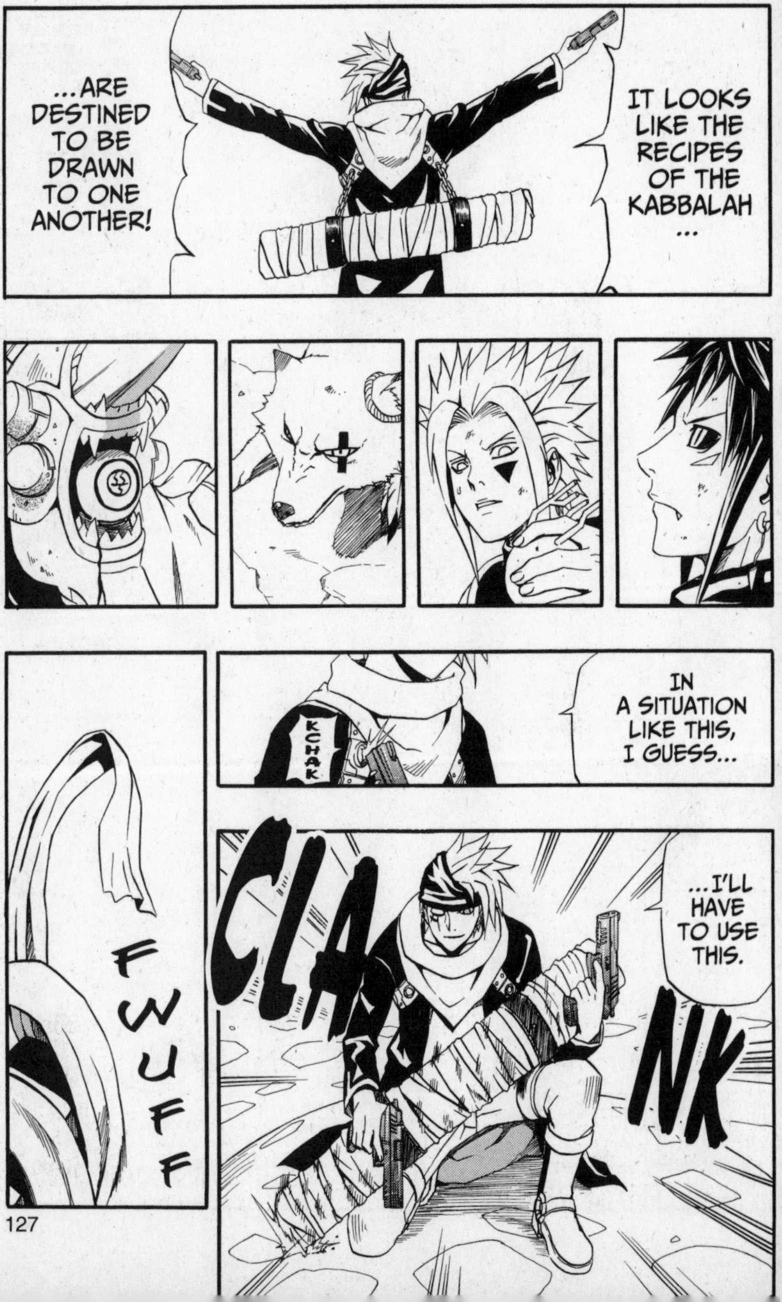

IT LOOKS LIKE THE RECIPES OF THE KABBALAH...
...ARE DESTINED TO BE DRAWN TO ONE ANOTHER!
IN A SITUATION LIKE THIS, I GUESS...
KCHAK
...I'LL HAVE TO USE THIS.
CLANK
FWUFF

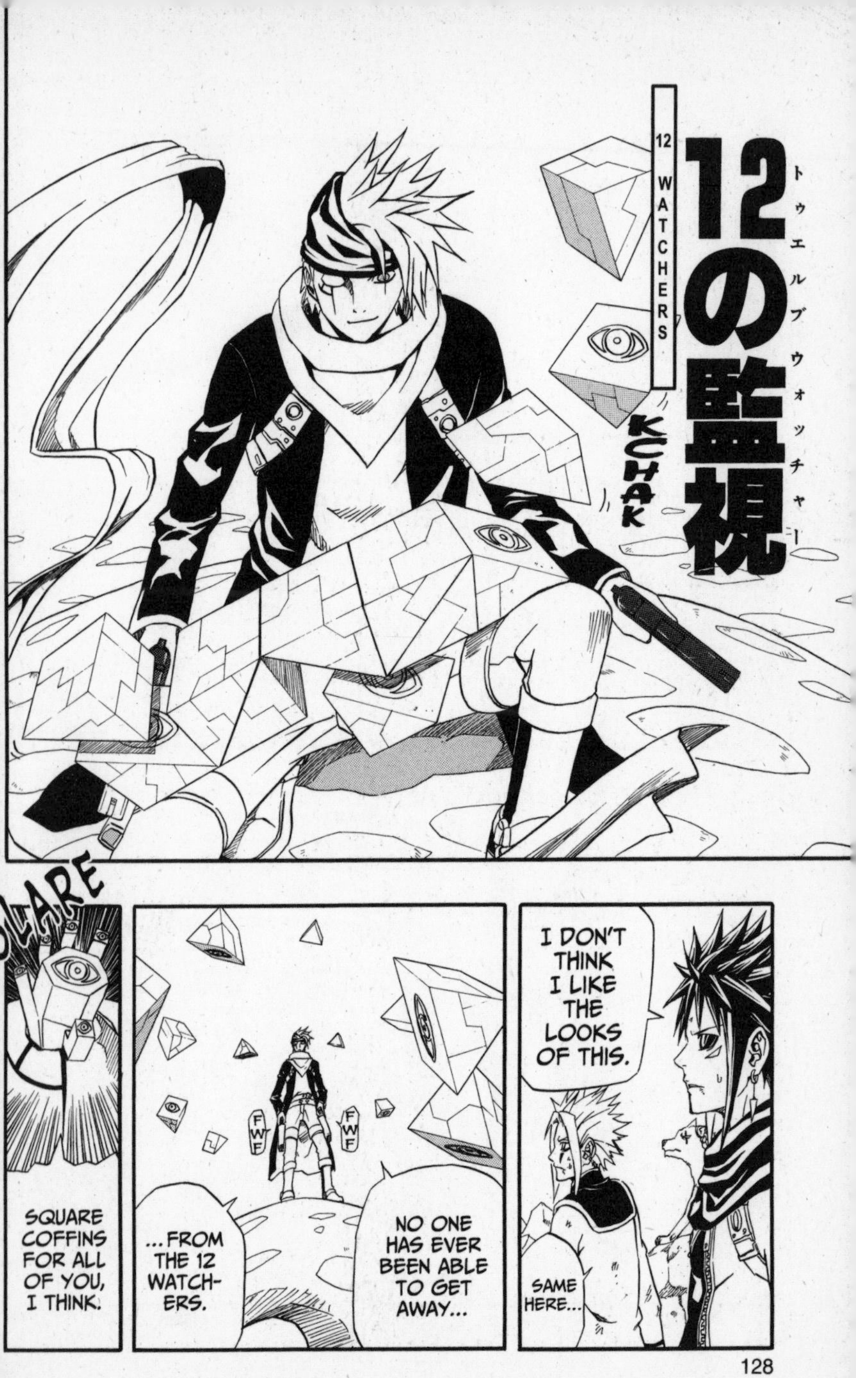
12の監視
トゥエルブウォッチャー
12 WATCHERS
KCHAK
I DON'T THINK I LIKE THE LOOKS OF THIS.
SAME HERE...
FWF
FWF
NO ONE HAS EVER BEEN ABLE TO GET AWAY...
...FROM THE 12 WATCHERS.
LARE
SQUARE COFFINS FOR ALL OF YOU, I THINK.

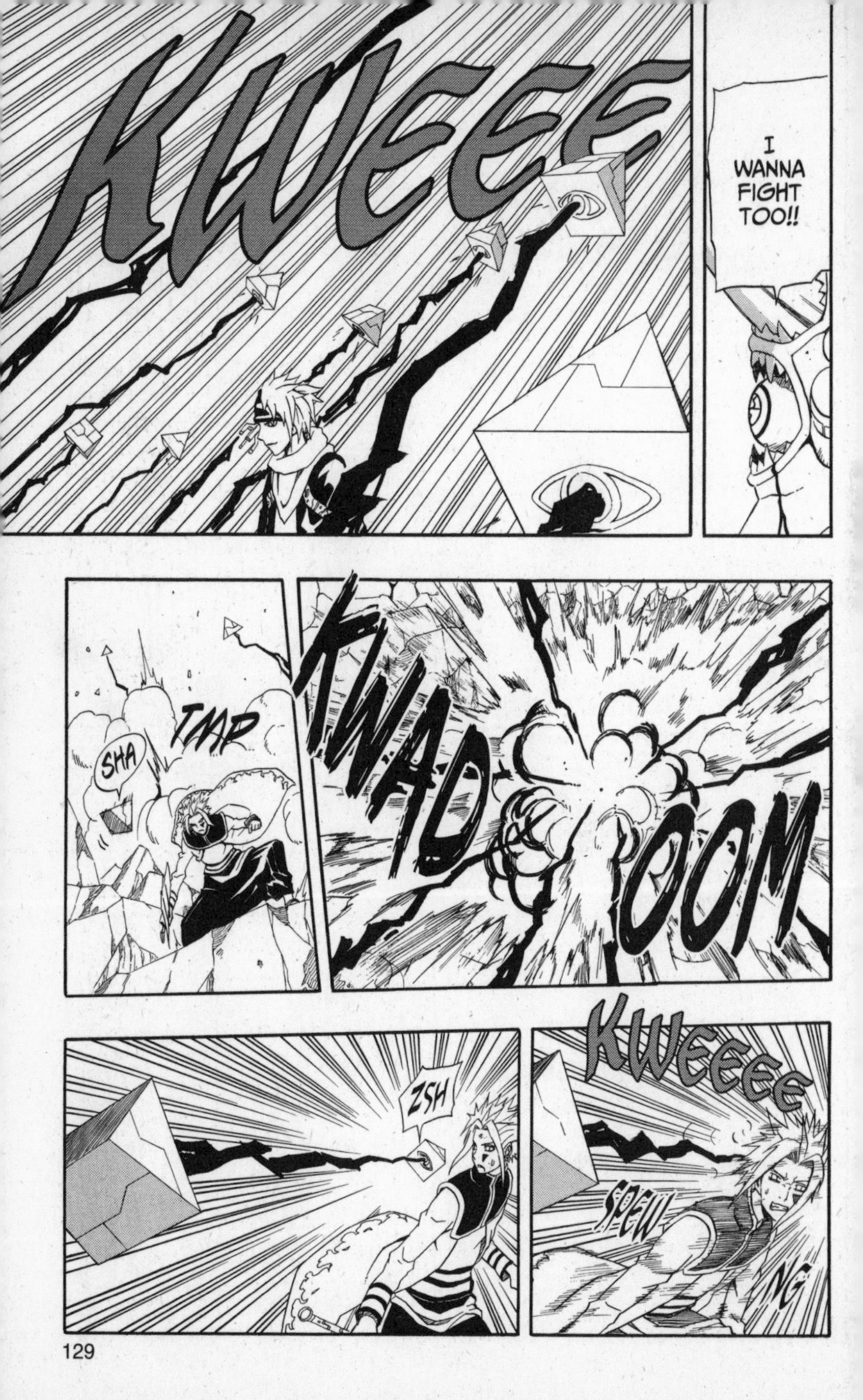
I WANNA FIGHT TOO!!
KWEEEE
KWADOOM
TMP
SHA
KWEEEE
SPEW
NG
ZSH

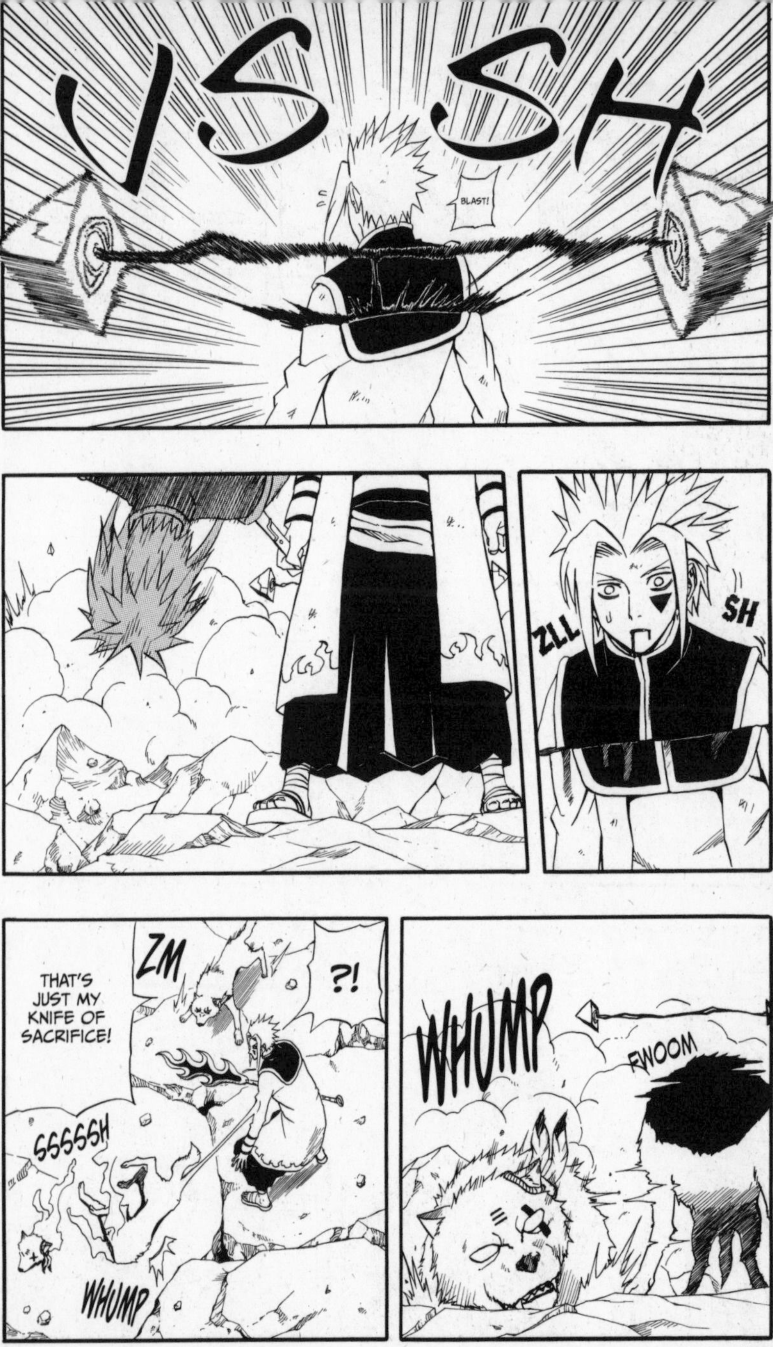
VSSH
BLAST!
SH
ZLL
WHUMP
FWOOM
?!
ZM
THAT'S JUST MY KNIFE OF SACRIFICE!
SSSSSH
WHUMP

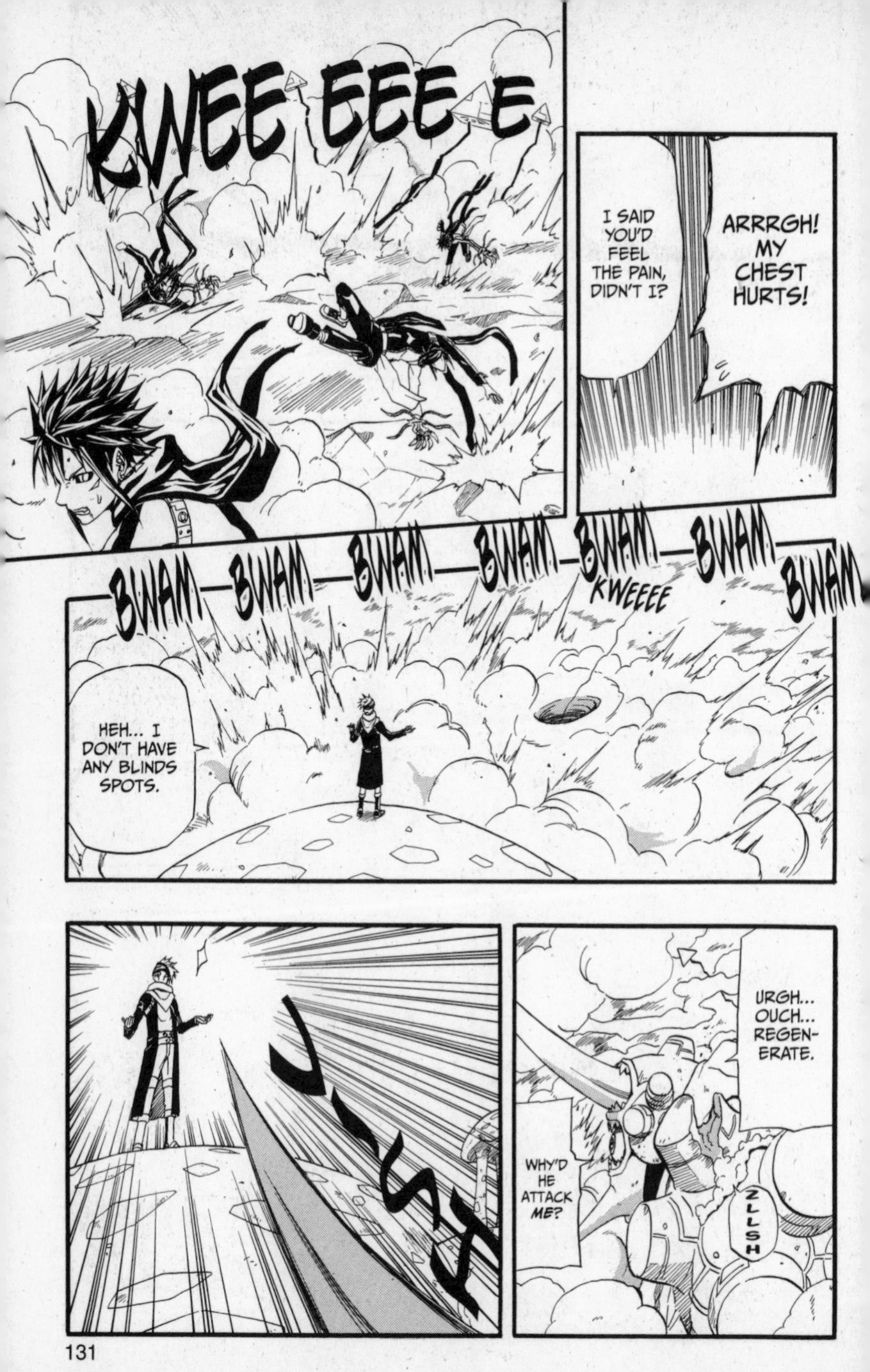
ARRRGH! MY CHEST HURTS!
I SAID YOU'D FEEL THE PAIN, DIDN'T I?
KWEE EEE E
BWAM BWAM BWAM BWAM BWAM BWAM BWAM
KWEEEE
HEH... I DON'T HAVE ANY BLINDS SPOTS.
URGH... OUCH... REGEN-ERATE.
WHY'D HE ATTACK *ME*?
ZLLSH

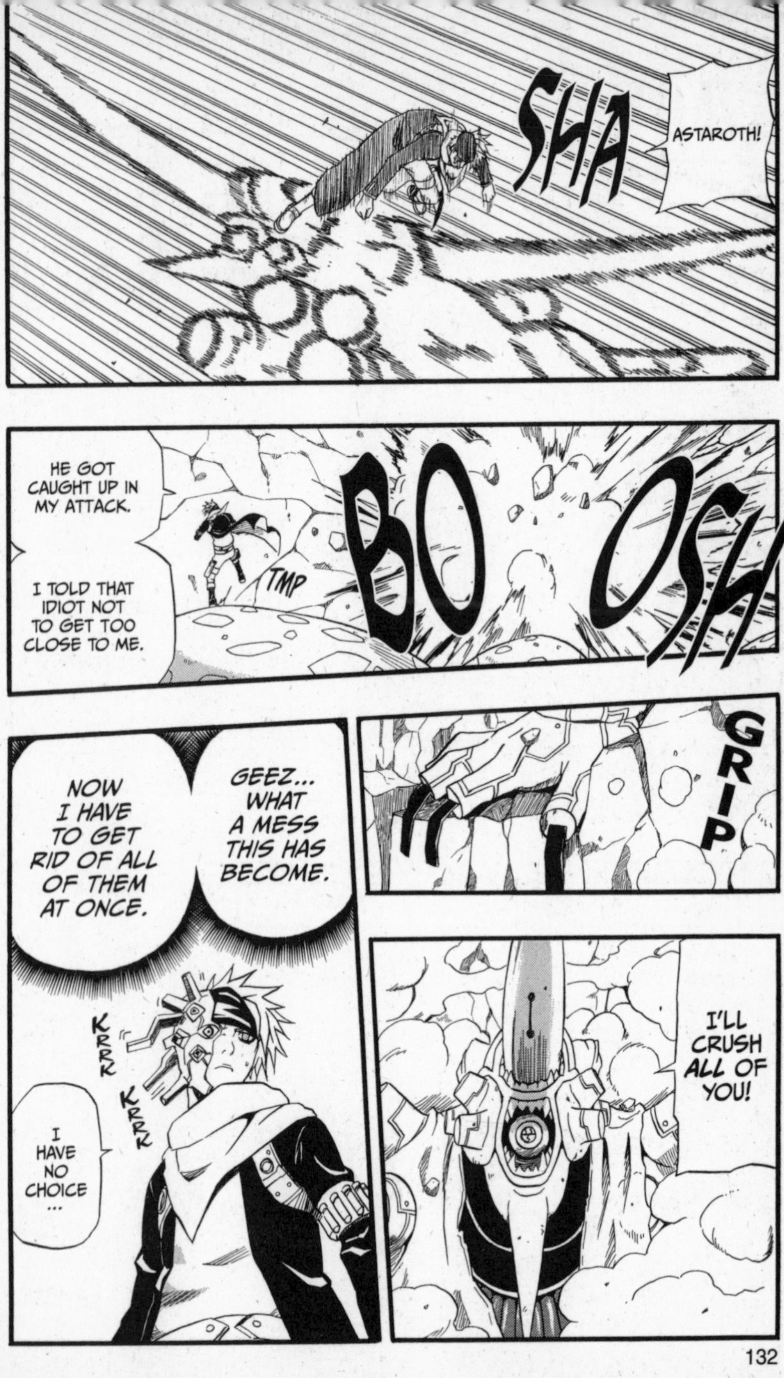
SHA
ASTAROTH!
BOOSH
HE GOT CAUGHT UP IN MY ATTACK.
I TOLD THAT IDIOT NOT TO GET TOO CLOSE TO ME.
TMP
GRIP
I'LL CRUSH ALL OF YOU!
GEEZ... WHAT A MESS THIS HAS BECOME.
NOW I HAVE TO GET RID OF ALL OF THEM AT ONCE.
KRRK
KRRK
I HAVE NO CHOICE...

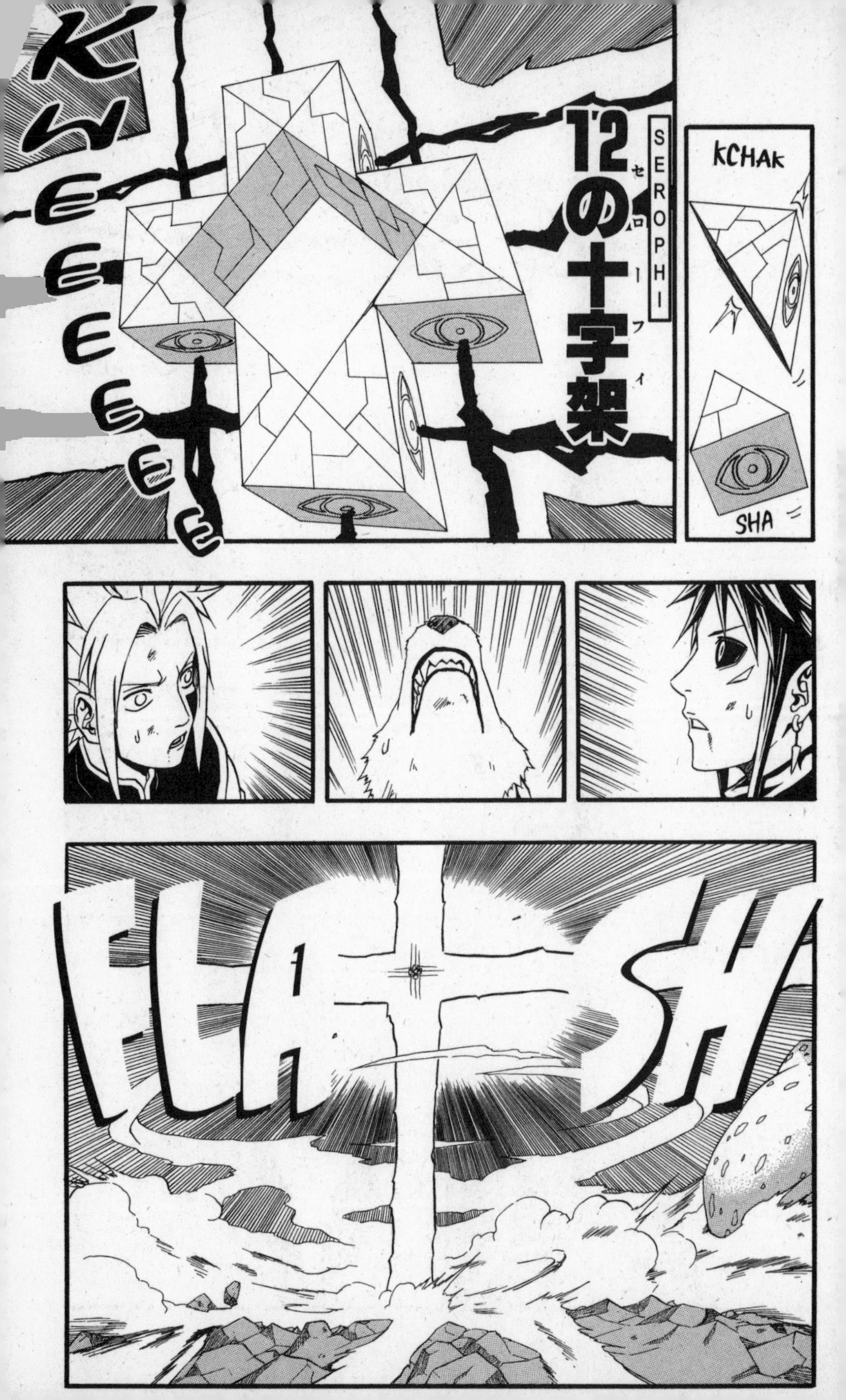
KCHAK
SHA
KWEEEEEE
12の十字架
SEROPHI
FLASH

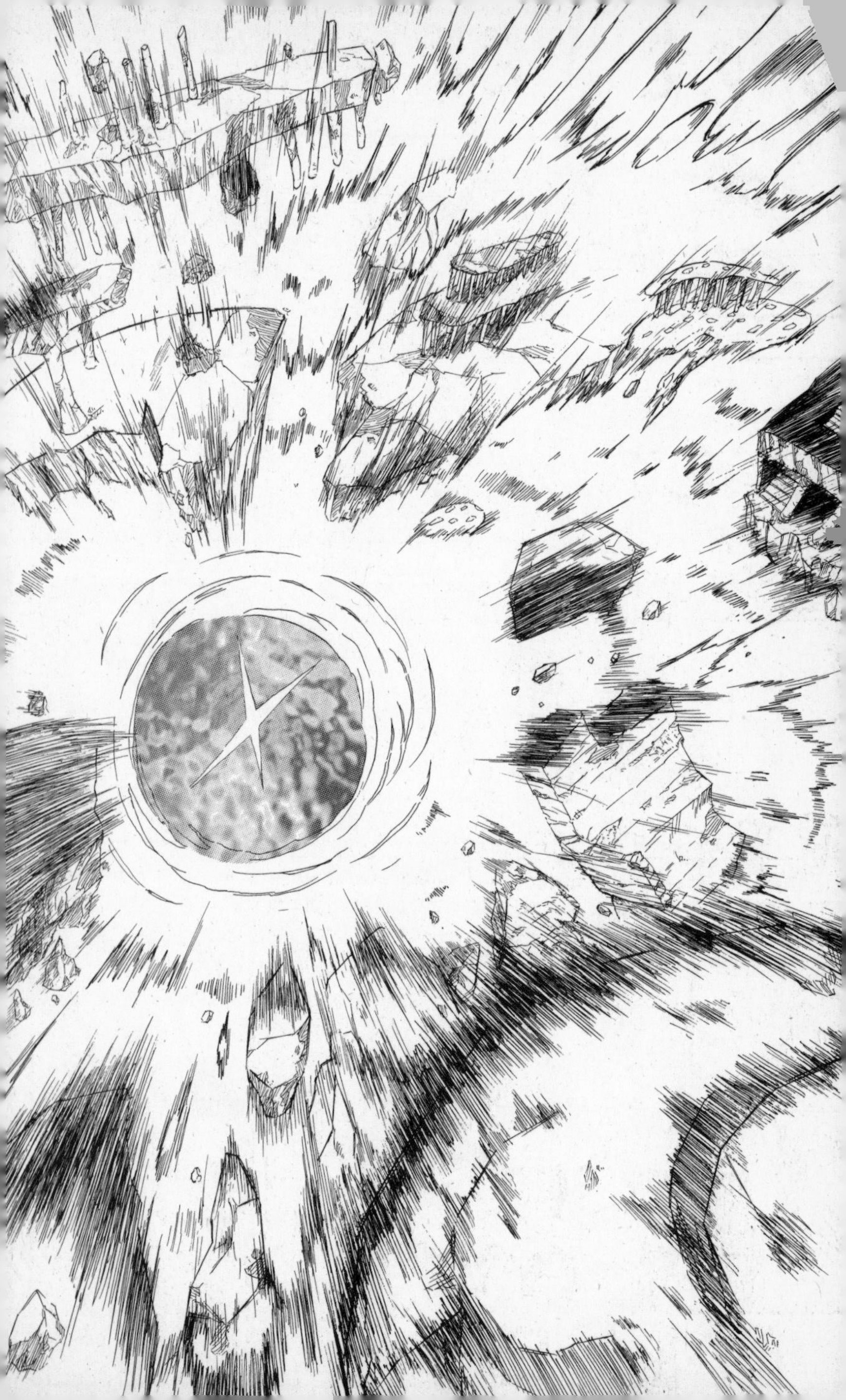

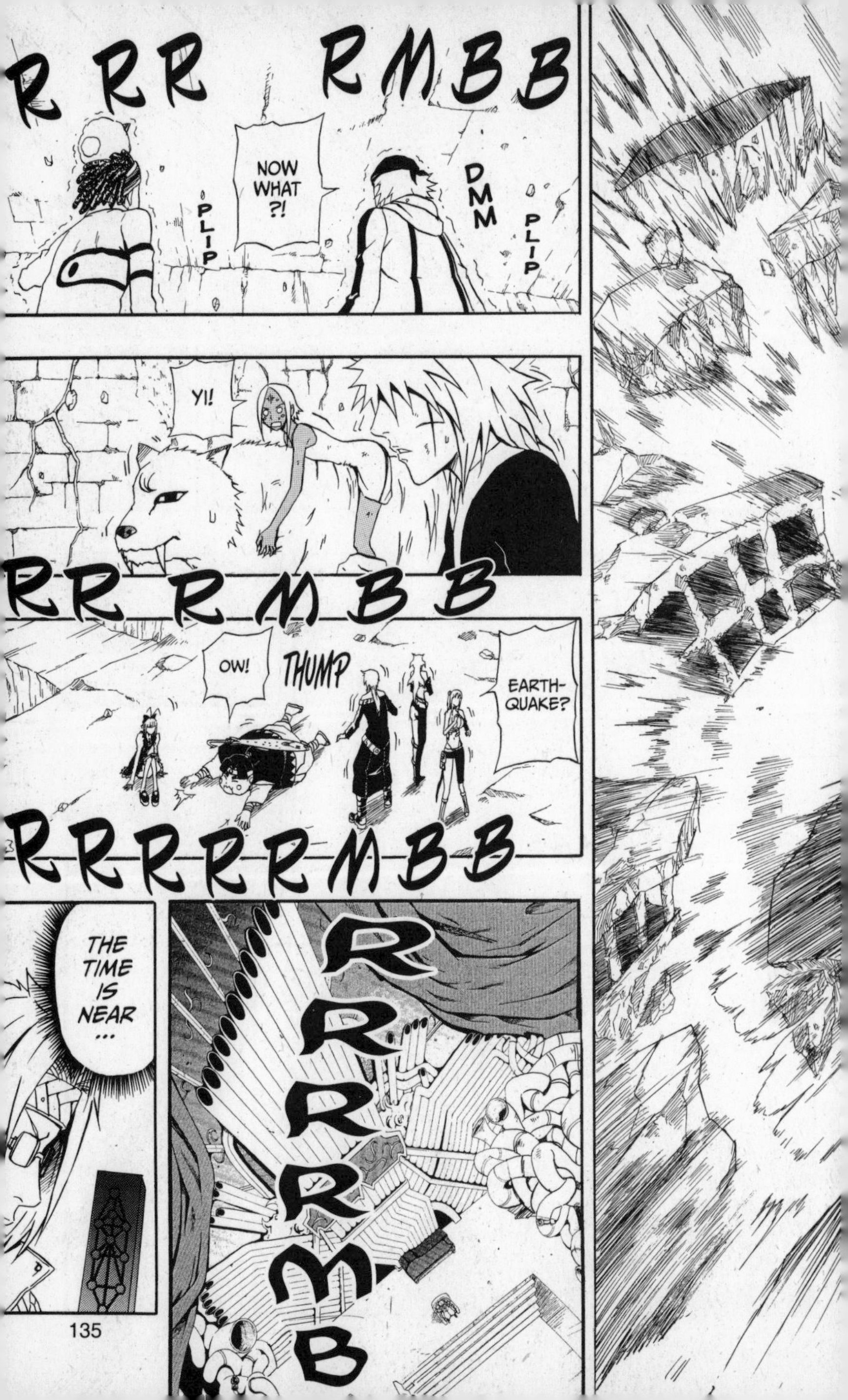
R R R RMBB
PLIP
DMM
NOW WHAT?!
PLIP
YI!
RR R M B B
EARTH-QUAKE?
THUMP
OW!
RRRRRRMBB
RRRRMB
THE TIME IS NEAR...

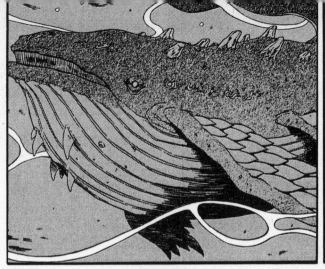

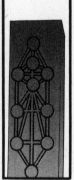

RRRMB

RRMB

TWCH

I ALMOST WANT TO FISH THEM UP.

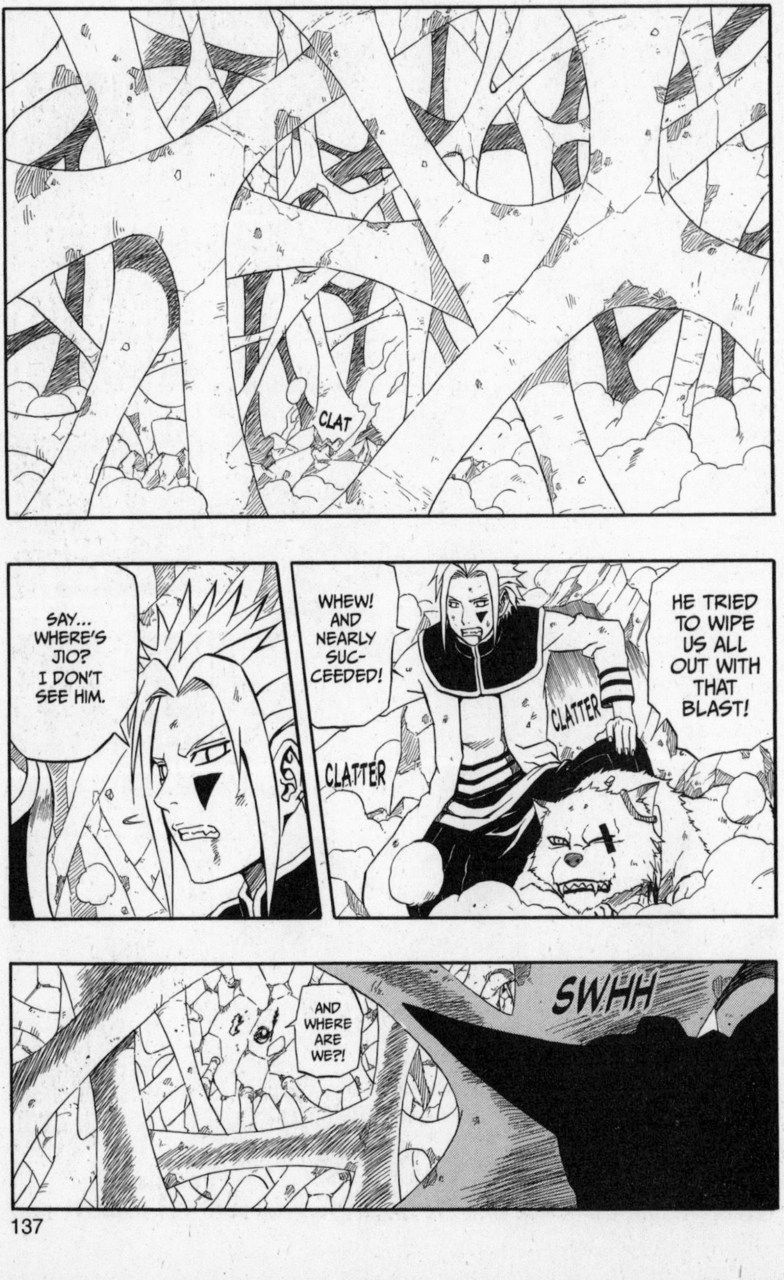
CLAT
HE TRIED TO WIPE US ALL OUT WITH THAT BLAST!
WHEW! AND NEARLY SUC-CEEDED!
CLATTER
CLATTER
SAY... WHERE'S JIO? I DON'T SEE HIM.
SWHH
AND WHERE ARE WE?!

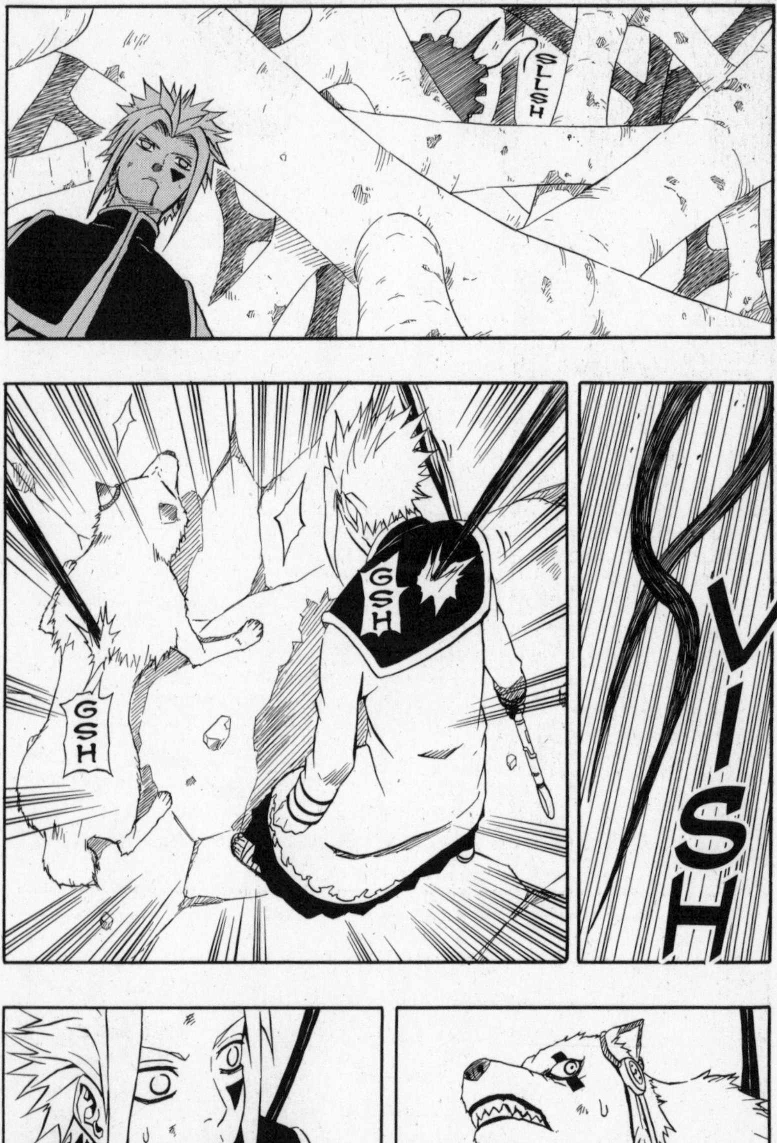
SLLSH
VISH
GSH
GSH

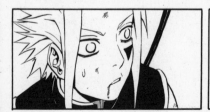

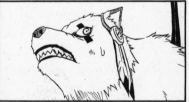

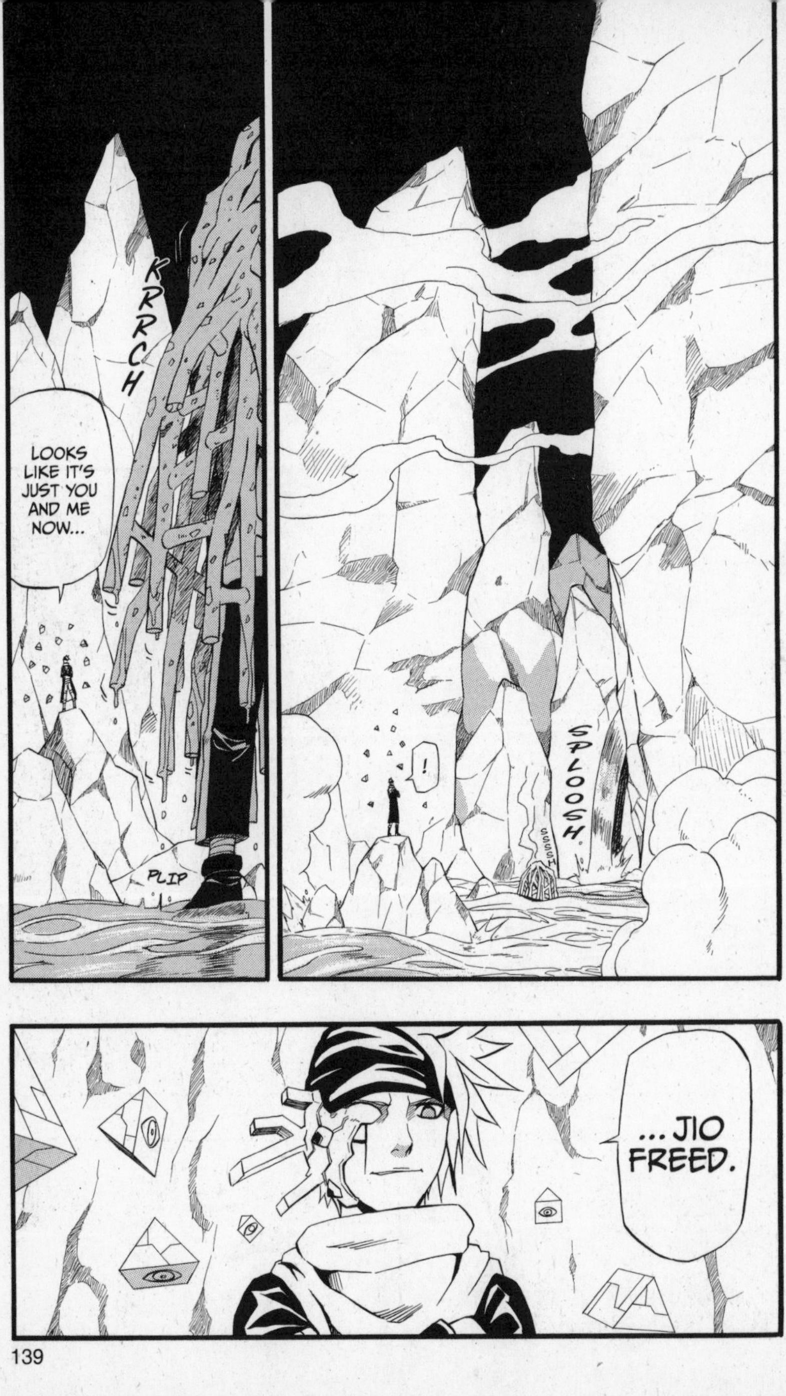
!
SSSH
SPLOOSH.
KRRCH
LOOKS LIKE IT'S JUST YOU AND ME NOW...
PLIP
...JIO FREED.

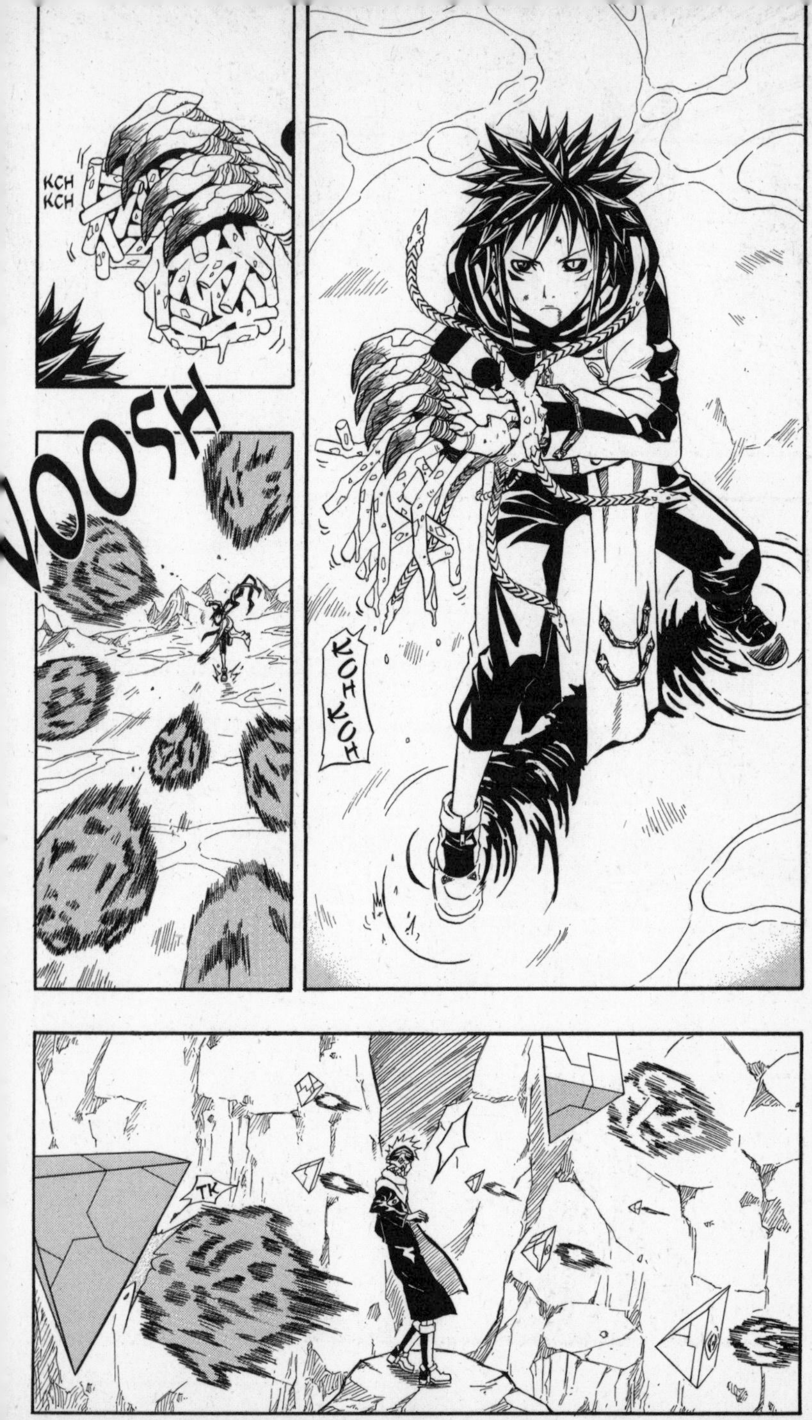
KOH KOH
KCH
KCH
VOOSH
TK

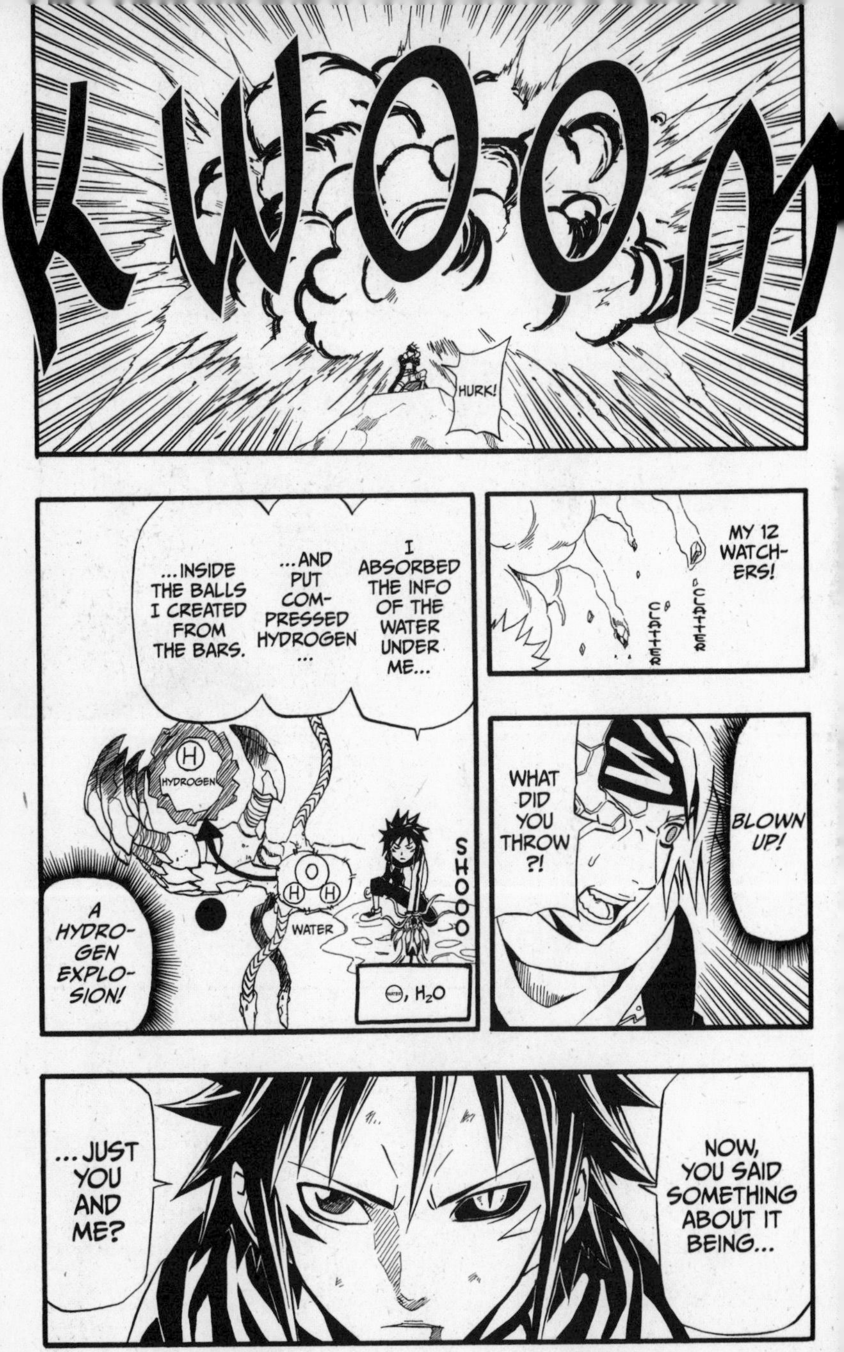
KWOOOM
HURK!
MY 12 WATCHERS!
CLATTER
CLATTER
BLOWN UP!
WHAT DID YOU THROW?!
I ABSORBED THE INFO OF THE WATER UNDER ME...
...AND PUT COMPRESSED HYDROGEN...
...INSIDE THE BALLS I CREATED FROM THE BARS.
H
HYDROGEN
O
H H
WATER
SHOOOO
WATER, H_2O
A HYDROGEN EXPLOSION!
NOW, YOU SAID SOMETHING ABOUT IT BEING...
...JUST YOU AND ME?

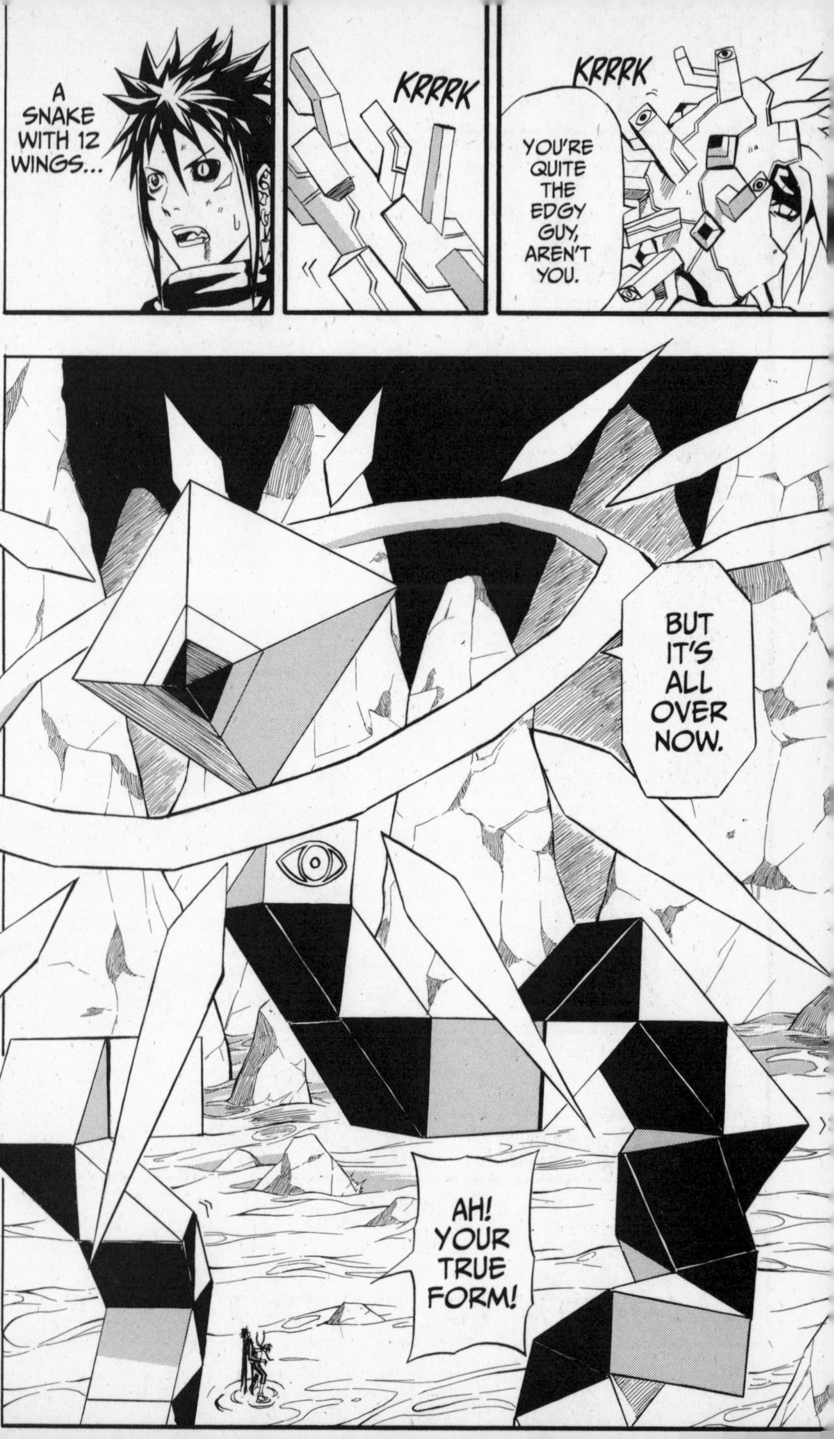
KRRRK
YOU'RE QUITE THE EDGY GUY, AREN'T YOU.
KRRRK
A SNAKE WITH 12 WINGS...
BUT IT'S ALL OVER NOW.
AH! YOUR TRUE FORM!

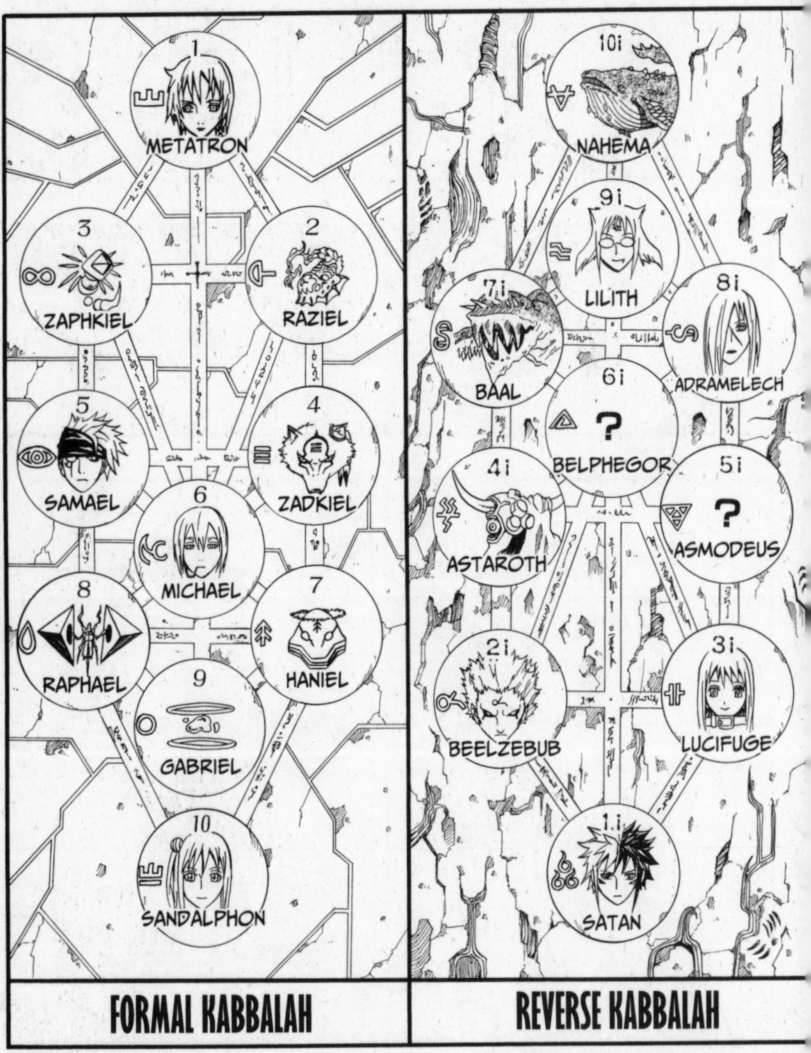
10i
NAHEMA
9i
LILITH
7i
BAAL
8i
ADRAMELECH
6i
?
BELPHEGOR
4i
ASTAROTH
5i
?
ASMODEUS
2i
BEELZEBUB
3i
LUCIFUGE
1i
SATAN
REVERSE KABBALAH
1
METATRON
3
ZAPHKIEL
2
RAZIEL
5
SAMAEL
4
ZADKIEL
6
MICHAEL
8
RAPHAEL
7
HANIEL
9
GABRIEL
10
SANDALPHON
FORMAL KABBALAH

CHAPTER 72 THE TWO BATTLES

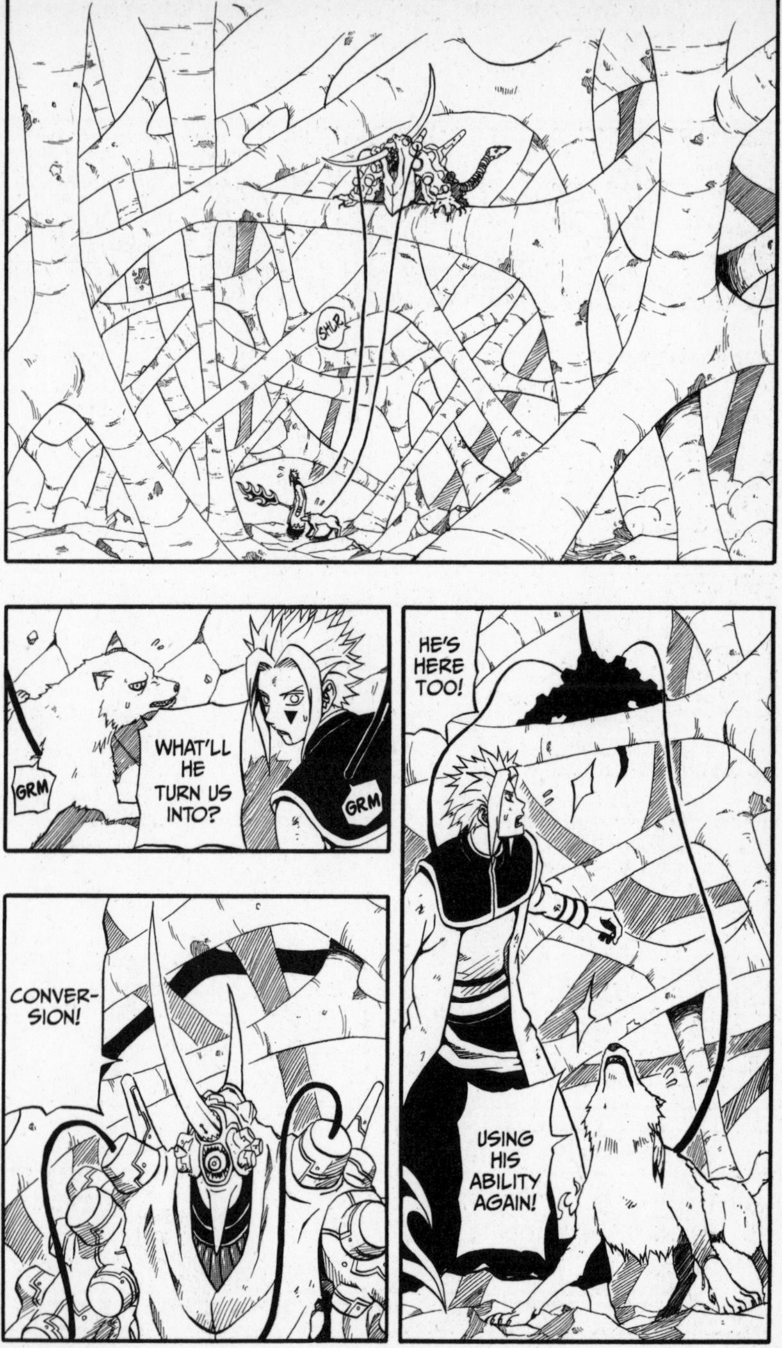
SMUR
HE'S HERE TOO!
USING HIS ABILITY AGAIN!
GRM
WHAT'LL HE TURN US INTO?
GRM
CONVER-SION!

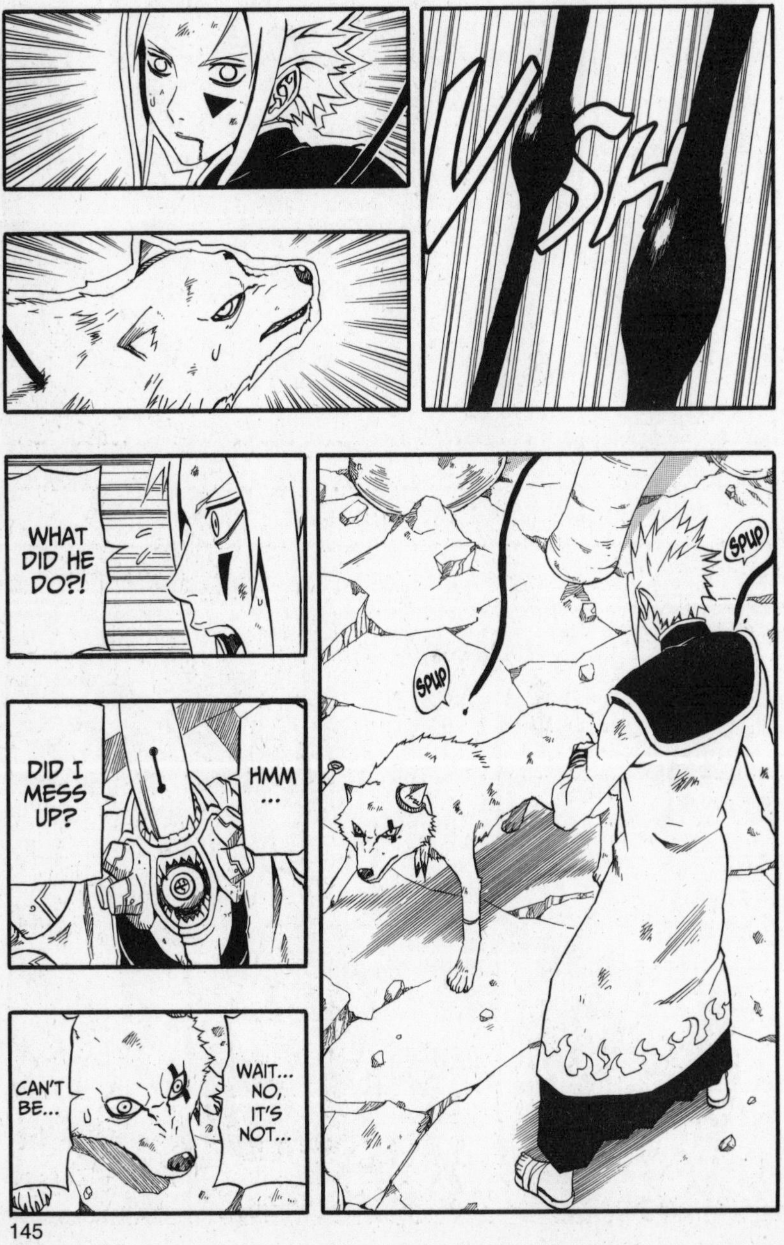
YSH
SPUP
SPUP
WHAT DID HE DO?!
HMM...
DID I MESS UP?
WAIT... NO, IT'S NOT...
CAN'T BE...

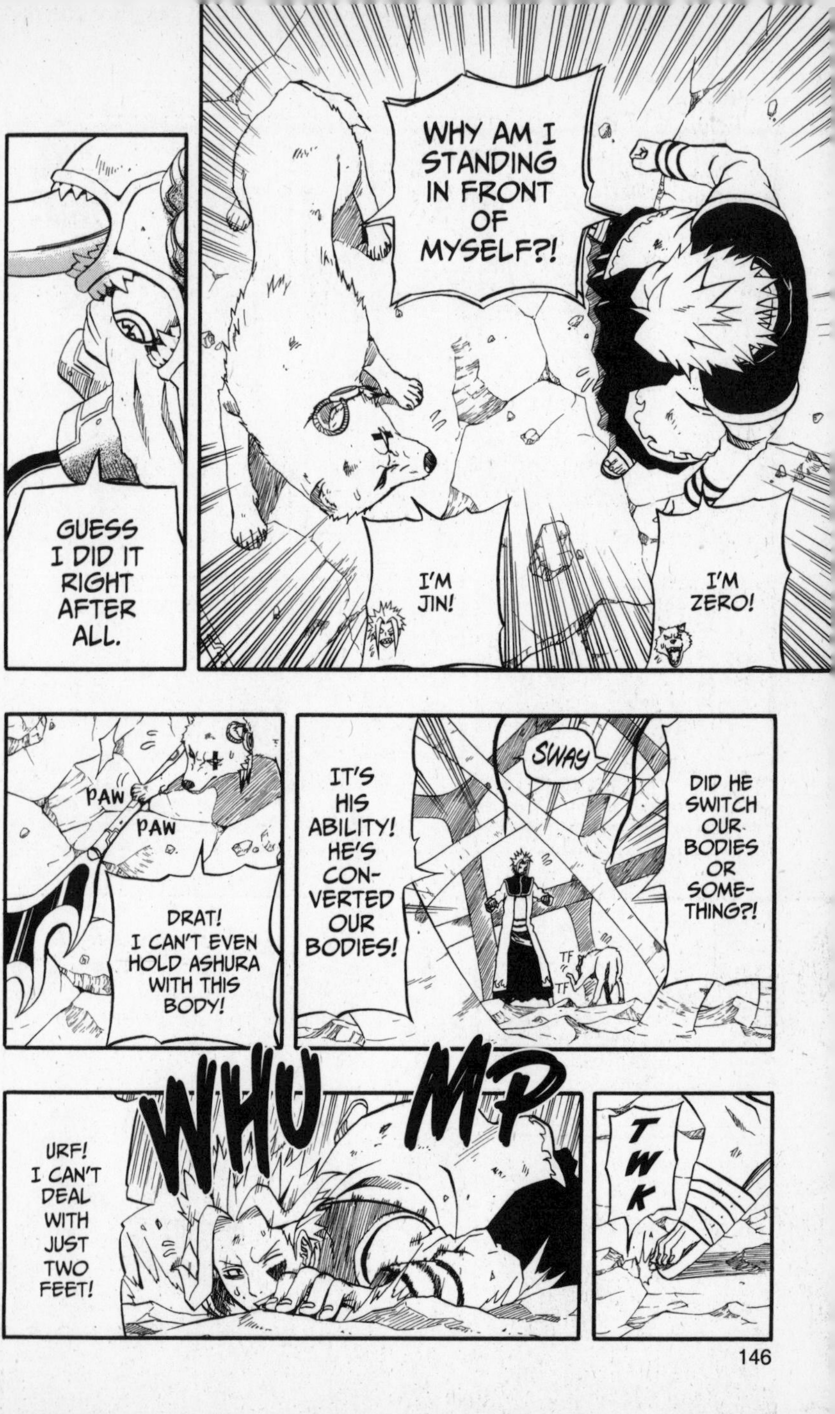
WHY AM I STANDING IN FRONT OF MYSELF?!
I'M ZERO!
I'M JIN!
GUESS I DID IT RIGHT AFTER ALL.
DID HE SWITCH OUR BODIES OR SOME-THING?!
SWAY
IT'S HIS ABILITY! HE'S CON-VERTED OUR BODIES!
TF
TF
PAW
PAW
DRAT! I CAN'T EVEN HOLD ASHURA WITH THIS BODY!
TWK
WHUMP
URF! I CAN'T DEAL WITH JUST TWO FEET!

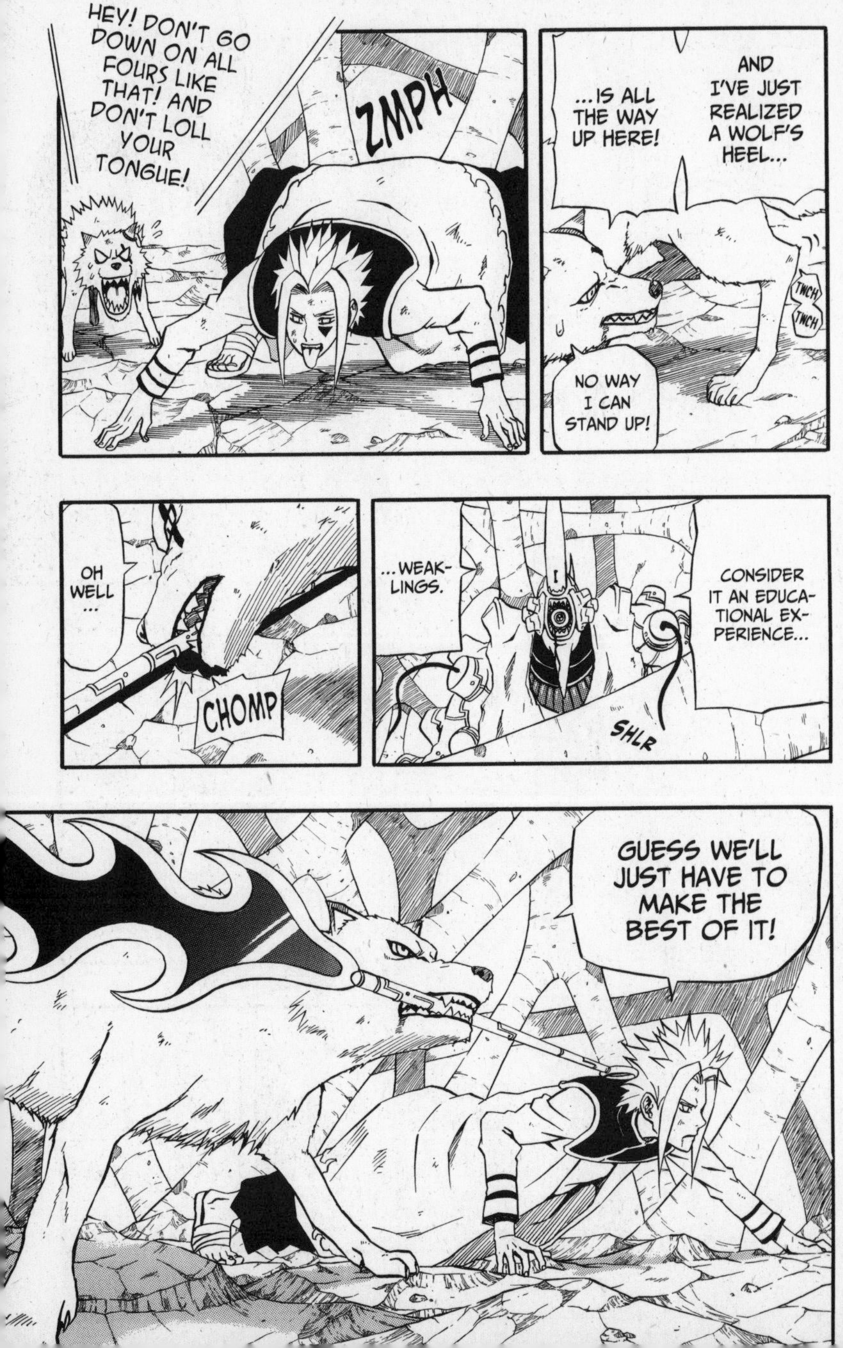
AND I'VE JUST REALIZED A WOLF'S HEEL...
...IS ALL THE WAY UP HERE!
TWCH
TWCH
NO WAY I CAN STAND UP!
HEY! DON'T GO DOWN ON ALL FOURS LIKE THAT! AND DON'T LOLL YOUR TONGUE!
ZMPH
CONSIDER IT AN EDUCATIONAL EXPERIENCE...
...WEAKLINGS.
SHLR
OH WELL ...
CHOMP
GUESS WE'LL JUST HAVE TO MAKE THE BEST OF IT!

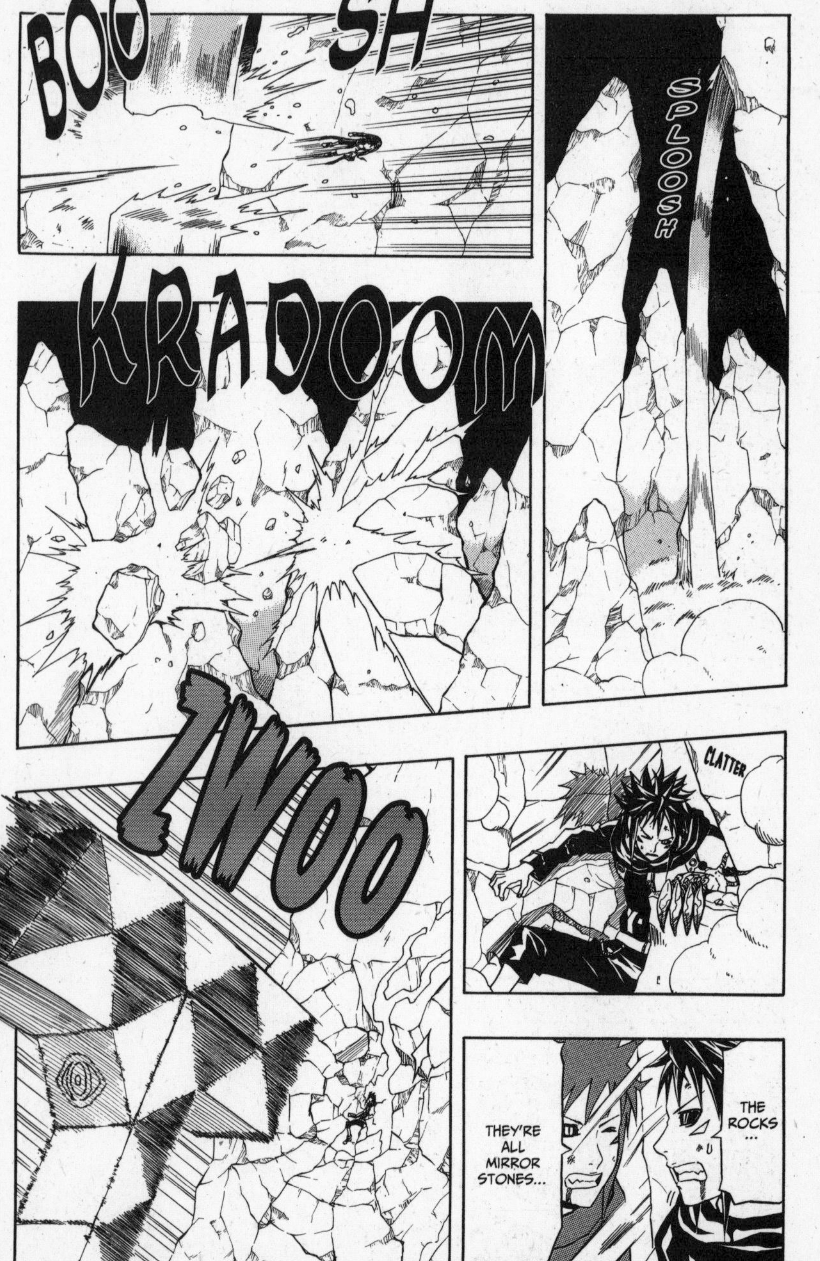
SPLOOSH
BOO SH
KRADOOM
CLATTER
THE ROCKS ...
THEY'RE ALL MIRROR STONES...
ZWOO

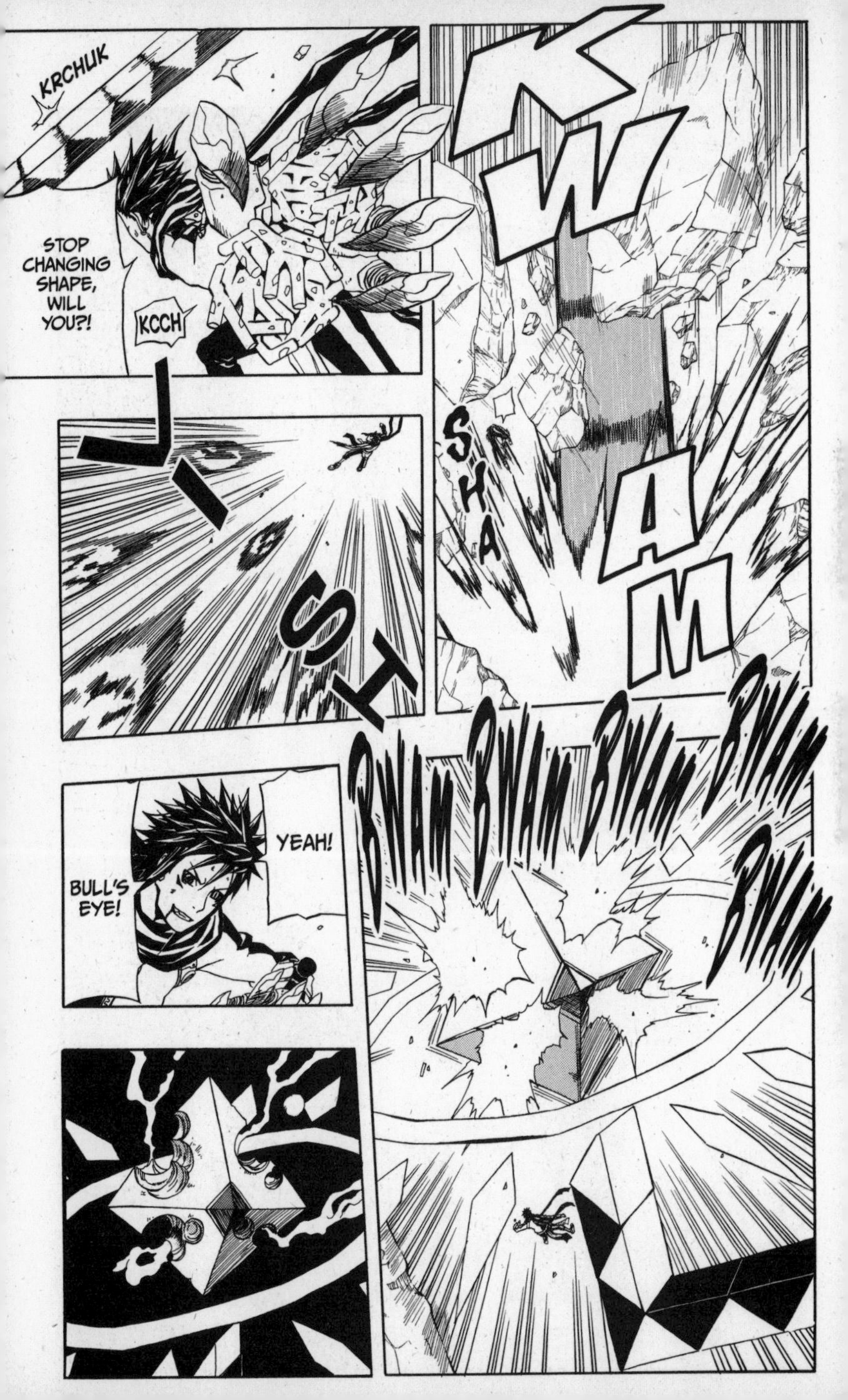
KWAM
SHA
KRCHUK
STOP CHANGING SHAPE, WILL YOU?!
KCCH
BWAM BWAM BWAM BWAM
BWAM BWAM
YEAH!
BULL'S EYE!

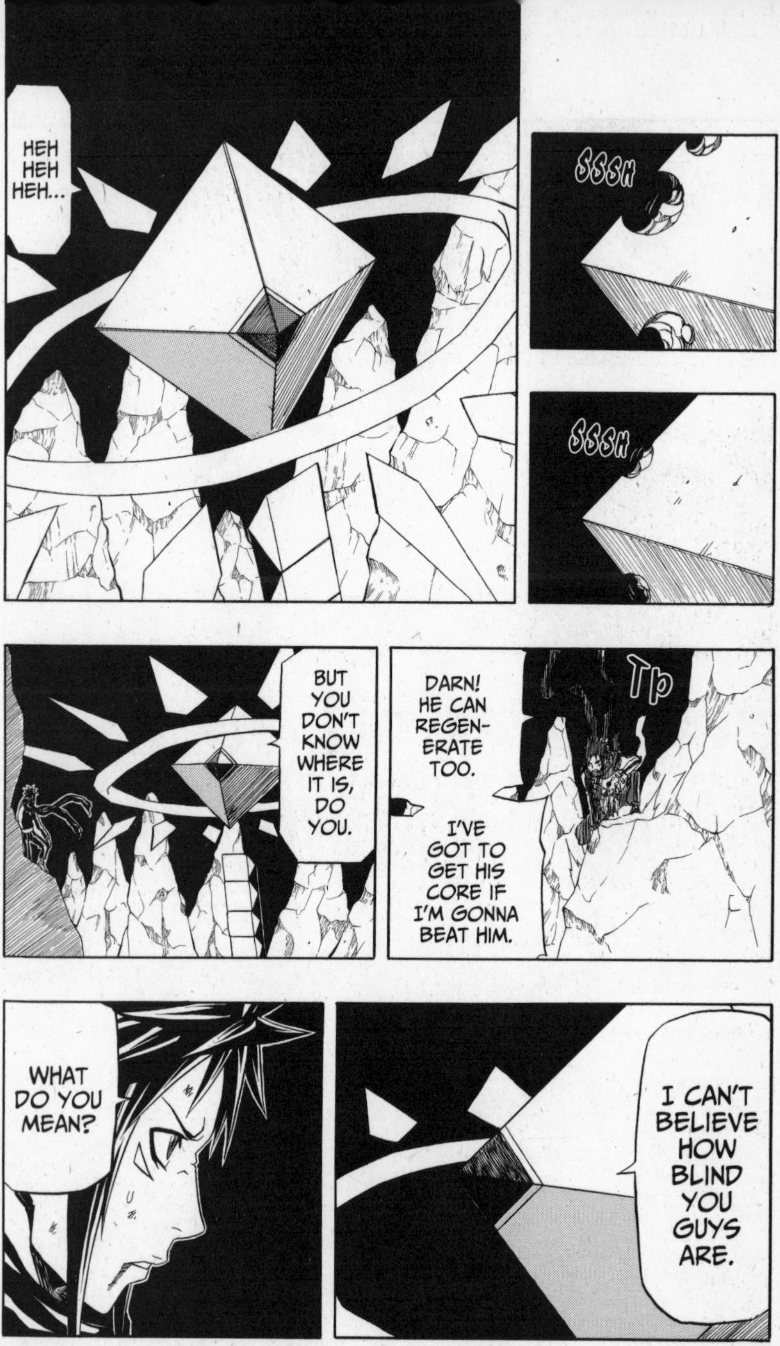
SSSH
SSSH
HEH HEH HEH...
Tp
DARN! HE CAN REGEN-ERATE TOO.
I'VE GOT TO GET HIS CORE IF I'M GONNA BEAT HIM.
BUT YOU DON'T KNOW WHERE IT IS, DO YOU.
I CAN'T BELIEVE HOW BLIND YOU GUYS ARE.
WHAT DO YOU MEAN?

ZENOM IS JUSTICE AND SHOULD RULE THIS WORLD.

WHAT?

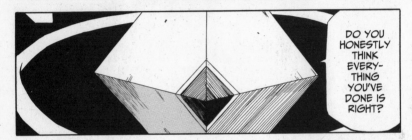

DO YOU HONESTLY THINK EVERY-THING YOU'VE DONE IS RIGHT?

ZENOM!

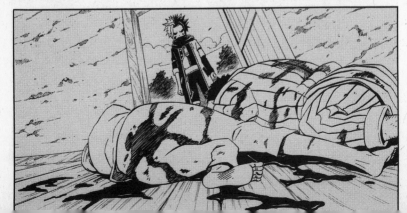

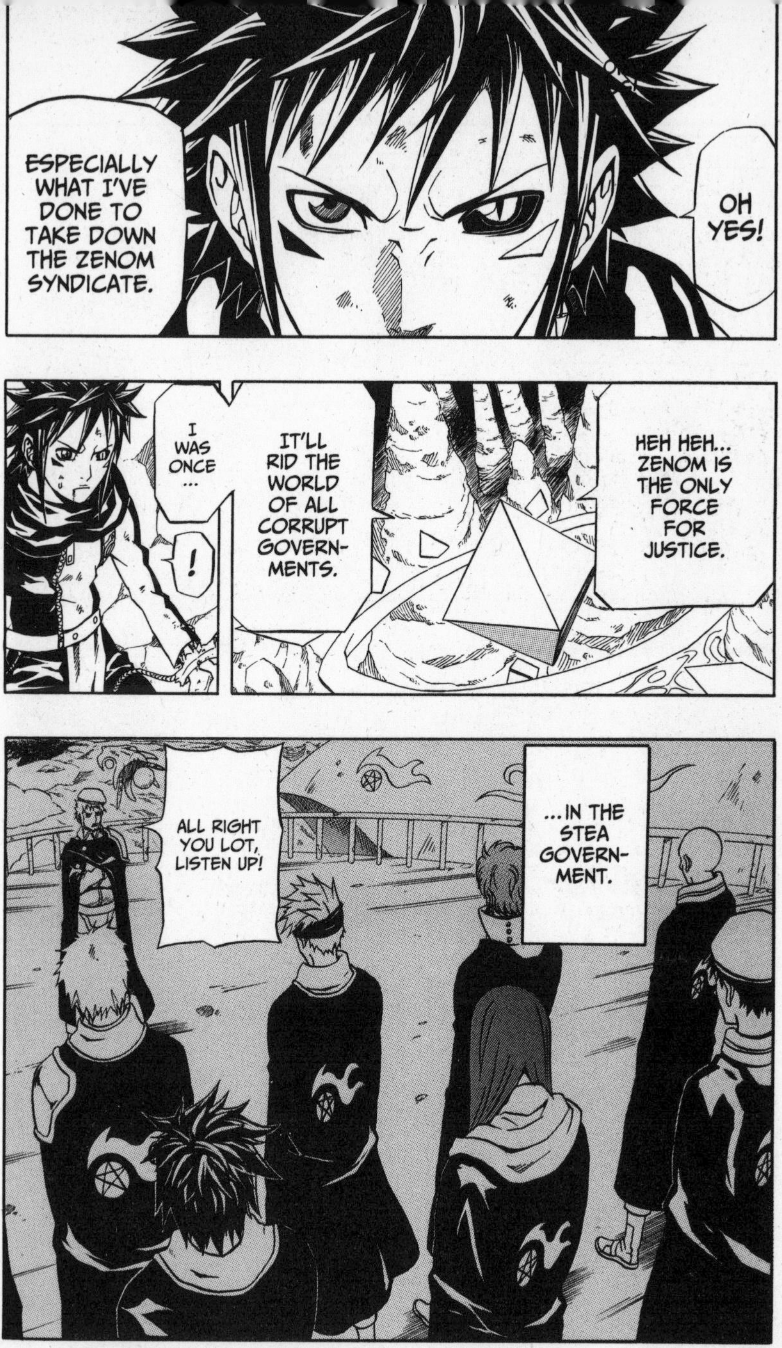
OH YES!
ESPECIALLY WHAT I'VE DONE TO TAKE DOWN THE ZENOM SYNDICATE.
HEH HEH... ZENOM IS THE ONLY FORCE FOR JUSTICE.
IT'LL RID THE WORLD OF ALL CORRUPT GOVERN-MENTS.
I WAS ONCE ...
!
...IN THE STEA GOVERN-MENT.
ALL RIGHT YOU LOT, LISTEN UP!

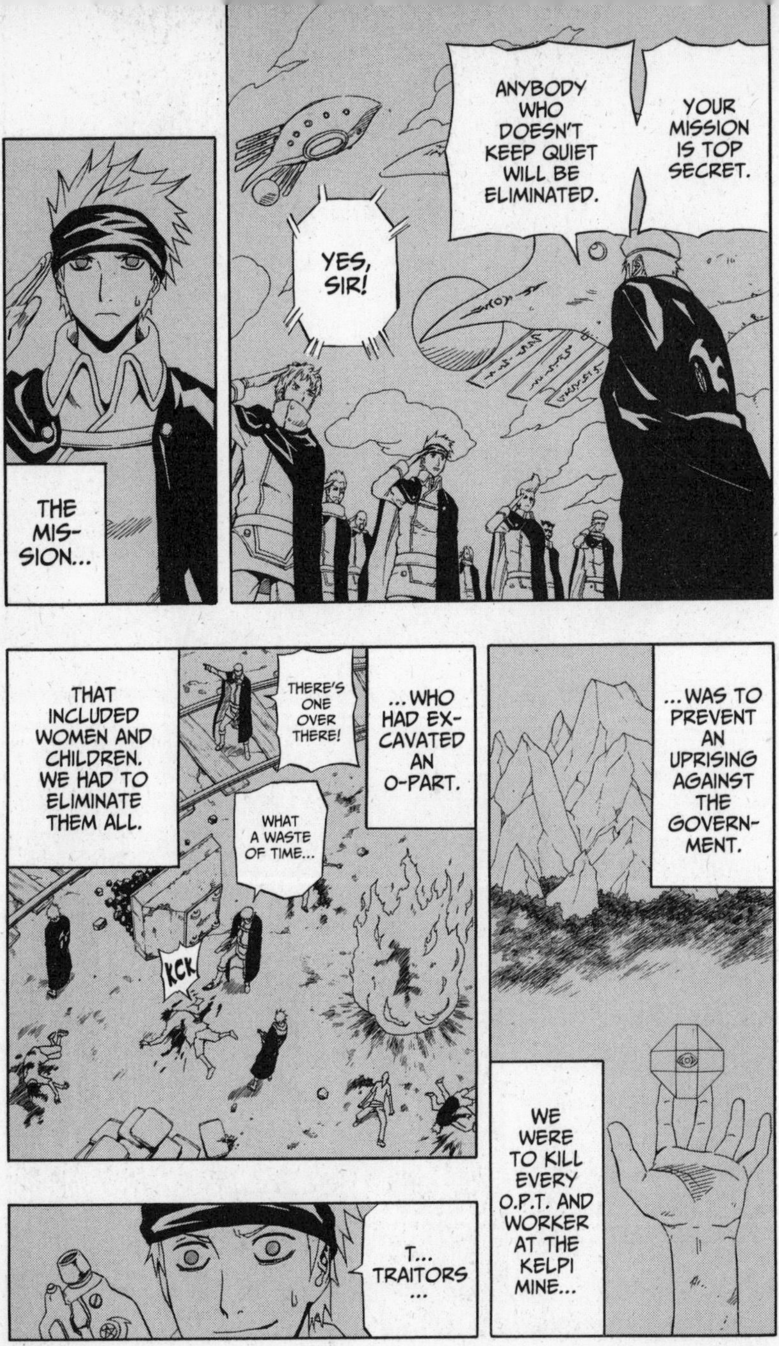
YOUR MISSION IS TOP SECRET.
ANYBODY WHO DOESN'T KEEP QUIET WILL BE ELIMINATED.
YES, SIR!
THE MIS-SION...
...WAS TO PREVENT AN UPRISING AGAINST THE GOVERN-MENT.
WE WERE TO KILL EVERY O.P.T. AND WORKER AT THE KELPI MINE...
...WHO HAD EX-CAVATED AN O-PART.
THERE'S ONE OVER THERE!
THAT INCLUDED WOMEN AND CHILDREN. WE HAD TO ELIMINATE THEM ALL.
WHAT A WASTE OF TIME...
KCK
T... TRAITORS ...

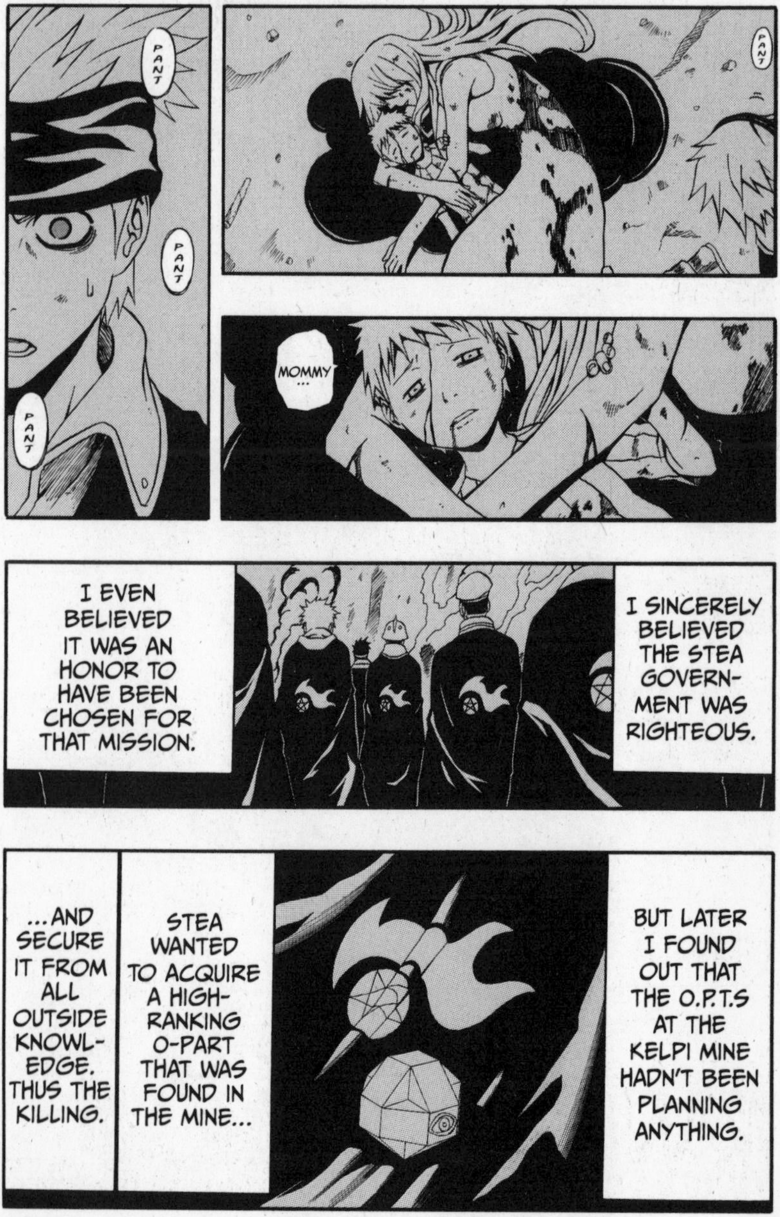
PANT
MOMMY...
PANT
PANT
PANT
I SINCERELY BELIEVED THE STEA GOVERNMENT WAS RIGHTEOUS.
I EVEN BELIEVED IT WAS AN HONOR TO HAVE BEEN CHOSEN FOR THAT MISSION.
BUT LATER I FOUND OUT THAT THE O.P.T.S AT THE KELPI MINE HADN'T BEEN PLANNING ANYTHING.
STEA WANTED TO ACQUIRE A HIGH-RANKING O-PART THAT WAS FOUND IN THE MINE...
...AND SECURE IT FROM ALL OUTSIDE KNOWLEDGE. THUS THE KILLING.

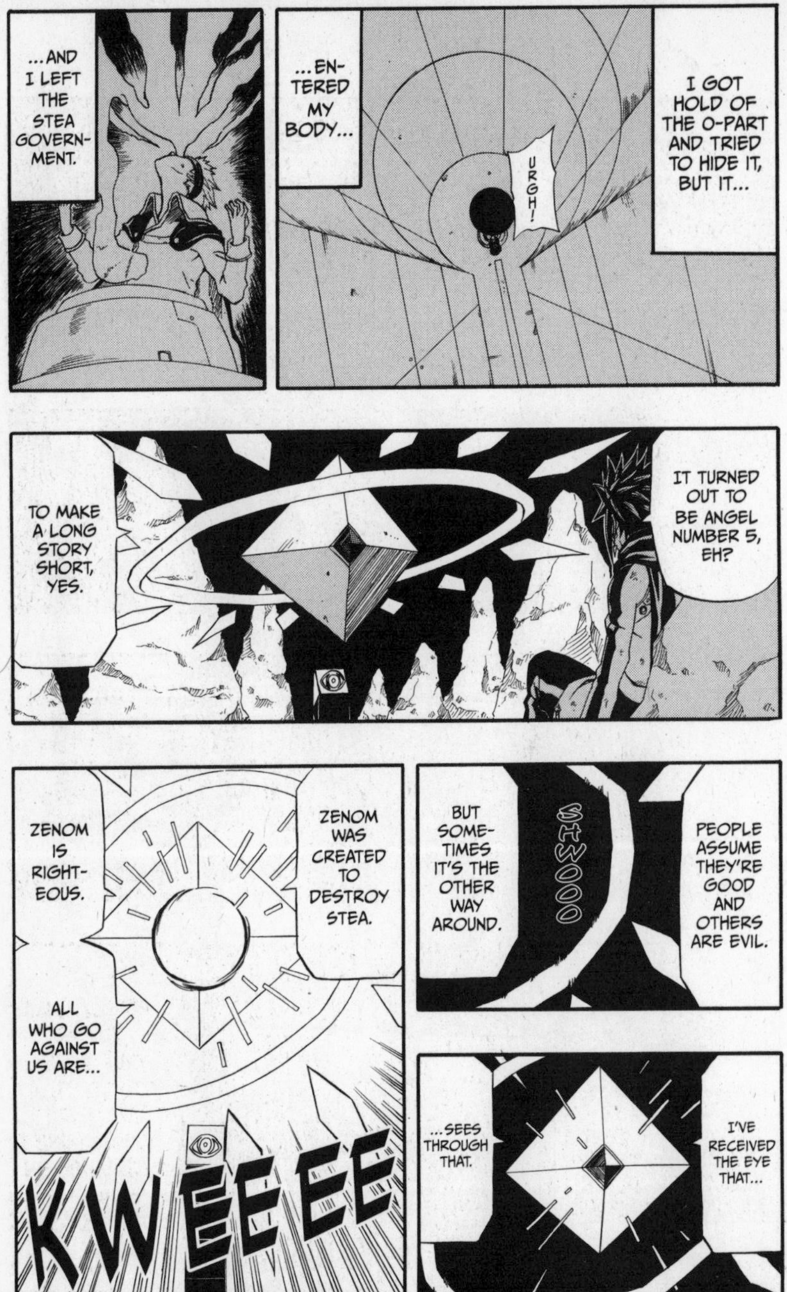
I GOT HOLD OF THE O-PART AND TRIED TO HIDE IT, BUT IT...
URGH!
...EN-TERED MY BODY...
...AND I LEFT THE STEA GOVERN-MENT.
IT TURNED OUT TO BE ANGEL NUMBER 5, EH?
TO MAKE A LONG STORY SHORT, YES.
PEOPLE ASSUME THEY'RE GOOD AND OTHERS ARE EVIL.
SHWOOO
BUT SOME-TIMES IT'S THE OTHER WAY AROUND.
I'VE RECEIVED THE EYE THAT...
...SEES THROUGH THAT.
ZENOM WAS CREATED TO DESTROY STEA.
ZENOM IS RIGHT-EOUS.
ALL WHO GO AGAINST US ARE...
KWEEEEE

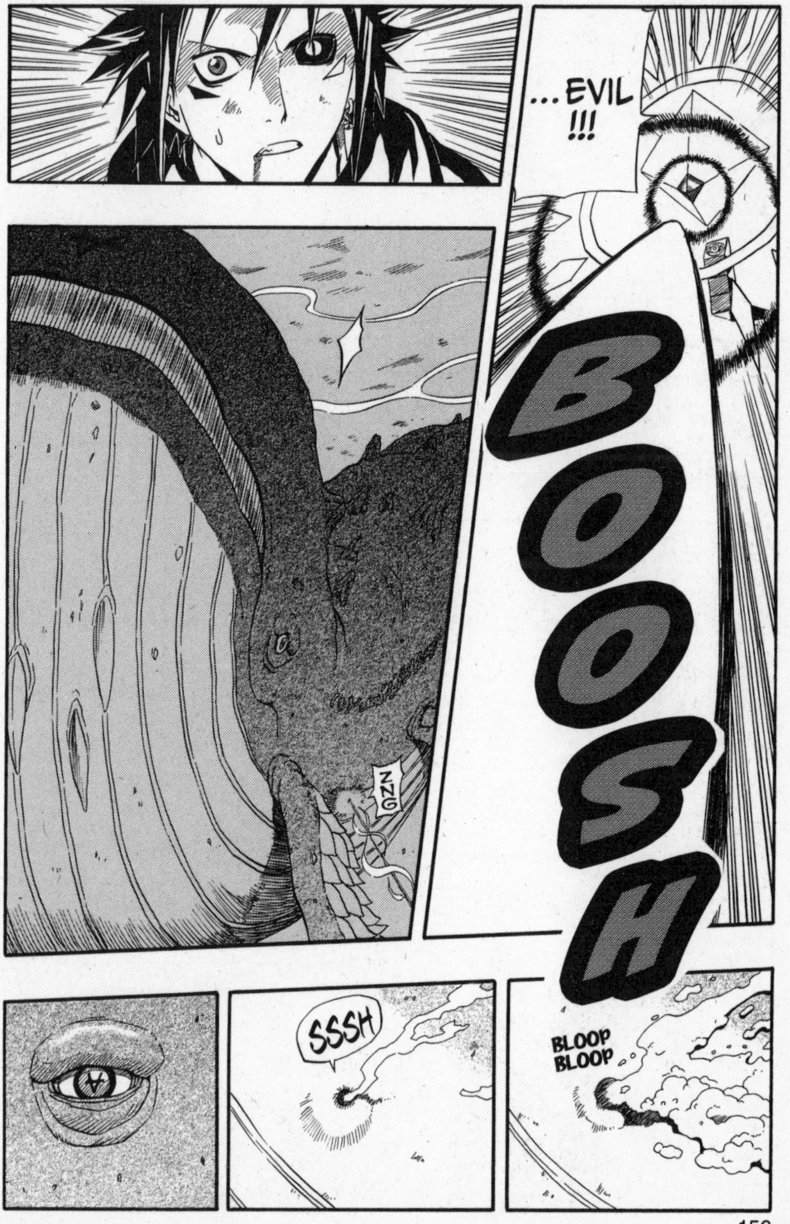
...EVIL !!!
BOOSH
ZNG
BLOOP BLOOP
SSSH

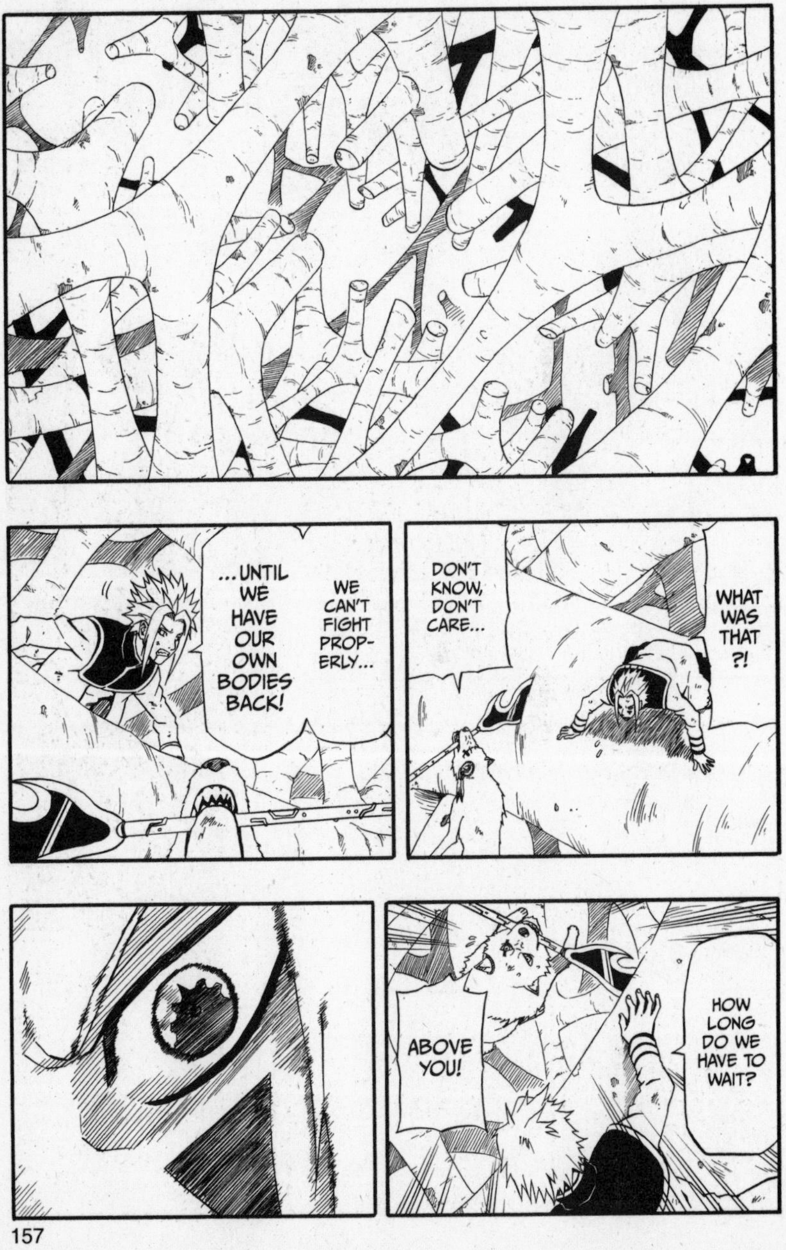
WHAT WAS THAT ?!
DON'T KNOW, DON'T CARE...
WE CAN'T FIGHT PROPERLY...
...UNTIL WE HAVE OUR OWN BODIES BACK!
HOW LONG DO WE HAVE TO WAIT?
ABOVE YOU!

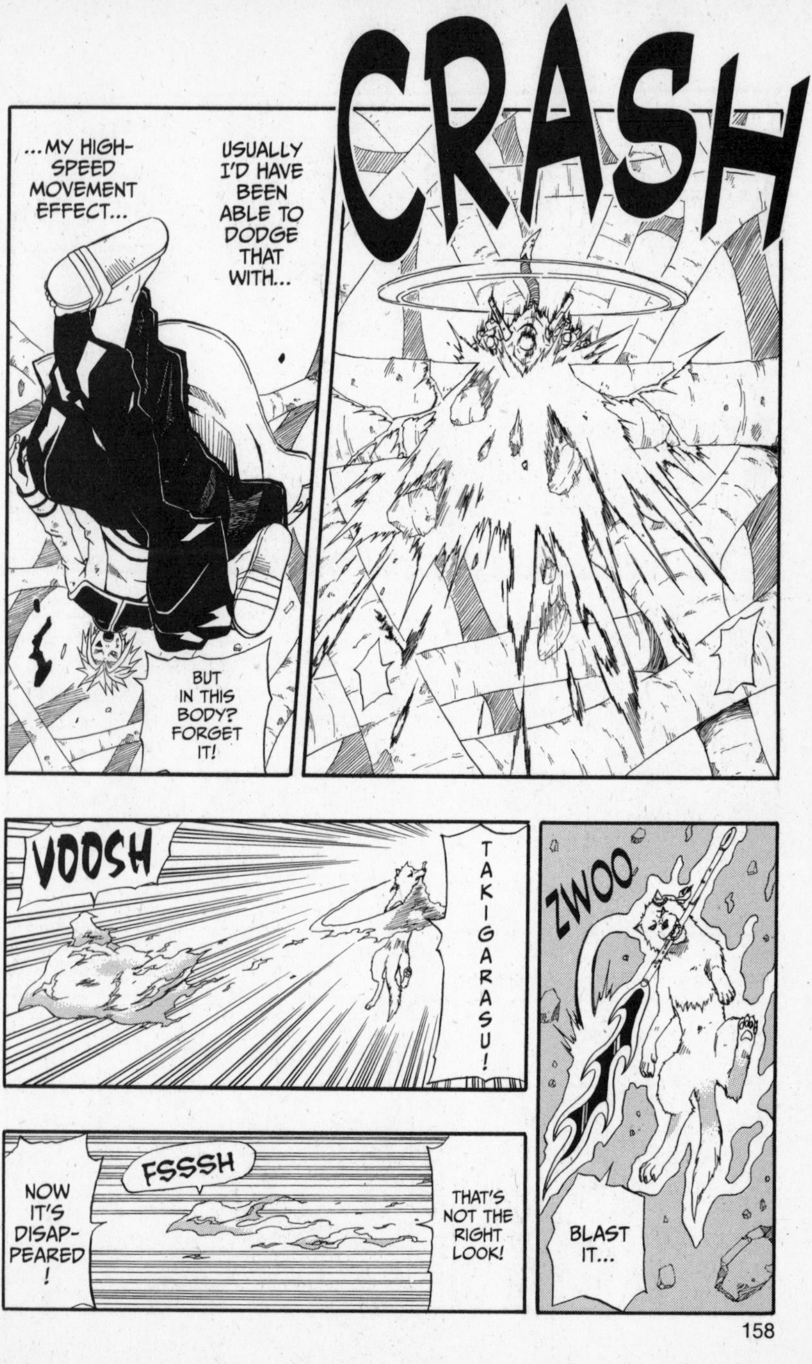
CRASH
USUALLY I'D HAVE BEEN ABLE TO DODGE THAT WITH...
...MY HIGH-SPEED MOVEMENT EFFECT...
BUT IN THIS BODY? FORGET IT!
ZWOO
BLAST IT...
TAKIGARASU!
VOOSH
FSSSH
THAT'S NOT THE RIGHT LOOK!
NOW IT'S DISAPPEARED!

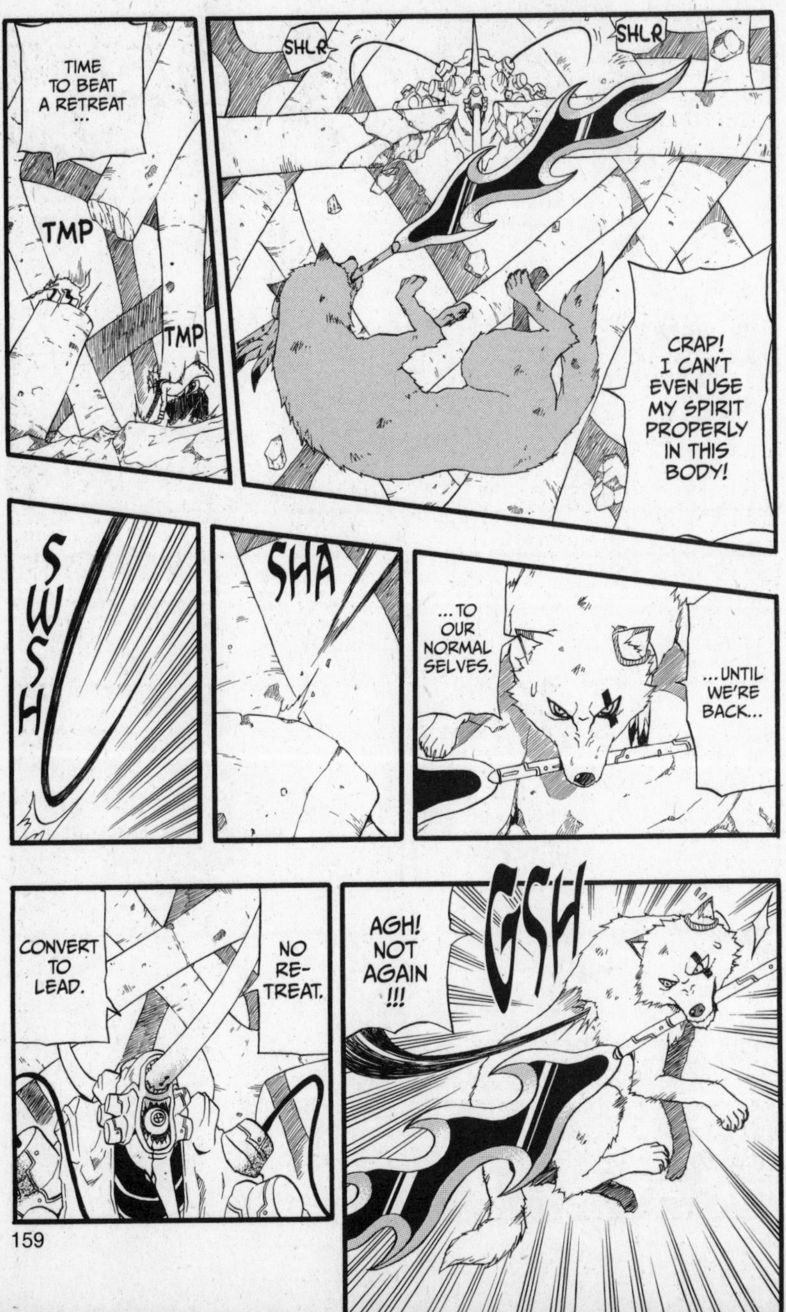
SHLR
SHLR
CRAP! I CAN'T EVEN USE MY SPIRIT PROPERLY IN THIS BODY!
TIME TO BEAT A RETREAT ...
TMP
TMP
...UNTIL WE'RE BACK...
...TO OUR NORMAL SELVES.
SHA
SWSH
GSH
AGH! NOT AGAIN !!!
NO RE-TREAT.
CONVERT TO LEAD.

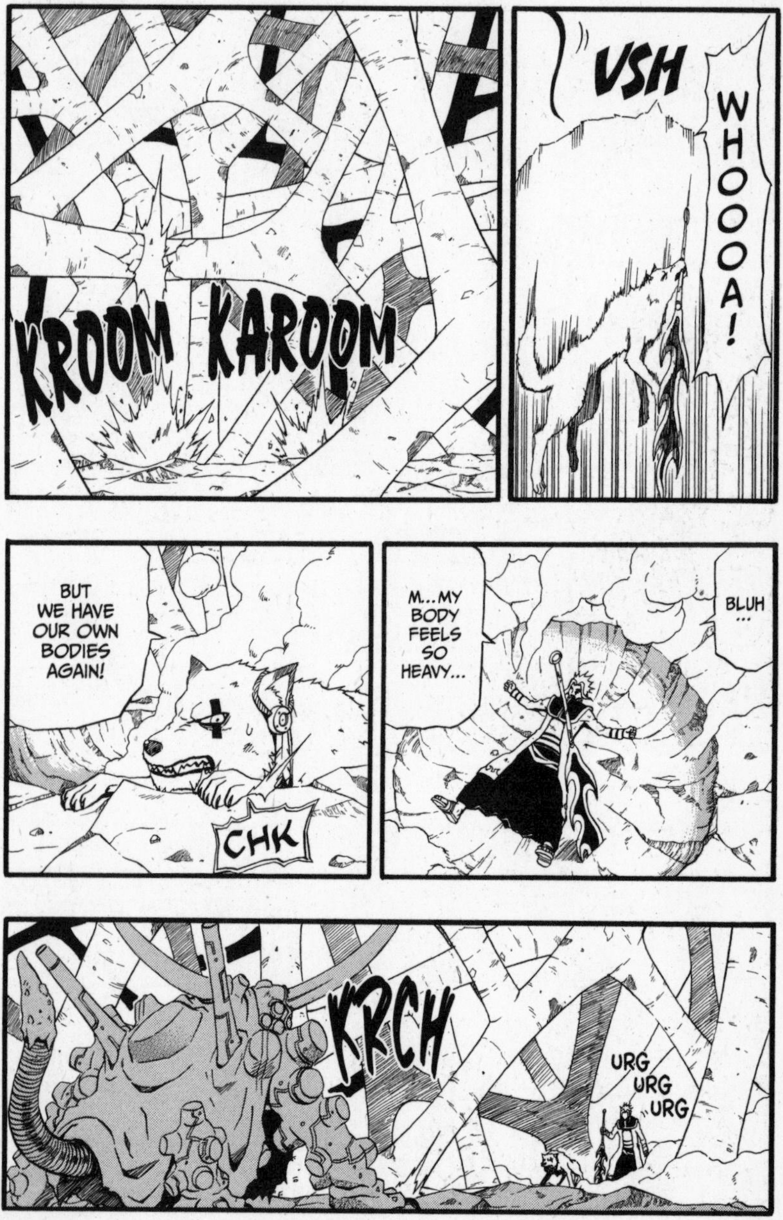
VSH
WHOOOA!
KROOM KAROOM
BLUH...
M...MY BODY FEELS SO HEAVY...
BUT WE HAVE OUR OWN BODIES AGAIN!
CHK
KRCH
URG URG URG

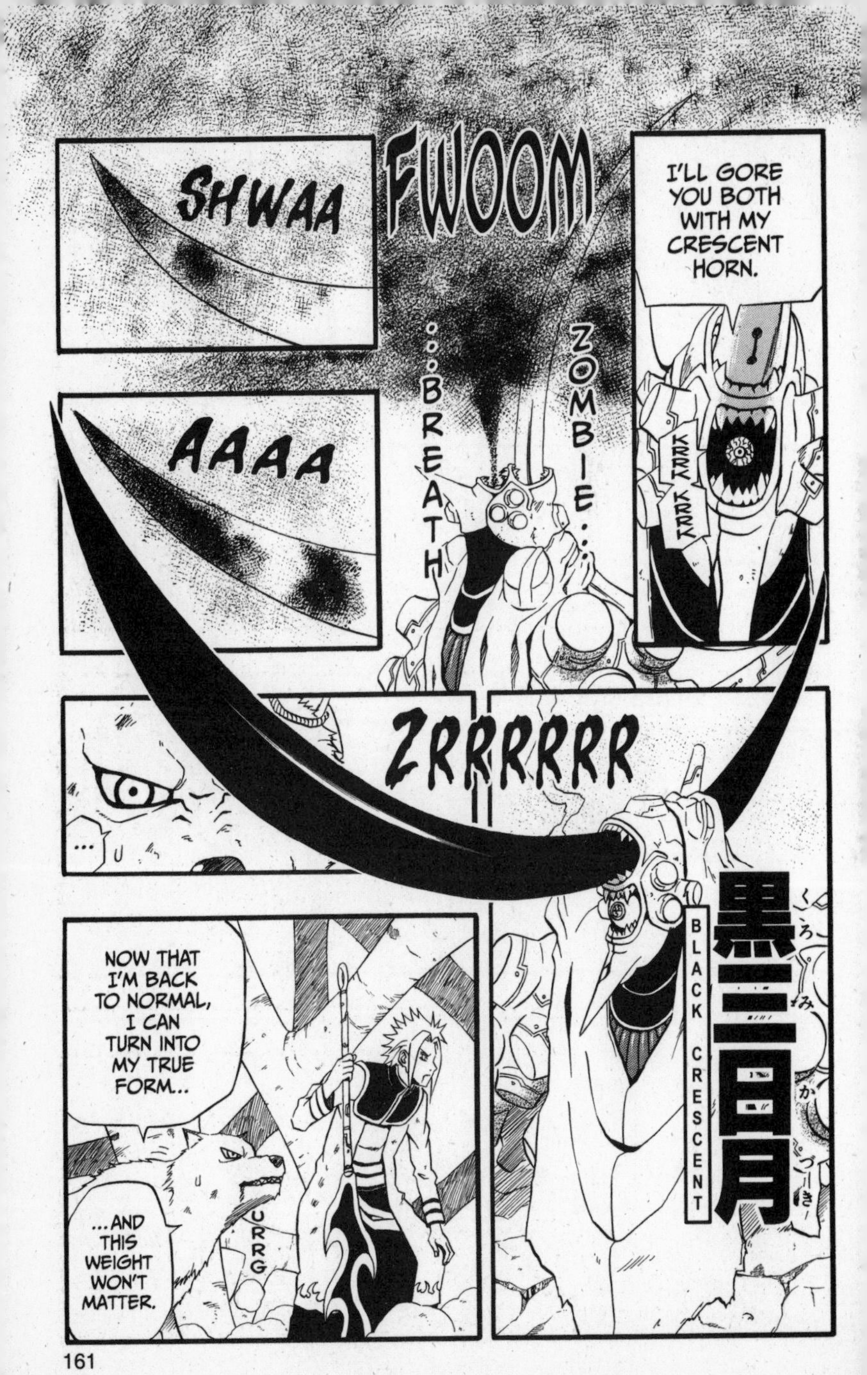
I'LL GORE YOU BOTH WITH MY CRESCENT HORN.
KRRK KRRK
ZOMBIE...
...BREATH
FWOOM
SHWAA
AAAA
ZRRRRRR
黒三日月
くろみかづき
BLACK CRESCENT
...
NOW THAT I'M BACK TO NORMAL, I CAN TURN INTO MY TRUE FORM...
URRG
...AND THIS WEIGHT WON'T MATTER.

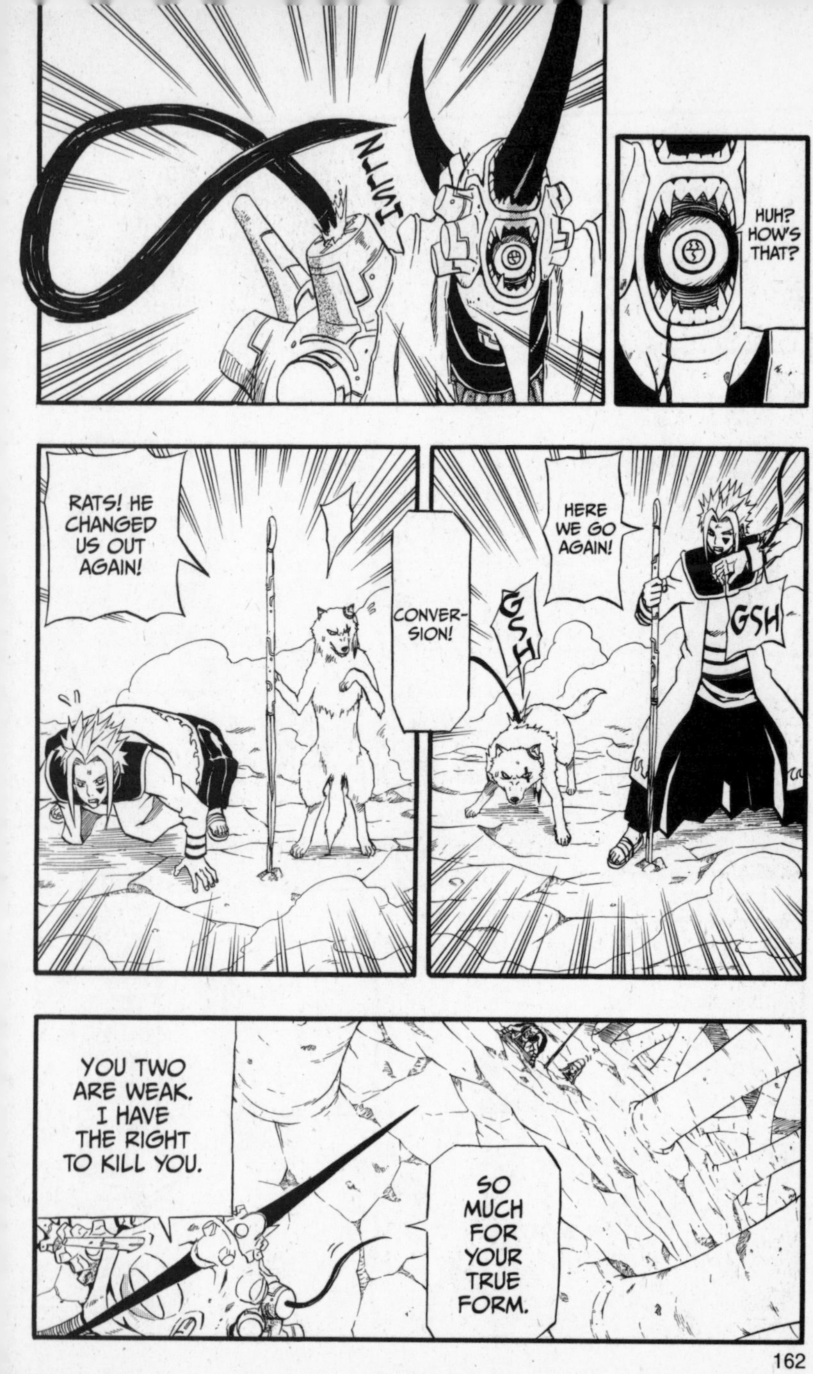
HUH? HOW'S THAT?
HERE WE GO AGAIN!
GSH
GSH
CONVERSION!
RATS! HE CHANGED US OUT AGAIN!
SO MUCH FOR YOUR TRUE FORM.
YOU TWO ARE WEAK. I HAVE THE RIGHT TO KILL YOU.

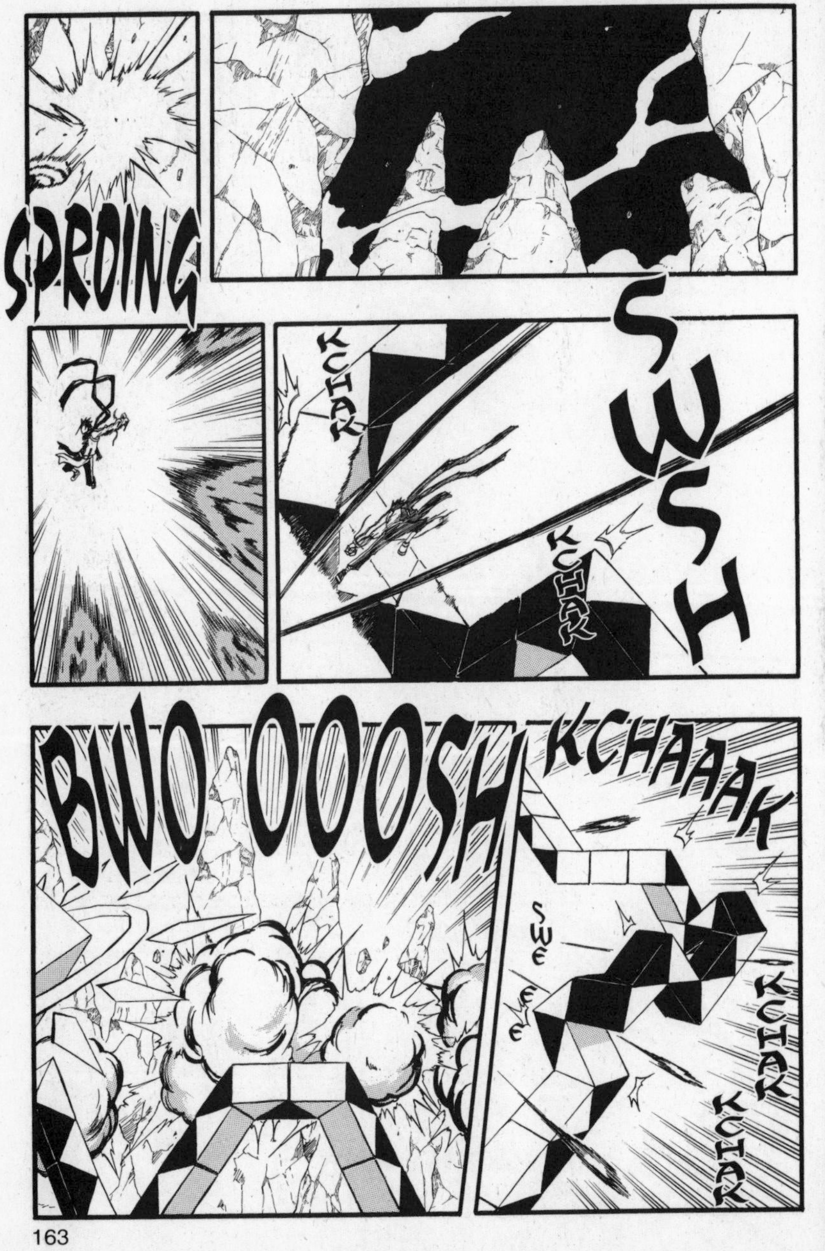
SPROING
SWSH
KCHAK
KCHAK
KCHAAAK
SWEEE
KCHAK
KCHAK
BWOOOOSH

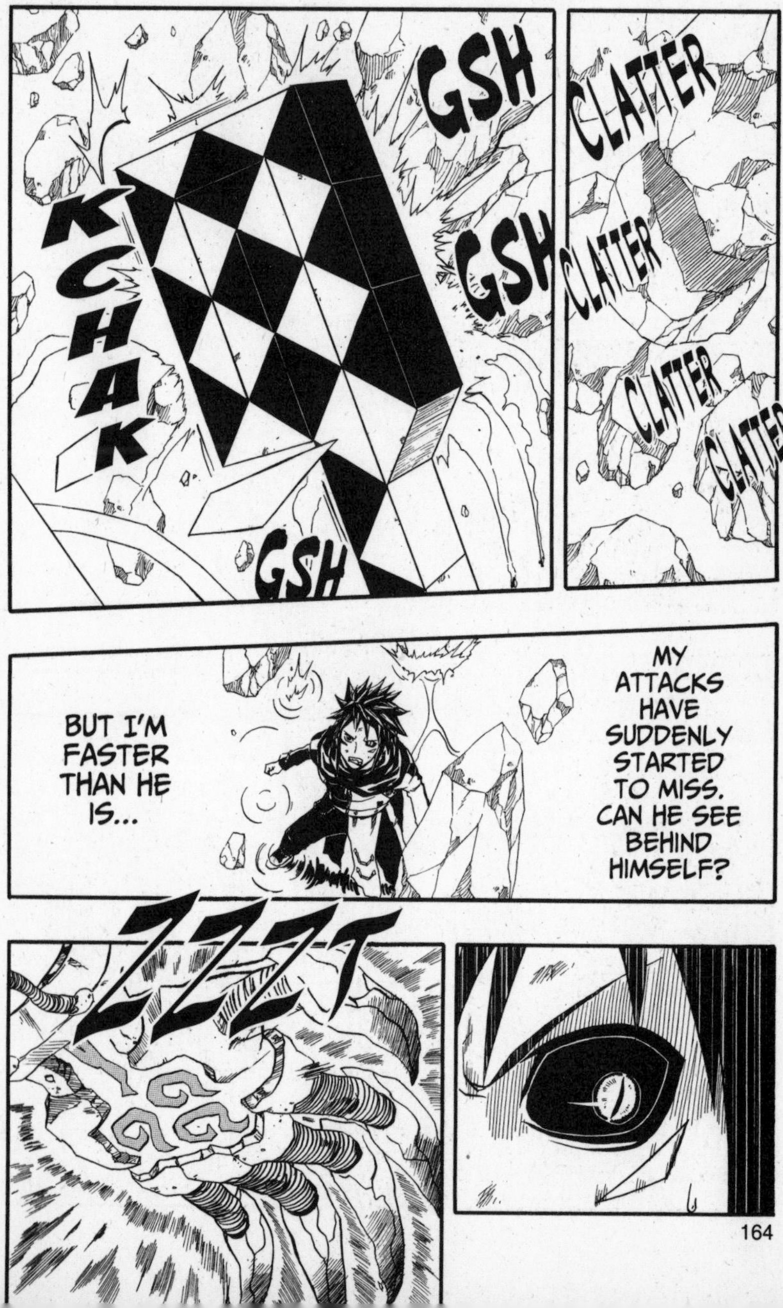
CLATTER
CLATTER
CLATTER
CLATTER
GSH
GSH
KCHAK
GSH
MY ATTACKS HAVE SUDDENLY STARTED TO MISS. CAN HE SEE BEHIND HIMSELF?
BUT I'M FASTER THAN HE IS...
ZZZT

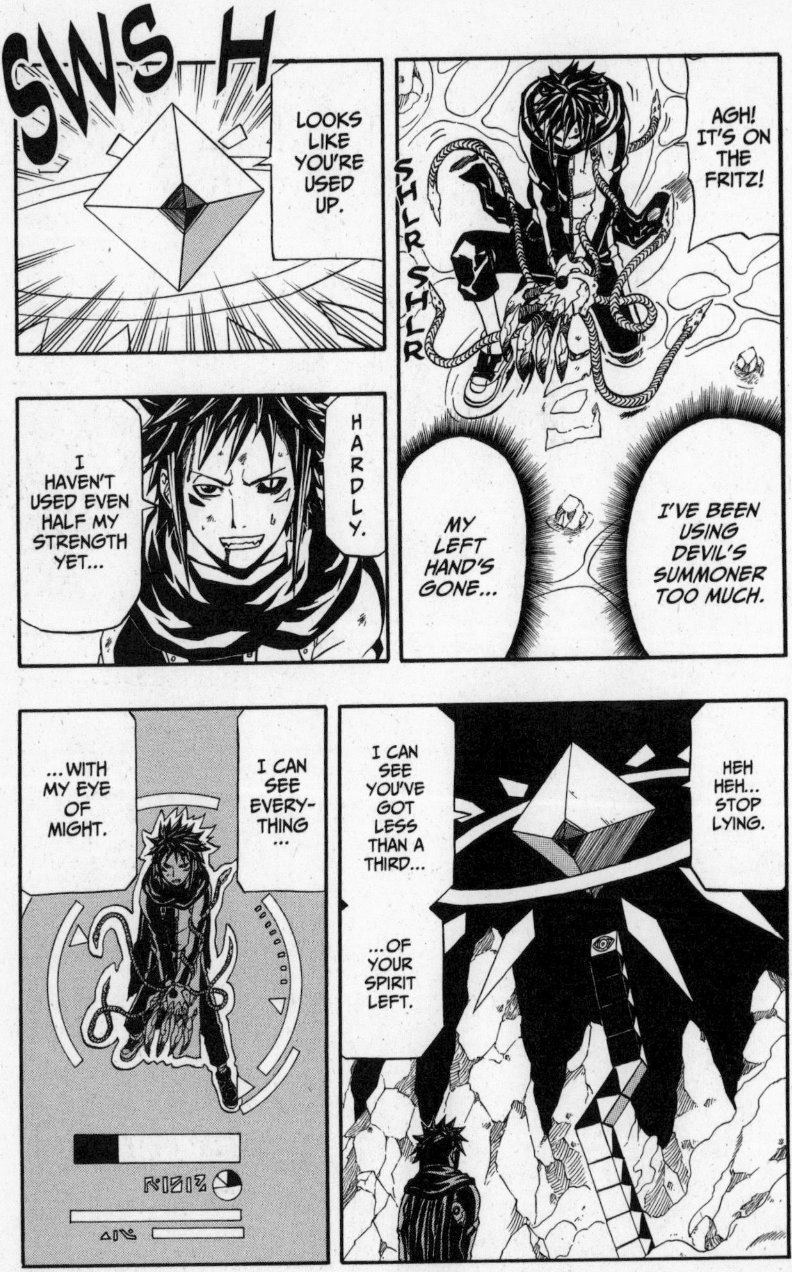
AGH! IT'S ON THE FRITZ!
SHLR SHLR
I'VE BEEN USING DEVIL'S SUMMONER TOO MUCH.
MY LEFT HAND'S GONE...
SWSH
LOOKS LIKE YOU'RE USED UP.
HARDLY.
I HAVEN'T USED EVEN HALF MY STRENGTH YET...
HEH HEH... STOP LYING.
I CAN SEE YOU'VE GOT LESS THAN A THIRD...
...OF YOUR SPIRIT LEFT.
I CAN SEE EVERYTHING...
...WITH MY EYE OF MIGHT.

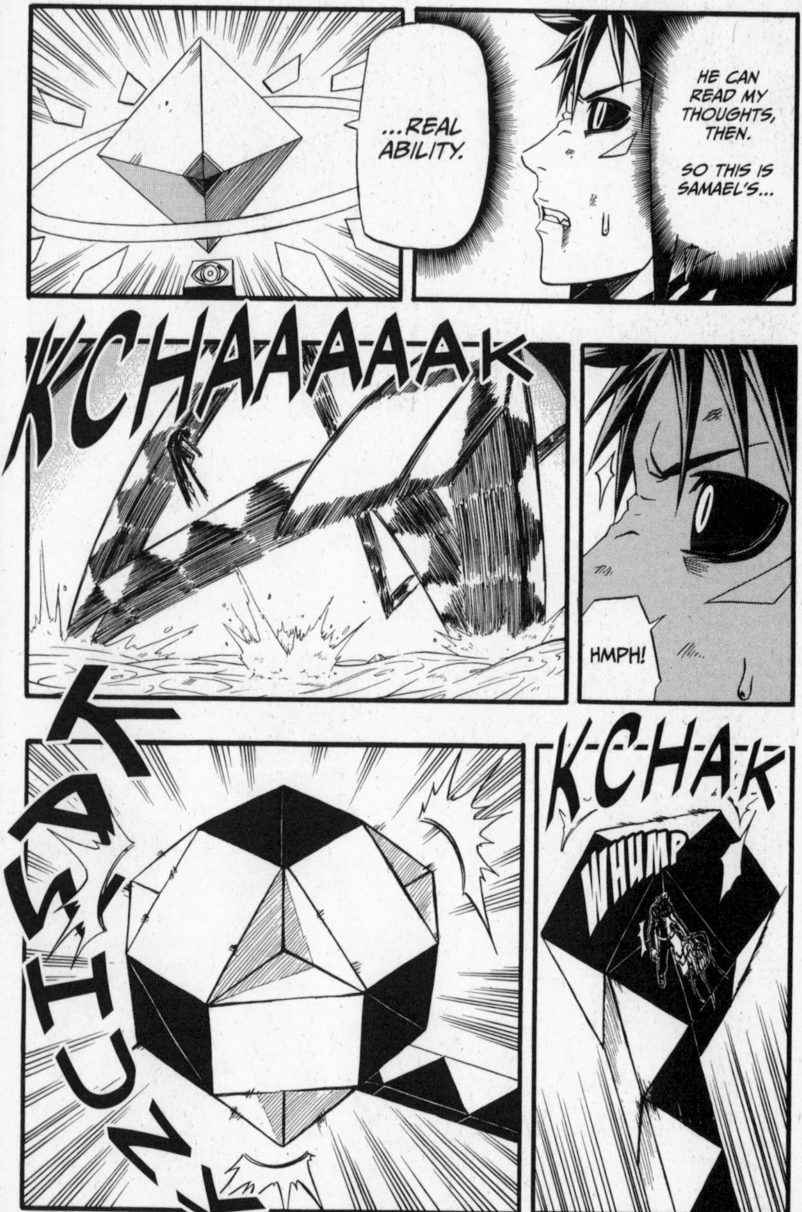
HE CAN READ MY THOUGHTS, THEN.
SO THIS IS SAMAEL'S...
...REAL ABILITY.
HMPH!
KCHAAAAAK
KCHAK
WHUMP
KASHUNK

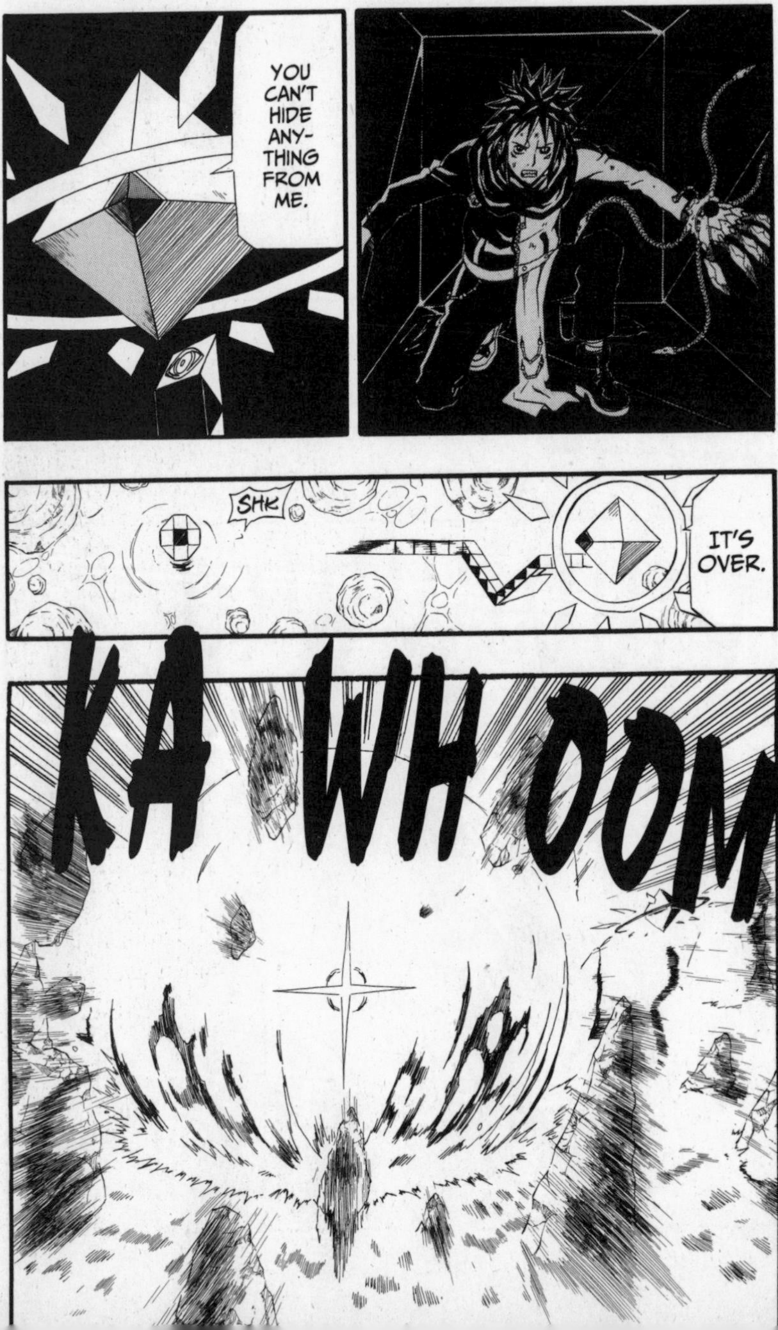
YOU CAN'T HIDE ANY-THING FROM ME.
IT'S OVER.
SHK
KA WH OOM

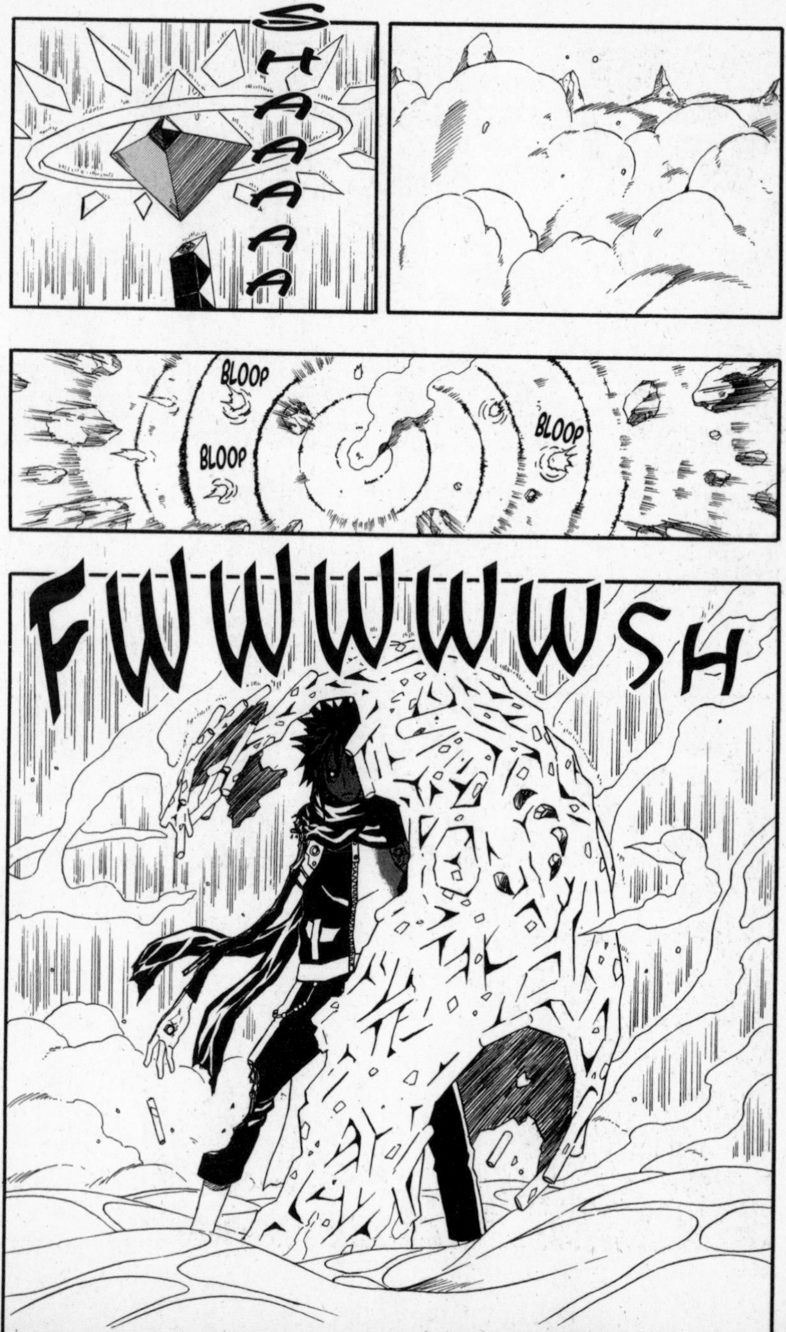
SHAAAAAA
BLOOP
BLOOP
BLOOP
FWWWWWSH

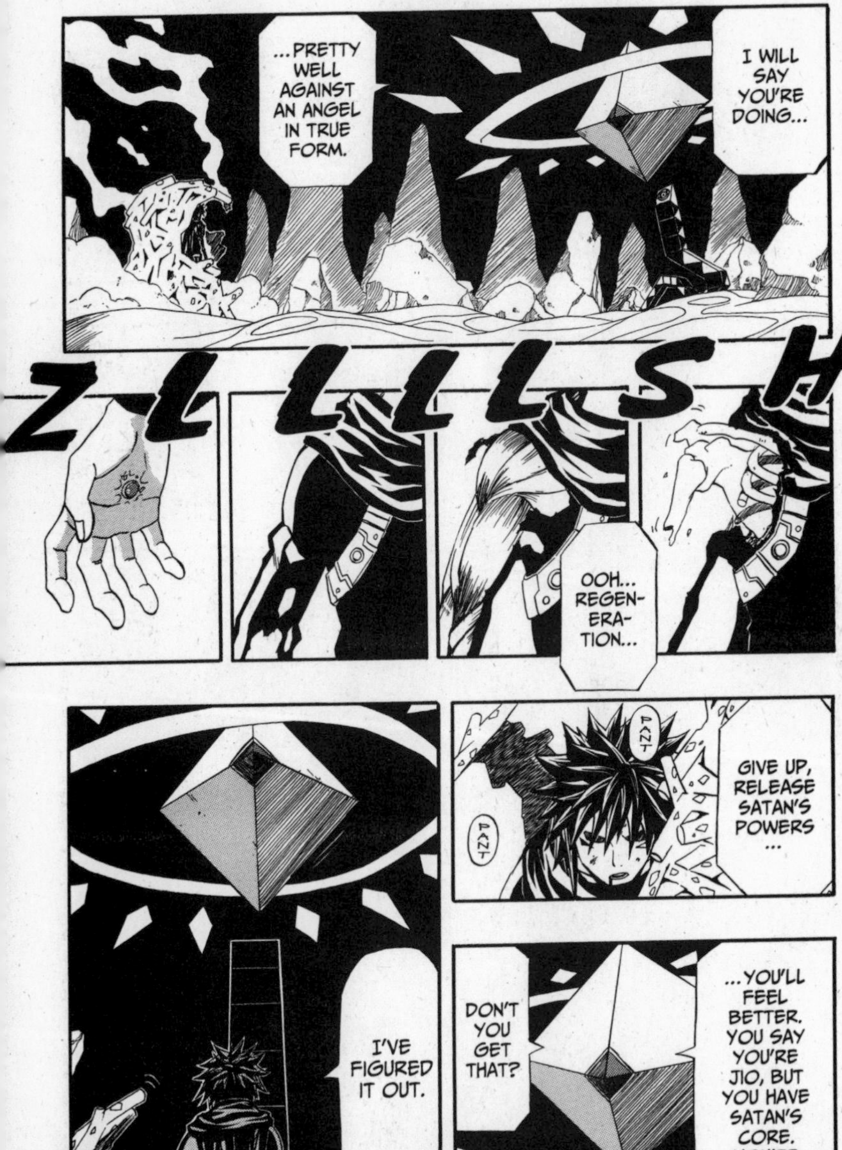
I WILL SAY YOU'RE DOING...
...PRETTY WELL AGAINST AN ANGEL IN TRUE FORM.
ZLLLLSH
OOH... REGEN-ERA-TION...
PANT
PANT
GIVE UP, RELEASE SATAN'S POWERS ...
...YOU'LL FEEL BETTER. YOU SAY YOU'RE JIO, BUT YOU HAVE SATAN'S CORE. YOU'RE EVIL.
DON'T YOU GET THAT?
I'VE FIGURED IT OUT.

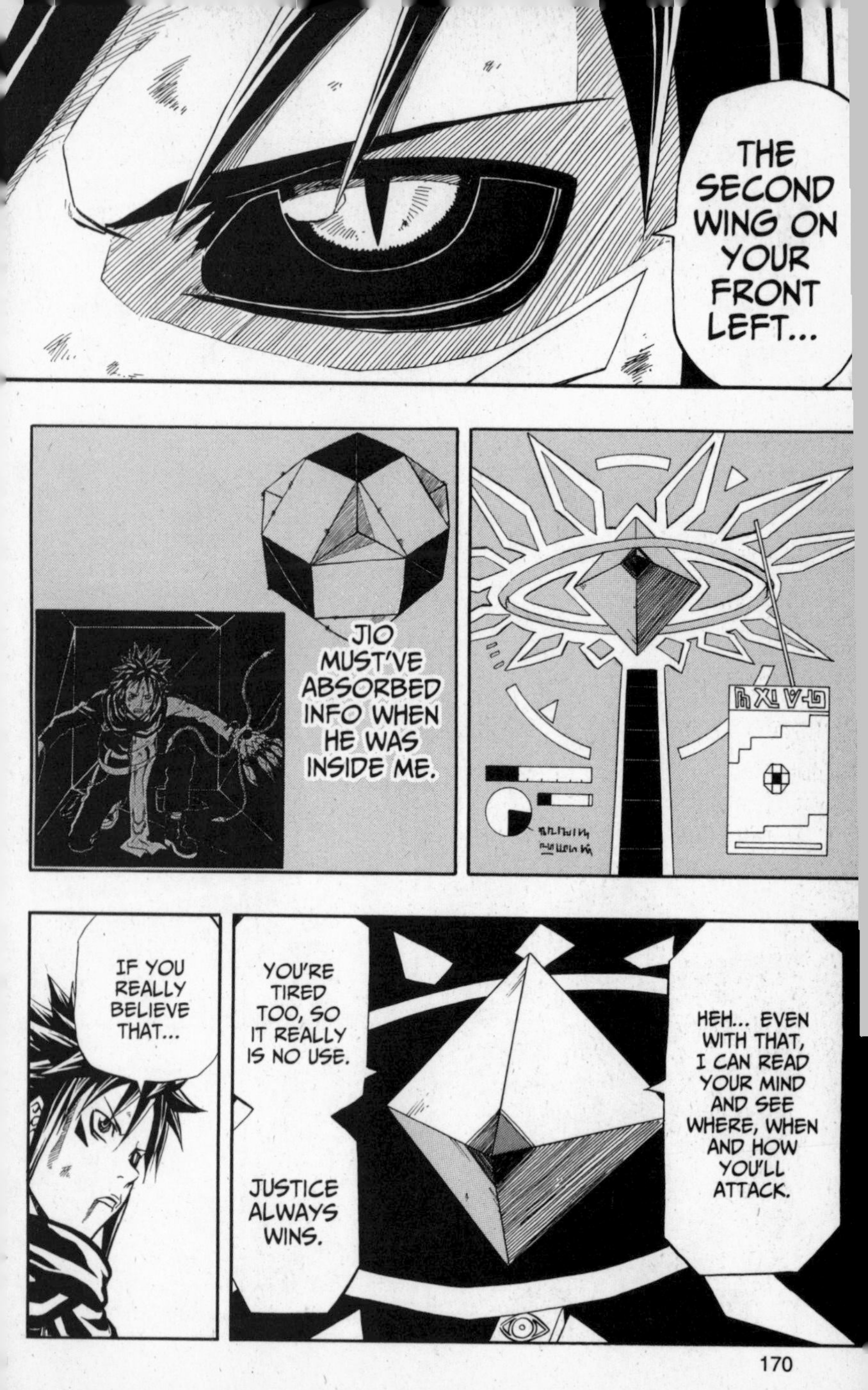
THE SECOND WING ON YOUR FRONT LEFT...
JIO MUST'VE ABSORBED INFO WHEN HE WAS INSIDE ME.
HEH... EVEN WITH THAT, I CAN READ YOUR MIND AND SEE WHERE, WHEN AND HOW YOU'LL ATTACK.
YOU'RE TIRED TOO, SO IT REALLY IS NO USE.
JUSTICE ALWAYS WINS.
IF YOU REALLY BELIEVE THAT...

YOUR CORE!!! THAT'S YOUR WEAK SPOT!

YOU KILLED ALL THOSE INNOCENTS... ...IN THAT STEA GOVERNMENT MISSION... ...BACK AT THE KELPI MINE.

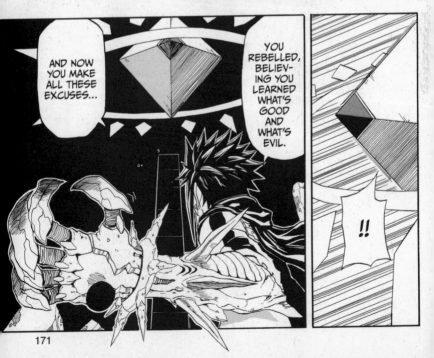

YOU REBELLED, BELIEVING YOU LEARNED WHAT'S GOOD AND WHAT'S EVIL.

AND NOW YOU MAKE ALL THESE EXCUSES...

!!

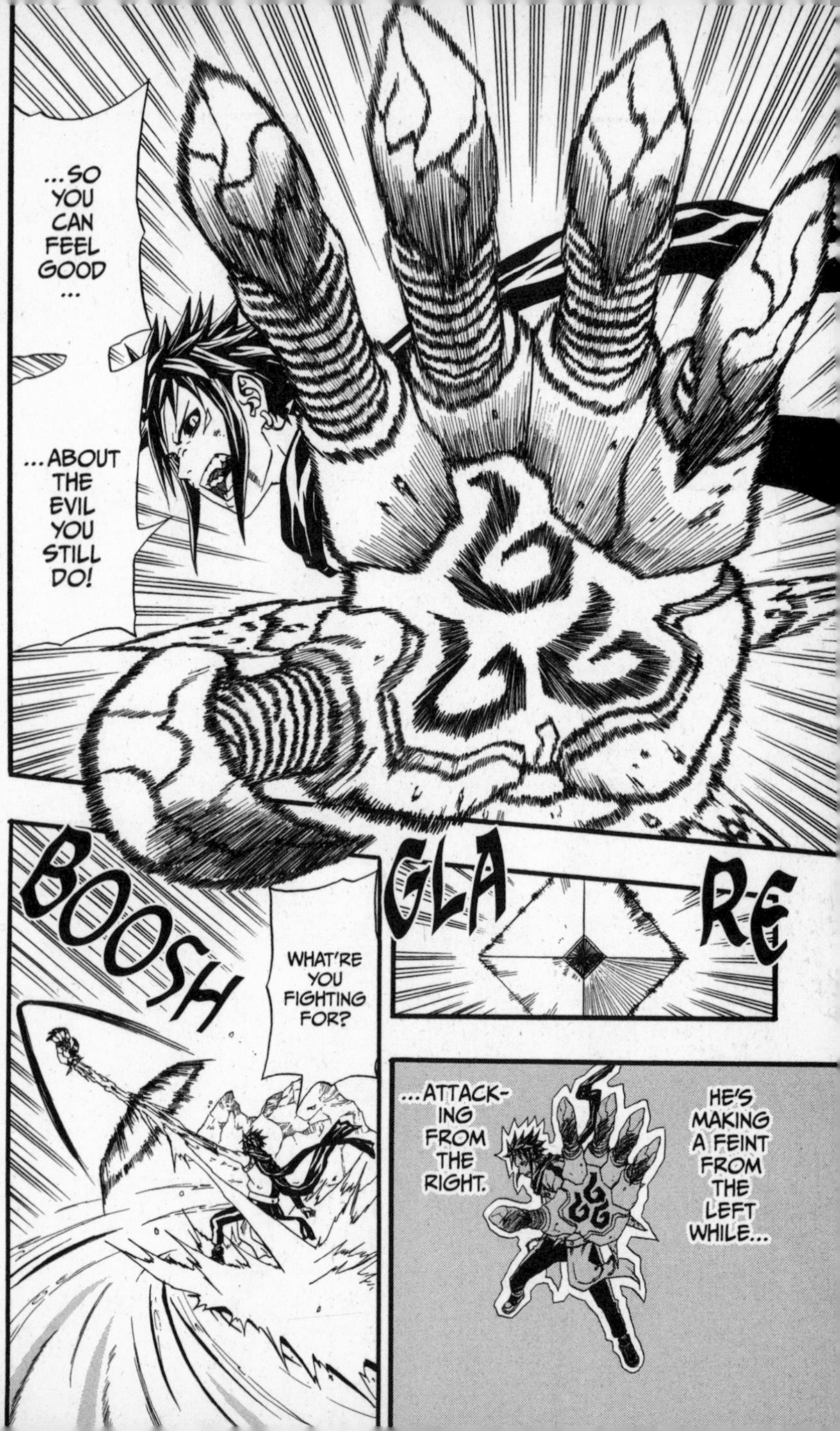
...SO YOU CAN FEEL GOOD...
...ABOUT THE EVIL YOU STILL DO!
GLARE
HE'S MAKING A FEINT FROM THE LEFT WHILE...
...ATTACK-ING FROM THE RIGHT.
BOOSH
WHAT'RE YOU FIGHTING FOR?

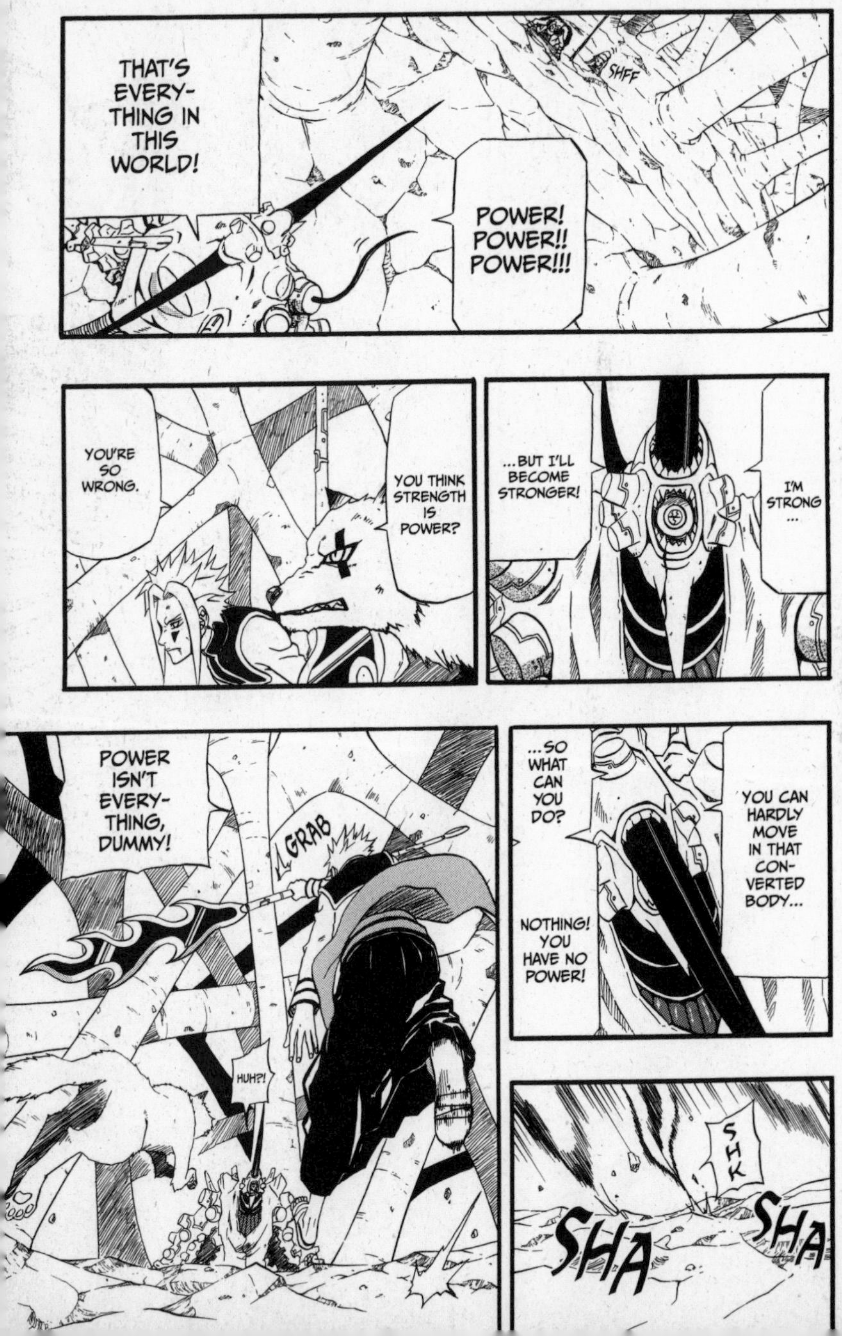
SHFF
POWER! POWER!! POWER!!!
THAT'S EVERY-THING IN THIS WORLD!
I'M STRONG...
...BUT I'LL BECOME STRONGER!
YOU THINK STRENGTH IS POWER?
YOU'RE SO WRONG.
YOU CAN HARDLY MOVE IN THAT CON-VERTED BODY...
...SO WHAT CAN YOU DO?
NOTHING! YOU HAVE NO POWER!
SHK
SHA
SHA
POWER ISN'T EVERY-THING, DUMMY!
GRAB
HUH?!

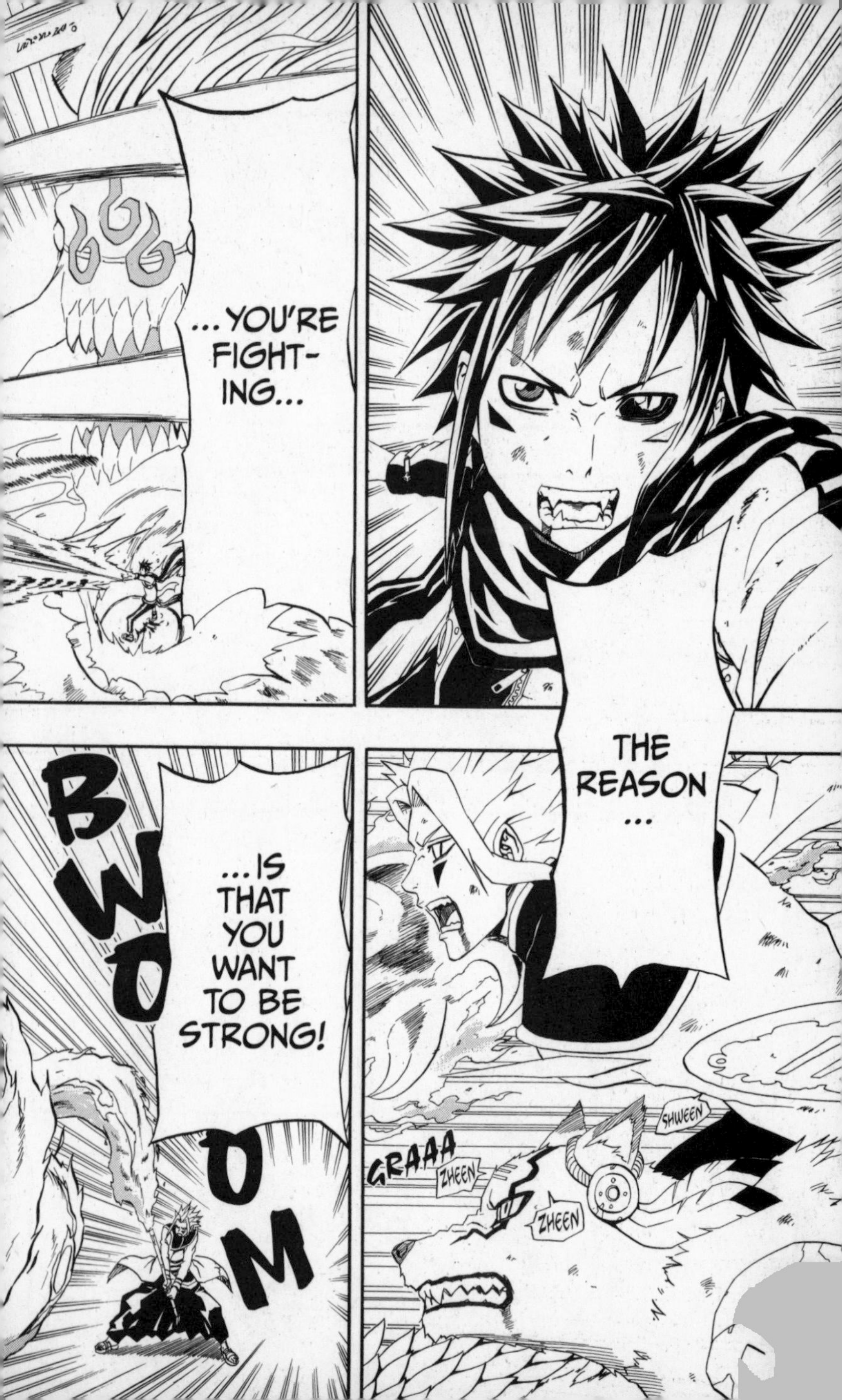
THE REASON ...
... YOU'RE FIGHT-ING...
SHWEEN
GRAAA
ZHEEN
ZHEEN
... IS THAT YOU WANT TO BE STRONG!
BWOOOM

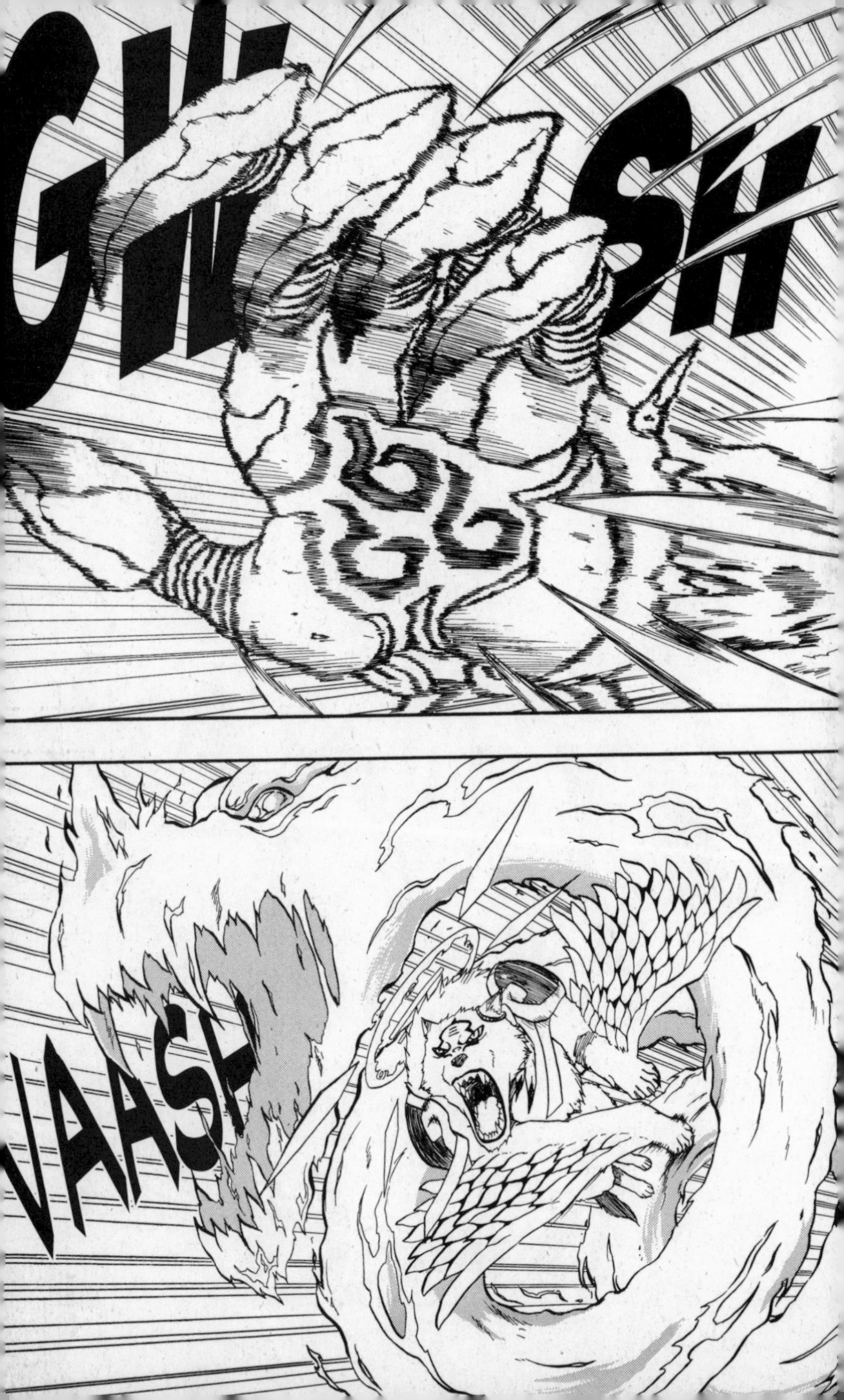
GW SH
VAASH

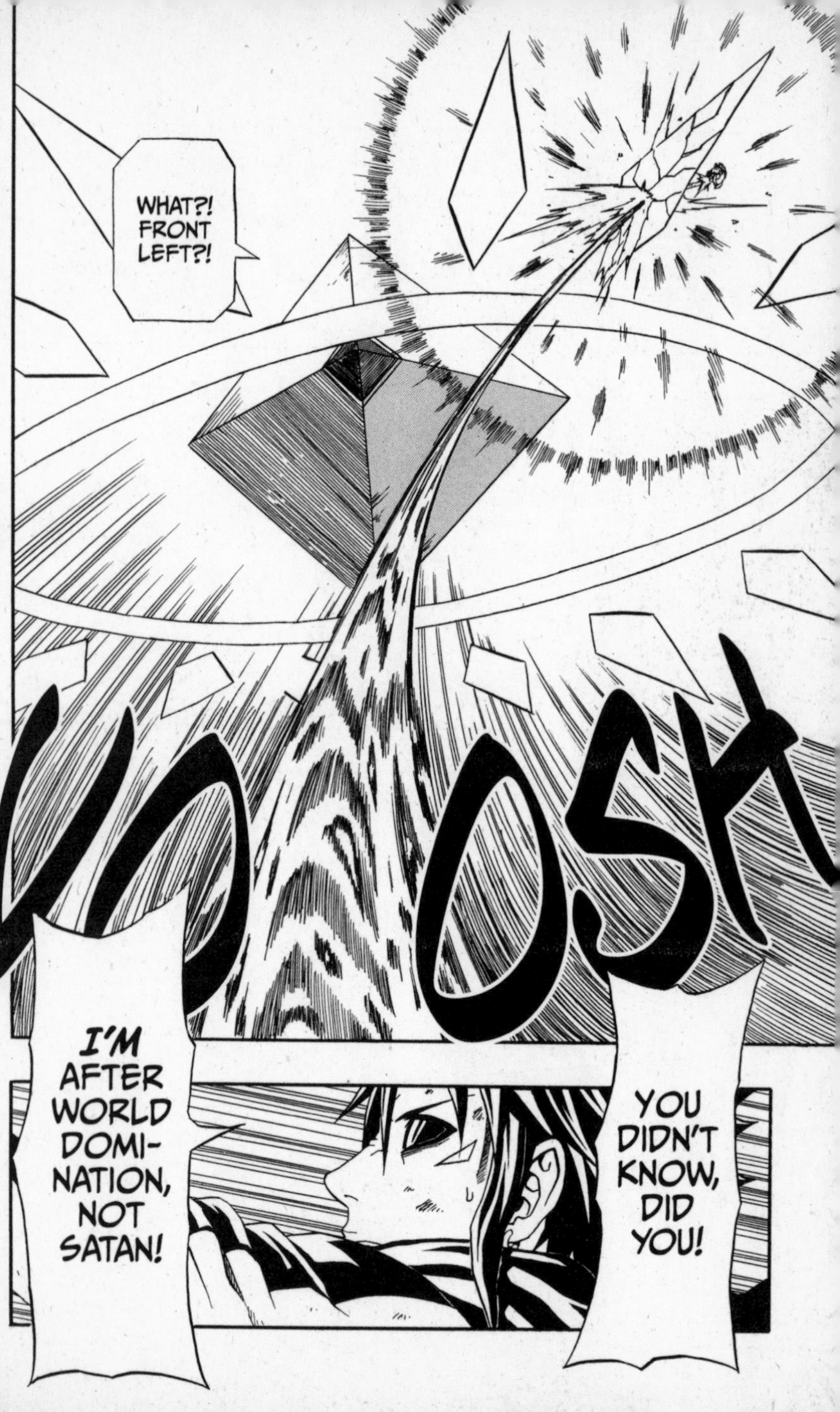
WHAT?! FRONT LEFT?!
YOU DIDN'T KNOW, DID YOU!
I'M AFTER WORLD DOMI-NATION, NOT SATAN!

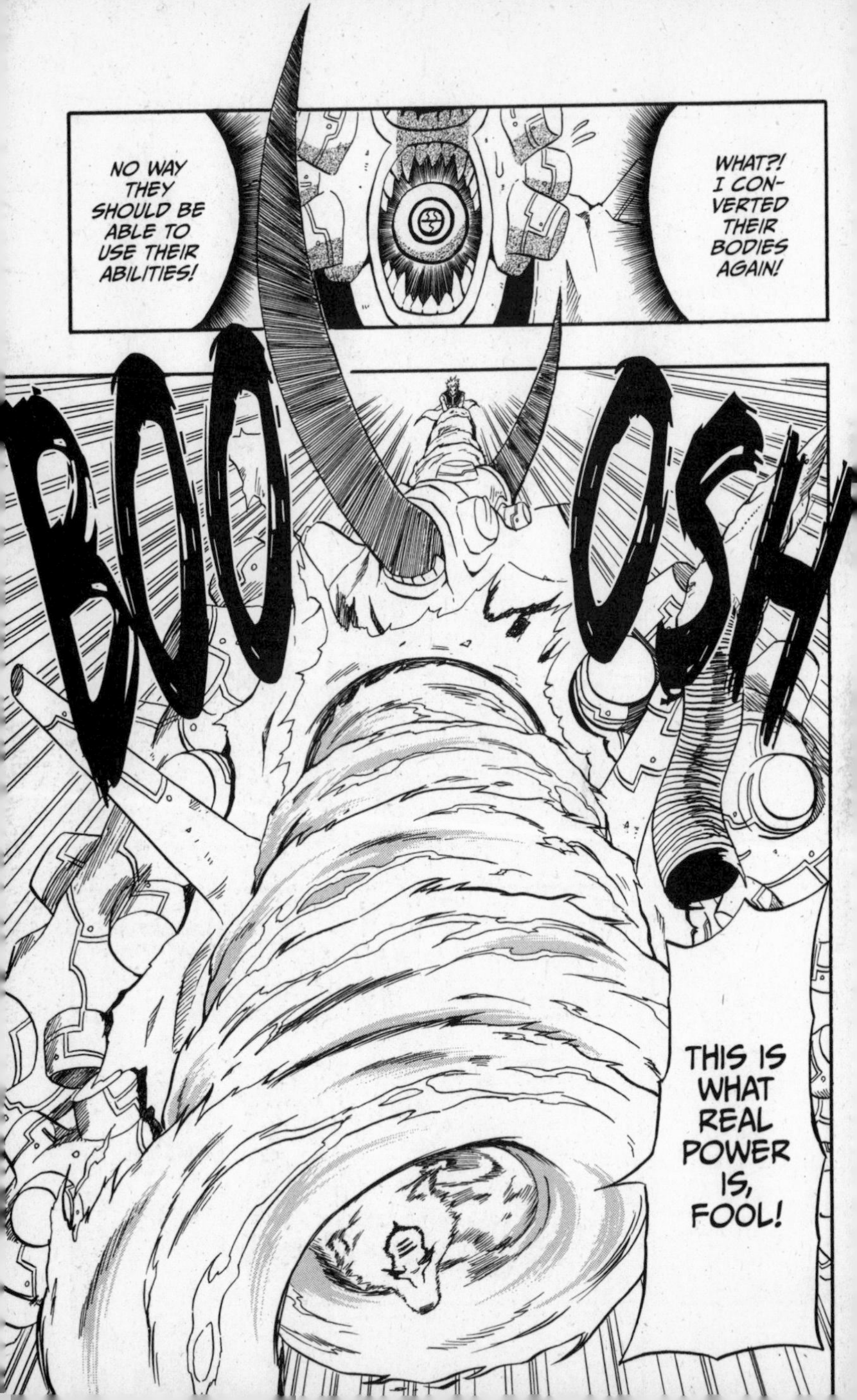
WHAT?! I CON-VERTED THEIR BODIES AGAIN!
NO WAY THEY SHOULD BE ABLE TO USE THEIR ABILITIES!
BOOOSH
THIS IS WHAT REAL POWER IS, FOOL!

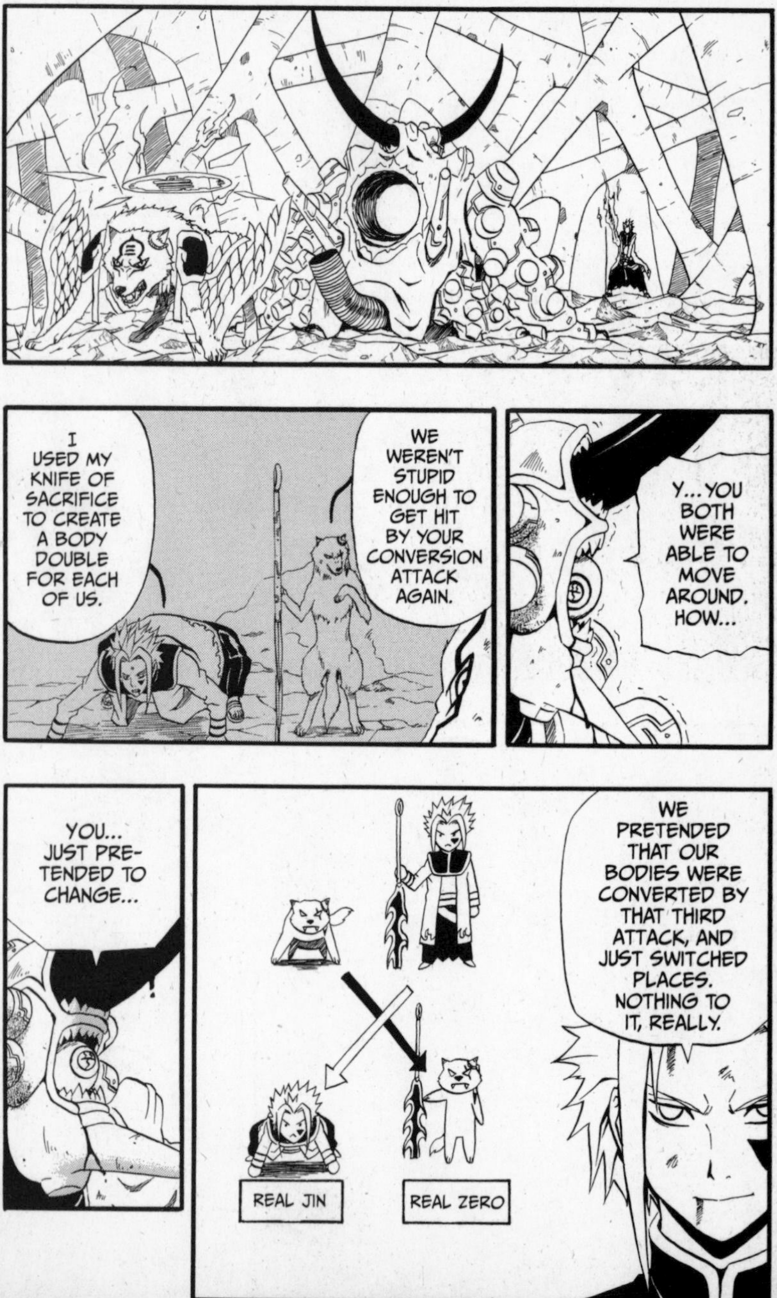
Y...YOU BOTH WERE ABLE TO MOVE AROUND. HOW...
WE WEREN'T STUPID ENOUGH TO GET HIT BY YOUR CONVERSION ATTACK AGAIN.
I USED MY KNIFE OF SACRIFICE TO CREATE A BODY DOUBLE FOR EACH OF US.
WE PRETENDED THAT OUR BODIES WERE CONVERTED BY THAT THIRD ATTACK, AND JUST SWITCHED PLACES. NOTHING TO IT, REALLY.
REAL ZERO
REAL JIN
YOU... JUST PRETENDED TO CHANGE...

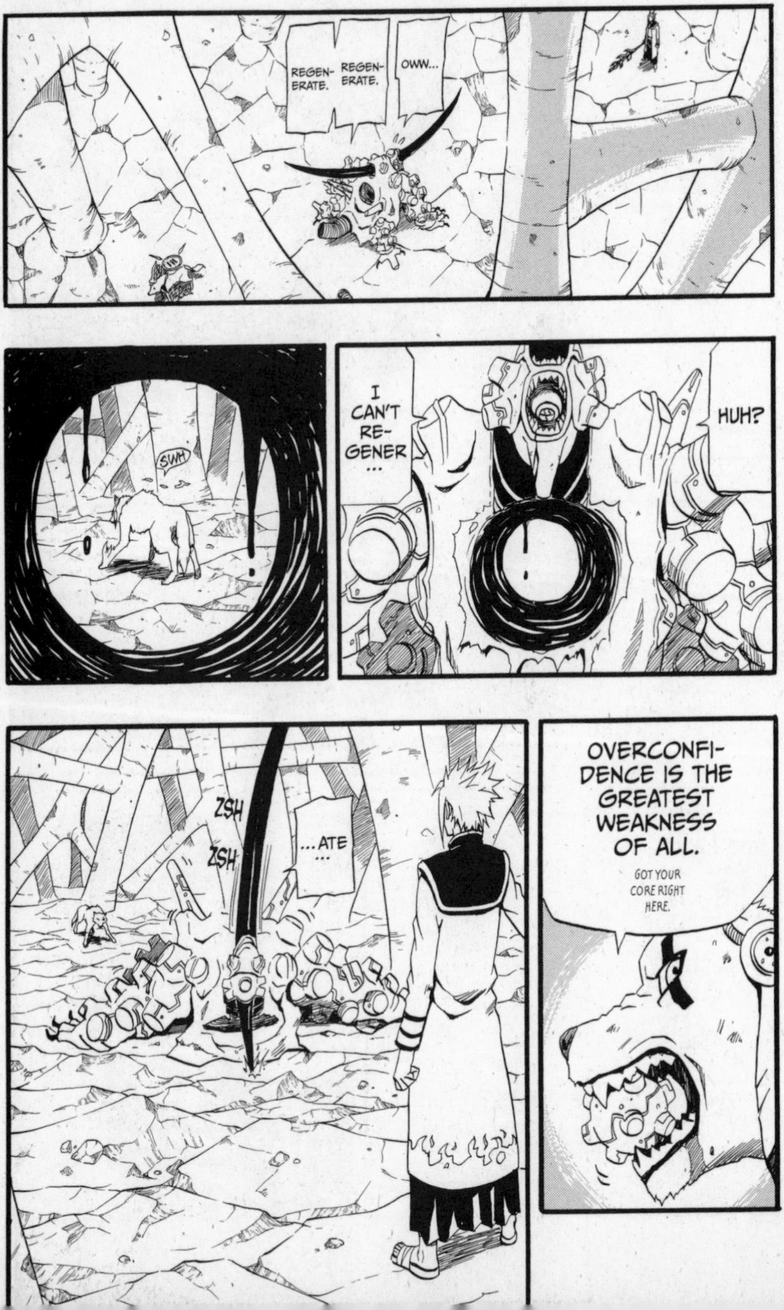
OWW...
REGEN-ERATE.
REGEN-ERATE.
HUH?
I CAN'T RE-GENER...
SWH
OVERCONFI-DENCE IS THE GREATEST WEAKNESS OF ALL.
GOT YOUR CORE RIGHT HERE.
...ATE...
ZSH
ZSH

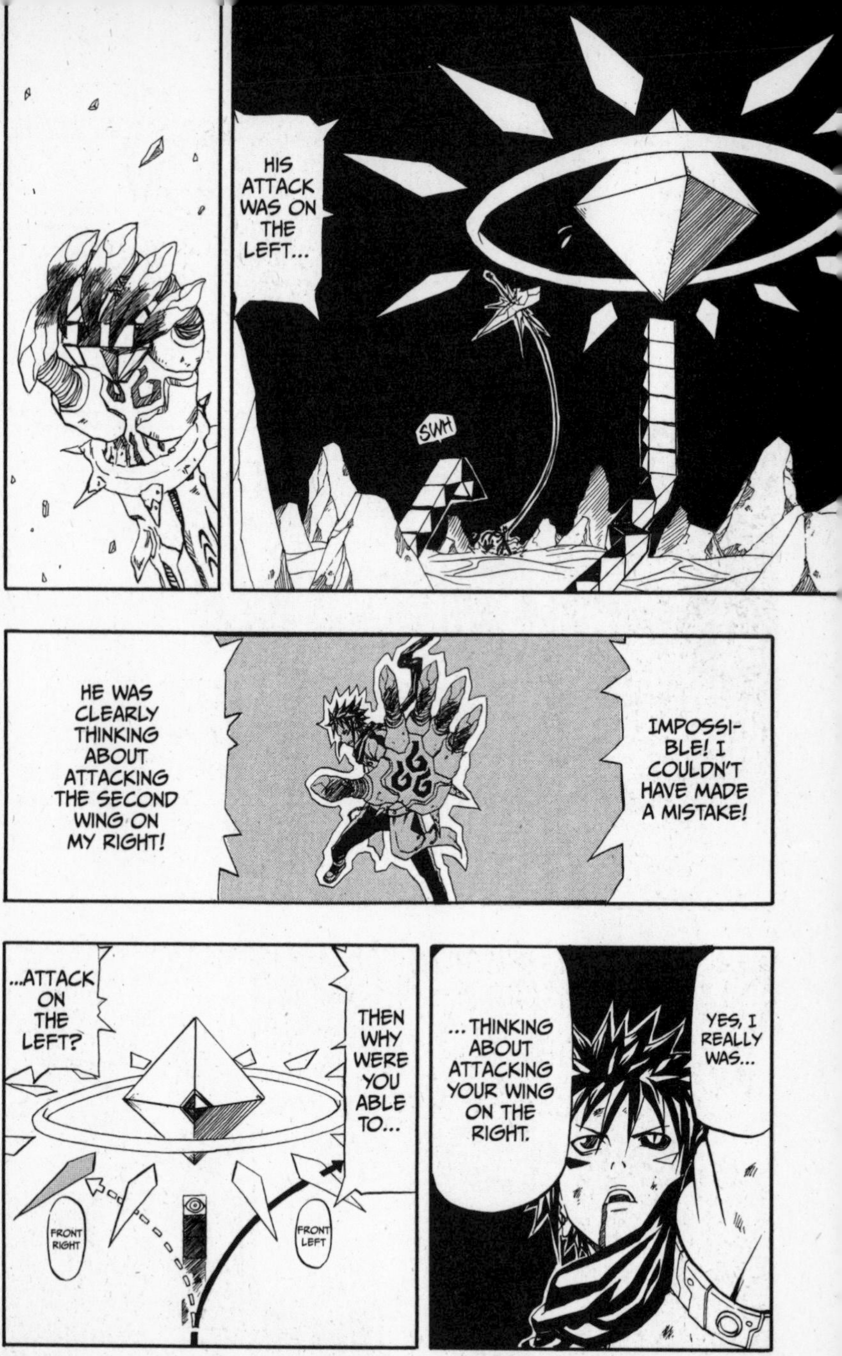
HIS ATTACK WAS ON THE LEFT...
SWH
IMPOSSIBLE! I COULDN'T HAVE MADE A MISTAKE!
HE WAS CLEARLY THINKING ABOUT ATTACKING THE SECOND WING ON MY RIGHT!
YES, I REALLY WAS...
...THINKING ABOUT ATTACKING YOUR WING ON THE RIGHT.
THEN WHY WERE YOU ABLE TO...
...ATTACK ON THE LEFT?
FRONT LEFT
FRONT RIGHT

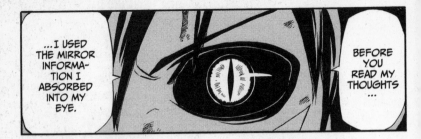

BEFORE YOU READ MY THOUGHTS...
...I USED THE MIRROR INFORMATION I ABSORBED INTO MY EYE.
SO EVERYTHING AROUND ME...
FLIP
...SEEMED INVERTED TO ME.
THE MIRROR INFORMATION?!
HOW... WHEN DID YOU ABSORB THAT?!
ZLLSH
YOU MEAN...
ZLLSH
ZLLSH
THAT'S RIGHT, THE ROCKS AROUND ME.
OF COURSE! THAT'S WHEN HE ABSORBED THE INFO!

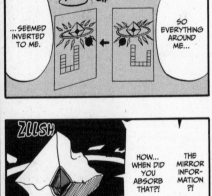

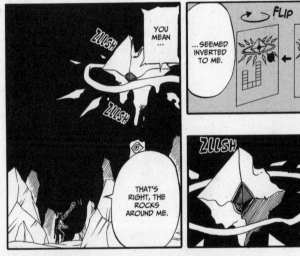

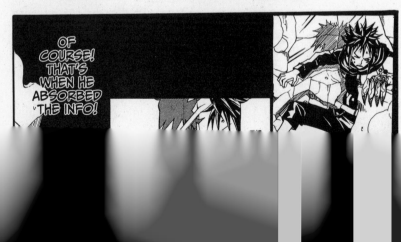

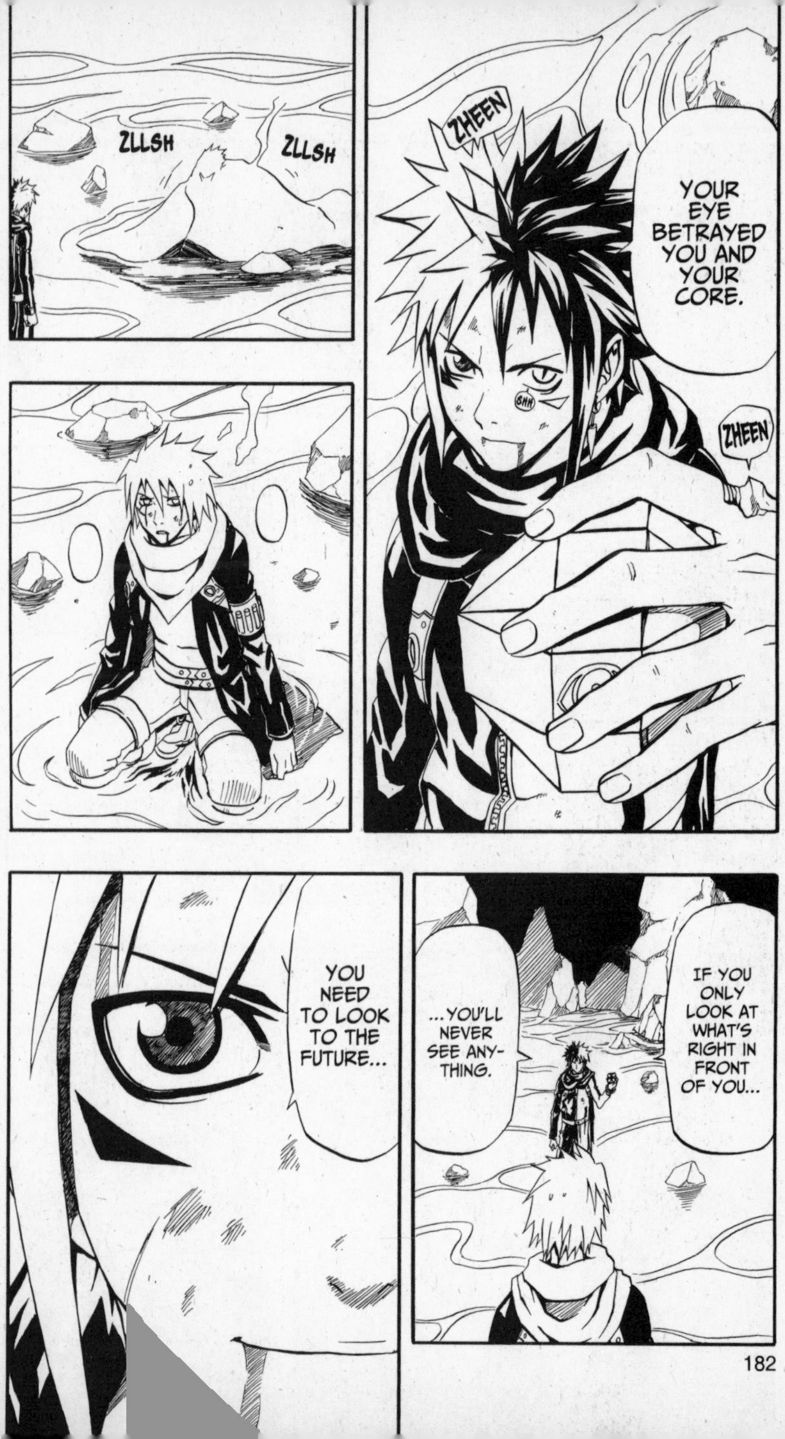
ZHEEN
YOUR EYE BETRAYED YOU AND YOUR CORE.
SHH
ZHEEN
ZLLSH
ZLLSH
IF YOU ONLY LOOK AT WHAT'S RIGHT IN FRONT OF YOU...
...YOU'LL NEVER SEE ANY-THING.
YOU NEED TO LOOK TO THE FUTURE...

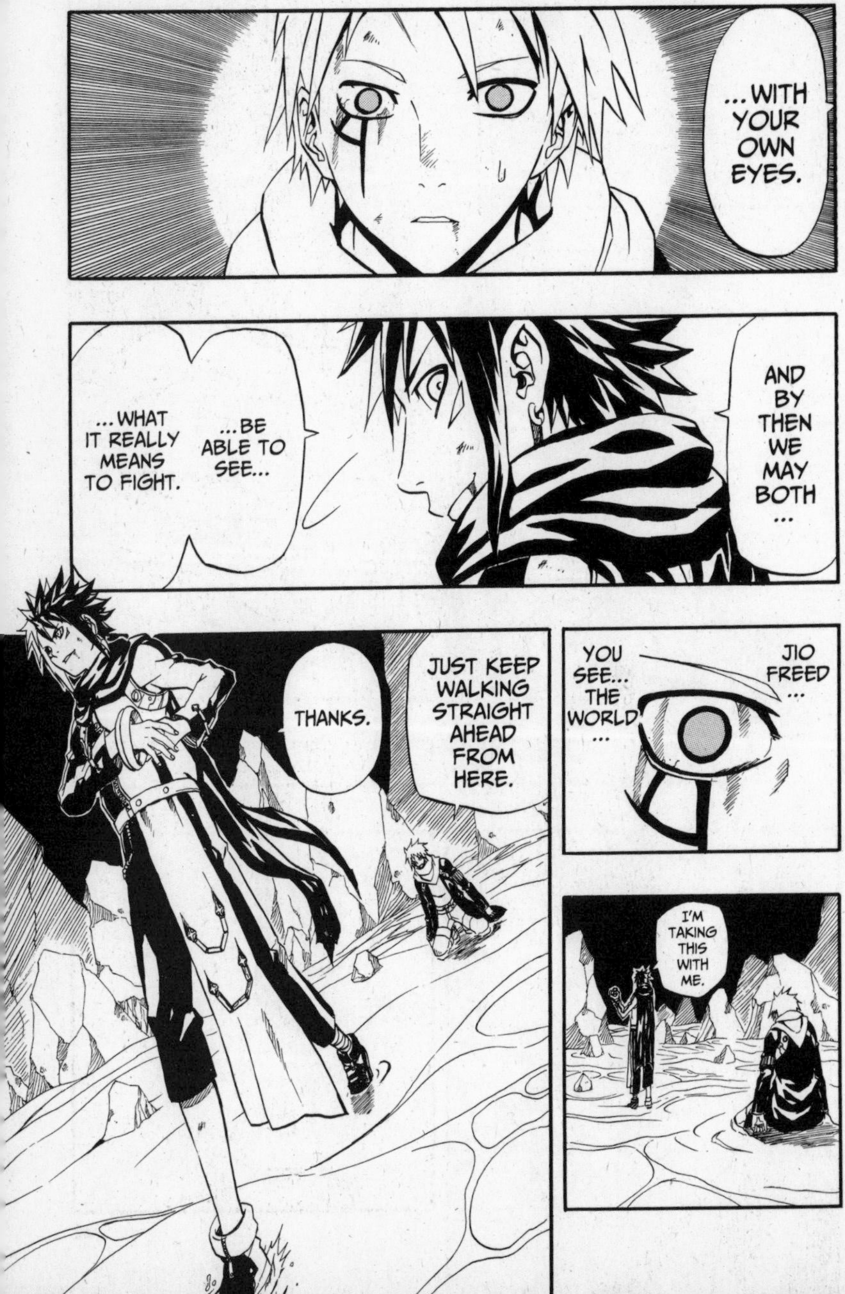
...WITH YOUR OWN EYES.
AND BY THEN WE MAY BOTH ...
...BE ABLE TO SEE...
...WHAT IT REALLY MEANS TO FIGHT.
JIO FREED ...
YOU SEE... THE WORLD ...
I'M TAKING THIS WITH ME.
JUST KEEP WALKING STRAIGHT AHEAD FROM HERE.
THANKS.

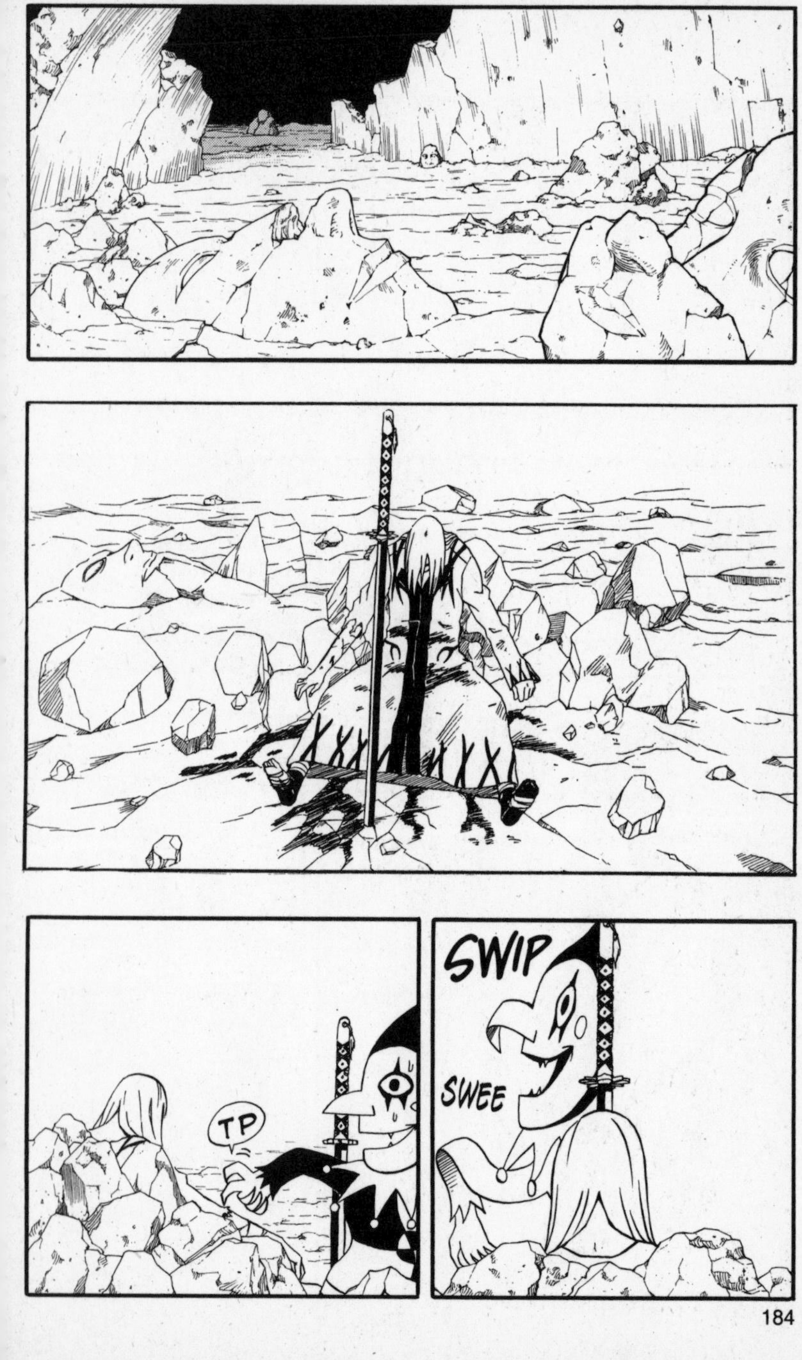
SWIP
SWEE
TP

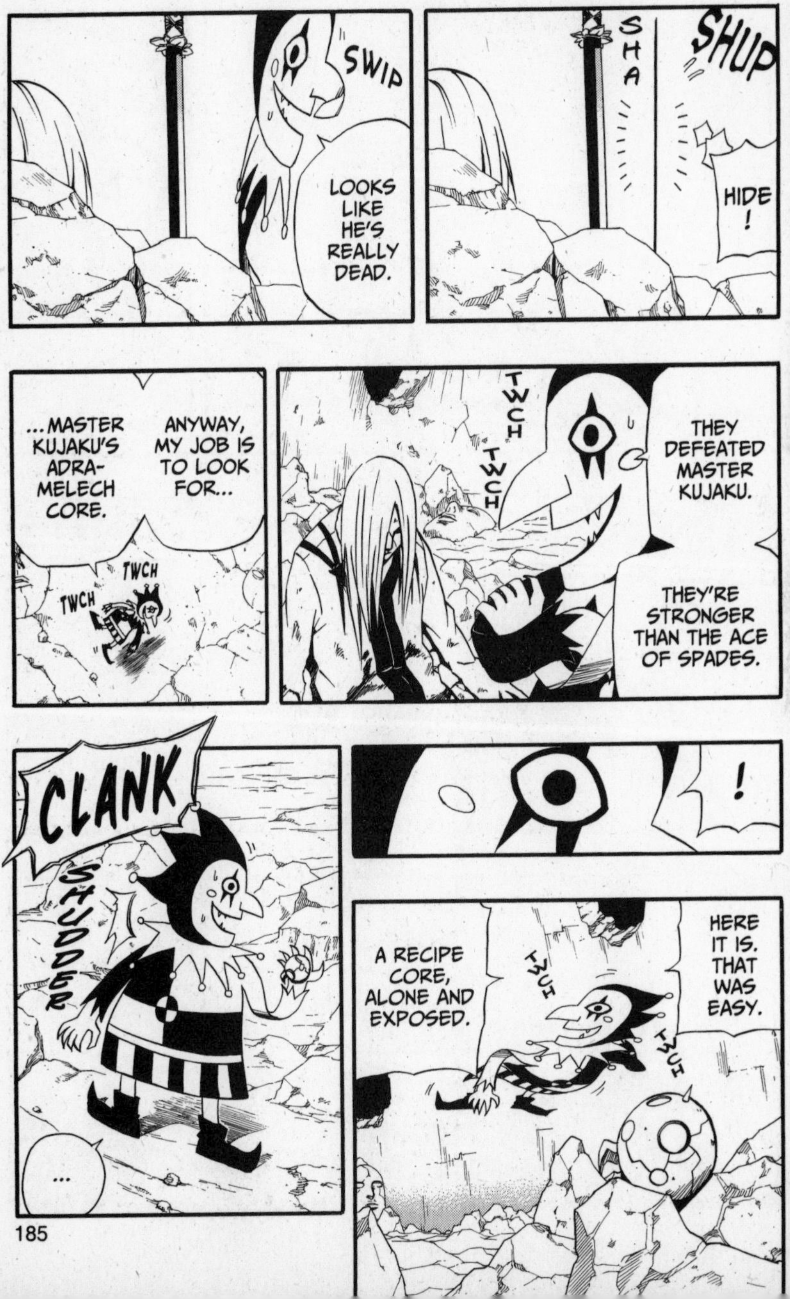
SHA
SHUP
HIDE!
SWIP
LOOKS LIKE HE'S REALLY DEAD.
TWCH TWCH
THEY DEFEATED MASTER KUJAKU.
THEY'RE STRONGER THAN THE ACE OF SPADES.
ANYWAY, MY JOB IS TO LOOK FOR...
...MASTER KUJAKU'S ADRA-MELECH CORE.
TWCH TWCH
!
HERE IT IS. THAT WAS EASY.
A RECIPE CORE, ALONE AND EXPOSED.
TWCH TWCH
CLANK
SHUDDER
...

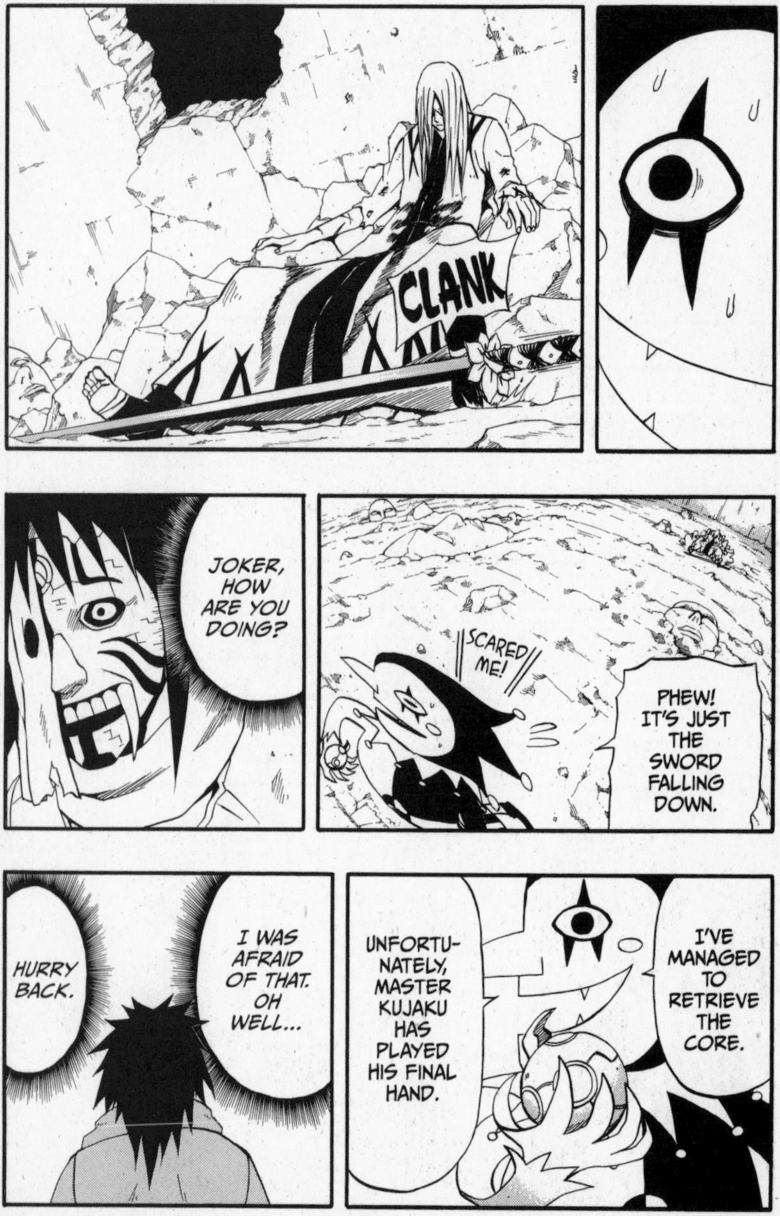
CLANK
SCARED ME!
PHEW! IT'S JUST THE SWORD FALLING DOWN.
JOKER, HOW ARE YOU DOING?
I'VE MANAGED TO RETRIEVE THE CORE.
UNFORTU-NATELY, MASTER KUJAKU HAS PLAYED HIS FINAL HAND.
I WAS AFRAID OF THAT. OH WELL...
HURRY BACK.

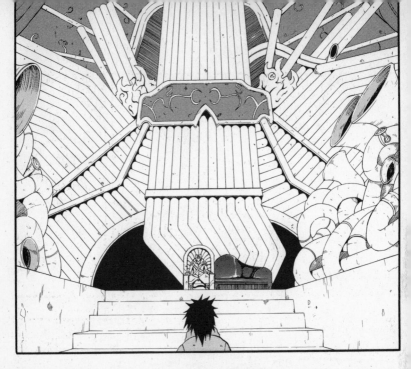

SO
THEY'RE
FINALLY
HERE.

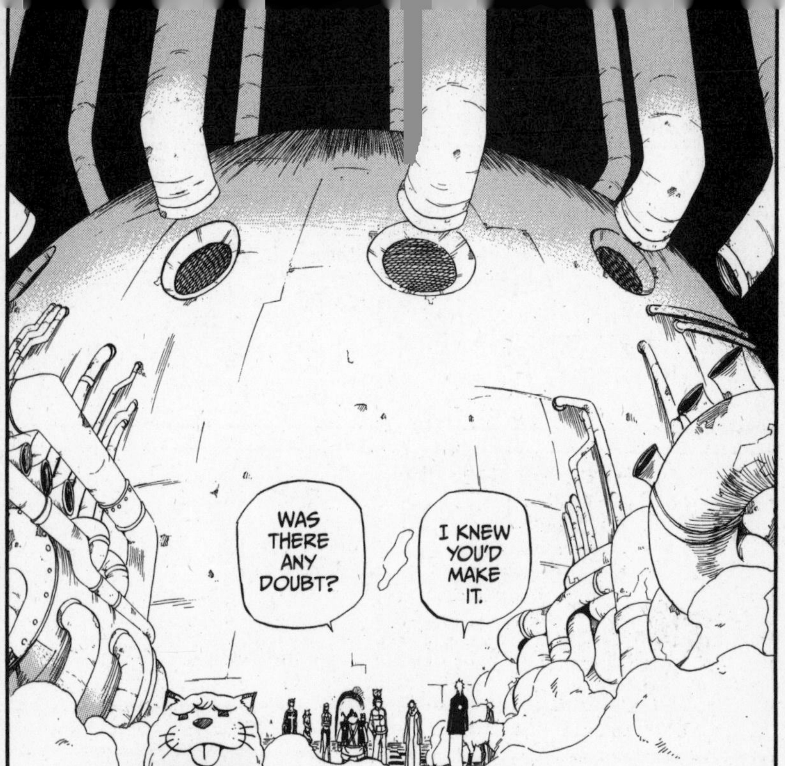
I KNEW YOU'D MAKE IT.
WAS THERE ANY DOUBT?

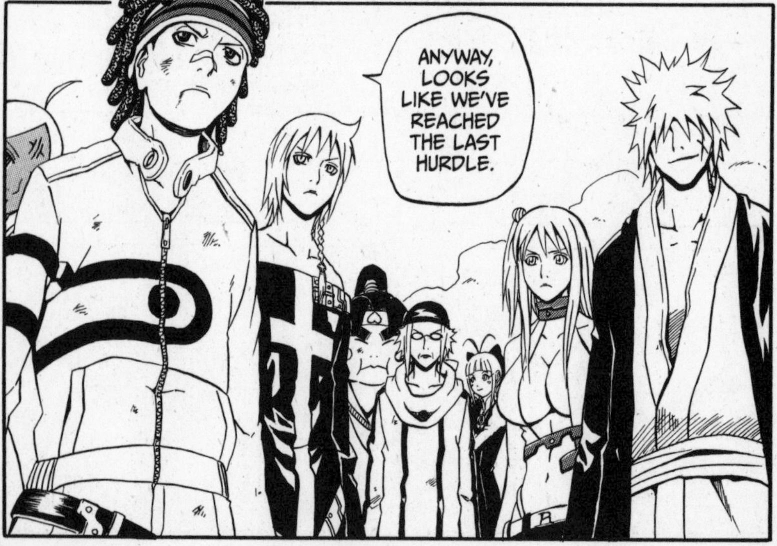
ANYWAY, LOOKS LIKE WE'VE REACHED THE LAST HURDLE.

SEISHI AND HIS CONTACT LENS

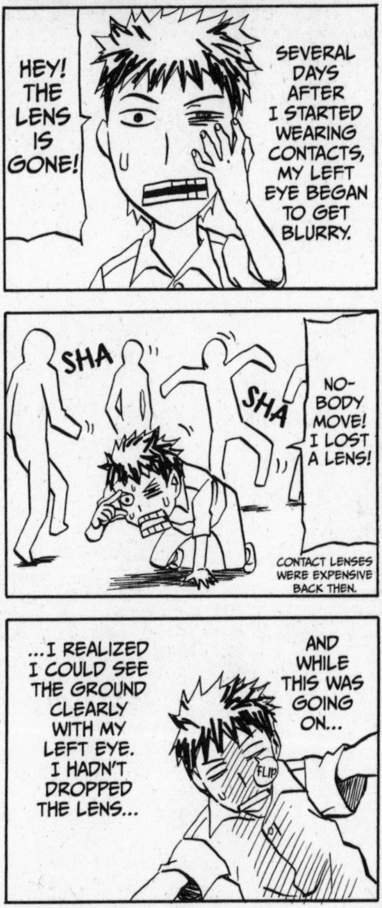
SEVERAL DAYS AFTER I STARTED WEARING CONTACTS, MY LEFT EYE BEGAN TO GET BLURRY.
HEY! THE LENS IS GONE!
NO-BODY MOVE! I LOST A LENS!
SHA
SHA
CONTACT LENSES WERE EXPENSIVE BACK THEN.
AND WHILE THIS WAS GOING ON...
FLIP
...I REALIZED I COULD SEE THE GROUND CLEARLY WITH MY LEFT EYE. I HADN'T DROPPED THE LENS...
...IT'D JUST SHIFTED OUT OF PLACE.
AW-RIGHT! I FOUND IT!
DASH
THANKS.
I RUSHED TO THE BATH-ROOM TO HIDE THE TRUTH!
OH, GOOD.
GLAD TO HEAR IT.

SEISHI AND HIS OLD SCAR

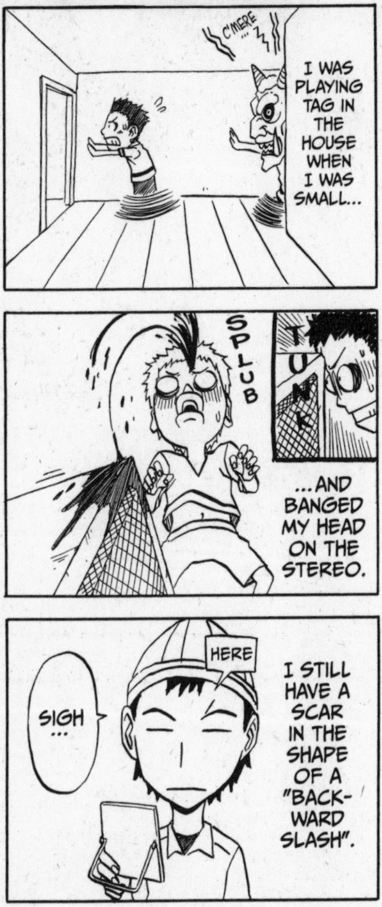
I WAS PLAYING TAG IN THE HOUSE WHEN I WAS SMALL...
C'MERE ...
TUNK
SPLUB
...AND BANGED MY HEAD ON THE STEREO.
I STILL HAVE A SCAR IN THE SHAPE OF A "BACK-WARD SLASH".
HERE
SIGH ...
MY FRIEND HAS A SIMILAR SCAR, BUT HE HAD IT STITCHED, SO HIS LOOKS LIKE A PERCENT-AGE SIGN.
HERE
OR A DIVISION SIGN IF I TILT MY HEAD.

O-Parts CATALOGUE⑱

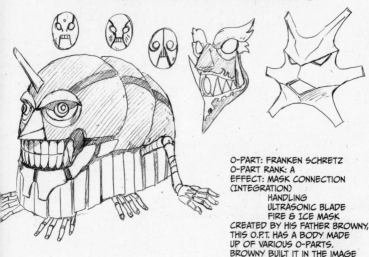

O-PART: FRANKEN SCHRETZ
O-PART RANK: A
EFFECT: MASK CONNECTION
(INTEGRATION)
HANDLING
ULTRASONIC BLADE
FIRE & ICE MASK
CREATED BY HIS FATHER BROWNY,
THIS O.P.T. HAS A BODY MADE
UP OF VARIOUS O-PARTS.
BROWNY BUILT IT IN THE IMAGE
OF FRANKEN'S FAVORITE MASK.

O-PART: KERBEROS × 2
O-PART RANK: C
EFFECT: POWER UP
IT CAN ENHANCE THE
POWER OF A 9MM
PARABELLUM BULLET TO
AN UNBELIEVABLE LEVEL.
IT'S LIKE HOLDING
A CANNON IN YOUR HAND.

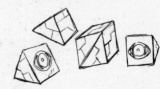

O-PART: TWELVE WATCHERS
O-PART RANK: A
EFFECT: BLACK LASER, HANDLING
EACH PIECE CAN SHOOT A BLACK,
HIGH-ENERGY LASER. PUTTING THE
PARTS INTO FIXED SHAPES CAN
INTENSIFY THE LASERS.

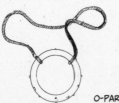

O-PART: FAIRING
O-PART RANK: A
EFFECT: SOUND MATERIALIZATION
IT HAS THE ABILITY TO
MATERIALIZE THE LETTERS
OF ALMOST ANY WORD
OR SOUND THAT GOES
THROUGH IT.

O-PART: TITHONIUM GUN
O-PART RANK: B
EFFECT: BROWNY SCHRETZ USED TITHONIUM, THE
HARDEST SUBSTANCE IN THE WORLD, TO CREATE HIS
RIGHT ARM. IT LOOKS LIKE AN ORDINARY ARM BUT IS
ACTUALLY A POWER COMPRESSOR THAT SHOOTS
HIGHLY COMPRESSED GAS. IT'S THE ONLY WEAPON
THAT CAN BREAK THROUGH TITHONIUM ITSELF.

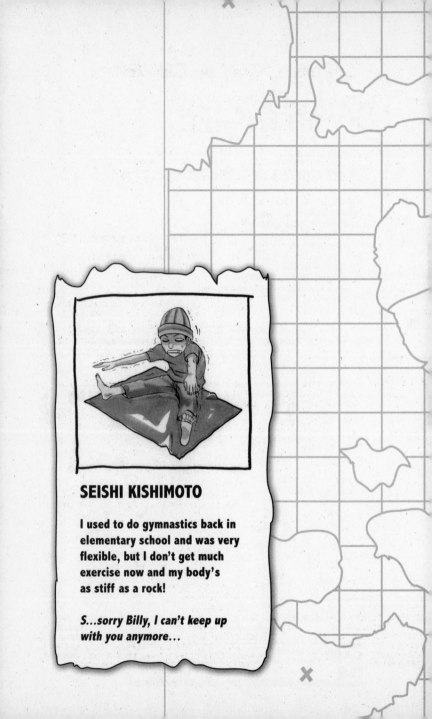

SEISHI KISHIMOTO

I used to do gymnastics back in
elementary school and was very
flexible, but I don't get much
exercise now and my body's
as stiff as a rock!

*S...sorry Billy, I can't keep up
with you anymore...*

O-Parts HUNTER™ 18

VIZ Media Edition
STORY AND ART BY SEISHI KISHIMOTO

English Adaptation/David R. Valois
Translation/Tetsuichiro Miyaki
Touch-up Art & Lettering/HudsonYards
Design/Andrea Rice
Editor/Gary Leach

VP, Production/Alvin Lu
VP, Publishing Licensing/Rika Inouye
VP, Sales & Product Marketing/Gonzalo Ferreyra
VP, Creative/Linda Espinosa
Publisher/Hyoe Narita

Printed in the U.S.A.

Published by VIZ Media, LLC
P.O. Box 77010
San Francisco, CA 94107

10 9 8 7 6 5 4 3 2 1
First printing, October 2009

www.viz.com

store.viz.com

PARENTAL ADVISORY
O-PARTS HUNTER is rated T+ for Older Teen and is recommended for ages 16 and up. This volume contains realistic and fantasy violence and adult situations.

ratings.viz.com